Working within the Law

A PRACTICAL GUIDE FOR EMPLOYERS AND EMPLOYEES

Frances Meenan

B. Comm., M.B.S. (N.U.I.)
Solicitor

FOREWORD BY

The Honourable Mr Justice Hugh Geoghegan

OAK TREE PRESS

DUBLIN

This book was typeset by
Gilbert Gough Typesetting for
Oak Tree Press
4 Arran Quay, Dublin 7.

A catalogue record for this book is
available from the British Library.

ISBN 1-872853-15-3 (pb)
ISBN 1-872853-24-2 (hb)

Printed in Ireland by
Colour Books Ltd., Dublin

Foreword

It has become a cliché for judicial foreword writers to celebrate the growth industry in Irish law books and to reminisce about the "bad old days" when the stock of Irish textbooks was largely confined to *O'Connor's Justice of the Peace* and *Babington's County Court Practice*. Such celebration is, however, fully justified and soundly based. Most practising barristers and solicitors have had to find considerable additional bookshelf space in recent years to accommodate the texts on almost every branch of Irish law regularly brought up-to-date with new editions. But in the main the target readership for this growth has been the lawyers and the law students.

Frances Meenan has rightly perceived that the entire body of employment law is of everyday practical interest to employers and employees who may want the information but not sufficiently to justify the time or expense of retaining professional legal advice. Ms Meenan has, therefore, written a law book directed at the lay person as well as the lawyer. She has achieved this by simple but clear exposition and an easily readable style. The subjects covered, however, are complex, each of them meriting a law book on its own. The chapter headings speak for themselves but I would particularly mention "Temporary Employment", "Maternity Leave", "Equal Pay", "Equal Treatment in Employment", "Transfer of a Business", "Unfair Dismissals" and "Redundancy" as subjects on which employers and employees may want quick guidance. I have selected these topics almost at random. The others are equally useful.

Ireland's entry into the European Community has had a dramatic effect on the law relating to employer/employee relationships. One has only to consider the European Communities (Safeguarding of Employees' Rights on Transfer of Undertakings) Regulations, 1980. The buyer of a business as a going concern may get a rude awakening upon discovery that he or she is legally obliged to retain existing employees on the same terms and conditions as pertained under the previous employer, the seller of the business. Frances Meenan's book will help to promulgate these newer laws among the business community. I very much welcome this book. In my opinion, it will be useful to both layman and lawyer, to the former for information and to the latter for reference. The appendixed forms and precedents should be immensely useful to all. I look forward to the success of this book and to further editions of it in due course.

Hugh Geoghegan

Four Courts
Dublin
May 1994

For my Mother and Father

Contents

SECTION THREE
TERMINATION OF EMPLOYMENT

Acknowledgements

I am indebted to so many people for their comments, assistance, time and encouragement. In particular I would like to thank Mr Justice Hugh Geoghegan for so generously agreeing to write the Foreword and placing Employment Law in its modern legal context. Brian O'Kane of Cork Publishing for asking me to write the book and for his constant help and encouragement throughout the long process. Eugene McCarthy and Albert Power for kindly agreeing to read an earlier draft and giving me the benefit of their precious time, academic knowledge and practical experience.

I would also like to thank Dan Horan, Secretary of the Employment Appeals Tribunal and his officials who are always obliging and helpful; Deirdre Sweeney, Head of the Employment Equality Service; Mary Honan, Legal Advisor of the Employment Equality Agency; Evan Brezzina of the Department of Enterprise and Employment, Colin Walker, Rights Commissioner; Gary Byrne, Rosheen Callender, Clare Carroll, Christopher Docksey, Dervilla Donnelly, Kyra Donnelly, Helen Doyle, Brian Hillery, Roddy Horan, Peter Kelly, Tony Kerr, Patrick McCann, Charles Meenan, Tom Mallon, Michael D. Murphy, Ciaran O'Mara, Orlagh O'Farrell, Mary Redmond and Ercus Stewart. I am sad that our family friend Eamon Smyth did not live to see the book published as he was always so kind, thoughtful and interested in my career.

Enormous gratitude is also deserving to Margaret Byrne of the Law Society Library and her staff who are always particularly helpful in providing sources of information. Julitta Clancy kindly agreed to the unenviable task of compiling the Tables of Statutes and Cases and also the Index. I owe her many thanks for all her professionalism and assistance.

David Givens, Gerard O'Connor and Emer Ryan provided me with considerable editorial and professional assistance in the preparation of the book. I sincerely thank them and their staff for their forbearance.

Nobody can write a book in isolation without the constant encouragement of their family. I am particularly fortunate in my parents who have been constantly understanding. Above all they have been generous with their time. I also thank Charles, Anita, John and Helen for their humour, kindness and patience.

Finally, all responsibility rests with me.

F.M.

Table of Cases

Table of Statutes, etc.

3. STATUTORY INSTRUMENTS

4. EUROPEAN COMMUNITIES LEGISLATION

Introduction

A quarter of a century has now passed since the coming into operation of the first major piece of Irish employment protection legislation, the Redundancy Payments Act, 1967. The subsequent decade witnessed a major growth in other legislation, which was influenced by our membership of the European Community and also by an awareness of the increasing need for employment protection. During the 1970s, legislation was passed for statutory minimum notice, written terms and conditions of employment, statutory holidays and public holidays (amending earlier legislation), statutory provision on the manner of the payment of wages, equal pay and equal treatment for men and women at work, amendments to the redundancy legislation and provision for redress for unfair dismissal.

The impetus for change was sustained up to the mid 1980s with provision for statutory maternity leave, guaranteed payments for employees in cases of employer insolvency, reduction in the hourly threshold for cover under certain protection legislation and a broadening of the scope of the trade disputes legislation. During the second half of the 1980s there were no developments of substance. In contrast, the early 1990s was a period of immense change for both individual employment and industrial relations legislation, providing protection for regular part-time employees and new legislation and procedures in respect of the payment of wages. After many years of debate the Edwardian Trade Disputes Act, 1906 (as amended by the Trade Disputes (Amendment) Act, 1982) was repealed which led to the Industrial Relations Act, 1990. That latter Act also amends Ireland's industrial relations procedures as contained in the Industrial Relations Act, 1946 (as amended).

The year 1993 saw the coming into effect of the Unfair Dismissals (Amendment) Act on 1 October. Also published in 1993 were the Adoptive Leave Bill and the Terms of Employment (Information) Bill. Their contents (as published) have been incorporated here. It is also envisaged that there will shortly be amendments in a consolidating statute of the equal pay and equal treatment legislation.

The purpose of this book is to encapsulate key employment law into a single text so that the reader will understand the contents of the legislation. Irish legislation is complicated by the many different Acts with subsequent amendments as well as by the fact that each group of Acts has different claims procedures. As an aid, the book contains various samples of statutory and non-statutory forms.

Working within the Law is for a universal audience — employers, employees, lawyers and industrial relations practitioners. To provide a total picture of the employment relationship, the book is divided into four sections: Recruitment and the Contract of Employment, Terms and Conditions of Employment, Termination of Employment, and Practice and Procedure. The first three sections set out the law and legislation and the final section explains in detail the practice and procedure under each piece of legislation. The various adjudicating bodies — the Employment Appeals Tribunal, the Labour Court and the Labour Relations Commission — are also considered.

At the time of going to press, the following developments had just taken place — the Terms of Employment (Information) Act, 1994 has been passed and will come into effect on 16 May 1994. The statutory redundancy ceiling has been changed from £250 to £300 per week and will apply to all redundancy notices from 1 May 1994 (Redundancy Payments (Lump Sum) Regulations, 1994 — SI No. 64 of 1994). The same limit of £300 per week shall also apply to calculating benefits under the Protection of Employees (Employers' Insolvency) Acts, 1984 to 1991 as and from 1 May 1994 (Protection of Employees (Employers' Insolvency) (Variation of Limit) Regulations, 1994 — SI No. 62 of 1994). The High Court decision of Costello J. concerned issues of alleged harassment and based upon the facts of this case an employer may not be vicariously liable for employees' wrongful acts (*The Heath Board v. BC and The Labour Court*, 19 January 1994). The Labour Court recently determined that dismissal arising from an employee's sexual orientation did not come within the scope of the Employment Equality Act, 1977 (*Brookfield Leisure Ltd. v. A Worker*, EEO 12/1993).

"The chief source of the law is the people" (Cicero, *De Legibus*); hence, it is my belief that the law, as it affects our working lives should be demystified and made accessible to everybody.

I hope this book plays some small part in that process.

Frances Meenan
May 1994

SECTION ONE

RECRUITMENT AND THE CONTRACT OF EMPLOYMENT

CHAPTER ONE

Recruitment and Equality

When a vacancy occurs the employer should draw up a job specification detailing the qualifications required for the position. All current employees, both male and female, should first be considered for the position, and the employer should explore the feasibility of various forms of work arrangement, such as job sharing, part-time work or working from home, if appropriate. Each would make the position available to a greater number of employees.

Once the employer has decided what the job requirements are, the best and most equitable form of recruitment should be considered. Initially it may be through internal recruitment by advising staff of the vacancy on the company notice board, and (if necessary) subsequently by advertising in the newspapers or through an employment agency. "Head-hunting" may be appropriate for certain vacancies.

No matter what recruitment method the employer uses, the most suitable person for the position must be found without resorting to sex or marital discrimination in the search.

EQUAL TREATMENT

The Employment Equality Act, 1977 provides that there cannot be "less favourable treatment" on the basis of sex or marital status. The Act applies equally to men and women. Such discrimination is called direct discrimination, for example, asking a married woman during an interview about childminding arrangements.

Indirect discrimination is more complex. Section 2(c) of the Act provides:

> For the purposes of this Act, discrimination shall be taken to occur in any of the following cases —
>
> where because of his sex or marital status a person is obliged to comply with a requirement, relating to employment . . ., which

is not an essential requirement for such employment . . . and in respect of which the proportion of persons of the other sex or (as the case may be) of a different marital status but of the same sex able to comply is substantially higher.

As this definition is difficult to understand its constituent parts need to be examined. The High Court in the case of *Vavasour and Another* v. *Bonnybrook Unemployment Action Group, FÁS and the Minister for Labour* [1993] ELR 112 at page 115 considered that there were four questions to be addressed to determine whether or not indirect discrimination occurred (on the basis of sex). In summary they are as follows:

(1) What is the requirement with which [the claimant] was obliged to comply?

(2) Is the requirement such that either a higher proportion of males than of females could comply with it, or a higher proportion of single females than married females can comply with it?

(3) If the answer to (2) is positive, is the fact that females are substantially more affected by the requirement than males a result of an attribute of their sex, or is the fact that married females are substantially more affected by the requirement than single females due to the circumstances of their marital status?

(4) Is the requirement for such employment essential?

In short, an employer cannot put a non-essential barrier to a job which could discriminate. An example of indirect discrimination would be the exclusion of pregnant women; obviously this is a non-essential requirement for the job and would thus be indirect discrimination against women. Another example would be an upper age limit of 27 years, which would exclude many women from applying for a position because at that age they may still be at home rearing their families.

While the 1977 Act specifically includes public servants within the definition of employee, the Act excludes the reference of certain disputes arising from recruitment competitions by the Civil Service and Local Appointments Commissioners. However, competitions for promotion within the public service fall within the scope of the Act and individuals who consider that they have been discriminated against may bring a claim (e.g. *Kearns* v. *Department of Industry and Commerce*, EE 3/1991 and *Revenue Commissioners* v. *Irish Tax*

Officials' Union, EE 6/1986, DEE 2/1987). The Top Level Appointments Committee (TLAC) is also subject to the provisions of the Act and individuals may bring claims arising from alleged discrimination.

ACCESS TO EMPLOYMENT

The 1977 Act provides that an employer cannot discriminate, either directly or indirectly, against prospective employees in relation to access to employment, classification of posts in employment, arrangements for recruitment, or entry requirements for employment. The Act also prohibits discrimination in respect of promotion.

ADVERTISING

Discriminatory advertising is also prohibited, whether intentional or where such an intention may be indicated. This includes newspaper, radio and television advertisements, as well as advertisements within a firm — notice boards or newsletters, for example. Advertisements cannot define or describe a position on the basis of gender, and if the job was previously carried on by one sex, it must be made clear that the job is now open to both.

The equality legislation not only applies to the prospective employer placing the advertisement, but also to the publisher (e.g. newspaper) and advertising agency. If the employer is advertising the position internally, the same equality rules apply and a statement that the position is open to both male and female candidates, married and single is required. If this section of the legislation is contravened there are monetary fines of up to £200 in the Act.

Examples of discriminatory advertising include "female supervisor" in a health and fitness clinic (*Cork Examiner Publications Ltd., Fitzsimons Flynn & Co., An Employer* v. *The Employment Equality Agency*, EE 13/1990). In this case, the Equality Officer recommended that a notice be published on the appointments pages of the *Cork Examiner* once every week for a period of four weeks, drawing the attention of employers to the 1977 Act and stating that certain sections of the Act in relation to occupational qualifications have been repealed (i.e. there was provision that certain establishments were excluded because persons of one sex required special care on the grounds of decency and privacy).

In another case a company was looking for full-time and part-

time store detectives in ladies' fashion stores. In the advertisement
there was a statement that "This position may be of particular
interest to married women" (*Independent Newspapers Ltd., Group 4
Securitas Ireland Ltd.* v. *The Employment Equality Agency*, EE
19/1991, DEE 1/1993). This advertisement was considered discriminatory and the Labour Court determined that Independent Newspapers publish four times a banner on the top of the job-advertising
page, stating "All positions advertised on this page are required to
be open to male and female candidates" and another advertisement
stating that "In accordance with the Employment Equality Act, 1977
the *Irish Independent* is committed to ensuring that recruitment
advertisements do not give the impression of a preference for candidates of one sex or marital status rather than the other". The
company placing the advertisement had to contribute £500 towards
the cost of the latter advertisement.

Employers also cannot discriminate in terms of education requirements for a job. In one particular case a certain certificate was
required, which a female candidate did not have, though she did have
a higher one. Women had been excluded from that particular training
course which the employer required. This was considered to be
discriminatory (*Landy* v. *CERT Ltd.*, EE 20/1983, DEE 2/1984).

EMPLOYMENT AGENCIES

Employment agencies and other employment-related services shall
not discriminate on the terms on which they offer their services. This
provision does not apply if the employer can lawfully refuse to offer
employment (see below) and the agency or service relies on such a
statement from the prospective employer. An employer who knowingly makes a discriminatory statement is liable to a fine not exceeding £200.

EXCLUSIONS

The 1977 Act provides an exclusion for people working outside
Ireland where there are laws and customs which only allow a person
of one sex to do the duties concerned. Such an exception might arise
in respect of women working in certain Middle Eastern countries, for
example.

There are also certain circumstances where a person's sex may
be taken as a genuine occupational qualification, such as modelling,
acting, the provision of personal services (e.g. nursing, though both

men and women can train as midwives), the prison service and the Garda Síochána (where the duties of the post include "guarding, escorting or controlling violent persons, or quelling riots or violent disturbances" and so forth). This would also include the direct supervision of prisoners dressing and undressing, the carrying out of personal searches and the interviewing of persons in relation to sexual offences.

JOB TITLE

The Act also provides that if there is a job description or job title which implies that the applicant should be of a particular sex, or that in the past the job was mainly carried on by a person of one sex, for example, a foreman or 'head waiter/manager', (*Independent Newspapers (Ireland) Ltd. and Irish Banqueting Services Ltd.* v. *Employment Equality Agency*, EE 17/1991, DEE 3/1993), then the advertisement should contain a statement that the position is open to both sexes.

APPLICATION FORMS

If application forms are used by an employer, all prospective employees who ask for a form should receive one. It is important that an employer briefs all staff who are in contact with prospective candidates on equality requirements, for example, a prospective candidate who telephones should not be told "the company is looking for men for this job". The form should not contain questions which are discriminatory or which could give rise to discrimination, for example, asking the prospective employee whether she is married or single or how many children she has (*Barrington* v. *The Medical Council*, EE 9/1988). Technically, it may not be unlawful to ask these questions on an application form, but one must consider whether the questions are necessary in order to find the best person for the position. By asking these questions, employers may be unnecessarily exposing themselves to claims of discrimination. Details of marital status and numbers of children are only appropriate when a candidate has accepted the job offer and the information is needed for pension/life assurance purposes.

INTERVIEWS

There have been several cases relating to access to employment and selection arrangements. The first key case was that of *Chaney* v.

University College, Dublin (EE 15/1983) where the claimant alleged that the prospective employer had refused her access to employment because she was married and had children. She maintained that she had been asked at the interview how many children she had and how she proposed to have them cared for. Apparently these questions were not asked of the male candidates, and it was considered that the questions were reasonable only if asked of both male and female candidates. In some situations it may be quite permissible for a prospective employer to find out if a candidate is married, for example, if the surname on the application is different from that on professional certificates (*Tuite* v. *The Coombe Lying-in Hospital*, EE 17/1985). However, questions such as "How will you be able to cope being a housewife and working?" or "What does your husband think about you working and studying?" (in relation to post-graduate study) or "Are you thinking of getting married?" or "Do you intend having children?" would be considered to be discriminatory on the basis of sex and marital status, as the case may be.

Of course, it is perfectly reasonable for an employer to assess whether a prospective employee will be able to carry out the job duties. At interview, therefore, the job and its requirements should be fully explained and all the candidates asked whether they believe they would have any difficulty in doing the job, obviously after a period of appropriate training. All candidates should also be asked if there is anything else that they wish to add to the interview or say to their prospective employer.

If there are further selection tests, it should be ensured that they are free of discriminatory bias.

Employers should ensure that they keep the notes of the interview for at least six months following a letter to an unsuccessful candidate, and the notes for a successful candidate should be placed in the personnel file. A person has six months within which to bring a claim under the Employment Equality Act. The time limit may be extended where a person has "reasonable cause" for the delay (see Chapter 24 — Equal Pay and Equal Treatment Claims).

"MARRIAGE BAR"

Prior to the early 1970s, in many employments, especially in the public service, women had to resign on marriage. In *Aer Lingus Teo* v. *The Labour Court* ([1990] ELR 125), the Supreme Court considered that the compulsory retirement of 24 air hostesses (the complain-ants) was a discriminatory act relating to marital status, but it was not illegal. This case concerned the subsequent re-employment of these air hostesses on first a temporary, then permanent basis, though all their previous service would not be considered for seniority purposes. The 1977 Act does not have a retrospective effect.

More recently, the "marriage bar" issue surfaced again as women who had to resign on marriage wished to return to their previous job in the public service. In one particular case the claimant, who had been employed as a Higher Tax Officer in the Revenue Commissioners, resigned on marriage in 1969. In 1973, the "marriage bar" was abolished and certain provisions permitted married women to be readmitted to their jobs on grounds of hardship or if they became widowed. The claimant applied for reinstatement in January, 1990. She was advised that she could only be reinstated on grounds of hardship (for which she would have to show evidence of her circumstances) or if she was widowed. She brought a claim under the 1977 Act, and the Employment Equality Agency also made a complaint to the Minister for Finance on her behalf, alleging that the Minister procured discrimination by having such discriminatory rules for reinstatement. The equality officer considered that there was discrimination towards the claimant arising from her marital status. However the equality officer ruling of reinstatement was overturned. The Labour Court did not award her compensation as it is not a case where compensation should be awarded to one claimant. The Minister for Finance was to repeal section 11 of the Civil Service Regulation Act, 1956 as amended by section 4 of the Civil Service (Employment of Married Women) Act, 1973 (*Moran* v. *The Revenue Commissioners*, EE 20/1991 and *Employment Equality Agency* v. *The Minister for Finance*, EE 21/1991, [1993] ELR 129).

MOBILITY

An employer must not discriminate on the presumption that a woman would be less able to travel as part of the terms and conditions of employment. In one particular case, the claimant considered that she had been discriminated against for the position of customer service agent. The employer had a condition of employment that employees must be mobile and be available for work both in Ireland and Great Britain. Interestingly, the equality officer accepted that the reason for her non-selection was that she was not able to comply with the mobility requirement which the equality officer accepted to be an essential requirement of the job. Nonetheless, the equality officer considered that there had been discrimination at the job interview, and the claimant was awarded a small sum of compensation (*A Prospective Female Employee* v. *A Company*, EE 12/1989).

AGE LIMITS

It can be discriminatory to have certain age limits for positions. This issue has arisen in particular where married women wish to return to the workforce having raised their family. The key case on age limits was *North Western Health Board* v. *Martyn* [1987] IR 565 where the upper age limit of 27 years was considered to be discriminatory because the age was too low for many married women to re-enter the workforce having fulfilled family responsibilities. Even though this decision was based on the actual facts of that particular case, the age limit requirement for such positions has now been raised.

PREGNANCY

An employer may not refuse a prospective employee a position solely on the basis that she is pregnant. The European Court of Justice in the Dekker case (Case 177/88) considered that an employer is in direct contravention of the principle of equal treatment if they refuse to enter into a contract of employment with a candidate solely because of possible adverse consequences of employing a pregnant woman. In Ireland, this has been considered to be indirect discrimination since this obviously affects more women than men. In *Geraghty-Williams* v. *An Foras Forbartha* (EE 6/1981, DEE 4/1982), the claimant was offered employment subject to a satisfactory medical report. The medical report stated that she was pregnant but otherwise in good health. The offer of employment was withdrawn. The Labour Court determined that the withdrawal of an offer of employment because the employee was pregnant was indirect discrimination. Also, the postponement of employment pending the completion of pregnancy was considered to be indirect discrimination (*Cassidy* v. *Pan American Airways Inc.*, EE 3/1989).

In another case, the claimant contended that she had been offered employment but when she told her prospective employer that she was expecting a baby within the next month, she was allegedly advised that the company could not guarantee her employment when the baby was born. There was considerable conflict of evidence in this case, but nonetheless the Labour Court considered that there was indirect discrimination and awarded the claimant £5,500, recommended that she be appointed to the next suitable vacancy in the branch concerned and that on reappointment her service be backdated to January 1988. The Labour Court reduced her financial award as, during the course of the proceedings, she had refused part-time work. (*Power Supermarkets Ltd. t/a Quinnsworth v. Long*, EE 15/1991, DEE 2/1993).

PHYSICAL REQUIREMENTS

If there is a stipulation that a person must be of a particular height, it must clearly be an essential requirement for the job. In one case, CIE had a requirement that bus conductors had to be at least 5' 5" tall and the claimant, who was smaller than 5' 5", claimed that she had worked for a number of years as a bus conductor in the UK and that it did not affect her doing the job. The Labour Court considered that the requirement to be 5' 5" was not an essential requirement (*Smith v. CIE*, EE 4/1979, DEE 1/1979).

However, in another case, physical strength was considered an essential requirement for the position of firefighter (*Gibney v. Dublin Corporation*, EE 5/1986).

TERMS AND CONDITIONS

Terms on which employment is offered cannot be discriminatory either. For example, there have been situations where married women were indirectly discriminated against in respect of their access to full-time employment by a requirement that there be a lay-off period between part-time and full-time employment. In *Employment Equality Agency v. Packard Electrical (Ireland) Ltd., the IT&GWU, and the AT&GWU* (EE 14/1985), female employees alleged that part-time employees on the twilight shift (mainly married women) were barred from entry to full-time employment. This practice arose from a clause in the union/management agreement which provided that employees who had been laid off or made redundant from the twilight shift were not permitted to apply for full-time work with the company until a period of 26 weeks had elapsed from the date of redundancy. Furthermore, if such employees made application for full-time work, they would automatically be removed from the twilight shift recall list. The equality officer considered that this clause was not an essential requirement and that it was indirectly discriminatory against married women. The practice was to be discontinued immediately and the next 30 appointments for full-time positions (subject to suitability) were to be made from the twilight shift within three months from the date of the recommendation.

PROCEDURE AND REDRESS

A person who believes there has been discrimination should first send a Section 28 form (which outlines the alleged discrimination) to their employer who should respond and return it within 21 days. If a person still considers that they have been discriminated against, they may refer their claim under the Act to the Labour Court within six months of the first act of alleged discrimination. This time limit may be extended where there is reasonable cause. The Labour Court normally refers the claim to an equality officer for investigation (see Chapter 24 — Equal Pay and Equal Treatment Claims).

If the equality officer considers that there was discrimination, the more usual form of redress is compensation which may be up to a maximum of 104 weeks pay. Monies awarded may vary and the award will obviously be larger where the equality officer considers that the claimant lost the job because of discrimination. Awards for this type of claim are relatively low — for example, a few hundred pounds — because it is generally considered that the prospective employee only lost the chance of the job and not the job itself. A claimant also has an obligation to mitigate or lessen his loss. In the case of *Power Supermarkets Ltd. t/a Quinnsworth* v. *Long* (above), the claimant refused part-time work, thus her award was reduced by the Labour Court from £15,500 to £5,500. If an employee loses out on promotional prospects, the award could be significantly higher. The successful claimant invariably also receives monies for "distress", although the term "distress" is not contained in the Act.

If there is discriminatory advertising, the Employment Equality Agency may pursue the matter to the Labour Court. Further, if a person makes a false statement in order to secure publication, or where there is an advertisement in breach of the Act, persons who contravene the Act may be guilty of an offence and be fined £200. An employer who makes a statement in breach of the Act will be guilty of an offence and may be fined up to £200.

There is no specific provision in the legislation to order an employer to enter into a contract of employment with a person. However, an equality officer or the Labour Court may recommend a specified course of action, for example, that part-time employees be considered for the next appointments to full-time vacancies (the Packard case, see above).

GENERAL REFERENCES

Callender, R. and Meenan, F., *Equality in Law between Men and Women in the European Community — Collection of Texts and Commentary on Irish Law*, Martinus Nijhoff Publishers and Office for Official Publications of the European Communities, 1994.

Curtin, D., *Irish Employment Equality Law*, The Round Hall Press, 1989.

CHAPTER TWO

The Contract of Employment

All employees work under a contract of employment which in legal terms is called a contract of service. Frequently employees state that they "have no contract". What they are really saying is that they "have no *written* contract". A contract may be in writing or verbally agreed between the parties. There are many different forms of contract:

(1) A written/oral contract providing ongoing employment

(2) A fixed-term contract (e.g. for one year or whatever period)

(3) A specified purpose contract (e.g. to work on a specific project)

(4) An independent contractor's agreement, which is not an employer/employee relationship.

It is always advisable to have a written contract or agreement between the parties. The Unfair Dismissals Acts, 1977 to 1993, contain particular requirements concerning fixed-term and specified purpose contracts which must be complied with if an employer seeks the exclusion under that Act for unfair dismissal claims at the end of those contracts. These provisions are considered in Chapter 3 — Temporary Employment.

Once the employer has made the decision to hire the successful candidate, a written offer of employment may be sent out. A contract of employment does not have to be long, complicated or very legalistic. It should set out in comprehensible language the key terms and conditions. The contract and agreement for employment only come into being once the contract has been accepted and signed by the employee. Obviously, a prospective employee does not have to accept the offer of employment and in the case of failure to do so, there is no employment contract between the parties. In other words, there must be offer and acceptance.

However, an employer can send out an offer of employment and then change their mind. It is extremely difficult for the employer to withdraw the offer at this time, yet it may be done if the employee has not accepted it. An employee who has accepted the contract would be entitled to the requisite notice period provided for in the contract should the employer wish to terminate the contract.

Before an offer of employment goes out, an employer should ask for the prospective employee's consent to check all relevant references. If this is not feasible, the employer should only send out the contract of employment subject to a satisfactory medical examination and satisfactory references. It is recommended that an employer requests an employee to undergo a general medical examination to determine that the employee is in good health. The employer may nominate the doctor and generally carries the cost of the examination. The doctor should be fully aware of the nature and requirements of the work concerned. If, for example, the prospective employee has a bad back and the job involves lifting heavy objects, the employer should be very cautious about hiring that person because this disability may cause problems later on in employment. It would then be arguable that any absenteeism arising from the condition would not be reason for a fair dismissal as the employer was in full knowledge of the condition and that this issue is implied into the contract of employment (see Chapter 17 — Unfair Dismissal). Should the potential employee be pregnant, this is not a sufficient reason for the employer to withdraw the offer of employment (see Chapter 1 — Recruitment and Equality).

In some cases there may be a union/management agreement in place which sets out all the terms and conditions of employment. In that case, the offer letter may only have to state the job title, date of commencement and salary of the prospective employee concerned. Of course, a copy of the agreement should be sent with the offer letter. Alternatively, if there is a staff manual setting out all the terms and conditions of employment, the same situation may apply.

WORK PERMIT

Should the employer wish to employ an "alien", that is, an individual who is neither Irish nor an EU national, application will have to be made to the Department of Enterprise and Employment. Before a work permit is issued, the Minister for Enterprise and Employment will have to be satisfied that every effort was made to recruit a

qualified Irish or EU national for the position. The proposed employment of such a person is usually in highly specialised positions.
Applications should be made at least six weeks before the proposed
employment is taken up and, when granted, work permits are usually for one year but may be renewed — see the form on pages 38-39.
It should be noted that a work permit does not necessarily allow such
a person to enter or reside within the State; that is under the control
of the immigration authorities at the Department of Justice.

EMPLOYEES OR INDEPENDENT CONTRACTORS

The difference between an employee and an independent contractor
is often difficult to interpret. A person who is an employee and works
under a contract of service falls within the scope of employment
protective legislation, namely, the Unfair Dismissals Acts, the Minimum Notice and Terms of Employment Acts, Redundancy Payments
Acts and the Maternity Protection of Employees Acts. An independent contractor is not an employee and thus does not fall within
the scope of protective legislation. Independent contractors are essentially in business themselves and sell their services to clients,
thus they work under a contract for services. Examples of independent contractors are generally professionals and tradespersons,
for example, solicitors, doctors, various other consultants, plumbers,
electricians and so forth.

Generally, courts and tribunals are more inclined towards considering a person an employee as distinct from an independent
contractor. In *E.P. Ó Coindealbháin (Inspector of Taxes)* v. *Mooney*
([1990] IR 422), the High Court considered the difference between a
contract of service and a contract for services. Blayney, J. considered
(in summary) that only the terms of the written contract could be
considered in deciding what the terms and conditions of employment
were. The extent and degree of control exercised by the employer and
whether the person was in business on his own account were also
factors in determining the form of contract. The Employment Appeals Tribunal also consider issues such as whether the "employee"
received holidays, sick pay and pensions. A person who is in receipt
of such benefits, it may be assumed, is an employee working under
a contract of service. In *Irish Press Limited* v. *Kelly* ((1986) 5 JISLL
170), the claimant had been an association football correspondent for
the *Sunday Press* since 1952. It was contended that he was not an
employee as he only worked part-time and he did not have income

tax or PRSI deducted from his earnings. The Circuit Court over-turned the Tribunal determination (which had held that he was an employee) and considered that Mr Kelly was not an employee. Clarke, J. in summary raised the following questions:

(1) Does the sports editor have to accept his articles?

(2) Would Mr Kelly be in breach of contract if he did not provide the newspaper with an article?

(3) Could the newspaper get an injunction if he gave the article to another journal?

The questions were answered in the negative as each party was a free agent. Each was free to accept or to refuse work. There was a fresh offer and acceptance on each occasion. Accordingly, there was a contract for services. Clarke, J. also considered the *Tribune* case ([1984] IR 505), and compared the *Sunday Press* contributor with a freelance contributor.

STATUTORY REQUIREMENTS

Written Statement of Terms and Conditions of Employment

Section 9 of the Minimum Notice and Terms of Employment Act, 1973 (this Act applies to all employees working over 18 hours and regular part-time employees) provides that an employer must give a written statement to an employee within one month of commencement providing the following information:

(1) The date of commencement of employment

(2) The rate or method of calculation of remuneration

(3) The intervals at which remuneration is paid, whether weekly, monthly or other period

(4) Any terms or conditions relating to the hours of work or overtime

(5) Any terms or conditions relating to:

    (a) holidays and holiday pay

    (b) incapacity for work due to sickness or injury and sick pay and

    (c) pensions and pension schemes.

(6) The period of notice which the employee is obliged to give, and entitled to receive, to determine their contract of employment, or (if the contract of employment is for a fixed term) the date on which the contract expires.

An employer is obliged within one month of an employee's request to give the employee the above written particulars or display them on a company noticeboard or wherever it is reasonably accessible for the employee.

Breach of this section may lead to a fine of £25 (s. 10). The Act does not provide for any other legal recourse.

The Terms of Employment (Information) Bill, 1993 was published on 25 November 1993 and makes provision to repeal sections 9 and 10 of the 1973 Act. It is envisaged that it will be enacted in early 1994. The proposed legislation arises from an EC Directive (91/533/EEC) which provides that an employer is obliged to inform an employee of the terms and conditions of employment. The Bill applies to employees who are normally expected to work over eight hours per week and have been in continuous employment for one month. It also applies to agency workers.

Section 3 of the Bill provides that an employer must give the following information in writing to an employee within two months of commencement of employment. This legislation only applies to employees recruited after the commencement of the Act unless a current employee requests such information, in which case the information would have to be provided within two months of the request. The information to be included is as follows:

(a) The full names of employer and employee

(b) The address of the employer in the State or, where appropriate, the address of the principal place of the relevant business of the employer in the State or the registered office (within the meaning of the Companies Act, 1963)

(c) The place of work or, where there is no fixed or main place of work, a statement specifying that the employee is required or permitted to work at various places

(d) The title of the job or nature of the work for which the employee is employed

(e) The date of commencement of the employee's contract of employment

(f) In the case of a temporary contract of employment, the expected duration thereof or, if the contract of employment is for a fixed term, the date on which the contract expires

(g) The rate or method of calculation of the employee's remuneration

(h) The length of the intervals between the times at which remuneration is paid, whether a week, a month or any other interval

(i) Any terms or conditions relating to hours of work (including overtime)

(j) Any terms or conditions relating to paid leave (other than paid sick leave)

(k) Any terms or conditions relating to —

(i) incapacity for work due to sickness or injury and paid sick leave, and

(ii) pensions and pension schemes

(l) The period of notice which the employee is required to give and entitled to receive (whether by or under statute or under the terms of the employee's contract of employment) to determine the employee's contract of employment, or where this cannot be indicated when the information is given, the method for determining such periods of notice

(m) A reference to any collective agreements which directly affect the terms and conditions of the employee's employment including, where the employer is not a party to such agreements, particulars of the bodies or institutions by whom they were made [e.g. Labour Court, joint labour committees — see Chapter 7 — Collective Bargaining].

This statement must be signed and dated by the employer. If there are changes in the terms and conditions, the employee must be so advised within one month. This provision does not apply to changes in legislation or collective agreements.

There are also detailed provisions for employees who will be working outside the State for over one month. Information such as the period of employment outside the State or the currency in which they will be paid must be given prior to departure.

The information provided under this Bill (when enacted) must be retained by the employer for one year following termination of the employee's employment. The Bill provides for a complaints procedure (see Chapters 22 and 23 — Labour Relations Commission and Employment Appeals Tribunal).

Dismissal Procedure

Section 14 of the Unfair Dismissals Act, 1977 provides that an employer must give an employee in writing the procedure which the employer must follow if the employee is going to be dismissed. This document must set out the agreed written procedure between the employer and a registered trade union (see Chapter 7 — Collective Bargaining) or what has been the custom and practice in the employment. If there is no written agreement, the employer may write one and when it is accepted by the employee it will be deemed as written procedure for the purposes of the Act. This must be given to the employee within 28 days of commencement. If the employer varies or alters the procedure, a written copy of the alteration must be provided to the employee within 28 days (see below for further details on dismissal procedures). The Unfair Dismissals (Amendment) Act, 1993 provides that if an employer fails to comply with the dismissal procedure, the failure will be taken into account when awarding redress to the unfairly dismissed employee.

LEGAL CONTRACT

Before one considers the terms of the contract of employment, it must above all be a legal contract. It cannot be tainted with an illegality, such as, an agreement between the employer and employee to avoid the payment of income tax/PRSI. If an agreement is tainted with such illegality, an employee will not be able to sue on the basis of the contract (see *Lewis* v. *Squash (Ireland) Ltd.* [1983] ILRM 363). The Unfair Dismissals (Amendment) Act, 1993 provides that, even if the contract is illegal, an unfairly dismissed employee will be entitled to redress for unfair dismissal. However, the Rights Commissioner, the Employment Appeals Tribunal or the Circuit Court will have authority to refer the file to the Revenue Commissioners or the Department of Social Welfare (see Chapter 17 — Unfair Dismissal).

EXPRESS AND IMPLIED TERMS

Express terms are the key terms unless legislation provides otherwise, for example, minimum statutory requirements for notice, holidays and maternity leave.

Implied terms are those that are taken as being in existence between the parties, to include that the employer will provide work for the employee; will pay wages to the employee; will indemnify the employee against all costs, expenses and any claims against the employee which arise from the employee's duties; and will provide a safe place of work and safe equipment. Equally, the employee will serve the employer (and not give the work to anybody else); will do the work in a competent manner; will be loyal to the employer and be confidential about the work; will not act in conflict of interest of the employer; will be honest and will work in a safe manner.

Legislation also imposes implied terms into the contract of employment, namely, the equal pay and equal treatment legislation. The Unfair Dismissal Acts provide that procedural agreements must be complied with and such compliance will be taken into account in awarding compensation under the Acts. Thus the employer must act in a reasonable and fair manner towards the employee and, of course, there is also the Constitutional right to fairness.

While the above are the statutory requirements, it is prudent for an employer to spell out completely the terms and conditions of employment.

It is advisable for an employer to provide an employee with a full contract of employment. This does not have to be a detailed legal document — it may be a letter, for example. However, it is recommended that it be given to the employee in writing and explained to the employee as well.

KEY CLAUSES IN THE CONTRACT OF EMPLOYMENT

Employer

The correct name and title of the employer should be fully stated, e.g. "ABC Limited having its registered office/business address at. . . ." If the employer has a number of companies, the employee should be advised that it will be necessary to work for such associate or subsidiary companies as the employer so decides.

Job Specification

The employer should also advise the employee as to what the job position is and provide the employee with a job specification. A job specification should set out all the duties that are required of the employee and may be an appendix to the contract of employment. While the job specification should set out all the duties, it should be acknowledged by both parties that, over time, the specific requirements of the job may change (e.g. upgrading of technology) and that the employee will carry out all reasonable requests of the employer. Of course, a genuine redundancy situation may arise if the employer requires a person with higher qualification (see Chapter 18 — Redundancy).

Date of Commencement and Job Title

An employer should always give a date for commencement of employment, that is, the date when the employee starts working for the employer. This point looks deceptively simple, but difficulties can arise because over the passage of time people can forget the date of commencement. It could be important should there be a claim for redundancy or unfair dismissal because of service requirements under these Acts.

The job title is usually clear enough because that was the position that was advertised, nonetheless it should be stated in the contract of employment. Also, the employee should be told to whom they will be reporting, that is, the title of the person who has responsibility over the department. It is advisable to state that this may change overtime.

Probation

A contract invariably includes a probationary period at commencement of employment, usually for a period of six months. The purpose of probation is to ensure that the employee is capable of doing the job and to assess whether the employee can work harmoniously with fellow workers in the employment concerned. An employer should have provision to extend the probationary period at the employer's discretion. Of course, during the probationary period the employer should ensure that the employee receives all necessary training and assistance in learning the new job. The Unfair Dismissals Acts provide that the probationary period cannot be longer than twelve months as an employee who is dismissed having one year's service can bring a claim under the Act. Thus, an employer cannot avoid the provisions of the Act by having an employee on continuing probation.

Hours of Work

An employer should specify the hours of work and the times which are allowed for breaks and lunch. If an employee is required to work overtime, it should be clearly stated as should the rate of pay for such overtime. It is important to note that all requests for overtime be reasonable, in other words, all employees must be given adequate notice. In executive positions, it is normally expected that the employee works in excess of the basic hours with no extra payment.

In industry an employee may have to work on shift. The shift rota should be clearly stated as well as breaks and whether overtime is required from time to time. Employers should also comply with the Conditions of Employment Acts, 1936 and 1944, the Shops (Conditions of Employment) Acts, 1938 and 1942, and various registered agreements (see Chapter 13 — Conditions of Employment in Industry and Services).

Remuneration

An employer has an obligation to pay an employee for their services. The contract should state the salary or the rate of pay per week/per hour, for example, £12,000 gross per annum subject to PAYE and PRSI. The timing of payment should be stated, e.g. on the last day of every month, on every Friday etc. An employer may state as to when the salary will be reviewed — every April, for example, or as agreed between management and the trade unions. The method of payment should also be agreed, for example, by credit transfer or by cheque as the case may be (see Chapter 6 — Payment of Wages). If there are bonus payments or commission paid, the method of calculation and when paid should be clearly spelt out. An employer may pay for VHI (up to a certain level of benefit or in full), provide for profit sharing, share options and so forth.

Any deductions from wages or salary (other than income tax or PRSI), must be clearly stated in the contract giving authorisation to the employer to deduct such monies.

Expenses

In some positions an employee may travel in connection with their employment, in the case of a salesperson, for example. If the employee is to use a company car, it should be noted whether they have a full driving licence with no endorsement(s). If the employee is to use their own car on company business, the company should be idemnified against any claim. The indemnity should be noted on the employee's insurance certificate which must be shown to management before the employee's car is used on company business. The rate of payment per mile should also be advised to the employee. There should be a statement to the effect that the company will only meet receipted expenses, and the procedures in place for claiming such outlay should be outlined.

If there is travel involved, the employer should specify whether it is to be economy or executive class (in the case of air and train travel), and whether there has to be prior written permission in the case of air travel.

Sick Pay

There is no statutory obligation on an employer to pay an employee sick pay in the event of absence from work due to illness. However, if there is a sick-pay scheme in place, an employer must give the employee the written details. Sick-pay schemes can be quite simple, for example, an employee may be entitled to six weeks full pay per year, but must reimburse the employer with the sum received for disability benefit. An employee ill for longer will have to rely on disability benefit only. Disability benefit is now subject to income tax. Some employers may provide that such arrangement lasts for the first 26 weeks of illness and then the employee moves on to the income continuance scheme where such scheme exists. An income continuance scheme is invariably linked into the pension scheme and is underwritten by an insurance company.

An employer should have certain rules in the event of an employee being sick and not available for work, such as having to contact a specified person by a certain time. Also, there is usually a requirement for employees to provide a medical certificate (stating the illness and the likely date of return to work) if they are out sick for more than three consecutive days. If an employee is out for a long period, an employer may require weekly certificates. If an employee has consistent intermittent absenteeism, or if through illness is no longer capable of performing their job, employment may be terminated (see Chapter 17 — Unfair Dismissal). It is a commonly held view that an employee's employment may not be terminated if they are out sick and have sent in medical certificates. This is not necessarily so, provided the employer has used fair procedures leading up to termination.

Holidays

Employees who have worked the requisite hours are entitled to statutory paid annual leave under the Holiday (Employees) Act, 1973. They are also entitled to public holidays. Regular part-time employees are entitled to paid annual leave pro-rata with hours worked, and to public holidays in accordance with the Worker Protection (Regular Part-Time Employees) Act. Most employments have holiday provisions over and above that contained in the holidays legislation. Holidays are considered in more detail in Chapter 4 — Annual Leave, Public Holidays and Jury Service.

Right to Search

An employer may incorporate into the contract the right to search an employee's person or property while on the company's premises or upon leaving the premises. An employer must obtain the employees' agreement to search either in the employment contract or through the company rules, as otherwise the employer would commit a trespass to the person. This type of clause is more typically used in manufacturing companies where there is a marketable company product.

Lay-off/Short-time

An employer cannot lay off or put staff on short-time if there is no such provision in the contract of employment (or in the union/management agreement). Lay-off or short-time usually arises where there is insufficient work as a result of an economic downturn, or where there has been a fire in the factory or a shortage of raw material or some other unexpected problem. Lay-off means that the employee is advised that there will be no work for a period of time, and short-time means that the employees could work half days or three days per week. Under the Redundancy Acts, short-time is defined as where an employee works for less than half their normal working hours. There is no statutory provision requiring that notice be given to the employees. However, it is good practice to give them as much notice as is reasonable. The employer should also advise employees why such lay-off/short-time is necessary, that it is a genuine intention that it will not continue for too long and that it will be reviewed within a specified period of time.

An employer should take care in the selection of employees for lay-off or short-time. For example, it would be discriminatory just to choose part-time women employees or a particular grade of employee. Of course, it can be justified to choose certain groups for specific reasons, as long as it is not discriminatory.

An employee who has been on lay-off/short-time for a period of time may claim a statutory redundancy payment (see Chapter 18 — Redundancy).

Also, if an employer realises that there is no work in the future for employees still on lay-off/short-time, then such employees must receive monies in lieu of notice and statutory redundancy. Lay-off/short-time may not be used as a means of avoiding notice entitlements (see Chapter 16 — Notice).

Health and Safety

The contract should have a positive statement that the company is committed to fulfilling its obligations under the Health, Safety and Welfare at Work Act, 1989 and that it has prepared a safety statement. The safety statement sets out the rights and responsibilities of both the company and its employees in achieving and maintaining a healthy and safe work place. The statement identifies the material hazards within the work place and the steps the company has taken to protect employees from them. The employee should receive and sign the safety statement on commencement of employment. (see Chapter 15 — Health and Safety in the Workplace).

Trade Union Membership

It may be a condition of employment that an employee remain at all times during the course of employment a benefit member of a particular trade union and that the employer recognises a particular union for negotiation purposes (see Chapter 7— Collective Bargaining). If there is to be a deduction of wages for union dues, the employee may acknowledge and agree to that in the contract of employment.

Retirement Age

Employment contracts should provide for the normal retirement age, particularly for permanent employees. Generally the normal retirement age in Ireland is the 65th birthday. Retirement age is not necessarily the same as pension age, as the pension scheme could technically provide for an earlier pension age than retirement age. For practical purposes, however, pension and retirement ages are the same. Upon reaching the retirement age, the employee's contract of employment comes to an end by operation of law so there can be no viable claim for unfair dismissal or redundancy.

Pension

There is no statutory obligation on an employer to provide a pension for employees. However, if there is a pension scheme either contributory or non-contributory, the employer must give the employee a copy of a summary of the key provisions (see Chapter 14 — Pensions).

Grievance Procedure

During the course of employment, an employee may have genuine grievances which they wish to raise with management. It is important that such matters be dealt with speedily in order to avoid an escalation of the issue. A grievance procedure should be simple and clear, and should provide that in larger employments the employee first goes to their supervisor and if the matter is not resolved at that level, then it may be referred to higher management. In smaller employments, such formality may not be necessary because there may only be two levels of employee, namely, management and staff. It is important that the employee has a right of representation at all times (e.g. a colleague or shop steward). If matters cannot be resolved locally, there should be provision to refer the matter to a rights commissioner, the Labour Relations Commission, an equality officer or the Employment Appeals Tribunal as appropriate (see Chapter 8 — Trade Disputes).

Notice

The contract may state that the Minimum Notice and Terms of Employment Acts will apply to this employment. This in effect means that the statutory notice provisions will apply. An employer may provide for a longer period of notice over and above the statutory minimum, for example, three months' notice. There should also be provision that the employer may pay monies in lieu of notice. It should also be stated for the purposes of clarification that an employee who is dismissed for reasons of gross misconduct is not entitled to notice or monies in lieu of notice. There may also be a provision that both parties may agree to waive the notice period or monies in lieu of notice (see Chapter 16 — Notice).

Even an employee who is dismissed during the probationary period is entitled to statutory minimum notice provided that the dismissal is not the result of misconduct. If an employer provides for a longer period of contractual notice, it may only apply once the probationary period is over and the employee is confirmed in employment.

Dismissal/Disciplinary Procedure

As discussed above, the Unfair Dismissals Acts require that the employer provide the employee with the dismissal procedure. Normally, the dismissal procedure also includes information concerning disciplinary actions. It should be noted that the purpose of the procedures is not to terminate employment, but to give the employee a warning that improvement is needed. It is recommended that the disciplinary/dismissal procedure be kept as simple as possible; if the procedure is unduly complicated it may result in ambiguity and unnecessary problems.

The employer should clearly state the grounds for dismissal, for example, misconduct to include theft, violence, falsifying clock-cards, being under the influence of alcohol while on the company premises, absenteeism both prolonged and intermittent, poor work performance, bad time-keeping, redundancy and any other substantial reason.

The essence of a disciplinary/dismissal procedure is balance and fairness to the employee concerned. It is a commonly held view by employees that one verbal and two written warnings can result in them being "fairly" dismissed. This is not necessarily the case, and if a claim under the Unfair Dismissals Acts were brought there might well be a finding of "unfair dismissal". It depends entirely on the facts and the circumstances. In cases of gross misconduct — theft of company property, for example — there is no necessity at all for warnings. A thorough and fair investigation of the issue with the opportunity for the employee to state their case (with representation) is called for. If the employer is satisfied that on the balance of probabilities the employee was involved in theft, the employment may then be terminated.

If matters cannot be resolved locally, there should be provision to refer the matter to a rights commissioner, the Labour Relations Commission, an equality officer or the Employment Appeals Tribunal as appropriate (see Chapter 10 — Trade Disputes).

The key parts to a disciplinary procedure are counselling, verbal warning, written warnings, a final written warning, suspension with or without pay (see Chapter 6 — Payment of Wages) and provision for representation. Procedural fairness is considered in more detail in Chapter 17 — Unfair Dismissal.

The Unfair Dismissals (Amendment) Act, 1993 provides that, when awarding compensation, the adjudicating bodies will take into account the compliance or the failure to comply by the employer with written dismissal procedures.

Secrecy and Confidentiality

While confidentiality about an employer's business is an implied term of the contract of employment, it is nonetheless prudent to include a clause stating that the employee shall not disclose any aspect of the employer's business to any third party except with the employer's prior written permission.

In some employments, the employer may have a separate agreement containing clauses relating to secrecy, confidentiality, restraint of trade or competition.

Competition

The Competition Act, 1991 has raised problems concerning restraint-of-trade or non-competition clauses in contracts of employment. The Act prohibits non-competitive clauses between undertakings — individuals or persons (companies, partnerships etc.) who provide goods or services for gain. The Competition Authority which "polices" the Act has issued guidelines in respect of such clauses in contracts of employment. These guidelines have no legal standing but are extremely useful. A non-competitive clause in a contract of employment is considered permissible because an individual who is an employee is not an "undertaking" — that person is working solely for the employer concerned. Thus there is no requirement for such contracts to be notified to the Authority.

However, an employee who leaves their employment to set up their own business would then be considered to be an "undertaking". If the employer then tried to enforce the non-competitive clause, it would restrict competition. The clause would also be notifiable under the Act. While it is arguable that such an agreement between a former employer and employee would not have a major effect on competition, nonetheless there could be considerable impact depending on the industry/service and the nature of the employee's work. A large number of restraint of trade clauses generally, or in one industry/service would restrict competition. In summary, an employer cannot have a clause that would distort competition in the market. Of course, the Authority can grant an exemption in respect of some clauses.

Leaving aside the Competition Act, one must also consider the general common law provisions on restraint-of-trade clauses. Generally speaking, the courts do not like enforcing such clauses and the clauses must be reasonable. Accordingly, it is generally provided that, if the courts delete such a clause, the balance of the contract remains enforceable.

Copyright/Patents

If the employee has to write or prepare materials in the course of their employment, the contract should clearly state that the copyright rests in the employer.

If it is envisaged that the employee will be writing articles for journals or will give lectures, there may be a statement that the employee may only do so with the prior written permission of the managing director. Further, if text is published it should clearly state that "any views expressed are the author's own".

If an employee is involved in designing or adapting products, it should be clearly stated that all inventions shall be assigned to the employer. There should be a statement that all documents (including copies) of all memoranda and other pertinent materials be handed over on termination of employment.

Company Directors

The Companies Act, 1990 provides that shareholders are entitled to inspect (without charge) a copy or a memorandum of the terms of a director's contract of employment. Such documents must be kept at the registered office, the principal place of business or the place where the register of shareholders is kept. A holding company must also keep such memoranda of directors of subsidiary companies. However, disclosure in such case is not required where the contract has less than three years to run or can be terminated within 12 months with no compensation.

Relocation

An employer may provide that the employee, if requested, work elsewhere in Ireland (or abroad), with x months' notice and that all reasonable relocation expenses will be paid.

Arbitration

Generally, contracts of employment do not provide for arbitration clauses because the Arbitration Acts, 1954 to 1980 do not apply to such contracts. There are special arrangements in the public and civil services. If a registered agreement forms part of the conditions of employment, the Labour Court may interpret the agreement (see Chapter 7 — Collective Bargaining).

Applicable Law

Should an employee have to work abroad for part of the contract, it is advisable to state the applicable law, i.e. that of the Republic of Ireland.

Attestation Clause

It is important for the employer to provide an attestation in the contract. Again, this can be extremely simple, with a statement that the employee accepts and agrees to be bound by the terms and conditions of employment. The employee should sign the letter/

agreement and it should also be signed by the employer. One must stress that the employee should be fully aware of and understand all the terms and conditions of employment before signing the contract.

The above are the key points in relation to a contract of employment. An employer may also wish to provide all the company rules within the contract of employment, such as shift-working, clocking procedure, details of notification if there is sickness, details of misconduct and gross misconduct, company cars, expenses, confidentiality, restraint-of-trade clauses and the safety statement.

Two copies of the contract should be sent to the prospective employee, one copy to be signed and returned to the employer by a particular date and the other to be held by the employee. If the terms and conditions are contained in a union/ management agreement or a staff manual, a written statement stating that the employee understands and accepts the terms and conditions as contained in the agreement or staff manual should be sent back to the employer.

The employer may also request the employee to send with the acceptance letter their birth certificate, P45 form from the previous employment, and written evidence of trade union membership (if appropriate).

Once everything is in order and the employee commences employment, it is advisable for an employer to have a period of induction/training for the employee, to be made aware of the custom and practice of the firm.

PERSONNEL RECORDS AND DATA PROTECTION

Personal data on employees kept on computer or word processor disk are covered by the Data Protection Act, 1988. Data kept on manual files are not covered under the Act. Personal data means "data relating to a living individual who can be identified either from the data or from the data in conjunction with other information in possession of the data controller". Such personal information may include details of an employee's health, family and social circumstances, political opinions, racial origin, religious or other beliefs, sexual life or criminal convictions. Certain data are exempt from the terms of the Act, such as data for the purpose of safeguarding the State, data required by law to be made available to the public and so forth.

Employers who keep ordinary personal data relating to employees including such matters as absence/injury records, disciplinary records, etc. are not covered under the Act as such data would not be deemed "sensitive".

The 1988 Act has a number of definitions to include the Data Controller (who can be an individual, firm or other body) who controls the contents and use of personal data. A Data Processor is a person who processes the personal data on behalf of the data controller. It does not include an employee of a data controller who processes such data in the course of their employment such as where data are sent out to third parties for processing.

The Act gives a right to every individual who establishes the existence of personal data to have access to such data and to have inaccurate data rectified or erased. It also imposes obligations on data controllers and data processors to ensure that such data are kept accurate and up to date and for lawful purposes. There must also be sufficient security measures taken so that data are not disclosed.

DATA PROTECTION COMMISSIONER

The Data Protection Commissioner has been appointed under the Act to supervise the operation of the legislation and to investigate complaints. Certain categories of data controllers and data processors are required to register with the Data Protection Commissioner. If an employer keeps normal personnel records (which do not comprise sensitive data) then there is no requirement to register.

Data controllers and data processors required to register include:

(1) All public authorities

(2) All financial institutions, life assurance and insurance companies or businesses which are wholly or mainly involved in direct marketing, credit referencing or collecting debts

(3) Data controllers who keep personal data relating to racial origin, political opinions, religious or other beliefs, physical or mental health, sexual life, or criminal convictions. This can be collectively called sensitive data

(4) Data processors whose business consists wholly or partly of processing personal data on behalf of data controllers, for example computer bureaux

(5) Data controllers or data processors who may be prescribed under

the Act by the Data Protection Commissioner with the consent of the Minister for Justice.

An employer who does not fall within the above categories is not obliged to register with the Data Protection Commissioner.

DUTIES OF DATA CONTROLLER

Data controllers and processors have a duty of care towards the individuals in regard to sensitive data, and must abide by the Data Protection Principles:

(1) "Fairly obtaining and processing" principle — an employee should be told why the information is needed and what use it may be put to, and assured that the information will not be used for any other purpose.

(2) The data will not be used or disclosed in any manner incompatible with those purposes, for example, data collected on employees for personnel administration should not be used for direct mailing.

(3) The data must be accurate, up to date, adequate, relevant and not excessive in relation to that purpose.

(4) The data must be in proportion to the use to which they are put or to be put, for example, some personal details may be irrelevant.

(5) The data must not be kept for longer than is necessary as they may become out of date or irrelevant.

Data controllers and processors are required by the Act to maintain appropriate security against unauthorised access to, alteration, disclosure or destruction of data. Examples of such security requirements would be the use of code words, passwords or restriction of physical access.

ACCESS TO DATA

An employee may request to find out data on their personnel file. In the normal course, this should not cause any problems because it may merely contain medical certificates or warnings. However, if there are "personal data" on the file, the employee may request access of such data under the provisions of the Act. If the request is not answered, the employee may refer the matter to the Data Protection Commissioner and the employer may be guilty of an offence.

GENERAL REFERENCES

Clark, R., *Data Protection Law in Ireland*, The Round Hall Press, 1990.

Data Protection Commissioner, *Guide to the Data Protection Act, 1988*, Dublin, December, 1988.

Forde, M., *Employment Law*, The Round Hall Press, 1992.

Harvey on Industrial Relations and Employment Law, Osman, C. and Napier B., Vol. 1, Individual Rights, The Contract of Employment, Butterworths.

O'Mara, C., Information on Terms of Employment, *Gazette of the Incorporated Law Society of Ireland*, January/February, 1993.

**DEPARTMENT OF ENTERPRISE
AND EMPLOYMENT
Davitt House, Adelaide Road,
Dublin 2.**

> Please
> affix
> Photos
> here

APPLICATION FOR A WORK PERMIT TO EMPLOY A Non-EC national

Ref:

Section A: Particulars of Employer

Employer's Name ——————————————————————————————————————

Registered name of employer's business ——————————————————————

Address ———

———

Nature of employer's business ——————————————————— Tel. No. ——————

Number of Irish/EC nationals employed ————— Number of non-EC nationals employed ——————

Section B: Particulars of non-EC national (who is the subject of this application)

Surname———————————————————————————————————Male/Female

Other Name (as on passport) ————————————————————————————

Present Address ——————————————————————————————————

———

Date of Birth ——————————— Place of Birth ——————————— Nationality ———

Number of Passport ————————————— Date and place of issue of passport ——————

Marital Status ————————————— Nationality of spouse ————————————
(if Married to an Irish or EC national, please furnish birth certificate of spouse and marriage certificate, or certified copies thereof)

Was the non-EC national previously employed in Ireland? ————— Name and address of previous employers; ——————.

Most recent Work Permit Number (if any) ———————————————————
(Please specify dates)

Details of dependants who will accompany the non-EC national

Name	Relationship to non-EC national	Age	Sex	Marital Status	Work Experience to date, if any

Section C: Title of post on offer_____

Main functions of the job _____

Proposed period of employment from _____ to _____
(please specify exact dates)

Salary or wages offered £................per ...... Other Benefits (Car, etc.)_____

Hours of work _____ Days per week _____

Reasons for employing the non-EC national._____

_____

Special qualifications for the job _____

_____

Section D: Detail any efforts made to recruit an Irish/EC national for the position, including
full details of advertisement.

(Documentary evidence should be attached)

_____

_____

_____

Detail any plans to train an Irish/EC national to fill this position in the future _____

_____

Which unions represented in your firm cater for the grade or category of worker to which this vacancy refers

_____

Have these trade unions been consulted re this application and, if so, with what result _____

Conditions for issue of a Work Permit

(A)   Issue of a work permit in respect of a named non-EC national does not in itself authorise such a person to enter or reside within the State. Admission to the State and authorised duration of stay is subject to the control of the Immigration Authorities. All non-EC nationals must be registered with the Aliens Registration Section of the Department of Justice.

(B)   Application for a work permit, including a renewal, should be made six weeks before the non-EC national is required to take up employment or a current permit expires.

(C)   Work permits are issued for a maximum period of one year.

(D)   A fee, as determined by the Department of Enterprise and Employment is payable by the employer, in respect of each work permit granted.

(E)   If the prospective employee is married to an EC national the marriage certificate and the spouse's birth certificate must be furnished unless Section D of this form has been completed satisfactorily.

I hereby solemnly declare that the particulars given in this application are true, to the best of my knowledge and belief and I apply to the Minister for Enterprise and Employment for a work permit as required under the provisions of the Aliens Act, 1935, the Aliens Order, 1946 and 1975 and the European Communities (Aliens) Regulations, 1977 in accordance with the conditions referred to in this form.
(Non-compliance with the provisions of the Aliens Act, 1935, and Orders made under that Act is an offence punishable by law).

Signature of Employer _____ Date _____
(In the case of an incorporated company this form must be signed by a director or the company secretary or other responsible person whose position must be stated.)

1tny3035.mb

CHAPTER THREE

Temporary Employment

The descriptions "part-time" employment, "temporary" employment, "casual" employment, "short-term" employment and "seasonal work" are not legal descriptions. Until recently it has frequently been assumed that such employees had no legal rights under either common law or protective legislation. This assumption is wrong and most temporary employment arrangements should have a written statement of terms and conditions, as previously discussed.

The Worker Protection (Regular Part-Time Employees) Act, 1991 came into force on 6 April 1991 (excluding redundancy and maternity, which was June 1991). This Act provided that employees not previously covered under employee protection legislation — namely, the Unfair Dismissals Act, 1977, the Redundancy Payments Acts, 1967 to 1984, the Minimum Notice and Terms of Employment Acts, 1973 to 1984 and the Maternity Protection of Employees Act, 1981 — are now covered under those Acts, provided that they are normally expected to work at least eight hours per week and they have the appropriate service. In this book, rather than providing a separate chapter on the 1991 Act, the amendments that have been made to the various pieces of protective legislation are included in the appropriate sections. However, there are still questions raised in relation to certain other types of employment which shall be considered.

"CASUALS"

There is no definition for "casual" employment. In practice, such workers are on stand-by to do work as required with no fixed hours or attendance arrangements. Nonetheless, it has been accepted that such workers are "employees" within the meaning of protective legislation. For example, the status of "permanent casuals" was considered in *Byrne* v. *Gartan Ltd.* (1048/1983) where it was held that the claimant, a "casual" waitress, was considered to be an employee since over the years the expectation arose of her availability for work. There is no provision which would stop a casual employee working for a number of different employers.

AGENCY WORKERS

Agency workers are persons who register with employment agencies that make temporary workers available to a third party (the hirer), the classic example being "agency temps", that is, secretaries. The legal status of such work is both complicated and unfortunate, and the law in Ireland (*The Minister for Labour* v. *PMPA Insurance Co. under administration* (1986) 5 JISLL 215) is that the agency temp is not an employee of the hiring company and thus does not have any protection under the legislation. If they were to be considered employees of anyone, it would be of the employment agency.

The Unfair Dismissals (Amendment) Act, 1993 provides that agency temps placed by an employment agency under the Employment Agency Act, 1971 shall be entitled to bring unfair dismissal claims for redress against the hiring company, i.e. the employer with whom they are placed. Of course, the agency temp must have the necessary service under the unfair dismissals legislation. The Terms of Employment (Information) Bill, 1993 makes provision for a written statement of terms and conditions of employment.

TEMPORARY EMPLOYMENT

In order to fall within the scope of protective legislation, a temporary worker must be an employee working under a contract of employment (of service) and must normally be expected to work at least eight hours per week. However, it should be noted that that worker is to have the requisite period of service under the relevant legislation namely: Unfair Dismissals Acts — one year; Redundancy Payments Acts — two years; and Minimum Notice and Terms of Employment Acts — 13 weeks. There must be continuity of service, and in relation to seasonal employment it is not sufficient for an employer to state that the contract comes to an end at the end of every season, for example in certain manufacturing industries and the hotel industry. The Employment Appeals Tribunal has considered that if the person works year in year out, or there is a pattern of such working, when that person is not working it is deemed to be a period of lay-off and continuity is preserved (*Roscrea Meat Products* v. *Mullins and Ors.* UD 347/1983 and *Cowman* v. *Bon Voyage Travel Ltd.*, 1054/1983). Furthermore, the 1993 Unfair Dismissals Act provides that if an employee is re-employed within 26 weeks of dismissal their continuity of service is not broken (see Chapter 16 — Notice). Employers cannot dismiss and re-employ employees in order to avoid liability under the Acts.

FIXED-TERM CONTRACTS

The Unfair Dismissals Act, 1977 does not apply to the non-renewal of a fixed-term or a specified purpose contract, provided the contract is in writing, signed by both parties and states that the Act will not apply to the termination of the contract.

Even though a contract is for a fixed term, it is strongly recommended that a notice clause be included in it. If, for example, the contract were for three years and the employer terminated it after six months, the employee would be entitled to sue for the balance of the contract, that is, for two-and-a-half-years' pay, in the absence of such a provision.

The main area of concern is the non-renewal of a second or subsequent fixed-term contract. From an employer's viewpoint, the issue is problematic as the Employment Appeals Tribunal may view the periods of employment as continuous unless there is good reason for the termination (or non-renewal) of the contract, and it could be held to be an unfair dismissal.

The Employment Appeals Tribunal has stated that employers may not use the device of a fixed term contract to avoid the unfair dismissals legislation. In *FitzGerald* v. *St Patrick's College* (UD 244/1978) where the claimant was a lecturer who had been employed on a series of fixed term contracts that were eventually not renewed, the Chairman of the Tribunal stated:

> if the mere expiry of a fixed term contract of employment were to be regarded as a substantial ground for the non-renewal of employment, the Unfair Dismissals Act, 1977 could be rendered abortive in many cases. An employer could side step its provisions by employing his employees on fixed term contracts only. Then, to get rid of an employee, on whatever grounds, be they trivial or substantial, fanciful or solid, fair or unfair, he need only wait until that employee's fixed term contract expired, and then refuse to renew it.

Accordingly, employees working on repeated fixed term contracts are covered under the unfair dismissals legislation, though they need to have at least one year's continuous service before they could bring a claim under the Unfair Dismissals Act.

The principles laid down by the Employment Appeals Tribunal have now been incorporated in the Unfair Dismissals (Amendment) Act, 1993. The Act provides that employers cannot avoid liability under the unfair dismissals legislation by employing their staff on such contracts. Thus, if there are two or more fixed-term contracts (i.e. re-employment within three months of the expiry of the first contract or any subsequent contract), then the adjudicating body may examine any second or subsequent contract to see if the employer was trying to avoid the legislation. Obviously, this only applies where the dismissal arises because the term of the contract has come to an end and there has been no renewal. These new rules are complicated and to date there is no determination from the Employment Appeals Tribunal interpreting them.

The maternity legislation does not apply to female employees who work under a fixed term contract of less than 26 weeks or if there are less than 26 weeks to run at the date of taking maternity leave.

SPECIFIED PURPOSE CONTRACTS

These are entered into in order to complete a special project. They must be used carefully, however, for if an employee were employed to do a specific job and he spent time doing other work it may render the contract void. The employee may then fall within the scope of the Unfair Dismissals Act if there is a claim on termination, presuming the employee has the requisite one year's service.

Of course, an employer could well use the defence of redundancy if a claim is brought for unfair dismissal following the non- renewal of a second or subsequent contract. Further, an employer could be liable for a redundancy payment if the employee has 104 weeks' continuous service and there is a genuine redundancy situation on the expiry of a specified purpose contract (see Chapter 20 — Redundancy).

The provisions under the Unfair Dismissals (Amendment) Act, 1993 equally apply to specified purpose contracts.

TEMPORARY OFFICERS

Officers of health boards, local authorities and so forth were excluded from the scope of the Unfair Dismissals Act, 1977. Problems have arisen in the case of temporary doctors and nurses and other temporary professional staff in the health boards as they are deemed officers, for example, in *Western Health Board* v. *Quigley* ([1982] ILRM 390) where the claimant, a nurse, had been employed as a temporary officer for many years and did not fall within the scope of the Act.

The Unfair Dismissals (Amendment) Act, 1993 makes provision that temporary officers will now fall within the scope of the unfair dismissals legislation.

APPRENTICES

The Unfair Dismissals Acts do not apply to the dismissal of a person who is or was employed under a statutory apprenticeship (i.e. an apprenticeship under the Industrial Training Act, 1967) if the dismissal takes place within six months after the commencement of the apprenticeship or within one month after the completion thereof. The 1993 Act provides that an apprentice can bring a claim if dismissed for trade union membership or activity even though the apprentice does not have one year's service.

The Redundancy Payments Act, 1967 provides that an apprentice can be dismissed within one month of the completion of the apprenticeship and not be entitled to a redundancy payment. Employers must ensure that when they look at the date of such dismissal they include the notice period — in other words, it must expire prior to the end of that one month.

It should also be noted that should an employee go on maternity leave during the apprenticeship period, the apprenticeship can be lengthened to cover the period of time which she has lost while out on maternity leave.

Some apprenticeships are called statutory apprenticeships under the Industrial Training Act, 1967. With its attendant regulations the Act provides for certain rules covering designated apprenticeships which include engineering, construction, electrical, printing, motor, furniture and dental craftspersons. These rules govern the length of the apprenticeship, age of entry and qualifications. An apprentice may be dismissed without notice for grave misconduct or wilful disobedience in the course of employment, either during or after the expiry of the period of probation. An apprentice may be dismissed for any other reason with one week's notice. In all other cases, an employer will have to give one month's notice to FÁS. This is considered in more detail in Chapters 17 and 18 on Unfair Dismissal and Redundancy.

EQUALITY

There are no service requirements for employees in respect of the equal pay or equal treatment legislation. The equal pay legislation provides that an employer can pay different rates of pay on grounds other than sex; however, an employee working part-time should not be paid on a lower pro-rata rate presuming that they are doing "like work" with a full-time male employee (e.g. *St. Patrick's College* v. *19 Female Employees*, EP 4/1984, DEP 10/1984). Equally, there cannot be any differentiation in treatment between part-time and full-time employees, for example, selecting part-time female employees for redundancy instead of male full-time employees (*Two Employees* v. *Michael O'Neill and Sons Ltd.*, DEE 1/1988).

JOB SHARING

Job sharing as a form of work arrangement has been receiving considerable attention in recent years. It may be defined as one full-time permanent post with benefits being shared by, more usually, two employees. There are many permutations and combinations of job sharing. It provides for considerable flexibility for employees who wish to work only part-time, though they are working within the confines of a full-time post.

EMPLOYEE PARTICIPATION

The Worker Participation (State Enterprises) Acts, 1977 to 1991 provide for the election of temporary employees of designated state enterprises to the board of directors. In order to vote in such elections, an employee must be aged between 18 and 65 years and have one year's service, and in order to stand for such election, the employee must have three years' service. Participating employees are normally expected to work eight hours per week (see Chapter 12 — Employee Participation).

GENERAL REFERENCES

Hepple and O'Higgins, Hepple. B., *Employment Law*, 4th ed., Sweet and
    Maxwell, 1981.
Leighton, P., "Job Sharing", *Industrial Law Journal*, No. 3, 1986.
Meenan, F., "Temporary and Part-time Employees", *Gazette of the
    Incorporated Law Society of Ireland*, July/August 1985.
Redmond, M., "Beyond the Net — Protecting the Individual Worker",
    (1983) JISLL 1.

SECTION TWO

TERMS AND CONDITIONS OF EMPLOYMENT

CHAPTER FOUR

Annual Leave, Public Holidays and Jury Service

Rest and relaxation are essential for everybody in employment and are so recognised by the legislation. However, the legislation only provides for three weeks' holidays in the year plus public holidays. Over the years, this basic entitlement has been extended through National Pay Agreements and other local agreements so that the norm now is 20 days plus public holidays. In some employments, the amount of annual leave is based on length of service or seniority within the employment. The legislation is complicated and has now been extended to cover regular part-time employees.

The Holidays (Employees) Acts, 1973 and 1991 provide entitlements for employees for both annual leave and public holidays as well as rights and obligations for the employer. The Worker Protection (Regular Part-Time Employees) Act, 1991 provides annual leave and public holiday benefits for regular part-time employees.

The Holidays (Employees) Act applies to all employees working under a contract of employment, with certain exceptions to include non-industrial state employees, fishermen, seagoing employees and employed relations who are maintained by and living with the employer on the employer's farm.

Agency "temps" are not entitled to holidays from the hiring company as they are not deemed to be employed by that company (*The Minister for Labour* v. *PMPA Insurance Co. under administration* (1986) 5 JISLL 215).

ANNUAL LEAVE

The statutory minimum for annual leave is three working weeks. However, the norm would be 20 days and many employees have in excess of that. An employee who has at least one qualifying month of service is entitled to paid annual leave.

An employee may qualify for annual leave under any of the following methods:

(1) Qualifying month basis. An employee who works 120 hours (110 hours if under 18 years) in any month qualifies for one twelfth of statutory annual entitlement in respect of each such month.

(2) Full leave year. An employee who works a total of 1,400 hours (1,300 hours if under 18 years) in any leave year (see below) qualifies for the full statutory entitlement for that year. This method of qualification for leave does not apply in the leave year during which an employee changes employment.

(3) Regular part-time employees. Prior to the enactment of the Worker Protection (Regular Part-Time Employees) Act, 1991, regular part-time employees did not have an entitlement to annual leave unless they had accrued 120 hours in each calendar month in accordance with the Act. (Again it should be noted that if a regular part-time employee falls within the provisions of the Holidays (Employees) Act, 1973, in that case it should be applied and the 1991 Act should not be applied.) Regular part-time employees with at least 13 weeks' continuous service are entitled to 6 hours for every 100 hours worked, and to proportionally less for periods of less than 100 hours in any leave year. The Worker Protection (Regular Part-Time Employees) Act came into force (in respect of holidays) on 6 April 1991 and the 13 weeks' service runs from that date. There is no entitlement to annual leave prior to that date.

Annual leave shall be increased to four weeks by November 1996 further to European Union Council Directive (93/104/EC).

Leave Year

In practice, the leave year may vary from employment to employment. Some employments use the statutory definition of the leave year which is 1 April to 31 March. Others may use the calendar year, 1 January to 31 December, and many manufacturing companies use 1 August to 31 July in the following year.

Entitlement

All "hours" that are worked, including overtime, are included for the purposes of calculating annual leave entitlement. Of course, time spent on annual leave is time worked. An employee with eight qualifying months is entitled to two unbroken weeks leave. Payment for annual leave must be made before annual leave actually begins.

If a female employee has 14 weeks' maternity leave, it is included for the purpose of building up holiday entitlement. Thus, she is entitled to annual leave as well as maternity leave. However, time spent on additional maternity leave, that is, the extra four weeks' (unpaid) leave, is not included for computation of leave.

Method of Calculating Pay for Annual Leave

Pay for annual leave must be paid in advance of going on leave and there are two ways of calculating it:

(1) Where normal remuneration does not vary, that is, where it is calculated completely by reference to time, pay for annual leave is the amount payable for normal working hours in the week immediately preceding annual leave. Overtime pay is excluded.

(2) Where normal remuneration is not calculated by reference to time, that is, where all or part of normal remuneration would vary in relation to work done, pay for annual leave is the average weekly payment for normal working hours in the 13 weeks ending on the date preceding the leave. Employees who have a basic salary plus a variable commission would fall into this category. Therefore, commission would be averaged over the 13 weeks prior to annual leave.

This method of calculation would also apply where an employee did some extra work and/or took extra responsibility. If this takes place during the 13 weeks prior to annual leave, the employee would get an average amount of that "extra pay".

There is no statutory provision for including earnings arising from overtime. However, it would be the general practice which the Labour Court has upheld that "regular and rostered" overtime should be included in pay for annual leave.

Sickness

If an employee has been absent through illness during the leave year and, for example, has not worked 120 hours in each calendar month, that employee may not be entitled to annual leave for that period. However, if the employee has worked 1,400 hours in the total leave year, then that employee would still be entitled to the full leave. An employee who does not work for the 1,400 hours is only entitled to pro-rata leave for the time actually worked.

If an employee claims to have been ill during annual leave and is so certified by a medical practitioner, then that day or those days shall not be included in the employee's annual leave. Accordingly, the employee would then have extra days' entitlement.

Timing of Leave

The Act provides that the employer decides when the employee can take annual leave, but the employee's opportunity for rest and relaxation must be taken into account.

The employer must consult with the employee or the employee's trade union at least one month before leave is to be given. Leave must be given in the annual leave year or in the six months following the leave year.

If an employer fails to give an employee annual leave within the appropriate time, the employer (a) commits an offence, and (b) must pay the employee an amount equivalent to the holiday pay which would have been received if the employee had been allowed to take holidays in the normal way.

An employee can recover monies for unpaid annual leave in the appropriate civil court, more usually the District Court which has jurisdiction up to £5,000 (see below).

There is no provision in the Act where an employee can get "double payment", that is, doing paid work for the employer during what should be holiday time and receiving holiday pay as well. Thus, assuming that the employer provides the employee with time off for annual leave (during the leave year or within six months of the end of the leave year) and the employee does not take it, the employee could forfeit the leave. Of course, employers must ensure that the employee has the opportunity to take leave.

In practice, a number of employments close (particularly manufacturing companies) for specified periods during the year, for example, the first two weeks in August and perhaps a week at Christmas. Generally, there can be flexibility about the timing of annual leave.

Regular Part-time Employees

A regular part-time employee who has eight months or more of service in a leave year is entitled to an unbroken period of leave on either of the following bases:

(1) The leave entitlement earned over the first eight months of service or of a subsequent leave year; or

(2) Two-thirds of the total leave entitlement earned in the first year of service or of a subsequent leave year.

A registered agreement, employment regulation order or collective agreement may vary these legal rules about the granting of the period of unbroken annual leave for various categories of employees.

When granting annual leave, account must be taken of the pattern the regular part-time employee works, for example, if the employee works three days per week, the annual leave would be over those three days. In other words, the annual leave must be given over the same days/hours that the employee works. Public holidays (see below) or sick days are not included for annual leave.

A regular part-time employee, who works over 120 hours in a given month, would fall within the provisions of the 1973 Act rather than the 1991 Act. That employee would receive one and one-quarter days' pay for the annual leave entitlement as only those employees who were previously not covered by legislation fall within the application of the 1991 Act.

Cessation of Employment The 1973 Act also provides that, when an employee ceases employment, any outstanding annual leave entitlement must be paid by the employer. It is calculated on the following basis:

(1) The employer shall pay compensation to the employee consisting of one-quarter of the normal weekly rate of remuneration for each qualifying month of service

(2) The employer shall pay the employee one and one-quarter days' pay where employment is on a day-to-day basis and the employee worked at least 120 hours (110 if under 18 years) during the 30 days ending on the day before termination of employment

(3) If a regular part-time employee is terminated with annual leave due, that employee is entitled to compensation at a proportionate rate to their normal weekly pay.

PUBLIC HOLIDAYS

There are nine public holidays:

- New Year's Day — 1 January

- St Patrick's Day — 17 March

- Easter Monday

- First Monday in May

- First Monday in June

- First Monday in August

- Last Monday in October

- Christmas Day — 25 December

- St Stephen's Day — 26 December

If a public holiday falls on a Sunday, it is automatically transferred to the next week day, that is, a Monday. Good Friday and Christmas Eve are not public holidays and an employee who does not work those days must treat them as days of annual leave. Some contracts of employment state that the employment will be closed on those days and they are deemed days of annual leave.

Public-holiday entitlement is not dependent on the length of service or hours worked, so those entitled to all nine public holidays include (a) all full-time employees and (b) part-time and day-to-day employees who have worked 120 hours in the five weeks preceding these public holidays.

The employer can decide the manner in which the public holiday shall be given. The employer's options are (a) a paid day off on the holiday, or (b) a paid day off within a month, or (c) an extra day's annual leave, or (d) an extra day's pay.

If the public holiday falls on a day on which the employee would not normally work a full day, the 1973 Act provides that the employee is still entitled to a "full day's pay".

Regular Part-time Employees

Regular part-time employees become entitled to public holidays in the normal way after 13 weeks continuous service. If the public holiday falls on a day on which the regular part-time employee normally works, the employer decides on the granting of the entitlement in the normal way. The regular part-time employee is entitled to a "full day's pay" even though a full day would not have been worked.

However, this entitlement can be problematic if the employee does not normally work on the day on which the public holiday falls. Both the 1973 and the 1991 Acts are silent as to whether a regular part-time employee is entitled to the benefit of a public holiday even though the employee would not normally have worked on that day. The general wording in the 1973 Act suggests that the employee should have the benefit of the public holiday even though the employee was not due to work that day. No doubt overtime custom and practice will provide an answer or a legal interpretation will be provided by the courts

Church Holidays

An employer may substitute a church holiday for a public holiday as long as the employee is given 14 days' advance notice (this is not applicable to Christmas Day or St Patrick's Day). Such church holidays include 6 January, Ascension Thursday, the Feast of Corpus Christi, 15 August, 1 November and 8 December. These days cannot be substituted when they fall on a Sunday (the feasts of Ascension and Corpus Christi always fall on a Thursday).

Bank Holidays / "EC" days

It is common usage for employees to talk about "bank holidays" or "EC" days. Such descriptions have no legal meaning whatsoever.

Cessation of Employment

A full-time employee leaving employment on the day before a public holiday can qualify for the public holiday if 120 hours have been worked in the preceding five weeks. Where a regular part-time employee ceases employment on the day before a public holiday, and the employee has during that five-week period worked for at least four weeks, the employer must give an extra day's pay in respect of the public holiday. Day-to-day and part-time employees must work a minimum of 120 hours (110 if under 18 years) during the five weeks ending prior to cessation of employment to obtain their entitlement.

Insolvency

If the employer has become insolvent, an employee can claim for holiday pay due under the Protection of Employees (Employers' Insolvency) Act, 1984. Up to a maximum of eight weeks' holiday pay due is allowed and the limit for any week's holidays due is £250 per week (see Chapter 23 — Employer Insolvency).

Maintenance of Entitlement

Employees who are on sick leave or maternity leave maintain their public-holiday entitlement.

RECORDS

All annual leave and public-holiday records should be maintained by the employer and retained for a period of at least three years for inspection by the Department of Enterprise and Employment.

OFFENCES

Failure to allow leave within a specified period, to pay for annual leave or public holidays, or to keep leave records are offences under the Act. Proceedings must be instituted within 12 months of the offence. The person prosecuting is technically the Minister for Enterprise and Employment. A person who is guilty of an offence is liable to a fine of £25 or in the case of a second or subsequent offence (under the same heading) the sum of £50.

PROCEDURES

An employee who has a complaint under the Act should refer the issue to the Conditions of Employment section of the Department of Enterprise and Employment with as much detail as possible (see the form on page 60). If there is a case to answer, the Department will write to the employer and may send an inspector to the employer's premises to look into the issue. The Department may decide to refer the matter to the Director of Public Prosecutions. If the DPP considers that there is a case to answer, the appropriate District Court Summons is issued and the matter proceeds.

The 1973 Act provides for recourse through the courts as stated above. However, in most unionised employments a dispute concerning annual leave or public holidays is referred to the Labour Relations Commission for conciliation. If there is no resolution at that stage, the dispute, with the permission of the Commission, may go on appeal to the Labour Court. The Labour Court would then issue its non-binding recommendation.

The 1991 Act does not change this position in respect of the holiday entitlements of regular part-time employees, although the Employment Appeals Tribunal does have jurisdiction in respect of any dispute relating to the weekly and hourly requirements.

The case of *O'Sullivan* v. *Dunnes Stores Ltd.* ([1991] ELR 86) illustrated this major drawback of the 1991 Act. In this case, a regular part-time employee who had been employed since 1985 requested her public-holiday entitlement for Monday 3 June 1991, which was the first public holiday after the coming into operation of the 1991 Act. The Tribunal stated that its jurisdiction was limited further to Section 5(1) which states:

> any dispute arising in respect of the calculation of the 13 weeks continuous service to which Section 2(1) of this Act relates, and any dispute relating to the number of hours a week actually worked or normally expected to be worked, shall be referred in the prescribed manner to the Tribunal.

Thus, the Tribunal can only make a declaration as to whether a person is a regular part-time employee or not.

Rights Commissioners are not permitted to hear disputes concerning holiday matters in relation to a group of employees, but there does not appear to be anything prohibiting a Rights Commissioner from hearing an individual grievance. The Rights Commissioner may issue a recommendation which may be appealed to the Labour Court. The Labour Court may issue a "binding" recommendation which is not enforceable in the courts. There is nothing to stop a claim under the industrial relations "path" and also a legal claim through the courts. However, procedures under the Payment of Wages Act, 1991 may be a more sensible recourse for a dispute.

An employee who considers that she has not got her full holiday entitlement while on maternity leave can refer the matter to a Rights Commissioner or the Employment Appeals Tribunal under the Maternity Protection of Employees Acts, 1981 and 1991 (see section 4 — Industrial Relations and Adjudicating Bodies).

Holiday pay is deemed to be "wages" under the Payment of Wages

Act, 1991, and an employee may pursue a claim for non-payment of holiday pay under that Act within six months of the contravention of the 1991 Act. This would seem the most sensible way for such claims to proceed (see Chapter 6 — Payment of Wages).

JURY SERVICE

Most individuals are called for jury service at some stage in their working lives unless they are ineligible for some reason. Jurors attend court in criminal and civil (e.g. defamation) proceedings in order to decide the facts of the case. Members of the Defence Forces, those concerned with the administration of justice and persons who are mentally or physically incapable are ineligible for jury service. There are other professional categories that are excused as of right, namely doctors, nurses and principals of schools and colleges. A person who has been in prison may be disqualified from jury service. A person who has served (or attended to serve) on a jury in the previous three years may be excused by the county registrar. A judge at the end of a trial may also excuse a juror from service for a period of time.

Thus, an individual who does not fall into one of the above categories may be called for jury service if they are aged between 18 and 70 years and are on the Dáil Electoral Register. The Juries Act, 1976 provides the legislation relating to the qualification for service and selection of jurors. The county registrar selects persons to be called for jury service.

Any person, summonsed as a juror, who fails without reasonable excuse to attend court shall be liable to a fine not exceeding £50.

It is an employer's duty to allow employees to attend for jury service. However, if it is not practicable because of the nature of an employee's work, or if it is an extremely busy time at work, a letter from the employer should be sent to the county registrar explaining the reason for the request to excuse the employee. A person who has not been excused by the county registrar may appeal to the court to which they have been summonsed to attend. The court's decision is final.

An employee or an apprentice shall be treated as employed or apprenticed during any period when absent from employment in order to comply with a jury summons. Thus, an employee or an apprentice is entitled to pay while on jury service. The Act does not provide a method of calculating such payment. Obviously, there is an entitlement to basic pay. It is more difficult to work out pay where an employee is at the loss of overtime pay, commission, shift premia or other bonuses. In such circumstances, it would be reasonable for the employer to average such pay. Another difficulty that can arise is if the employee is working on night shift and is called to jury service during the day. Clearly both may not be possible, so an employee should not be expected to work all night after attending in court during the day.

Frequently an employee may be excused from jury service by the court at 11 a.m. in any morning of required service. Obviously the employee should report to work as soon as reasonable that same day. The county registrar's office can provide a statement with details of an employee's attendance on jury duty if so requested.

GENERAL REFERENCES

Kerr, T., *Irish Law Statutes Annotated, Worker Protection (Regular Part-Time) Employees Act, 1991*, Sweet and Maxwell.

Wayne, Naomi, *Labour Law in Ireland*, Chapter 4, The Right to Holidays, IT&GWU, Kincora Press.

DEPARTMENT OF ENTERPRISE AND EMPLOYMENT

Holidays (Employees) Acts 1973 and 1991

Complaint Form

1. Name:

   Address:

Telephone No.: _____   2. R.S.I. No.: _____

3. Employee's age (if under 18): _____   4. Occupation: _____

5. Employer's full legal name and address
   (If in doubt, consult your P60)

6(a) Date of Commencement of this Employment ____/____/____   (b) Date of termination: ____/____/____

7. Date of termination of previous employment, if any: ____/____/____

8. Date of commencement of current employment, if any: ____/____/____

9. Details (date and duration) of Annual Holidays received during the period of employment:

DATES		
From	To	No. of Days

10. Did you receive entitlement for all the public holidays that occurred during your employment: (Please tick(√))

Yes	No

    If No please give details: _____

    _____

11. Details (dates and duration) of any absences from work:

DATES		DURATION
From	To	

12. Net rate of Pay (exclusive of overtime): _____   13. Did your employer provide board and/or lodgings: (Please tick(√))

Yes	No

14. How long was your working week?   Hours per week [   ]   Days per week [   ]

15. In what way has your employer failed to comply with the Act? _____

    _____

I hereby declare that the information which I have given herein is to the best of my knowledge correct and complete.

Employee's signature: _____   Date: _____

WHEN COMPLETED, PLEASE RETURN TO ROOM G03, DEPARTMENT OF ENTERPRISE AND EMPLOYMENT, DAVITT HOUSE, ADELAIDE ROAD, DUBLIN 2.

CHAPTER FIVE

Maternity Leave

The Maternity Protection of Employees Acts, 1981 and 1991 established a statutory right to unpaid maternity leave (14 weeks plus additional leave) and the right to return to work after such leave for women in employment. These rights are subject to detailed notification requirements with which an employee must comply. There is also provision for unpaid time off for antenatal and postnatal medical care.

APPLICATION OF THE ACT

Employees are covered from the first day of employment, except for regular part-time employees. The maternity legislation has applied to regular part-time employees since 17 June 1991 further to the Worker Protection (Regular Part-Time Employees) Act, 1991.

Thus, the Act covers all female employees in:

(1) Insurable employment (this means Class A PRSI), for which they must be earning £30 or more per week, or

(2) Regular part-time employment who normally work for eight hours per week and have 13 weeks' service in such insurable employment, or

(3) Insurable employment under a contract of employment for a fixed term of at least 26 weeks of which there are at least 26 weeks still to run.

ENTITLEMENT TO SOCIAL WELFARE MATERNITY ALLOWANCE

The social welfare scheme provides that women get 70 per cent of their earnings subject to a maximum payment of £154 (that is, based on earnings up to £11,000 per annum) per week and a minimum payment of £60 per week. There are certain requirements for PRSI contribution conditions (see form on pages 71–74). This form must be completed and sent to the Maternity Benefits Section of the Department of Social Welfare at least 10 weeks before confinement. In the case of an early miscarriage, there is no maternity benefit payable. The normal cut-off point is 28 weeks, so if a child is born after that (even if born dead) the benefit is payable. However, if a child is born prior to the 28 weeks and is born alive (if only for a short period), benefit may be payable. Unfortunately, if the baby is born dead, there may be no benefit payable but this should be checked with the Department of Social Welfare.

A number of employers actually "pay" their female employees while on maternity leave. In other words, they "top-up" the social welfare monies, usually by paying the employee's salary in the normal way and having her reimburse the employer with the social welfare monies. It should be noted that there is absolutely no obligation on the employer to pay monies to an employee while on maternity leave.

ENTITLEMENTS AND PROTECTION

All employees covered by the Maternity Act are entitled to a minimum period of 14 weeks' "maternity leave', which is usually four weeks before the date of confinement and 10 weeks after. The maternity benefit is payable during maternity leave to persons meeting the required contribution conditions.

The maternity leave period can be extended in certain circumstances, for example if the birth is late. This is fairly rare and only arises where the employee does not have four weeks leave left after the birth of the child before she is due to return to work.

ADDITIONAL MATERNITY LEAVE

This is frequently known as "unpaid maternity leave" because there is no social welfare payment during this period. An additional period of four weeks may be taken immediately following the maternity leave period. It should not be confused with extended maternity leave as described above. The employee is entitled to take additional maternity leave, regardless of whether her maternity leave has been extended or not.

TIME-OFF

An employee is entitled to unpaid time-off during "normal working time" for prenatal and postnatal medical checks. The right to time-off for "medical or related appointment" is subject to an employee giving written notification of the date and time of the appointment to her employer at least two weeks beforehand. If the appointment was urgent, the employee must advise her employer within one week after the appointment.

In addition, the employer may require the employee to produce an appointment card or similar document indicating the date and time of the appointment, confirm the pregnancy and specify the expected week of confinement. This provision does not apply to the first medical appointment in relation to the pregnancy.

As stated above, this is unpaid "time-off" but in a number of employments, through union management negotiation or by agreement, the time-off may be paid in the normal way. The Regulations covering such time-off are the Maternity Protection (Time-Off for Ante — Natal and Post — Natal Care) Regulations, 1981 — SI No. 358 of 1981.

EMPLOYMENT PROTECTION DURING LEAVE

The employee remains in the employment during any leave or time-off under the Act so her statutory and contractual rights are protected by the Act during this time. Notices of termination of employment (from employer or employee) given during maternity leave and to take effect during leave or after the end of maternity leave are void, and thus the employee would remain in employment. An employee cannot resign during a period of leave or time-off, and an employer cannot terminate an employee's employment during such leave or time-off.

The Maternity Act also gives protection against the imposition of certain disciplinary measures against an employee on leave or time-off. An employee cannot receive a disciplinary suspension while on leave or time-off.

If notice of termination is given to an employee before she has given notice of taking maternity leave, and if the termination notice is to take effect during maternity leave then the notice is extended for any balance period after maternity leave and additional maternity leave. This can arise in a redundancy situation where the employer issues a Notice of Redundancy (the Form RP1) (see Chapter 18 — Redundancy).

Employment during maternity leave is continuous and reckonable for all protective legislation, and all employment rights arising from the contract of employment are retained. The employee retains all her future redundancy payment rights for the maternity leave period as well as her annual leave and public-holiday entitlements. Also, the employer cannot deem maternity leave as sick leave.

During the period of additional maternity leave the protection afforded to the employee is more limited. An employee's continuity of employment for statutory rights — unfair dismissal, minimum notice, etc. — is protected. However, the four-week additional leave period would not be included as reckonable service for redundancy payment purposes. There would be no entitlement to annual leave in respect of this four weeks, but the public-holiday entitlement remains, by virtue of the person still being in employment. Additional maternity leave cannot be deemed sick leave.

REMUNERATION

An employee is not entitled to any remuneration from her employer when she is on leave or on time-off. Unfortunately, there is no definition of "remuneration" in the Act. So far, "remuneration" has been broadly interpreted by the Tribunal to include a company car and attendance bonuses. In one particular case, the Tribunal considered that a company car was remuneration and thus it could be withheld from the employee during maternity leave (*McGivern* v. *Irish National Insurance Co. Ltd.*, P 5/1982). An attendance bonus was not considered payable during maternity leave even though an employee is deemed to be in employment during such leave (*Memorex Media Products* v. *Byrne and Others*, P 9/1986).

THE RIGHT TO RETURN TO WORK

There is a general right to return to the same job for employees who have been on maternity leave. This also applies if there has been a transfer of the business while the employee was on leave. If, for example, in order to give an employee suitable work during pregnancy she had been in a job different from her usual one, she is still entitled to return to her old job.

However, what happens if an employer cannot give the employee back her old job? An employer must provide suitable alternative work (see below) if it is not reasonably practicable to permit an employee to return to work in the same job, for example, if there was a reorganisation of work.

Should there be a stoppage of work due to a strike or lay-off on the day the employee is due to go back to work, the employee must be allowed to resume work as soon as possible after the work interruption.

ALTERNATIVE WORK

Alternative work must be work that is suitable to the particular employee and appropriate for her in the circumstances. The Act does not define "suitable alternative work", but it specifies that the terms and conditions of the new contract as regards the place of employment, the capacity in which she is to be employed and the monetary and other terms of employment, must not be substantially less favourable than those of her previous job.

A number of cases have gone to the Tribunal under this particular heading. In one case, the employee had worked as a switchboard operator and upon returning from maternity leave was offered alternative work in the company's accounts department, in the same grade with no loss of pay. The company had originally advertised her position internally as a temporary position but found nobody suitable. They then approached the National Manpower Service but their applicants only wanted permanent employment. The employer then offered someone the position on a permanent basis. The claimant was unhappy with this decision and sought reinstatement to her original position. The Tribunal considered that the inconvenience arising out of the new arrangement was greater to the employee than the inconvenience to the employer, and thus awarded her her job back as a switchboard operator (*O'Brien* v. *Harrington and Goodlass Wall Ltd.*, P 2/1981).

In another case, an employee had originally worked as an accounts clerk and was offered the position of receptionist on her return from leave. She did not want to work as a receptionist and resigned her employment. In this particular case, the claimant was awarded £8,000 by the Tribunal (*Butler* v. *Smurfit Ireland Ltd. t/a Paclene Co. Ltd.*, P 3/1988).

NOTIFICATION REQUIREMENTS

For an employee to preserve her rights to take leave and to return to work under the Act, she must comply with certain notification requirements. There is no obligation on the employer to advise the employee of these requirements (see form on page 75).

Maternity Leave

Entitlement to maternity leave is subject to compliance with the notification procedures laid down by the Act. There is a considerable volume of case law which has determined that an employee has no entitlement to maternity leave if she has not complied with the procedures (see below). An employee must fulfil the following conditions in notifying her employer of her intention to take maternity leave:

(1) It must be in writing

(2) It must be given not later than four weeks before the commencement of the maternity leave

(3) It must be specific, in other words the employee must state her intention to take maternity leave and the date on which the leave is to commence

(4) She must produce a medical certificate for inspection by her employer, certifying the pregnancy and the estimated week of commencement.

An employee who wishes to obtain maternity benefits should complete parts 1–7 of the Social Welfare form and have her employer complete part 8. The Social Welfare form is not sufficient on its own, however, as she must comply with the above points and state her intention of returning to work by a specific date.

If an employee wishes to extend her maternity leave, she must give written notification as soon as it is practicable, stating that the confinement was late and that she wishes to extend her leave. As stated above, this typically only arises when an employee is left with less than four weeks after the birth of the child before she is due to return to work.

An employee can decide not to go on maternity leave. She should confirm her decision in writing to her employer, but, assuming that she takes time off, it will have to be with the agreement of her employer.

If an employee has an early confinement which takes place at least four weeks or more before the expected date and before she has gone on leave, the employer must be notified in writing at least 14 days after the birth. The employee is entitled to 14-weeks maternity leave commencing from the date of birth.

Additional Maternity Leave

An employee is entitled to take up to four weeks additional maternity leave which must follow immediately after the end of ordinary maternity leave. The entitlement to additional maternity leave is not prejudiced in any way by the extension of the 14-week period of maternity leave (i.e. if she has less than four weeks after the birth of the baby). Entitlement to additional maternity leave is also subject to written notification by or on behalf of the employee. Frequently, the intention to take additional maternity leave is declared at the same time as the employee's written notification that she is actually going to take leave.

Resignation after Maternity Leave

An employee who does not wish to return to work after maternity leave may give written notice to her employer prior to leave that her resignation is to take effect from the date that she is due back to work. This is in order provided that the employee works the necessary notice period. Alternatively, she may give notice to her employer on the day she is due back to work. In that situation, she may have to work the notice period or she could take such period as annual leave provided there is sufficient leave left. She would then be entitled to be paid for the notice period. Alternatively, the employer may pay in lieu of notice.

Returning to Work

An employee who has taken maternity leave is entitled to return to work provided that she notifies her employer in writing at least four weeks before her expected date of return of her intention to return to work on a specific date. This requirement is mandatory and the notification may be given before or during maternity leave.

There is a second confirmatory notification due two weeks before the employee's expected date of return. If she does not give this notice, she does not lose her right to return to work, however. (Harrington and Goodlass Wall case, above).

Extreme caution is advised. If an employee fails to give the mandatory four-week notification, she may lose her entitlement to return to work. The High Court has held that if the employee fails to give the four-week mandatory notice then it is a fair reason for her dismissal by her employer (*Ivory* v. *Ski-Line Ltd.* [1988] IR 399).

No Notification

There is no obligation on the employer to advise the employee of the notification requirements. Obviously, an employee who does not give the proper notification that she wishes to take maternity leave is not entitled to such leave. However, the employer frequently agrees to waive his rights to notification. The employer may decide to do this automatically or it may be done at the employee's request. The Employment Appeals Tribunal is conscious of the strict notification requirements under the Act and generally tries to find a contractual arrangement so that the employee will not lose her job.

A history of the employer waiving such requirements would make it difficult to terminate an employee for not complying with them. In a recent case, a claimant who did not comply with the Maternity Act for two previous confinements and was allowed back to work, submitted a notice that she would be going on maternity leave. She informed the company by telephone that she would be returning on 13 May 1991. Her employer told her not to return to work as she had failed to comply with the provisions of the Maternity Act. She brought a claim under both the Maternity Act and also the Unfair Dismissals Act. The Tribunal accepted that the *Ivory* v. *Ski-Line Ltd.* judgment applied and thus dismissed the claim under the Maternity Act but held that there was agreed contractual leave based on the previous confinements. Thus, the Tribunal considered she was unfairly dismissed. She was only awarded re-engagement, however, since she was at fault for not complying with the Maternity Act. She was awarded monies in lieu of notice so her continuity of employment was broken (*Scott* v. *Yeates & Sons Opticians Ltd.* [1991] ELR 83).

Of course, employees should not rely on this situation. One would advise both employers and employees that the relevant notifications should be provided.

Indeed, it would be fairer to all parties to amend this legislation to place an obligation on employers to provide a statutory notice for employees who wish to take maternity leave. It would avoid a great deal of confusion.

EC DIRECTIVE

A recent EC Directive (Council Directive, 92/85/EEC) introduces measures to encourage improvements in the safety and health at work of pregnant workers and workers who have recently given birth or are breast-feeding. With no radical departures from our present law, this Directive provides for 14-weeks unpaid maternity leave with at least two weeks prior to confinement and at least two weeks after. Time off for antenatal care will be paid time off, presuming that the examinations have to take place during working hours. Provision is made for necessary measures to adjust the working conditions for pregnant and nursing mothers, that they may move to another job within the same employment or be granted leave for the entire period. Equally, such employees may not have their employment terminated. Furthermore, pregnant employees may not do nightwork.

All payments follow the normal course, which in our instance will be linked into the social welfare legislation. Two annexes to this Directive set out certain agents and processes which may cause a danger to such working women. This Directive should come into Irish national law by October 1994.

ADOPTIVE LEAVE

The Adoptive Leave Bill, 1993 was published on 20 October 1993 and it is expected that it will be enacted in early 1994. The Bill grants adoptive leave to women employees on a similar basis to maternity leave. It also applies to male employees in certain circumstances. The minimum period of leave provided in the Bill is ten weeks, during which the employee will receive a social welfare payment. There is also an optional four weeks additional unpaid leave. The principles of the Bill and the notification requirements are similar to those of the Maternity Act.

Leave commences on the day the child is placed for adoption. An employee who wishes to avail of leave must give to her employer four weeks' notice in writing of her intention to take leave and the expected date of placement. Evidence of placement must be furnished within four weeks of the placement. If the employee wishes to take the additional leave, four weeks' notice must be given to the employer. The employee has a right of returning to work, subject to four weeks' written notification before her expected date of return. This notification shall be confirmed at least two weeks before the expected date of return. There is provision for the rights commissioner or the Employment Appeals Tribunal to extend these time limits.

There are special rules for foreign adoptions and also in circumstances where the adopting mother dies.

Disputes may be referred to the rights commissioner or the Employment Appeals Tribunal within six months (with provision for extension of time in exceptional circumstances) from the date the employer receives notification from the adopting parent. The rights commissioner's recommendation may be appealed to the Tribunal within four weeks of the date of communication of the recommendation. The Tribunal determination may be appealed to the High Court on a point of law only, or the Tribunal may request the Minister to refer the matter to the High Court on a question of law. Compensation may be up to a maximum of 20 weeks' remuneration.

PROCEDURES

Disputes (other than dismissal) which have arisen within 156 weeks of the date of confinement under the 1981 Act must be referred to a rights commissioner or the Employment Appeals Tribunal within six months of the commencement of the dispute. This would cover claims concerning remuneration during leave or the issue of "suitable alternative work" if their job has been changed following completion of leave. This time limit may be extended where there are exceptional reasons. The Regulations that apply are Maternity Protection (Disputes and Appeals) Regulations — SI No. 357 of 1981.

If employment has been terminated by the employer, or the employee has resigned and claimed constructive dismissal (see Chapter 17 — Unfair Dismissal), not only should she bring a claim under the Maternity Acts but also under the Unfair Dismissals Acts. A claim for unfair dismissal must be instituted, within six months of the date of dismissal, to a rights commissioner or the Employment Appeals Tribunal under the Unfair Dismissals Acts, 1977 to 1993 (See Chapter 23 — Employment Appeals Tribunal).

1. Your Own Details

- Please state your:

  Full Name _____

  Address _____

  _____

  _____

  Telephone No. _____

	Day	Month	Year
Date of Birth			

  RSI Number (same as Tax No.)

Figures						Letters	

- Was your RSI Number changed within the last 2 years?   YES ☐   NO ☐

  If 'YES', state your previous RSI Number:

Figures						Letters	

- State whether you are:

  Married ☐   Single ☐

  If a married woman, state Maiden Name:

  _____

	Day	Month	Year
Date of Marriage:			

  RSI Number before marriage:

Figures						Letters	

2. Your Employment Details

- Are you working at present?
  YES ☐   NO ☐

  If 'YES', when do you intend to start Maternity Leave?

Day	Month	Year

  If 'NO', when did you last work?

Day	Month	Year

- When did you first start working?

Day	Month	Year

- Is your work?

  Full-time ☐   Part-time ☐

  If 'Part-time', state your gross weekly earnings

  £ _____

- State your present (or last) Employer's Name and Address:

  _____

  _____

  _____

- What is your occupation/type of employment?

  _____

- Are you related to your Employer?
  YES ☐   NO ☐

  If 'YES', state relationship:

  _____

3. Working in another EC Country

● Did you ever work in the United Kingdom, or any other EC country?

YES ☐   NO ☐

If 'YES', state

Social Insurance Number	Period of Employment	Country

Employer's Name _____

Address _____

● Have you worked in Ireland since your return?   YES ☐   NO ☐

4. Other Claims/FÁS Courses

● If you have claimed any weekly Social Welfare payments or completed a FÁS course, in the last 2 years, you may be entitled to credits to help you qualify for Maternity Benefit.

Please state dates of FÁS course: From _____ To _____

● If you signed for unemployment benefit/assistance or credited contributions, state Employment Exchange / Office where you 'signed on': _____

Day	Month	Year

Please state the date you last signed:

● Are you getting/claiming a weekly payment from the Department of Social Welfare?

YES ☐   NO ☐

If 'YES', state   Date you were last paid: _____

Type of Payment: _____

Pension/Claim No.:   _____

Weekly amount: £ _____

● Are you getting a weekly payment from a Health Board?   YES ☐   NO ☐

If 'YES', give the name of Health Centre from which you are receiving payment:

_____

5. Your Husband's Details

● Is your Husband getting a weekly payment from the Department of Social Welfare?

YES ☐   NO ☐

If 'YES', state Type of payment: _____

Pension/Claim No.:_____

● Name of Employment Exchange/Office if he gets an Unemployment payment:

_____

6. Declaration

I claim Maternity Benefit and declare that the details I have given are true and complete.
I undertake to notify the Department if there is any change in the details given.

Signed _____   Date _____
Claimant

WARNING
Penalty for false statement: Fine or imprisonment, or both.

---

7. To be Completed by a Registered Medical Practitioner

To (Name of Claimant) _____

I certify that I have examined you
and that in my opinion you may expect to be confined on:

Day	Month	Year

Date of examination:

Day	Month	Year

Signature of Doctor _____

Address _____

Any other remarks by the doctor _____

8.	To be Completed by Your Employer

WARNING:

EMPLOYERS PLEASE NOTE: False or misleading statements made in order to obtain Maternity Benefit for another person can result in a fine of up to £10,000 or imprisonment for up to 3 years - or both.

The employee must give her employer at least 4 weeks notice of her intention to take maternity leave.

Name of Employee: _____

RSI
Number

	Figures						Letters	

Is employee entitled to resume employment with you after Maternity Leave?

YES ☐   NO ☐

If 'YES', please complete the following:

I/We certify that the above-named has given notice of her intention to apply for maternity leave from _____ to _____

If 'NO', please complete the following:

I/We certify that the above-named has given notice of her intention to cease employment for reasons of maternity on _____

	FROM	TO	No. of Weeks of Insurable employment	PRSI CLASS
Details of her employment with me during the 12 months immediately before the first date of her Maternity Leave are:				

SIGNED BY OR ON BEHALF OF EMPLOYER

Name _____
Address _____
Employer's Registered No. _____ Employer's Tel. No._____
Date _____

Send this completed form to:

Maternity Benefit Section, Social Welfare Services Office,
Gandon House, Amiens Street, Dublin 1.
Telephone (01) 748444

MATERNITY PROTECTION OF EMPLOYEES ACTS, 1981 and 1991

LETTER TO EMPLOYER

I, ... intend taking maternity leave from .... to ....I intend returning to work on .... (date of end of maternity leave).

I will confirm my intention to return to work on ....

Additional maternity leave

I now advise you that I have added an extra 4 weeks to the end of my normal maternity leave for the purpose of taking additional maternity leave.

Alternatively

I understand that I am entitled to take additional maternity leave and should I wish to take such leave, I agree to give you at least 4 weeks notice of taking such leave. I will also advise you of the date I intend to return to work giving you at least 4 weeks notice and also confirm that 2 weeks in advance of my return to work.

Should I have to extend or shorten my maternity leave, I shall advise you and I will also advise you of my new date for returning to work.

I wish to advise you that it is my clear intention to return to work.

IF IN DOUBT, PLEASE CONSULT YOUR ADVISOR

CHAPTER SIX

Payment of Wages

Happily, the manner of the payment of wages and procedures for resolution of disputes have now reached the twentieth century. Prior to the enactment of the Payment of Wages Act, 1991, the previous legislation governing deductions from wages rested in laws passed in the Georgian and Victorian eras. Known as the Truck Acts, which have since been repealed, they provided that the payment of wages to manual workers was to be in "coin of the realm". They also limited the circumstances in which deductions could be made from manual workers' wages so that certain abuses could be limited.

PAYMENT OF WAGES ACTS

The Irish Payment of Wages Act, 1979 (see below) provided a more modern manner of payment of wages for manual workers than previously, as long as there was an agreement between employers and employees. Nonetheless, this legislation did not provide very practicable procedures for the modern cashless environment. Cheques and credit transfers were now acceptable as long as there was an agreement. It also established that all employees were entitled to a written statement of deductions from their pay, for example, PAYE, PRSI and other deductions such as VHI and trade union dues.

The 1979 Act has now been repealed (with all the previous legislation), but it must be noted that all agreements for manual workers that came into force under the 1979 Act are still applicable unless agreed otherwise.

The Payment of Wages Act, 1991 came into force on 1 January 1992. The 1991 Act provides for transitional arrangements for employees who were paid their wages in cash before the coming into operation of the Act. Such employees are entitled to continue to receive cash wages until they reach an agreement with the employer for the payment of wages by one of the accepted methods of payment in the new Act. An employee who enters into an agreement to be paid wages by cheque under the 1979 Act and now wishes to revert to cash payment may do so. The right to change payment to cash would be at the end of the agreement. If there was no termination date to the agreement, there must be four weeks notice to end the agreement. It is an offence for an employer to be in breach of these provisions and a breach may result in a fine of up to £1,000.

Thus, from 1 January 1992,. the method of payment for all manual employees shall be what is agreed between employer and employee as stated in the employment contract (or the union/management agreement where this is incorporated into the contract of employment).

The 1991 Act establishes for the first time a range of rights for all employees relating to the payment of wages. Neither an employer nor an employee can "contract out" of the provisions of this Act. The key rights established under the Act are:

(1) A right to a readily negotiable mode of wage payment (e.g., cheque, credit transfer, payable order or such other methods that may be added to the list from time to time),

(2) A right to a written statement of wages, conditions and deductions, and

(3) Protection against unlawful deductions from wages.

The Act covers all employees who are:

(1) Working under a contract of employment or apprenticeship,

(2) Employed through an employment agency or through a sub-contractor, and

(3) In the service of the State, including members of the Garda Síochána, the Defence Forces, civil servants, employees of any local authority, health board, harbour authority or vocational education committee.

MEANING OF WAGES

Wages are defined as:

(1) Normal basic pay as well as any overtime

(2) Shift allowances or other similar payments

(3) Any fee, bonus or commission

(4) Any holiday, sick pay or maternity pay

(5) Any other form of payment

(6) Any sum payable to an employee in lieu of notice on termination of employment.

However, the following payments are not regarded as wages:

(1) Expense payments incurred by employees in carrying out their employment

(2) Any payment by way of pension, allowance or gratuity in connection with the death, retirement, or resignation of the employee or compensation for loss of office

(3) Any payment relating to the employee's redundancy

(4) Any payment to the employee otherwise than in the employee's capacity as an employee, and

(5) Any payment-in-kind or benefit-in-kind.

Repayment of loans to employees as individuals — other than as a benefit under a loan scheme — would fall outside the scope of the legislation.

MODES OR METHODS OF WAGE PAYMENTS

The legally acceptable modes of wage payment include:

(1) Cheque and bank draft drawn on any of the commercial banks or a Trustee Savings Bank

(2) Payable order warrant issued by a Minister of the Government or a public authority

(3) Postal order, money order, paying order warrant issued by or drawn on An Post

(4) Credit transfer to an account specified by the employee

(5) Cash.

Employers are required to make alternative arrangements for wage payment where a strike or other industrial action affects banks or other financial institutions so that cash is not readily available to employees who are paid by a non-cash method. In these circumstances, wages must be paid with the employee's consent by one of the other legally acceptable modes of wage payment. If the employee does not agree to same, the employer must pay the wages in cash.

If an employer pays wages to an employee otherwise than by one of the above-stated methods, or contravenes these special arrangements in the event of a bank dispute, it shall be an offence and the employer is liable to a fine of up to £1,000.

RIGHT TO A WRITTEN STATEMENT

All employees are entitled to a written statement showing (a) the gross amount of wages payable and (b) the nature and amount of any deduction from that gross amount. This statement must be given at the time of payment when the employee is paid by cheque, cash, postal or money order. If the employee is being paid by way of credit transfer, this statement must be given to the employee as soon as possible after payment.

There is an obligation on the employer to treat the information contained in the pay statement as confidential. A statement of wages which includes an error or omission is a valid statement of wages provided that it can be shown that the error or omission was due to a clerical mistake or was made accidentally and in good faith. Obviously the mistake should be rectified as soon as possible.

An employer who contravenes this provision can be liable to a fine of up to £1,000.

DEDUCTION FROM WAGES

An employer may only make deductions from wages (or receive any payment from an employee) if:

(1) The deduction or payment is required or authorised to be made by or under statute, e.g., PAYE or PRSI, or

(2) The deduction or payment is required or authorised to be made under the term of the contract of employment (this term must have been in force at the time the deduction was made or the payment received, e.g. employee pension contributions, deductions for till shortages), or

(3) There is an advance written agreement from the employee, e.g. VHI premia, trade union dues.

In *Murphy* v. *Ryanair plc.* (PW 2/92) the employee was suspended without pay for one week. There was no provision for the deduction in the contract of employment or in a written statement prior to the suspension. The EAT held that the employee was entitled to be paid for that week.

Special restrictions are placed on employers in relation to deductions (or the receipt of payments) from wages which:

(1) Arise from any act of the employee, e.g. till shortages, bad workmanship, breakages, or

(2) Are in respect of the supply to the employee by the employer of goods or services which are necessary to the employment, e.g. the provision or cleaning of uniforms.

Any deduction (or payment) from wages of the kind described above must satisfy the following conditions:

(1) The deduction (or payment to the employer) must be provided for in the contract of employment, either in writing or orally

(2) The amount of the deduction (or payment to the employer) from wages must be fair and reasonable having regard to all the circumstances, including the amount of the wages of the employee

(3) The employee must be given at some time prior to the act or omission (e.g. till shortage) or the provision of the goods or services (e.g. uniform cleaning) written details of the terms of the contract of employment governing the deduction (or payment to the employer) from wages.

Where a written contract exists, a copy of the terms of the contract which provides the deduction (or payment) must be given to the employee. In any other case, the employee must be given written notice of the existence and effect of the terms. Written notice must be given in the case of each deduction. The deduction cannot take place more than six months after the employee's act or omission has become known to the employer. Where there is a series of deductions arising from the same incident, the first deduction must take place within six months of the incident. The deduction in respect of a service provided by the employer must also take place within six months.

An employer making a deduction arising from a till shortage (for example), must give the employee a written statement at least one week before the deduction takes place, including the reason for, and the amount of, the deduction. Of course, the deduction cannot exceed the amount of the employer's loss.

Similarly, a deduction arising from a service provided to the employee, for example, uniform cleaning, cannot be for more than the cost of the service. The employer must give a receipt for the amount of the deduction.

DEDUCTIONS AND PAYMENTS OUTSIDE THE APPLICATION OF THE ACT

The provisions on deductions do not apply to:

(1) Statutory deductions, e.g. PAYE, PRSI, reimbursement of social welfare payments to the Minister for Social Welfare. The employer must have authorisation for such deductions, e.g. Certificate of Tax Free Allowances.

(2) Deductions paid over to a third party, e.g. trade union subscriptions, VHI premia, contributions to a group savings scheme etc. This kind of deduction remains outside the application of the Act provided that the employer pays the correct amount over to the third party by the appropriate date. The employer should also be in receipt of a notice from the third party (e.g. the VHI) that such monies are due and owing by the employee.

(3) Deductions for the overpayment of wages or expenses, as long as the amount deducted does not exceed the amount due to the employer.

(4) Deductions or payments arising from a strike or industrial action in which the employee has been involved. The deduction or payment must arise because of the employee's involvement in such action.

(5) Statutory disciplinary proceedings. A deduction from the wages of an employee in consequence of any disciplinary procedure if those proceedings were held by virtue of a statutory provision, for example, the Garda Síochána (Discipline) Regulations, 1989.

(6) Deductions or payments arising from a court order in the unusual cases where a court has awarded damages to an employer against an employee, e.g. statutory redundancy monies paid back to the employer after an employee has been reinstated following a redundancy dismissal. There must, of course, be prior written consent from the employee.

(7) Deductions or payments arising from certain specific court orders,

for example, an Attachment of Earnings Order to pay maintenance
to the wife of an employee.

WAGE DEFICIENCY

Non-payment of wages, or any deficiency in the amount of wages due
to an employee on any occasion, are regarded as unlawful unless the
deficiency or non-payment is attributable to an error of computation.

INSPECTION PROCEDURE

Authorised officers appointed by the Minister for Enterprise and
Employment will have inspection powers under the 1991 Act. They
have power of entry to the employer's premises at all reasonable
times, and the power of inspection to see if the Act has been complied
with. The time limit for subsequent criminal proceedings is 12
months from the date of the offence.

COMPLAINTS PROCEDURE

An employee may complain to a rights commissioner where there has
been an alleged unlawful deduction or the employer required an
unlawful payment from the wages of the employee. Such complaint
must be made within six months of the alleged breach of the Act. The
rights commissioner's recommendation may be appealed to the Employment Appeals Tribunal (see Chapters 22 and 23 — The Labour
Relations Commission and The Employment Appeals Tribunal).

GENERAL REFERENCES

Department of Enterprise and Employment, Explanatory Booklet on the
    Payment of Wages Act, 1991.
Kerr, T., *Irish Law Statutes Annotated, The Payment of Wages Act, 1991*,
    Sweet and Maxwell.

CHAPTER SEVEN

Collective Bargaining

Collective bargaining and its voluntary nature is the keystone of Irish industrial relations. The term "collective agreement" is defined in the Anti-Discrimination (Pay) Act, 1974 as "an agreement relating to terms and conditions of employment made between parties who are or represent employers and parties who are or represent employees".

In essence, industrial relations in Ireland have been characterised by legal abstention, whereby both employers and employees are free to enter into negotiations and to regulate their own respective rights and behaviour. An employee has the constitutional right to join a trade union (Article 40.4.1). However, there is no duty placed on an employer to negotiate with a trade union (*Abbott and Whelan v. ITGWU and Ors.* [1982] 1 JISLL 56). "Voluntarism" is becoming more and more of a misnomer because individual employment rights are increasingly protected by statute with a basic "floor of rights". Such basic rights as holidays and redundancy payments can be increased by negotiation, but such payments must be within the statutory framework.

Negotiations on the amount of salary and wages are "voluntary", yet in recent years centralised bargaining has resulted in the Programme for National Recovery (PNR) and the current Programme for Economic and Social Progress (PESP). The PESP did provide for some amount of local bargaining and included not only pay matters but also provision to amend various pieces of employment legislation, for example, equal pay, equal treatment and unfair dismissal. Generally, employment legislation provides for more and more reference of issues to third parties at the instigation of the parties involved.

INDUSTRIAL RELATIONS ACTS

The Industrial Relations Acts, 1946 to 1990 provide the framework for the collective bargaining process. The 1990 Act provides for the definition of "worker" as:

any person aged 15 years or more who has entered into or works under a contract with an employer, whether the contract be for manual labour, clerical work or otherwise, whether it be expressed or implied, oral or in writing, and whether it be a contract of service or of apprenticeship or a contract personally to execute any work or labour including, in particular, a psychiatric nurse employed by a health board and any person designated for the time being . . . [employed under the Defence Act, 1954 or employed under the State (other than established civil servants)] but does not include —

(a) a person who is employed by or under the State
(b) a teacher in a secondary school
(c) a teacher in a national school
(d) an officer of a local authority
(e) an officer of a vocational education committee, or
(f) an officer of a school attendance committee.

In order to give an overview of the Irish system of collective bargaining, we must refer back to the enactment of the Industrial Relations Act, 1946, which essentially legislated for industrial relations dispute resolution machinery within the framework of "voluntarism". That Act is extremely significant in our history and, despite some amendments, is still the key Industrial Relations Act for dispute resolution, leaving aside issues of trade disputes within the context of strikes. The Act, which was novel for its time, set up the Labour Court to deal with a rush of wage claims expected following the price/wages freeze and the lifting of the statutory orders after the Second World War.

The Labour Court's key function is in the settlement of trade disputes. The Court is arranged into three divisions consisting of a chairperson and two deputy chairpersons with six ordinary members, three employer representatives and three employee representatives. Such persons are appointed by the Minister for Enterprise and Employment, though the Irish Business and Employers' Confederation and the Irish Congress of Trade Unions provide the Minister with their nominees. While it may be called the "Labour Court", it is not a court of law and its recommendations are not legally binding. Nonetheless, the Court has power to summon witnesses, hear evidence on oath and in certain circumstances issue binding recommendations.

The key provision of the Industrial Relations Act, 1969 was the establishment of the office of Rights Commissioner which hears matters relating to individual grievances.

The Industrial Relations Act, 1990 set up the new industrial relations framework under the Labour Relations Commission and amended various parts of the earlier Acts. The 1990 Act provides new trade dispute legislation, having repealed the Trade Disputes Act, 1906 (as amended in 1982) (considered in the next chapter). The Labour Relations Commission comprises a chairperson, representatives of both sides of industry and two independent members who are appointed by the Minister for Enterprise and Employment. The Commission also appoints a chief executive. The Commission has under its umbrella the conciliation, rights commissioner and equality services (see section 4 — Industrial Relations and Adjudicating Bodies — where all aspects are considered in more detail). The Commission also has power to publish Codes of Practice (see Chapter 8 — Trade Disputes). A dispute which affects the public interest may be referred by the Minister to the Commission or to the Labour Court. However, it should be noted that the Labour Court is essentially a "court of appeal" within the industrial relations framework.

The Labour Relations Commission investigates and conciliates disputes. The Labour Court may not investigate a dispute until it has received a report from the Commission stating that it cannot resolve the matter and that both parties request the Court to investigate it. In certain circumstances, there may be direct reference to the Labour Court either by the workers concerned or by both parties (in respect of a certain issue in a dispute). There has to be agreement to accept the Court's recommendation.

TRADE UNIONS

The Trade Union Act, 1941 sets out the provisions for registration of trade unions and the granting of a licence which authorises negotiation on terms and conditions of employment. There are certain "excepted bodies" that do not need a negotiation licence, for example, the civil service, teachers groups and so forth.

It should be noted that if a union failed to have a balloting procedure by 18 July 1992, in accordance with the 1990 Act, it lost its negotiation licence.

In order to obtain a licence, a trade union must have rules on the entry and cessation of membership. The list of members must be

available for inspection. At least 18 months before a new union
applies for a licence, it must notify the Minister for Enterprise and
Employment, the ICTU and any trade union to which its members
also belong, as well as place the appropriate notice in the press. There
must also be an appropriate balloting procedure. The new union
must have at least 1,000 members resident in the State for the previous 18 months and at the date of application, and deposit between
£20,000 and £60,000 (depending on the size of the membership) with
the Registrar of Friendly Societies.

JOINT LABOUR COMMITTEES

The Industrial Relations Act, 1946 empowered the Labour Court to
set up a Joint Labour Committee (JLC) on the application of an
organisation representing workers, a trade union or the Minister for
Enterprise and Employment. The purpose of a JLC is to regulate
conditions of employment and minimum rates of pay for workers
engaged in certain forms of activity. There are JLCs covering some
of the following forms of activity: Contract Cleaning (City and County
of Dublin), Retail Grocery and Allied Trades, Law Clerks, Hairdress-
ing (Dublin and Cork), Provender Milling and so forth.

The Labour Court will not establish a JLC unless it considers
that the application is well founded and is made by an organisation
or a group representing such workers or employers, and that either:

> there is substantial agreement between such workers and their
> employers to the establishment of a joint labour committee, or

> the existing machinery for effective regulation of remuneration
> and other conditions of employment of such workers is inade-
> quate or is likely to cease or to cease to be adequate, or

> having regard to the existing rates of remuneration or condi-
> tions of employment of such workers or any others that it is
> expedient that a joint labour committee be established.

The Labour Court will consider the issue and, after consultation
with the parties, prepare a draft establishment order. Then the Court
will publish a notice stating that it intends to hold an inquiry into
the application for a JLC, the day, time and place where the inquiry
will be held (not earlier than 30 days or later than 60 days from the

date of publication) and where draft copies of the establishment order can be obtained.

All objections to the draft must be in writing, listing the grounds of objection to the establishment of the JLC. The objections will be considered by the Court on the day of the inquiry. If the Court is satisfied about matters, the order will be published and become effective not later than 42 days afterwards.

The constitution and proceedings of JLCs are governed by the Fifth Schedule to the 1990 Act. A JLC comprises an independent chairperson appointed by the Minister for Enterprise and Employment and an equal number of employer and worker representatives who are appointed by the Labour Court.

JLCs issue Employment Regulation Orders (EROs) which set out minimum rates of pay for all workers covered by the JLC. The proposals for an ERO must be published, stating where copies of the proposals may be obtained and that representations may be made within 21 days of the publication. The proposed ERO is then submitted to the Labour Court, which may refer the proposals back to the JLC or give effect to them from whatever date the Court considers appropriate. The JLC does not have to republish its amended proposals, though they do have to go back to the Court for the making of an order.

If there is already a registered employment agreement (see below) in place and there is agreement with both sides, the provision of an ERO may be waived as long as the terms and conditions of employment are not less favourable than those of the ERO.

An inspector may institute proceedings against an employer for breach of an ERO and a worker may also institute civil proceedings against their employer. Breach of an ERO is an offence and the employer may be liable to a fine of £750.

The Labour Relations Commission may carry out periodic reviews to see whether new JLCs should be established and to review existing committees. Also, the Labour Court may ask a JLC for a report on the industry for which it was established. The independent chairman may also ask the members for such report.

JOINT INDUSTRIAL COUNCILS

Joint Industrial Councils (JICs) are permanent, voluntary joint negotiating bodies whose main purpose is the promotion of harmonious relations between employers and employees. The procedures of the Council must provide that during the course of a trade dispute, a lockout or a strike cannot take place until the matter has been considered by the Council. The Labour Court does not register such groups unless it is satisfied that they are substantially representative of a particular class, type or group of worker and their respective employers.

REGISTRATION OF COLLECTIVE AGREEMENTS

The Industrial Relations Act, 1946 (as amended by the 1990 Act) provides that a collective agreement may be registered with the Labour Court, making it legally binding upon the parties. These are known as registered agreements and they provide for certain basic terms and conditions of employment. Such agreement is defined in the 1946 Act as

> an agreement relating to the remuneration or the conditions of employment of workers of any class, type or group made between a trade union of workers and an employer or trade union of employers, or made at a meeting of a joint industrial council between members of the council representative of workers and members of the council representative of employers.

The Acts provide for certain requirements to be complied with before these agreements can be registered. The agreements apply to all workers of the particular category who need not necessarily be represented at the negotiation process before the Labour Court.

Before an agreement can be registered, the Labour Court must be satisfied that the parties to the agreement are substantially representative of such workers and employers. All practical details of applicants must be given (e.g. names and addresses) the extent to which there is agreement and the grounds for establishing that the applicants are substantially representative of such employees.

Recently, a High Court judgment declared the registered agreement in the security industry as null and void due to "rubber stamping" by the Labour Court. It was also considered that neither fair procedures nor appropriate registration formalities were complied with. The parties were represented by the Federated Union of Employers (FUE) (now IBEC), who represented five firms where 1,000 of the 2,700 static guards were employed, and the Irish Transport and General Workers' Union (now Scientific Industrial and

Professional Trade Union). An organisation called the National Union of Security Employers (NUSE) challenged the validity of the agreement, which was registered in 1984, on the basis that the objections of certain employers in the security industry were not considered by the Court and that FUE did not substantially represent the majority of employers in the security industry (*National Union of Security Employers* v. *The Labour Court, Ireland and the Attorney General*, High Court, Flood, J., 4 December 1992).

There has been an ongoing concern over the years that such agreements are not constitutional, but this issue was not addressed in this judgment.

Two parties may consent to such registration or, where there are more than two parties involved, there must be substantial agreement between them. The agreement must apply to all workers of a particular type, group or class and their respective employers. The Court must be satisfied that it would be a desirable practice or that it would be expedient to have a separate agreement for that group, class or type of worker. The agreement cannot have the intention of restricting employment or causing unduly costly work practices. The agreement must provide that if there is a trade dispute, a strike or lockout shall not occur until the dispute resolution provisions in the agreement have taken place. The contents of the agreement become the contractual provisions of the employment contract.

Before the agreement is registered, the Labour Court must ask the parties to publish particulars of the agreement so that it will be brought to the attention of all the parties who will be covered by it. This is extremely important because all employers and employees who may not be party to the original application will be covered by the agreement when it is registered. The Court will not register the agreement until 14 days have elapsed from the date of the publication. If there is an objection to the registration of the agreement, the Court will have to hear all such objections and then make its decision. Once the Court is satisfied that all aspects of the Act have been complied with, the agreement shall be placed on the Register of Employment Agreements.

The Labour Court is considered the body for the interpretation of registered agreements. If the interpretation of a registered agreement arises before a court of law, it may be referred to the Labour Court if the court so wishes.

There is provision for the variation or amendment to registered agreements. If variation is requested the Court shall hear all the parties and then decide. This is a frequent occurrence in matters such as pay. A variation order is then registered along with the original agreement and becomes part of the registered agreement.

If there is a breach of the agreement and a complaint to the Court, both parties will be heard (should they so wish) and the Court shall make the appropriate order so that the agreement is complied with if the complaint is well founded.

The 1990 Act provides that an employer must keep all the necessary records to show that a registered agreement is being complied with. Such records must be kept for three years and an employer who fails to do so may be liable to a fine of £500. If records are falsified, there is liability to a fine of £1,000.

If a sum is due to a worker by an employer arising from a registered employment agreement, or if there is a breach of such an agreement, an inspector can institute proceedings for the recovery of the sum or the enforcement of the condition on behalf of the worker. A worker can also institute proceedings on their own behalf.

There are also provisions stating that there cannot be the maintenance of a strike (out of the union funds) where an employer is being made to agree to pay levels or work conditions other than those contained in the agreement. In such situations, the Court may order the union not to assist the maintenance of such a strike or may cancel the agreement. If there is a breach of this order, the party may be guilty of a criminal offence (£1,000 and £200 fines per day for a continuing offence). If a strike continues after such an order, and the issue does not relate to pay or conditions of employment, then the payment of strike benefits is not considered to be "assistance or maintenance" within the meaning of the Act.

A registered agreement may be cancelled by a joint voluntary application of the parties concerned. Also, the Court may cancel an agreement if there is a substantial change in the trade or industry covered. Equally, an agreement registered for a specific period and still in force at the end of the period will continue to remain in force until it is formally cancelled. It can be cancelled after three months notification to the Court where there is agreement between the parties.

GENERAL REFERENCES

Industrial Relations in Ireland: Contemporary Issues and Developments, Department of Industrial Relations, UCD, 1989.

Report of the Commission of Inquiry on Industrial Relations, Stationery Office, Dublin, 1981.

Kerr, A., *The Trade Union and Industrial Relations Acts of Ireland*, Sweet and Maxwell, 1991.

McCarthy, C., *Trade Unions in Ireland, 1894–1960*, Institute of Public Administration, 1977.

CHAPTER EIGHT

Trade Disputes

INDUSTRIAL RELATIONS ACT, 1990

The Industrial Relations Act, 1990 came into operation on 18 July 1990. This complex legislation is the outcome of various different proposals and much discussion, including recommendations by the Commission of Inquiry on Industrial Relations which reported in July 1981. The Trade Disputes Act 1906 as amended (the 1982 Act extended the scope of the 1906 Act) has been repealed in full.

As the Act is of recent origin and there have been few cases, there is little judicial interpretation. Interestingly, many of the rulings of the High Court during the 1970s and 1980s have now become statutory provisions in the 1990 Act, for example, the provisions relating to places where picketing is permitted and the numbers that may be involved.

The purpose of the Act is to make better provision for promoting harmonious relations between workers and employers and to amend the industrial relations and trade union legislation generally. In this chapter, trade or industrial disputes are considered. Legislation affecting trade unions themselves and general industrial relations (collective) bargaining have already been considered.

DEFINITIONS

As with all pieces of legislation, the definitions in the Act are important and considered first.

Employer

"A person for whom one or more workers work or have worked or normally work or seek to work having previously worked for that person".

Worker

"Any person who is or was employed whether or not in the employment of the employer with whom a trade dispute arises, but does not include a member of the Defence Forces or of the Garda Síochána".

This appears to be a very loose definition and one fears it will be open to wide interpretation. There is no specific reference to a contract of service (contract of employment). Accordingly, the courts may consider that independent contractors fall within the definition of "worker". If that is the case, there is no major change from the 1906 Act. However, individuals who are seeking employment would appear to be excluded.

In *Westman Holdings Ltd.* v. *McCormack and Ors.* ([1991] ILRM 833), six of the defendants were employed by a company called Alma Taverns Ltd. as bar and restaurant staff in an establishment in Dublin known as Judge Roy Beans, occupied by that company under a lease. The lease expired on 1 March 1991 and the business was taken over by the immediate landlords, Westhall Property Co. Ltd., which also took over the employment of the worker defendants.

On 15 March 1991 Westhall entered into a contract with Westman Holdings to sell the premises. Westhall terminated the employment of all its employees and business ceased on 5 April 1991. Prior to that, each of the employees had received a sum of money and signed a form acknowledging that this was in full discharge of all claims that they may have against Alma and Westhall. An official of the workers' trade union, INUVGATA, made a claim that its member employees of Westhall were entitled to continue in the employment of Westman under the provisions of the European Communities (Safeguarding of Employees on the Transfer of Undertakings) Regulations, 1980. Westman rejected the claim and the worker defendants commenced an official union picket of the premises.

Westman made a successful ex parte application to have the picketing removed on 11 April. On the hearing of the matter, an interlocutory injunction was granted, restraining the defendants from picketing the premises. That decision was appealed to the Supreme Court, which considered that, on the balance of convenience, the injunction against picketing should continue until the full hearing of the case. The Court acknowledged that there were fair reasons for such a hearing, however, including consideration as to whether Westman would be deemed to be their employer and whether there was a transfer of business within the meaning of the 1980 Regulations.

Trade Dispute

"Any dispute between employers and workers which is connected with the employment or non-employment, or the terms or conditions of, or affecting the employment of any person".

This definition excludes "worker *v.* worker" disputes. It obviously does not only apply to "employer *v.* worker" disputes, however, as it can include disputes involving former workers (thus, including dismissal in the widest sense, e.g. employees having a dispute over future redundancy payments) or indeed workers employed by some other employer. The terms or conditions of employment include all matters either expressed or implied in the contract of employment.

Industrial Action

"Any action which affects or is likely to affect, the terms or conditions, whether express or implied, of a contract and which is taken by any number or body of workers acting in combination or under a common understanding as a means of compelling their employer, or to aid other workers in compelling their employer, to accept or not to accept terms or conditions of or affecting employment".

This definition is extremely broad, even broader than a similar definition contained in the Unfair Dismissals Acts, 1977 to 1993. It also refers to collective industrial action as opposed to action by an individual employee. The definition encompasses action such as "work-to-rule" and a "go slow". If employees wish to engage in such industrial action they will have to comply with requirements of the legislation, such as holding secret ballots which are discussed below.

Strike

"A cessation of work by any number or body of workers acting in combination or a concerted refusal or a refusal under common understanding of any number of workers to continue to work for their employer done as a means of compelling their employer, or to aid other workers in compelling their employer, to accept or not to accept terms or conditions of or affecting employment".

The key issue in this definition is that the purpose of the strike must be to compel an employer to accept or not to accept certain terms and conditions of or affecting employment. By implication it excludes strikes which are purely political, such as a general strike or demonstration concerning income tax matters.

IMMUNITIES

The new legislation does not give a positive right to strike, but trade union members, officials of trade unions and trade unions themselves who take industrial action in furtherance or contemplation of a trade dispute have immunity or protection under the legislation. In other words, they cannot be sued for taking part in such action. Of course, such persons are required to comply with the balloting and notice requirements as provided for in the legislation.

This immunity or protection applies only to "authorised" trade unions (including its officials and members), that is, trade unions which hold negotiation licences. There is no change on this point from the previous legislation.

However, like all general rules there are exceptions. Accordingly, such persons in dispute may be sued for damages or there may be proceedings by way of injunction if, for example:

(1) It is not a genuine trade dispute, e.g. a political action as discussed above (see definition of strike/industrial action);

(2) The balloting and notice procedures have not been complied with;

(3) Non-peaceful picketing takes place;

(4) The industrial action amounts to an inducement to breach a commercial contract or there is an unlawful interference with a trade or business.

Trade unions themselves cannot be sued for damages in respect of a tort (a civil wrong) pursued in contemplation or furtherance of a trade dispute, provided, of course, that they have an honest and reasonable belief that the action is in contemplation or furtherance of such trade dispute. Of course, if it is an action for defamation or for breach of contract, the trade union can be sued.

INDIVIDUAL WORKERS

One of the major changes in the 1990 legislation concerns disputes relating to an individual worker. The legislation is quite clear in that it refers to "one individual worker" and not to group disputes.

Section 9 (2) states:

Where in relation to the employment or non-employment or the terms or conditions of or affecting the employment of one indi-

vidual worker, there are agreed procedures availed of by custom
or in practice in the employment concerned, are provided for in
a collective agreement, for the resolution of individual grievances, including dismissals. . . .

Thus, if such procedures are not applied, the employee will not
have the benefit of the immunity. This means that the employer may
seek an injunction to stop the picketing and may sue for damages
caused by it.

If at any stage an employer fails or refuses to comply with such
procedures, the employee will have the benefit of the immunity even
though the full procedure will not have been exhausted. The procedures referred to in the Act are not specified, but would include
reference to such persons or bodies as a rights commissioner, Labour
Relations Commission, the Labour Court, an equality officer and the
Employment Appeals Tribunal.

Thus, it is important and indeed practicable for both employer
and employee to include a specific reference to the mandatory referral of disputes to third parties in the contract of employment and/or
collective agreement. Indeed, having such mandatory referral can
assist the speedy defusion and resolution of disputes. Interestingly,
even though the Unfair Dismissals Acts, 1977 to 1993 provide for an
appeal from the Employment Appeals Tribunal to the Circuit Court,
such appeal to the courts is excluded under the provisions of the 1990
Act. Thus, following on the hearing of unfair dismissals case by the
Employment Appeals Tribunal, the former worker can picket the
premises of their former employer and have immunity under the Act.

SECRET BALLOTS

A major change in Irish trade dispute legislation concerns the provision of secret ballots. Trade unions now have to have a pre-strike
secret ballot rule in their rule books. Every trade union operating in
this country had to send a copy of its rules incorporating balloting
procedures by 18 July 1992 to the Registrar of Friendly Societies. If
a trade union fails to provide for such rules, the union shall cease to
be entitled to hold a negotiation licence.

The Act has complicated rules in respect of balloting procedures,
which are in summary:

(1) No strike or other industrial action will take place without a secret
ballot;

(2) All members whom it is reasonable for the union to believe will be called upon to engage in the strike or other industrial action must be given a fair opportunity of voting;

(3) Notwithstanding a majority vote favouring industrial action, the committee of management of a trade union will have full discretion in relation to the organisation of industrial action; and

(4) A trade union must make known to the members entitled to vote in the ballot the results as soon as practicable after the vote.

Obviously, balloting must take place before primary or secondary picketing (see below) takes place. There may be a number of ballots, for example, one in the employment where the original trade dispute exists and a second ballot in another work place if there is to be secondary picketing.

Following a ballot for industrial/strike action, the trade union must give an employer one week (seven days) notice of such action.

AGGREGATE BALLOTING

The issue of aggregate balloting can arise where there are a number of trade unions in a work place. The Act does not require that aggregate balloting take place, however. If only one union votes, members of other unions would be expected to work in the normal way, that is, pass the picket and not take part in industrial action.

The Act contains complex provisions on the aggregation of votes in a multi-union ballot. The effect of these provisions is to give a trade union the right to allow its members to take industrial action where a majority of all the workers in the plant have voted in favour of such action, but where the members of the union concerned have voted against it.

A union that is affiliated to the Irish Congress of Trade Unions cannot vote in favour of supporting a strike organised by another trade union unless such action has been sanctioned by ICTU.

BALLOTING SANCTIONS

If a trade union fails to hold a secret ballot, or if one week's strike notice is not given, or if the ballot is flawed (e.g. the proper electorate was not balloted, members were not notified or if the members balloted on a different issue), the strike/industrial action may not attract the immunities under the legislation. The employer may seek an ex parte injunction (i.e. without notifying the trade union/members in dispute) restraining such action.

The Registrar of Friendly Societies may revoke the licence of a trade union if it fails to hold a secret ballot in accordance with legislation after being instructed to do so.

PICKETING

Section 11(1) of the Act provides:

> It shall be lawful for one or more persons, acting on their own behalf or on behalf of a trade union in contemplation or furtherance of a trade dispute, to attend at, or where that is not practicable, at the approaches to, a place where their employer works or carries on business, if they so attend merely for the purpose of peacefully obtaining or communicating information or of peacefully persuading any person to work or abstain from working.

Workers are thus confined to picketing at their place of work (unless they fall within the secondary picketing exemption which is considered below). The picketers must be attending "in contemplation or furtherance of a trade dispute" and they must also be "acting on their own behalf or on behalf of a trade union". This applies to both official and unofficial picketing. They can only picket their employer, not associated companies of their employer. Again, this provision reflects the stated position of the High Court over the last number of years. An employee can picket at branches of their employer's business, but not at premises of associated companies.

This provision raises a question about the position of workers who are employed by one company but who work at the premises of another. It is likely to provide major scope for interpretation. For example, it would affect an employer with a small head office and workers in various locations, such as in the catering and cleaning industries. Accordingly, can such workers only picket the head office of their employer or can they picket the various sites where they work? If, for example, all the service workers were employed in Dublin it would be [reasonably] practicable for them to picket the head office in Dublin. However, if the employer had employees scattered all over the country, it would not be practicable for them to travel to Dublin to picket the head office. It would make more sense for them to picket the place where their employer "carries on business". The next wording we have to consider is the meaning of "carries on business". Is it merely the business functions of a head office or is it where the business contracts are actually performed?

The courts will likely take a wide interpretation of where "it is practicable" to picket. In other words, if there are numerous country locations or city centre locations, picketing would be allowed in the place where the employee works and carries out the business of the employer. At this time, however, we do not have any interpretation from the courts.

The definition of "employer" also raises the issue of what happens to a prospective employee who has unsuccessfully sought employment. The position would appear to be that the prospective employee cannot picket the employer as the prospective employer was never actually in employment.

Industrial Estates and Shopping Centres

The Act provides that an employee must picket at the premises where the employer carries on business or if that is not practicable "at the approaches to" the premises.

In the past few years, the picketing of shopping centres or industrial estates has been problematic. Such complexes are invariably owned by financial institutions, investment companies or other bodies, and the employers who have shops or factories in the complex are their tenants. Thus, for example, staff picketing outside a shop within the shopping centre were trespassing, and picketing outside the shopping centre obviously affected all other traders. Usually, the matter was resolved by the owners of the centres giving permission to picket on the premises, thus resolving the issue of trespass and the effect it might have had on general business in the centre.

In effect, the 1990 Act is stating the existing legal position and providing a right to picket the approaches to a complex. Of course, picketers at various entrances would clearly have to name the employer with whom they were in dispute. Further, it would be reasonable to have only two picketers at each entrance.

Secondary Picketing

Secondary picketing occurs where workers in dispute with company X picket company Y with a view to bringing about a withdrawal of labour or a disruption of business, thus adding to the pressure on company X to come to a settlement. Company Y will normally have a connection with company X, whether as a customer, a supplier or a competitor.

Generally, under the 1990 Act, all secondary picketing is unlawful. However, secondary picketing may be lawful if the picketers "believe at the commencement of their attendance and throughout the continuance of their attendance that that employer has directly assisted their employer who is a party to the trade dispute for the purpose of frustrating the strike or other industrial action".

For example, if company Y was merely trying to gain more business at the expense of a competitor, then the secondary picketing would not be lawful. It would only be lawful where the "second" employer frustrated the strike by actively providing services on behalf of the employer.

Persons who wish to engage in secondary picketing have to prove that the "second" employer is trying to frustrate the strike. In other words, the onus of proof will be on the picketers and must be sustained throughout the period of secondary picketing.

Balloting provisions are of particular importance to secondary picketing. Not only will the issue be balloted on by the employees in the primary dispute, but the union members in the secondary employment will have to ballot.

There is one exception to the general provisions on secondary picketing. Action taken by an employer in the health services in order to maintain life-preserving services shall not constitute action which "assists" an employer who is party to a dispute.

Both the wording of the Act on secondary picketing and also balloting provisions in relation thereto will undoubtedly provide ample scope for litigation and judicial interpretation.

CODES OF PRACTICE

In February 1991, the Minister for Labour requested the Labour Relations Commission to prepare codes of practice on disputes procedures and levels of cover which should be provided in the event of disputes arising in essential services. In preparing this Code, the Commission had consulted with and taken into account the views of ICTU, FIE (now IBEC), the Department of Finance, the Department of Labour, the Local Government Staff Negotiations Board, the Labour Court and representatives of the International Labour Or ganisation. The draft code was accepted by the Minister for Labour who made an order under Section 42 of the Industrial Relations Act, 1990, namely Industrial Relations Act, 1990, Code of Practice on Dispute Procedures (Declaration) Order, 1992 (S.I. No. 1 of 1992).

The Code "recognises that the primary responsibility for dealing with industrial relations issues and the resolution of disputes rests with employers, employer organisations and trade unions". The Code covers disputes procedures, including procedures in essential services. The Act provides that such Code(s) shall be admissible in evidence before a court, the Labour Court, the Labour Relations Commission, a rights commissioner or an equality officer and shall be used in deciding on the issue concerned.

The key issues were to make provision for written procedures which would resolve the matters in dispute in a peaceful manner and to avoid the need for any of the parties to resort to actions which would lead to a disruption of supplies and services, or a loss of income to employees and of revenue to employers. In order to achieve this aim, the procedures provide for discussion at the earliest possible stage with a view to the parties reaching agreement and thus avoiding industrial action. These principles cover all employments irrespective of their sector and size, and written procedures should be given and explained to all employees. There should also be an appropriate timescale within which the procedures should be effected. The procedures should also take into account the use of the State industrial relations machinery, namely the Labour Relations Commission, the Labour Court, the rights commissioner service, the equality service and the Employment Appeals Tribunal. Of course, the procedures should be reviewed from time to time to ensure that the procedures remain effective.

Dispute procedures should provide:

(1) That the parties will refrain from any action which might impede the effective functioning of these procedures;

(2) For co-operation between trade union and employers on appropriate arrangements and facilities for trade union representatives to take part in agreed dispute procedures;

(3) For appropriate arrangements to facilitate employees to consider any proposals emanating from the operation of the procedures.

The Code also provides general guidance to employers and trade unions on the arrangements necessary to ensure minimum cover of service for disputes that could have serious or adverse consequences for the community or the business/service concerned and its employees. There is also a joint obligation on employers and trade unions to have contingency plans to deal with any emergency that may happen in an industrial dispute.

In employments providing an essential service in particular, management and unions should make arrangements covering:

(1) The maintenance of plant and equipment;

(2) All matters concerning health, safety and security;

(3) Special operational problems which exist in continuous process industries;

(4) The provision of urgent medical services and supplies; and

(5) The provision of emergency services required on humanitarian grounds.

If there are no dispute procedures in place, the Code provides that they should be put in place and that they should cover both individual and collective procedures. If procedures are in place, both employers and trade unions should take whatever steps are required to ensure that the principles in the Code are incorporated within them. The agreements should include appropriate levels of management and trade union representation at various stages in the procedure.

ESSENTIAL SERVICES

The Code of Practice described above provides additional procedures and safeguards for the peaceful resolution of disputes involving essential services. These would include services whose cessation or interruption could endanger life, or cause major damage to the national economy or widespread hardship to the community, such as the health services, energy supplies (including gas and electricity), water and sewage services, fire ambulance and rescue services and certain elements of public transport. Additional procedures should be introduced in these employments, recognising the joint responsibility of employers and employees in trying to resolve disputes without recourse to strikes or other forms of industrial action. Employees should be fully aware of the nature of the service that they are providing and its relationship with the community. Also, any major changes affecting employees' interests should include consultation with the trade unions within the agreed procedures. Unless there are other procedures in place, agreements negotiated on a voluntary basis should include one of the following provisions to eliminate or reduce the risk to essential supplies or services arising from industrial disputes:

(1) Acceptance by the parties of awards, decisions and recommendations which result from the final stage of the dispute settlement procedure where these include investigation by an independent expert body such as the Labour Court, an agreed arbitration board or tribunal or an independent person appointed by the parties (some semi-state bodies, the ESB, for example, have internal industrial relations machinery); or

(2) A specific undertaking in agreements that, should one of the parties decide that an award, decision or recommendation emerging from the final stage of the dispute settlement procedure is unsatisfactory, it will agree on the means of resolving the issue without recourse to strike or other forms of industrial action; such agreements to include a provision for a review of the case by an agreed recognised body after 12 months, which would represent a final determination of the issue; or

(3) Provision that the parties to an agreement would accept awards, decisions or recommendations resulting from the operation of the final stage of the dispute procedure on the basis that an independent review would take place at five-year intervals to examine whether the employees covered by the agreement had been placed at a disadvantage and, if so, to advise on the changes necessary to redress the position, taking into account economic and financial considerations.

If the parties have not concluded an agreement taking into account one of the above options and there is a serious threat to the continuity of essential supplies and services, and if the Labour Relations Commission is satisfied that all available disputes procedures have been used to try to effect a settlement, the Commission shall then consult with the Irish Business and Employers' Confederation (formerly FIE) and the ICTU. The objective would be to secure their assistance and co-operation for whatever measures may be necessary to resolve the dispute. This may include a continuation of normal working for a period of not less than six months in order for the parties or the State industrial relations machinery to effect a full and final settlement of the issues concerned.

In general, it is difficult to predict how the courts will interpret various sections of this Act. It will take a number of years before a body of Irish case law is built up, partly because balloting provisions and certain sanctions arising from it only became operative in July 1992.

GENERAL REFERENCES

Forde, M., *Industrial Relations Law*, The Round Hall Press, 1991.

Kerr, A., *The Trade Union and Industrial Relations Acts of Ireland with Commentary*, Sweet and Maxwell, 1991.

Kerr, A. and Whyte, G., *Trade Union Law in Ireland*, Professional Books, 1985.

McCarthy, C. and von Prondzynski, F., *Employment Law in Ireland*, 2nd ed., 1988.

Report of the Commission of Inquiry on Industrial Relations, Stationery Office, Dublin, July 1981.

CHAPTER NINE

Equal Pay

THE ANTI-DISCRIMINATION (PAY) ACT, 1974

Article 119 of the Treaty of Rome provides that men and women should receive equal pay for equal work. In Ireland, equal pay legislation came into effect on 31 December 1975 as a result of the application of EC Directive 75/117/EEC. In addition, the Anti-Discrimination (Pay) Act, 1974 contains an equal pay clause which is implied into each and every contract of employment. Thus there cannot be unfavourable treatment in relation to pay between men and women. Over the last two decades a large number of women have successfully claimed equal pay against their employer, and such claims (with arrears of "equal pay") have cost employers substantial sums.

The 1974 Act (as amended) provides the right of men and women to receive the same rate of remuneration if employed on "like work" by the same (or an associated) employer in the same city, town or locality. A man and a woman perform "like work" where both perform the same duties under the same or similar conditions; where the work performed is of a similar nature with any differences being infrequent or of small importance in relation to the work as a whole; or where the work is equal in value, judged by the demands it makes in terms of skill, responsibility, working conditions and physical or mental effort.

The 1974 Act provides that there cannot be direct discrimination in relation to pay. There is no reference to indirect discrimination. There is a definition of indirect discrimination in the Employment Equality Act, 1977, however (see Chapter 10 — Equal Treatment in Employment). A provision in the 1977 Act that both the 1974 and 1977 Acts be read as one means that the concept of indirect discrimination has been imported into the 1974 Act. Thus, a group of workers who feel that they are being discriminated against in matters of pay by reason of their sex or marital status can bring a claim under this Act. For example, part-time women workers cannot be discriminated against on pay matters just because they are part-time; it must be justified on other grounds (*Bilka Kaufhaus GmbH* v. *Weber von Hartz* Case 170/1984).

In *St Patrick's College, Maynooth* v. *19 Female Employees* (EP 4/1984, DEP 10/1984), the Equality Officer considered that their lower rate of pay was on the basis of indirect discrimination because they were part-time employees. They were successful in their claim which was upheld by the Labour Court. In the case of *Kowalska* v. *Freie und Hansestadt Hamburg* (Case 33/1989), the Advocate General of the ECJ in summary considered that Article 119 must be interpreted as prohibiting provisions in a collective agreement which would indirectly discriminate against a group of workers in matters of pay. Thus they must be treated the same way as full time workers on a proportional basis. Of course, pay can be different as long as it is "on grounds other than sex". The Second Commission on the Status of Women has recommended that both the 1974 and 1977 Acts should be consolidated in one statute and that the concept of indirect discrimination should apply to equal pay.

This legislation applies to both men and women. Marital status of the claimant or the comparator does not matter. Claims are initially referred to an equality officer; if either party is dissatisfied with an equality officer's recommendation, they may appeal it to the Labour Court. A claimant who is awarded equal pay is entitled to three years' difference (between themselves and the comparator) in the rate of pay prior to the referral of the claim to the equality officer and all pay differences from the date of referral. Section 4 explains procedures in equal pay claims before equality officers and the Labour Court.

APPLICATION

The Act has a wide application and covers all employed persons in both the public and private sector. "Employed" means employed under a contract of service (i.e. a contract of employment either oral or in writing) or apprenticeship or a contract personally to execute any work or labour.

The definition of "employed" would appear to apply to certain self-employed persons and independent contractors as long as such persons "personally execute" the work concerned, in other words it would not cover the staff of an independent contractor. A solicitor who was a partner in a firm was not covered under the Act (*P.C.*

Moore & Co. v. *Flanagan* EP 13/1978, DEP 12/ 1978), but a senator of the Oireachtas was (*Department of Public Service* v. *Robinson* EP 36/1978, DEP 7/1979). "Agency temps" are not currently included under the legislation because in law they are deemed to be neither employees of the hiring company (i.e. the place where they work) or of the employment agency. This issue has not yet been tested under the equality legislation. The husband of a deceased employee bringing a claim would be entitled to the same pension benefits as those enjoyed by the survivors of the married male employees (*EEA* v. *University College, Galway*, EP 18/1984, DEP 2/1985).

A former employee can also bring a claim (*Revenue Commissioners* v. *O'Sullivan*, EE and EP 10/1983, DEP 7/1983). In addition, the equality officer in *Byrne* v. *Champion Fire Defence Ltd.* (EP 8/1985) considered that a woman is entitled to the same rate of pay as a man who previously performed the same job, and furthermore that both persons do not have to be employed at the same time.

The definition of employer is broad and includes associated employers (e.g. a company with a subsidiary or a holding company with a number of subsidiaries). Thus, for example, a woman may work in one company and the male comparator in another company. In the case of *Clonskeagh Hospital* v. *Two Telephonists* (EP 40/1979), the equality officer considered that the women who worked in one hospital could compare themselves with the male comparator who worked in another of the same health board.

REMUNERATION

The definition of remuneration in the Irish legislation is virtually the same as Article 119 of the EC Treaty, namely that remuneration

> includes any consideration whether in cash or in kind, which an employee receives either directly or indirectly in respect of his employment from his employer.

Thus remuneration includes not only basic pay but also accommodation, bonus earnings, commission payments, marriage gratuities, overtime payments, pensions, permanent health insurance, redundancy payments and sickness payments.

Article 1 of EEC Directive 117/1975 is also important and it states:

The principles of equal pay for men and women outlined in Article 119 of the Treaty . . . mean for the same work or for work to which equal value is attributed, the elimination of all discrimination on grounds of sex with regard to all aspects and conditions of remuneration.

The Labour Court has interpreted this to mean that the employee's total package is not the issue but instead each and every aspect of remuneration must be equal where there is "like work" unless there are "grounds other than sex".

Accommodation

In a number of cases it has been established that accommodation which is "part and parcel" of a job should be seen as part of remuneration (*CIE* v. *IT&GWU* DEP 1/1978). In *Metropole Hotel* v. *Seven Female Waitresses* (EP 19/1986, DEP 4/1987) the waitresses were in receipt of a lower basic rate of pay than the waiter comparator, but they received accommodation and thus the hotel argued that they were in fact receiving equal remuneration. The Labour Court determined that this view was incorrect as the Act provided for "the same rate" of remuneration. The claimants were awarded the same basic rate of pay.

Bonus Payments

Bonus payments should be the same for men and women who are doing "like work". In one particular case, female workers maintained that they were discriminated against because their production bonus commenced at 80 per cent performance while the male comparators were at 70 per cent, and women could only earn their maximum bonus at 117 per cent performance while the men did so at 120 per cent. The Labour Court considered that the women were entitled to be paid their production bonus at the same minimum level of performance (*Lissadell Towels Ltd.* v. *IT&GWU*, EP 10/1986, DEP 3/1989).

Commission

Commission is clearly part of remuneration so it must be applied in the same way.

Marriage Gratuities

Before the removal of the "marriage" bar which formally required women employees to resign upon marrying, many public and private sector employments paid to those women marriage gratuities based on pay and service. Following the removal of the "marriage bar" during the 1970s, many employers continued to pay the gratuities in certain circumstances, for example, to women who had been in employment prior to the changes and who still wished to avail of the gratuity on marriage.

In a number of cases, men maintained that they were entitled to the marriage gratuity and were thus being discriminated against. In the Bank of Ireland case, the claimant was employed from 1969 until his retirement in 1984, he married in 1980 and, before he left the Bank, wrote requesting payment of his marriage gratuity. At that time, the marriage gratuity was only payable to certain female employees. He then brought a claim under the 1974 Act and both the equality officer and the Labour Court held in his favour. The Bank appealed the case to the High Court. Costello, J. held that this higher payment to such female officials was not because they were women but because they fulfilled certain conditions, namely (a) they were married and (b) had entered the service of the Bank before 1974. Thus the difference in pay was "on grounds other than sex". (*Bank of Ireland v. Kavanagh* (1987) 6 JISLL 192, EP 11/1985, DEP 10/1985 and since followed, e.g., *Deeney* v. *National Irish Bank*, EP/1991).

Overtime Payments

These have been accepted as part of remuneration, but like bonus and commission payments must be applied equally where employees are doing "like work".

Permanent Health Insurance

Membership of a permanent health insurance scheme or income continuance plan has also been clearly established as part of remuneration. The practice of excluding female employees in respect of disabilities arising from pregnancy or childbirth was considered discriminatory (*Shield Insurance Co. Ltd.* v. *Two Female Employees* EP 8/1984 and *McCarren & Co. Ltd.* v. *Jackson* EP 5/1987).

Redundancy Payments

Lump sum redundancy payments in excess of statutory redundancy are part of remuneration and thus cannot be discriminatory on the basis of gender.

However, situations can arise where different payments are made to men and women and such payments may not be discriminatory. In the case of *Grant, Barnett and Co.* v. *Leonard* (EE 7/1983, DEE 7/1983), ten of the staff were declared redundant. Union and management negotiated a severance package of two and a half weeks' pay per year of service, which was accepted by a number of employees. However, three others, including two men, rejected the offer and negotiated a higher package for themselves. The claimant then contended that she had been discriminated against compared to her male colleagues as they got a higher package. The claim was brought under the 1977 Act and the equality officer considered that the claim did not fall within the scope of that Act. On appeal, the Labour Court agreed that the payment did not come within the scope of the 1977 Act, but the criteria used to calculate the payment did. Nevertheless, the Court did not consider that the payment was discriminatory as it had nothing to do with the claimant's sex.

The payment of ex-gratia payment to female part-time workers was at issue in another case where the claimants maintained that the computation of their voluntary redundancy package was unfair because they only received credit for one year's service for two years' part-time work. The male comparators were full-time employees and at the date of redundancy the women were also in full-time employment. The equality officer considered the claim fell within the scope of the 1974 Act, but the claim was not upheld as the company was actually calculating the ex-gratia payment on the basis of the full weekly rate of pay. The equality officer calculated that if the claimants' package were calculated on the same basis as the men, they would in fact be in receipt of a higher payment and no account would be taken of the fact that part of their service was part-time (*Packard Electric (Ireland) Ltd.* v. *38 Female Employees* EP 3/1992).

Uniforms

The definition of remuneration includes "any consideration . . .which an employee receives . . . in respect of his employment from his employer". In a number of cases the meaning of "consideration" was discussed and in one case was defined as "some advantage moving from one party to a contract to the other party to the contract in return for something given or promised by the other party under the contract" (*Educational Building Society* v. *Male Employees*, EP 9/1987and para. 18).

In that case the female employees received a jacket, two skirts and five blouses or £45 in lieu of the blouses on an annual basis. The male employees considered that they were entitled to a uniform or monies as well. The equality officer considered that the employer was not giving the women uniforms in return for something given or promised under the contract because they were employed in the first instance subject to the condition that, where provided, uniforms must be worn. Thus the provision of free uniforms does not constitute remuneration where it is a condition of employment.

In another case there was a dispute concerning a claim by female catering employees who had to wash their own "easy-care" overalls while the male catering assistants" cotton coats were laundered free of charge. As a result of this arrangement, the women considered they received less pay than the men even though they were doing "like work". The equality officer stated:

> I consider that irrespective of whether or not the employer, in laundering the uniforms of the males, is giving the males an advantage or benefit, the employer is not providing the launder- ing of the uniforms in return for something given or promised by the employee under the contract. In fact, both the male and female employees are employed in the first instance subject to the condition that they wear the uniforms provided by the employer in the course of their duty and that they must appear clean at all times in order to comply with the hygienic standards set by the employer. Consequently, I find that as the male comparators were employed subject to the condition that they wore a uniform which had to be clean, the provision of laundered uniforms to the male employees concerned did not constitute any part of the consideration which they received in respect of their employment.

Accordingly, the female claimants did not have an entitlement under the Act to have their uniforms laundered by the company or to be reimbursed for the expenses incurred in laundering the uni- forms (*British Home Stores (Dublin) Ltd.* v. *127 Female Catering*

Assistants EP 1/1988). However, a weekly uniform cleaning allowance was considered to be remuneration as it was a monetary payment (*Group 4 Securitas (I) Ltd.* v. *26 Female Store Detectives* EP 3/1991 — part of this recommendation was appealed (DEP 6/1991) but the Labour Court determination did not affect the uniform payment).

Pensions

The inclusion of pension arrangements within remuneration was first established in 1977 (*Linson Ltd.* v. *ASTMS*, EP 1/1977 and DEP 2/ 1977). It has also been considered that membership of a death benefit plan, a non-contributory pension scheme and an income-continuance scheme all constituted remuneration, and that the non-provision of a widower's pension (and benefits to children) for a female contributor was discriminatory (*Department of Public Service* v. *Robinson*, EP 36/1978, DEP 7/1979). Survivors' benefits are also part of an employee's remuneration, and the fact that they are paid after the death of the employee does not put them outside the scope of the Act (*EEA* v. *University College, Galway*, EP 18/1984, DEP 2/1985).

Contributions made by employers towards pension schemes have been viewed as remuneration, as have contributions towards permanent health insurance plans and other fringe benefits (see above). The question of whether employee contributions towards pension schemes or other fringe benefits constitute remuneration for the purposes of the 1974 Act has not arisen.

A claim for survivors' benefits may be brought by a widower of a deceased female employee. A husband was entitled to the same benefits as those enjoyed by the survivors of male employees.

No cases have yet arisen in respect of benefits which continue to be payable after the cessation of employment. However, benefits which commence to be paid after the employment has ended, namely, survivors' pensions, have been held to be part of the employee's remuneration.

The Pensions Act 1990 gave effect to the provisions of EC Directive 86/378/EEC which provides equal treatment in occupational pension schemes. This is considered in Chapter 14 — Pensions.

Voluntary Health Insurance

Many employers provide VHI cover for employees as part of their remuneration package. In the case of *Gypsum Industries plc* v. *Ormiston* (EE 16/1992) the employer agreed to pay the VHI subscription for employees whose earnings exceeded the limit for free medical care. If an employee's earnings fell below the limit for one year, the company would fund VHI cover for that year only. In this case the employee had been earning more than the health service limit in 1988 but, because of maternity leave, fell below the limit in 1990, and the special concession was then applied for 1991. In 1991 the health service income limit was abolished and the company provided one year's transitional arrangement after which this arrangement was to cease. The claimant was not entitled to this transitional year as her cover at the time arose from the special concession. She claimed that her loss of that transitional year was discriminatory, as the reason for her reduced earnings was her maternity leave. The equality officer accepted her argument and she succeeded in her claim of discrimination (although this was a case under the Employment Equality Act, 1977 nonetheless she received the same value of the VHI cover).

COLLECTIVE AGREEMENTS

Most collective agreements which form part of an employee's contract of employment simply describe the rates of pay, hours of work, leave arrangements, fringe benefits, work practices, disciplinary procedures and related matters. It is implied into each contract of employment that there is an entitlement to equal pay. If there is a discriminatory clause in the agreement, it shall be deemed null and void. As the legislation is presently drafted at present, there is no mechanism to have such a clause deleted. Thus, an employee would have to bring an equal pay or equality claim to have the matter resolved. The Second Commission on the Status of Women recommended that any party to such an agreement, or a person affected by it, can apply to the Labour Court to make a declaration that it is null and void.

"SAME PLACE"

Both the claimant(s) and the comparator(s) must work in the "same place", which is defined as including "a city, town or locality". However, the "same place" requirement has given rise to a number of cases whose outcome has been far from consistent or conclusive.

Several cases have arisen where comparators were employed by the same company or organisation but in different locations. In one case, a comparator located 18 miles away was considered to be in the same place (*Midland Health Board* v. *Stokes*, EP 26/1982, DEP 2/1983). In another case it was held that since salaries were determined on a national rather than local or regional basis in the company concerned, the fact that the comparator was 30 miles away was immaterial and the comparison was valid (MIPMPA Insurance Co. Ltd. (Waterford) v. *Three Women Insurance Officials*, EP 29/1981). Clonmel and Carrick-on-Suir, 12 miles apart and in different counties, were considered the "same place" (*Schiesser International (Ireland) Ltd.* v. *217 Female Employees*, EP 11 and 15/1988, DEP 1/1989).

In *Leaf Ltd.* v. *49 Female Employees* (EP 10/1988, DEP 4/1989), the claimants were employed in County Kildare and they compared themselves with ten male comparators, five who worked in Kildare and five who worked in the company's Roscommon premises. The equality officer considered that Roscommon was not the "same place". However, in the case of an employer whose pay rates were determined nationally, the same argument was rejected on the basis that it implied that the "same place" could mean the entire State which rendered the definition meaningless (*North Western Health Board* v. *Brady*, EP 12/1985, DEP 9/1985).

COMPARATOR

Section 2(1) of the Act provides that a comparator(s) must be employed in the same place by the same (or an associated) employer(s). This means that a comparator must be a real individual rather than a hypothetical member of the opposite sex. The comparator need not have been employed at the same time, however. In the Polymark case, it was considered that claimants cannot change their comparator once the claim has commenced, as to do so would constitute a new claim (*State Polymark (Ireland) Ltd.* v. *The Labour Court and IT&GWU* [1987] ILRM 357)

CONTEMPORANEOUS EMPLOYMENT

The 1974 Act contains no specific requirement that a comparator must be employed at the same time as a claimant. In one case in which this issue arose, the equality officer concluded that "nothing in the Act" suggested "that a woman cannot be entitled to the same rate of pay as a man who had previously performed the same job as her" (see Champion Fire Defence, above). Though it was held that the man and woman need not be employed at the same time, the job cannot have significantly changed and must still be of equal value.

"LIKE WORK"

There are three definitions of "like work" in Section 3 of the Act:

Two persons shall be regarded as employed on like work:

(a) where both perform the same work under the same or similar conditions, or where each is in every respect interchangeable with the other in relation to the work, or

(b) where the work performed by one is of a similar nature to that performed by the other and any differences between the work performed or the conditions under which it is performed by each occur only infrequently or are of small importance in relation to the work as a whole, or

(c) where the work performed by one is equal in value to that performed by the other in terms of the demands it makes in relation to such matters as skill, physical or mental effort, responsibility and working conditions.

The three definitions of "like work" are considered separately.

Exactly the Same Work

The work actually performed and the conditions under which it is performed by the claimant and the comparator must be virtually identical. In the early years of the Act there were a large number of claims under this heading, though now claims are far more likely to be brought on grounds of similar work or work of equal value. (Generally speaking, claimants would be wiser to claim all three forms of "like work" if they are unsure.) In one case where the employer argued that a claimant's work was not the same as that of her comparator because the comparator had a liability for additional attendance and duties, it was found that in practice the work performed was substantially the same. Equal pay was therefore awarded on the basis of the actual work situation rather than additional work which rarely occurred (*Department of Posts and Telegraphs* v. *Kennefick*, EP 9/1979, DEP 2/1980).

Similar Work

This definition in the Act applies where work is broadly similar; where differences occur only infrequently and are of small importance in relation to the work as a whole. This means that there can be frequent differences as long as they remain "of small importance". However, even an occasional difference can make the work dissimilar if it is sufficiently important in relation to the job as a whole.

There have been several key cases in this area, such as *Toyota Motor Distributors Ireland Ltd.* v. *Kavanagh* (EP 17/1985, DEP 1/1986) and *Dowdall O'Mahony & Co. Ltd.* v. *9 Female Employees* (EP 2/1987, DEP 6/1987). In the Dowdall O'Mahony case, women on a lower grade maintained that they were doing like work under section 3(b) with men in a higher grade. The Labour Court considered the following points:

(1) Was the work performed by each claimant similar in nature to that performed by each comparator?

(2) Were there any differences between the work performed by each claimant and each comparator?

(3) Did the differences occur infrequently?

(4) Were the differences of small importance in relation to the work as a whole?

The Labour Court found as follows:

(1) The work performed was of a similar nature. The claimants and comparators each performed general operative factory work and the Court took the view that the intention of section 3(b) is to cover claims from persons employed in such situations, as opposed to persons employed on the same work which is covered by section 3(a) — two bus conductors, for example — or work that is not the same or similar which is covered by section 3(c) — a clerical worker and a general operative worker, for example.

(2) The Court found that there were differences between the work performed by each claimant and each comparator.

(3) These differences occurred on an ongoing basis and therefore occurred frequently.

The Court further stated that the Act did not state a basis for assessing what is or is not of small importance. Therefore, this must be a matter for judgment. If the company had a job classification system which was free of sex bias, then that would be used. In the Dowdall O'Mahoncy case, the Court had difficulty in assessing what criteria were used in assessing the work classified as grade 1 (the claimants) and that of grade 2 (the male comparators). Thus, in the absence of such criteria, the Court decided that it had to examine the work and make a judgment based on its own experience of grading structures, salary scales and rates of pay. The Court then sought (a) to identify the differences and (b) to decide whether or not these differences were of such importance that they would normally be used as the basis for establishing a different grade, salary scale or rate of pay irrespective of the sex of the workers concerned.

In this case, the major difference that the Labour Court saw related to the physical demands of the jobs performed by the claimants and comparators. The Court considered that this difference was not that significant and did not justify a difference in pay. Thus the claimants and the comparators were doing "like work" and equal pay was awarded.

Ms Justice Carroll in *An Comhairle Oiliúna Talmhaíochta* v. *Doyle and Ors.* (High Court, unreported, 13 April 1989) considered that, in order to make a finding under section 3(b), the Labour Court must find

(1) That the work is of a similar nature, and

(2) That (a) either there are no differences in the work performed or the conditions under which it is performed by each or (b) any differences are either infrequent or of small importance in relation to the work as a whole.

Equal Value

This definition allows for comparisons to be made between jobs which are radically different in content. For example, the claimant and the comparator may be in different grades and, indeed, may have different value to the employer, but their jobs require the same skill, responsibility, physical or mental effort and equality of working conditions.

The issue of work of higher value arose in the case of *Murphy and Others* v. *An Bord Telecom Éireann* (EP 28/1983, DEP 6/1984, [1986] ILRM 483, [1988] 1 CMLR 1 879, High Court, unreported, April 1988 and DEP 7/1988). This equal pay case was referred by High Court to the European Court of Justice for its opinion, after both the equality officer and the Labour Court held that "work of higher value" does not come within the scope of the Act. In this case, the claimant andand 28 other women were employed as factory workers engaged in such tasks as dismantling, cleaning, oiling and reassembling telephones and other equipment. They were claiming the right to be paid at the same rate as a male worker employed in the same factory as a stores labourer who was engaged in cleaning, collecting and delivering equipment. The key point here was whether "work of higher value" came within the meaning of the principle in the EC Treaty of equal pay for equal work. Keane, J. stated that "the words [equal in value] should not be used so as to require a mathematical exactitude of equality having regard to the statutory context in which they are used" (at page 486).

The High Court asked the ECJ for its interpretation of Article 119 as follows:

> Does the community law principle of equal pay for equal work extend to a claim for equal pay on the basis of work of equal value in circumstances where the work of the claimant has been assessed to be of higher value than that of the person with whom the claimant sought comparison?

The ECJ considered that:

> Article 119 of the EEC Treaty must be interpreted as covering the case where a worker who relies on that provision to obtain equal pay within the meaning thereof is engaged in work of higher value than that of the person with whom a comparison is to be made.

Thus such employees did fall within the scope of Article 119 and therefore the 1974 Act. The High Court then referred the case back to the Labour Court for determination on the basis that the claimants and the comparators were doing "like work".

JOB EVALUATION

The 1974 Act does not either require or prohibit the use of job evaluation. Such schemes have been considered in a number of cases, but they have not generally formed the basis of any recommendation or determination from equality officers or the Labour Court. Invariably, both the employer and the claimant(s) provide their own job evaluation reports and use such reports as the basis of their arguments.

The Court made its attitude to job evaluations clear at a relatively early stage, when it said that, in effect, in assessing a case, evaluations would be one of a number of considerations to be borne in mind, but not the determining one. The results may, or may not, contain an element of bias based on sex but they should not be ignored.

The Act does not provide any assistance as to how jobs should be assessed and compared in terms of the provisions of section 3(c), namely, skill, responsibility, mental and physical effort and working conditions. In every case, the equality officer and the Labour Court (as the case may be) compare and contrast the claimant and the comparator under each heading and then weigh up all the factors to see if the work is equal in value. It is not a mathematical process, so objective judgment must be used. In the *Pauwels Trafo (Ireland) Ltd.* v. *15 Women Catering Machine Operators* case (EP 48/1981), the equality officer stated:

> There is no method by which the Equality Officer nor any assessor can determine with mathematical precision that the woman's work and the man's work come out exactly the same. The Equality Officer must therefore take a practical approach to the work under examination and determine whether the total package of every individual's work under examination can be reckoned as being of equal value in terms of section 3(c).

All rates of pay should be objectively justifiable. The European Court of Justice made it clear in the Danfoss case (see below) that where an employer had a system of remuneration which was not "transparent" (i.e. there were no clear grounds for assessing the pay structure) it must prove that its salary practice was not discriminatory if a woman showed that for a relatively large number of employees the average wages of women were less than those of men. In this case the employer paid the same basic salary to employees in the same salary class, but there was a collective agreement between the employers' association and the trade union which provided for salary supplements to employees based on their mobility, training and length of service. The result was that the average wage of men was 6.85 per cent higher than that of the women (*Handelsandog Kontor-funkionaerenes Forbund i Danmark* v. *Dansk Arbedsgiverforening (for Danfoss)* Case 109/88).

GROUNDS OTHER THAN SEX

Section 2(3) of the Act provides that there may be differences in pay where there are "grounds other than sex". There have been numerous examples where equality officers or the Labour Court have considered this defence which has been raised by employers. Examples of such grounds would be as follows:

(1) Service. This may be applied where rates of pay are tied into annual increments (e.g. *Inter-Beauty (Ireland) Ltd.* v. *Bobbett* EP 41/1981).

(2) Age. An age-related structure would not constitute discrimination as long as it was based on age and not sex (*Irish Plastic Packaging* v. *IT&GWU* EP 25/1978), but extreme caution must be exercised so that there is no indirect discrimination.

(3) Attendance duties. A liability to work extra hours may justify a higher rate of pay. In *Department of Posts and Telegraphs* v. *POMSA* (EP 7/1977), the male telephonists were paid a higher rate of pay because they had a more onerous attendance liability. This was rejected by the equality officer as (*inter alia*) the male night telephonists retained a higher basic rate of pay while on day duty and the female day telephonists also had a liability to work unsociable hours.

(4) Capacity for extra duties. In *Dunnes Stores (Parkway) Limerick Ltd.* v. *28 Female Employees* (EP 6/1987), the male comparators performed extra duties over and above their main work and thus the claimants were not entitled to equal pay. It should be noted that the extra duties must actually be performed; it is not sufficient to have a liability to do extra duties.

(5) "Red-circling". Frequently employees have a personal rate of pay because of particular circumstances which are not based on sex, for example, in Schiesser Ireland Ltd. (above) one of the male comparators was not working the full range of duties because of illness, yet

he retained his original rate of pay. Hence an employee whose work is overvalued is said to be "red-circled".

In *Micromotors Groschopp (Ireland) Ltd.* v. *IT&GWU* (EP 18/1986, DEP 5/1987), there was a new job evaluation scheme following the introduction of equal pay. At that time, it was found that 16 men and one woman were overrated. They were allowed to retain their "old" rates of pay on a personal basis. The claim concerned four women who compared themselves with a number of the "red-circled" males. In the case of three of the claimants, they had been appointed to their existing grades subsequent to the job evaluation exercise. This was accepted by the equality officer as grounds other than sex, hence their claims failed. However, the fourth claimant had been employed at the time of the job evaluation and her work had not changed since. It was accepted that she was doing "like work" with the male comparators and that if she had been male her rate of pay prior to the job evaluation would have been the same as the men's and she would have retained the "male rate of pay" on a personal basis. She was awarded equal pay with the men and the Labour Court upheld this decision.

In *Eastern Health Board / St Brendan's Hospital* v. *Coffey and Others*, EP 8/1990, DEP 5/1991, the male comparators stated that they were not aware of any red-circling agreement. Thus, the defence of grounds other than sex failed.

(6) Part-time employees. Such employees are entitled to a pro rata payment for the same work done by full-time employees (e.g. St Patrick's College, Maynooth, case above).

(7) Actuarial factors. There cannot be sex-based differential factors in the calculation of benefits under an income continuance scheme. Furthermore, as a result of the EC Directive on Equal Treatment in Occupational Social Security Schemes, there can be different premium payments for men and women but they cannot result in different payments.

(8) Grading structure. The employer must be able to show that the work in all grades has been evaluated in a non-discriminatory manner and that pay differences would be the same if men were in the lower grades and women in the higher ones. In such situations there would be no discrimination. However, there have been a number of successful "equal value" claims brought by women in lower grades against men in higher ones.

(9) Qualifications. It has been considered that superior qualifications can be grounds for higher pay (*Department of Agriculture* v. *Instructors in Farm Home Management and in Poultry Keeping*, EP 32/1978, DEP 10/1979 and see also *An Comhairle Oiliúna Talmhaíochta* v. *Doyle and Ors.*, High Court, unreported, Carroll, J., 13 April 1989). However, if there is an all-female wage scale, such differences cannot be relied on.

Many employers have used the defence of economic necessity or market forces in the defence of an equal pay claim. To date, neither equality officers nor the Labour Court have accepted these defences.

CONTRACTING OUT

An employer cannot contract out of an equal pay claim, for example by settling a potential claim, because an individual cannot sign away their statutory rights.

VICTIMISATION AND DISMISSAL

An employee cannot be dismissed for bringing a claim under the 1974 Act, giving evidence in such proceedings, or giving notice that they are going to bring a claim or give such evidence. If dismissed, an employee can either be reinstated (i.e. get their job back with no loss), re-engaged (i.e. get a similar position with or without loss of pay) or awarded up to two years' pay. Such a dismissal is also a criminal offence.

The recent case of *SIPTU* v. *Dunne* (EE 9/1993) concerned the victimisation which resulted from the denial of promotion after the referral of an equal pay claim. The equality officer considered that the onus was on the employer to give a reasonably credible explanation for the interview board's selection, which it failed to do. The claimant succeeded in her claim and the equality officer recommended the creation of a new post with the difference in pay from the date of the non-promotion. She was also awarded £3,000 for distress and loss of status.

PROCEDURES

An equal pay claim can be referred to an equality officer for investigation after the matter is brought to the attention of the employer concerned. Either the employee or the employee's union (or any other representative) can contact the employer and raise the equal pay issue. The matter does not have to be raised in writing, but the claimant(s) and the comparator(s) should be named and the grounds on which the equal pay claim is based. Procedures are considered in detail in section 4.

GENERAL REFERENCES

Callender, R. and Meenan, F., *Equality in Law between Men and Women in the European Community, Collection of Texts and Commentary on Irish Law*, Martinus Nijhoff Publishers and Office for Official Publications of the European Communities, 1994.

Curtin, D., *Irish Employment Equality Law*, The Round Hall Press, 1989.

CHAPTER TEN

Equal Treatment in Employment

The purpose of the Employment Equality Act, 1977 is to ensure equal treatment in relation to certain employment matters. This Act came into force on 1 July 1977 and was enacted on foot of EC Directive (76/207/EEC) on the implementation of the principle of equal treatment for men and women as regards access to employment, vocational training and promotion and working conditions. That directive recites the purpose of the social-action programme of achieving equality between men and women and identifies the principle of equal treatment (Article 2(1)) as meaning "that there should be no discrimination whatsoever on grounds of sex either directly or indirectly by reference in particular to marital or family status".

The recent European Court of Justice judgment in the case of *Marleasing SA* v. *La Commercial Internationale de Aliamentacion SA* [1990] ECR 4135) confirmed that national courts are bound to interpret their national laws in the light of the wording and purpose of the relevant EC directive (this was accepted by Murphy, J. in *Nathan* v. *Bailey Gibson Ltd., The Irish Print Union and the Minister for Labour* [1993] ELR 106 under appeal to Supreme Court).

It should be noted that the 1977 Act does not refer to family status, however. Since any reference to childminding arrangements is discriminatory, it would logically follow that reference to matters of status or children is also discriminatory.

The Act does not cover pay matters as they are specifically covered under the Anti-Discrimination (Pay) Act, 1974. As previously discussed in Chapter 1, it is unlawful to have discrimination on grounds of sex or marital status either direct or indirect. Unlike the 1974 Act, there is no requirement for a specific male comparator and neither Act makes provision for a "hypothetical male", though under the 1977 Act there must be some evidence that the claimant was treated in a materially different manner from somebody of the other sex or of the same sex but of a different marital status. In Chapter 1 on Recruitment and Equality, the key principles of the Act were considered on the basis of how they relate to recruitment and access to employment generally.

All employees fall within the scope of the Act. There are no restrictions in respect of length of service, hours of work, or place of employment. Although not tested, it would appear that independent contractors providing services to an employer fall within the scope of the Act, as do their employees in respect of services to another employer.

The definition of indirect discrimination, which has already been considered, introduces proportionality into indirect discrimination cases. Statistics have become part of the evidence in such cases. Statistics typically relate to company figures, though in some cases national statistics have been used. Barron J. in *North Western Health Board* v. *Martyn* ([1985] ILRM 226 (HC)) stated that statistics must be used in evidence. He stated:

> There must be evidence and generally this evidence will be statistical. For example, if a condition is imposed which makes it difficult for women to comply, then two sets of statistics must be considered:
>
> 1. the statistics of the particular application for employment;
>
> 2. the actual statistics of an application for similar employment on the same conditions but without the impugned condition.
>
> If it is found that the proportion of men to women applicants in the first set of statistics is 80/20 and the second set of statistics 60/40, then as a matter of fact the particular requirement is one which discriminates against women. Obviously, it may be extremely difficult in practice to obtain the latter set of statistics but that does not absolve the Tribunal hearing the matter from seeking to obtain evidence which is as near as possible to such statistics.

This case concerned the issue of age limits and recruitment to employment for women who had been affected by the "marriage bar". The ruling was overturned by the Supreme Court, but that Court did not overturn the requirement to have proper statistical evidence. The case of *Employment Equality Agency* v. *Packard Electric (Ireland)*

Ltd. (EE 14/1985) concerned an allegation that there was indirect discrimination because of a "condition" that persons who worked on the twilight shift had to be laid off for 26 weeks before they could apply for full-time employment. The twilight shift mainly comprised married women and thus they felt that they were being discriminated against. The equality officer's recommendation showed the detailed statistical evidence required, namely the numbers of single men and women, married men and women employed and the number of persons who normally would apply for full-time employment broken down into the person's sex and marital status and those that could apply for full-time employment if the offending condition were dispensed with.

The case of the *Revenue Commissioners* v. *Irish Tax Officials' Union* (EE 6/1986, DEE 2/1987) used a more sophisticated statistical technique, the chi-square test. This case concerned an allegation that there was discrimination in relation to promotion where there was a panel of suitable persons drawn up for promotion and more men than women were placed on the panel. The Labour Court considered that the outcome of the interviews did not make statistical sense as there had been more female applicants than men. This particular test was used in order to find out whether the observed frequencies (i.e. of successful applications) differed substantially from the expected frequencies (or results). The test showed that a higher number of women should have been successful, thus there was an indication that discrimination was likely to have been present at interview. The Labour Court subsequently determined that two women, in order of merit, be placed on the panel for promotion.

In the case of the *Central Statistics Office (CSO)* v. *O'Shea* (EE 7/1987), national unemployment statistics were considered, as the claimant maintained that she was discriminated against in obtaining employment with the CSO as she was required to have been in receipt of unemployment benefits. This requirement was found to have been indirectly discriminatory against women because of social welfare regulations which made it difficult for married women to be registered as unemployed (see Callender and Meenan, below).

More recently, the High Court has accepted the use of statistics in assessing proportionality in looking at the requirement to hold a union card in order to be available for promotion. The figures considered include the number of existing employees in the company who were members of the Irish Print Union (all male) and the membership of the IPU broken down into male and female which showed that there was a much higher number of males. This showed that the requirement to hold an IPU card had a disproportionately greater impact on women than it did on men (though this case was decided against the employee appellant on different grounds) (*Nathan* v. *Bailey Gibson Ltd. and the Minister for Labour*, above).

EFFECTS OF PAST DISCRIMINATION

We are still contending with the effects of past discrimination and undoubtedly it will take a working generation before it is resolved. In particular, reference must be made to the "marriage bar" where women who married in the late 1960s and early 1970s now want to return to the workforce after having reared their children. The issue of age limits and the effect of losing seniority on return to work has already been considered.

However, there is another form of alleged discrimination arising from the fact that women frequently did not become tradespersons in the past. The recent High Court decision in the *Bailey Gibson* case (above) highlights this problem. In summary, the claimant applied for a promotional position but it was a custom and practice in the company that only a card-carrying member of the Irish Print Union could hold such a job. However, the Union itself had certain rules before a Union card was granted, namely that the job must first be advertised and that there was no suitable (e.g. unemployed) IPU member applicant for the position. The company had requested the IPU to issue a card for the claimant but it refused. The Union and its unemployed members were practically all men — at the time there were 2,337 male and 283 female members — but it maintained that it did not discriminate. Mr. Justice Murphy accepted that this was not discriminatory within the meaning of the Act. The case at present on appeal to the Supreme Court. Murphy, J. (at page 111) stated that there must be a

> causal connection between the sex or marital status of a person and the treatment afforded to him ... the 1977 Act requires this basic connection between sex and treatment and does not deem discrimination to have occurred merely because historical factors (other than sex or marital status) have limited the eligible candidates to a pool which contains a larger number of the members of one sex than another.

He considered that the 1977 Act did not, either in its purpose or in its terms, attempt to address this wider issue of historical factors.

EQUAL OPPORTUNITIES AND POSITIVE ACTION

There is no definition of positive action in the equality legislation. In the introduction to its "Model Equal Opportunities Policy" (1991), the Employment Equality Agency (EEA) states: "Our legislation is a useful standard-setter, but it does not by itself tackle the systematic discriminatory character of a traditional sex-segregated labour market."

The Second Commission on the Status of Women recommended that the EEA (or the Commission's proposed Equality Commission) have statutory powers under the legislation to draw up a Code of Practice on equality matters. Such a Code would be admissible in any equality proceedings.

The EEA defines the positive approach as one that

> in the first instance means management and unions working to create a climate where all staff are aware that the sex and marital status of a person is not a factor in any management decision regarding, for example, who to recruit, who to train, who to promote.

> The second feature of a genuinely positive approach involves management and unions taking positive action to remove any existing discrimination or imbalance based on sex and to promote equal opportunities in the organisation.

There is limited provision for positive action in the 1977 Act. All it provides is that, if there have been few or no persons of one sex in a particular type of work in the previous 12 months, specific training be provided for members of that sex in an attempt to redress the balance.

In its Model Policy, the EEA includes draft statements in relation to the following: selection, advertising, application forms, shortlisting for interview, testing, interviewing, promotion, training, placement, mobility, work experience, work and family responsibility, pay and benefits in kind and so forth. There is also a guide to assist in the monitoring of an Equal Opportunities Policy.

In recent years, large employments (in particular semi-state companies) have introduced positive action programmes, for example, RTE, the ESB and Bank of Ireland.

Trade unions have been continually highlighting the importance of equality in the workplace and employ women's officers and hold women's conferences. Furthermore, all the unions have been particularly active in bringing equal pay and equal treatment cases. The main employers' body, FIE (now IBEC) issued Guidelines on Equal Opportunities in December 1990 which includes reference to positive action.

SEXUAL HARASSMENT

Although sexual harassment is not specifically defined or mentioned in the 1977 Act, there have been numerous cases concerning alleged sexual harassment brought before the equality officers and the Labour Court. The Labour Court has stated that

> freedom from sexual harassment is a condition of work which an employee of either sex is entitled to expect, and that denial of such freedom contravenes the 1977 Act (*Garage Proprietor* v. *A Worker*, EEO 2/1985).

The EEA has defined sexual harassment as behaviour which includes:

> unreciprocated and unwelcome comments; looks; jokes; suggestions or physical contact which might threaten a person's job security or create a stressful or intimidating working environment (A Model Sexual Harassment Policy — Sample Policy Outline, 1991).

Equality officers and the Labour Court have considered sexual harassment to be direct discrimination. Most cases to date have concerned sexual harassment between men and women — the matter of harassment between members of the same sex is unclear. Such harassment was claimed between women (as a second allegation against the company) in one case, but the Labour Court made its decision on the basis of harassment by a male visitor who was not an employee of the company (*A Company* v. *A Worker*, EEO 3/1991 — see below). In another case, the alleged harassment had been by the managing director's husband who was an independent contractor who frequently visited the premises (*A Company* v. *A Worker* DEE 2/1988).

The types of behaviour which have been held to constitute sexual harassment vary widely. It can range from direct, persistent, unwanted physical contact and sexual advances, to unsolicited comments, suggestions, jokes and looks of a sexual nature. It need not be physical or verbal. It can even be symbolic in form to have the effect of intention and psychological effects (see *A Limited Company* v. *One Female Employee*, 1989 — Confidential Recommendation). However, the key point is that the activity must be unwanted, unwelcome and unsolicited. Agreement between employees obviously would not constitute harassment. In summary, it must undermine the person's job security and provide an intimidating working environment.

The first Irish case involving sexual harassment concerned a 15-year-old girl working as a shop assistant/petrol pump attendant. She worked there for about seven months and maintained that she had been sexually harassed by her employer. She resigned and claimed constructive dismissal. The Labour Court awarded her £1,000 (above, EEO 2/1985).

A more recent case concerned the alleged harassment of the secretary to a general manager where she alleged that she had been continually harassed by both the company secretary and the general manager. She maintained that the harassment had been so bad that it adversely affected her health and that she was left with no option but to resign and claim constructive dismissal. The alleged harassment in this case involved instances of physical touching and assault, the use of crude language with sexual connotation, the display of an offensive calendar and a Christmas card with a double meaning. The employee had complained to a previous general manager, but matters got worse on the appointment of a new one (the employee was awarded £4,000 as she had incurred little loss having obtained alternative employment (*A Company* v. *A Worker*, EEO 3/1991).

The Labour Court has taken a wide view of sexual harassment, and it is not necessarily caused directly by the employer or an employee within the company. In fact, it can happen where a person enters the premises at the invitation of the employer and harasses an employee (*A Company* v. *A Worker*, DEE 3/1991).

An employee who considers that she is being harassed at work should invoke the grievance procedure and report the matter to her manager, if at all possible. In smaller employments, this may not be possible, particularly if the person who is harassing her is her manager. Nonetheless, the matter should be reported in order to try to avoid resigning. In one case, the Labour Court determined that the claimant had produced no evidence that she had complained to her employer that she was being harassed (DEE 2/1988 above).

The Employment Equality Agency has published a Model Policy in order for employers to recognise that sexual harassment will not be tolerated in the workplace. The Model provides a positive statement stating that sexual harassment will not be tolerated, definitions of sexual harassment, an outline of the responsibility of management and staff and procedures should an employee consider that they have a grievance in this regard.

The EC Recommendation on Sexual Harassment may also be applied through a voluntary Code of Practice agreed between employers and employees (probably under the aegis of the Labour Relations Commission).

The Second Commission on the Status of Women recommended that there be further promotion of active measures to combat sexual harassment in the work place; that equal opportunities programmes in the work place should refer to sexual harassment and the procedures for dealing with it; that the Minister for Labour (as the title then was) should direct the Labour Relations Commission to adopt in its practice the EC Code on protection of the dignity of women and men at work; and that the Department of Labour or the EEA should run a media campaign to combat sexual harassment.

VOCATIONAL TRAINING

The Employment Equality Act, 1977 provides that no vocational education body can discriminate in respect of courses offered, including access to the courses and the terms and manner in which they are offered to persons over the statutory school leaving age of 16 years. The key case in this area concerns access to physiotherapy training at University College, Dublin, which used to be available only to female students. In *UCD* v. *Corrigan* (EE 13/1979, DEE 6/1980), the male claimant was denied access to the physiotherapy school. The Labour Court considered that this was discriminatory and determined that the claimant be accepted for the course in the next academic year. In *Trinity College, Dublin* v. *McGhee* (EE 1/1989), the claimant successfully maintained that she was discriminated against at interview for a place in the college's Diploma in

Theatre Studies course because she was asked questions concerning her marital status.

Section 11 of the Act has been amended so that men can train as midwives.

PERSONAL SERVICES AND OCCUPATIONAL QUALIFICATIONS

The Act provides that there are certain circumstances where "personal services" are performed, making it "necessary to have persons of both sexes engaged in such duties" (Section 17(2)(b)). Both men and women can work as nurses, for example, but there may be certain circumstances where only male nurses are appropriate, for example, in some areas of psychiatric nursing.

As stated in Chapter 1, there are certain circumstances where a person of a particular sex is required for a job — modelling or acting, for example — and also in respect of certain duties in the Garda Síochána and the Defence Forces. The Second Commission on the Status of Women recommends that the Defence Forces should be fully covered under the 1977 Act and thus have no exemptions.

DRESS

The issue of discrimination can arise in respect of "dress". For example, in one case it was considered discriminatory where women were not allowed to wear trousers or jeans at work (*Norwich Union Insurance* v. *131 Female Clerical Staff* EE 19/1981). In another case, where women were provided with free uniforms but men were not (or given compensation in lieu of uniforms), it was not considered discriminatory. The equality officer decided that since it was a condition of the women's employment to wear uniforms or "appropriate dress" it was not discrimination within the meaning of the Anti-Discrimination (Pay) Act, 1974 (*Educational Building Society* v. *Male Employees*, EP 9/1987; see Chapter 9 — Equal Pay).

PREGNANCY, MATERNITY AND RELATED MATTERS

The Unfair Dismissals Acts, 1977 to 1993 provide that if a dismissal results from pregnancy or matters connected therewith, it is an unfair dismissal provided that there is no other suitable employment. This also refers to pregnancy-related illnesses which may arise before or after the baby is born. If, during the course of the pregnancy, a woman is not able to carry out her normal work and there is no suitable alternative, the dismissal may not be unfair. However, extreme caution must be exercised in this regard. It is generally advisable not to dismiss the employee but to place her on "sick leave" and allow her to return to her normal job after maternity leave (see also the reference to the EC Pregnancy Directive in Chapter 5).

The Second Commission on the Status of Women recommended that there be adoptive leave of ten weeks with accompanying benefits (the Adoptive Leave Bill, 1993 has now been published and is considered in Chapter 5). Many larger employments provide for adoptive leave on the same terms as maternity leave, namely, the ten-week period after the arrival of the child. Some employers may pay the employee during this time, but the employee has no such legal entitlement and most often the leave is unpaid.

The issue of adoptive paternity leave arose in *Aer Rianta* v. *37 Male Employees* (EE 11/1987, [1990] ILRM 193, DEE 3/1990) where male employees considered that the failure to provide for paternity leave was discriminatory. The Labour Court did not agree, however.

The Second Commission on the Status of Women recommended that statutory paternity leave be introduced in order to allow fathers to fulfil their family responsibilities on the birth of their child, and that statutory leave for family reasons be introduced by 1995.

Pregnancy and access to employment has already been discussed in Chapter 1. In summary, an employer may not have a requirement that an employee "not be pregnant" as this could constitute indirect discrimination since it only affects women.

In *University College, Dublin* v. *Zeuli* (EE 4/1987), it was considered that rostering arrangements should be made that facilitated a nursing mother.

MOBILITY AND TRANSFER

The issue of mobility has arisen from a particular case involving a claim of alleged discriminatory questions at interview. However, the equality officer considered that there was a requirement for mobility in the job, and that the reason for the applicant's non-selection was that she was unable to comply with the mobility requirement. This was seen as an "essential requirement" for the job (*A Company* v. *A Prospective Female Employee*, EE 12/1989; see Chapter 1 — Recruitment and Equality).

Internal transfers within a company or organisation would fall within the scope of this legislation. In one particular case, a claimant was refused a transfer because the employer did not consider it appropriate that a secretary should work in the same sensitive area as her husband. The equality officer considered that such a policy was intended to apply to all relatives and was not confined to married women. Thus there was no direct or indirect discrimination (*NIHE* v. *Bolton*, EE 7/1984).

A policy of transferring employees from one location to another in Ireland or abroad must apply to both male and female employees. All employees must get equal chances of promotion and experience. One exception would be sending female employees to a country outside the State where there are laws and customs allowing a person of only one sex to do the duties concerned, for example, certain Middle Eastern countries.

SENIORITY

Loss of seniority has caused difficulties for women, in particular where they had been obliged to resign on marriage and subsequently return to work. For example, if they were re-employed, previous service was excluded for seniority purposes (see *Aer Lingus Teo.* v. *Labour Court and Ors.* [1990] ELR 113, e.g. as the claimants had "less" service, they were not working on the "better" routes as their service prior to marriage was excluded for seniority purposes).

OVERTIME

Both male and female employees should have equal access to overtime. There cannot be rostering arrangements which would discriminate against women and deny them equal access to overtime (*Cork Corporation* v. *Cahill and Ors.*, EE 17/1984, DEE 1/1985, (1987) 6 JISLL 172). The same situation applies to shift rosters.

SHORT-TIME/LAY-OFF

If an employer finds that, because of economic circumstances, staff have been put on short-time or lay-off, the employer must ensure that the same rules for selection are applied to both male and female employees. For example, it would be discriminatory for an employer to put a female employee on lay-off or short-time because the employer takes the view that her husband may be working.

SAFETY

An employer must comply with the Conditions of Employment Acts, 1936 to 1944 and the Safety in Industry Acts, 1955 and 1980 (and also the Safety, Health and Welfare at Work Act, 1989). Night work for women is permitted. The safety legislation states that women may only lift 16 kilos. However, an employer must take reasonable steps to provide for the employment of women without being in breach of the Acts, for example, by providing lifting equipment so that there will not be a breach of the 16-kilo weight limit (see *Tayto Ltd.* v. *O'Keeffe and Ors.*, EE13/1985 and Factories Act, 1955 (Manual Labour) Maximum Weights and Transport Regulations, 1972, SI No. 283 of 1972). The Second Commission on the Status of Women recommended that the weightlifting exemption (16 kilos) be valid where an employer can show that all necessary steps have been taken to reduce the incidence of manual handling and the carrying of loads. This would include the organisation of teamwork and the provision of mechanical aids and devices.

There are other discriminatory provisions in force, for example, the prohibition of women working underground in a mine (Employment Equality Act, 1977 (Employment of Females in Mines Order 1985, SI No. 176 of 1985)) and the requirement to provide seating arrangements for women shop assistants (Shops (Conditions of Employment) Acts, 1938 and 1942).

REDUNDANCY

There must be fair selection for redundancy. In one key case the selection for redundancy of part-time women employees instead of full-time male employees was considered to be indirect discrimination as more married women worked on a part-time basis than men (*Michael O'Neill and Sons Ltd.* v. *Two Female Employees*, DEE 1/1988).

Discrimination in respect of age limits, minimum height and strength have already been considered in Chapter 1.

DISCIPLINARY MEASURES

A disciplinary or dismissal procedure should be exactly the same for male and female employees. Furthermore, disciplinary measures which are more strict than those applied to male employees cannot be imposed on a female employee.

VICTIMISATION

A person cannot be victimised for having brought an equal pay or equal treatment claim (see Chapter 9). The case of *SIPTU* v. *Dunne* ([1993] ELR 65) as previously discussed in Chapter 9 highlighted this issue. This case concerned the subsequent non-promotion of an employee because she had previously brought an equal pay claim. She was successful as the employer could not give a credible explanation for her non-appointment.

DISMISSAL

There have been relatively few cases of employees claiming retaliatory or discriminatory dismissal, constructive or otherwise. These cases mainly concerned employees who were dismissed within the one-year period from the commencement of their employment. More usually, persons who are claiming that they were unfairly dismissed will bring their claim under the Unfair Dismissals Acts, 1977 to 1993, as the ostensible reason for their dismissal may be something else — lack of performance, for example. An employee is not entitled to receive redress for dismissal under both the equality and the unfair dismissals legislation.

In one case, an employee dismissed from temporary employment contended that the company had a preference for a male employee; the dismissal was considered discriminatory and she was awarded £4,000 (*Irish TV Rentals* v. *Brady*, EEO 1/1984, EE 5/1985, DEE 8/1985). In another case, an allegation of retaliatory dismissal arose from a part-time employee who had applied for full-time employment. She brought proceedings to the effect that she was discriminated against at interview, and succeeded in that claim. She was subsequently dismissed from her temporary employment and brought successful dismissal proceedings (*University College, Dublin* v. *A Female Worker*, EEO 5/1983, and *University College, Dublin* v. *Chaney*, EE 15/1983; see Chapter 1 — Recruitment and Equality).

Constructive dismissal claims have primarily arisen in the context of allegations of sexual harassment.

PROCUREMENT OF DISCRIMINATION

The 1977 Act provides that a person cannot persuade or induce another person to discriminate. Section 9 states that "a person shall not procure or attempt to procure another person to do in relation to employment anything which constitutes discrimination".

Union/management agreements can unintentionally give rise to discrimination where certain practices are agreed between an employer and the trade union. For example, in the case of the *Employment Equality Agency* v. *Packard Electric Ireland Ltd., the IT&GWU, and the AT&GWU* (EE 14/1985) part-time women were denied immediate access to full-time employment on foot of the union/management agreement. In another case, both employer and union required the employees to hold a certain union card for specific jobs (see the Bailey Gibson case, above). More recently, the Minister for Finance in his supervisory role over the public service was considered to procure discrimination in relation to the re-employment of married women who had resigned because of the "marriage bar" (*Department of Finance, the Revenue Commissioners* v. *A Worker*, EE 20 and 21/1991 and DEE 5/1993).

The Second Commission on the Status of Women recommended that there be a mechanism that would allow the Labour Court to declare null and void any collective agreement that was contrary to the provisions of the 1974 or 1977 Acts.

PROCEDURES

An equality claim must be referred in writing to the Labour Court within six months of the first act of alleged discrimination, except where reasonable cause can be shown for the delay. The Labour Court typically then refers the claim to an equality officer, or occasionally to an industrial relations officer of the Labour Relations Commission. The claim is then investigated by the equality officer who makes a recommendation. That recommendation may be appealed to the Labour Court which investigates the claim and issues a determination. Procedures are considered in detail in section 4.

GENERAL REFERENCES

Callender, R. and Meenan, F., *Equality in Law between Men and Women in the European Community — Collection of Texts and Commentary on Irish Law*, Martinus Nijhoff Publishers and Office for Official Publications of the European Communities, 1994.

Curtin, D., *Irish Employment Equality Law*, The Round Hall Press, 1989.

Employment Equality Agency, *Equality at Work, A Model Equal Opportunities Policy* (including a grievance procedure for sexual harassment), 1991.

Second Commission on the Status of Women, *Report to Government*, Stationery Office, Dublin, January 1993.

CHAPTER ELEVEN

Transfer of a Business

Decades ago, an employee had no rights on the transfer of a business. When a business was sold (and there was a new employer), the employee's contract of employment was terminated. Subsequently, redundancy, minimum notice and unfair dismissals legislation provided limited protection in ensuring continuity of service for an employee in the case of a transfer of a business. The European Communities (Safeguarding of Employees' Rights on Transfer of Undertakings Regulations, 1980 — SI No. 306 of 1980) now attempts to protect employees' statutory and contractual rights in the event that the business is transferred as a going concern. These regulations (which arose from the EC Transfer of Undertakings Directive — 77/187/EEC) have succeeded to a limited extent, but they do suffer somewhat in their drafting from EC law into Irish law.

The purpose of these regulations is to protect employees' rights in the event of a transfer. They are almost identical to the original EC Council Directive, which is somewhat clearer and provides that the regulations apply to the transfer of an undertaking, business, or part of a business to another employer as a result of a legal transfer or merger. The Council Directive also states that it is necessary to provide for the protection of employees' rights in the event of a change of employer. In other words, they will retain their jobs and also seniority and continuity of service. These regulations also place an obligation on employers to inform and consult their employees' representatives in the event of a proposed transfer.

A TRANSFER

The term "transfers" is not defined in the regulations. However, the key point in relation to the transfer of a business is that there must be a change in the identity of the employer, and that the business be transferred as a going concern, as was considered by Barron, J. in *Nova Colour Graphic Supplies Ltd.* v. *EAT and Another* ((1987) 6 JISLL 142).

It is generally considered that transfers of control in companies by means of share ownership or the mere transfer of assets does not constitute a transfer, for example, the lease of property or the sale of machinery. More recently, the case of *Guidon* v. *Farrington* ([1993] ELR 98) highlighted that the reversion of a lease from a lessee back to the lessor of a property constituted a transfer of a business where the business was carried on. The facts of the case are that the claimant worked as a "night owl" in the Westmoreland Street premises of Local Stores (Trading) Ltd. trading as Seven Eleven from 18 June 1990 until 23 March 1991. A receiver was appointed to the group of shops and the claimant was transferred to the Seven Eleven in the BP Petrol Station at Usher's Island where she worked until 14 June 1991. Her employment was terminated on 17 June even though there were other employees there. On 14 June the lease of the petrol station reverted back to the landlords, Richard and Hugh Farrington, who were now running the business. The claimant maintained that the Transfer of Undertakings Regulations applied and also that she was entitled to one week's notice which would bring her within the scope of the unfair dismissals legislation (see Chapter 19). The Tribunal considered that both the EC Directive and the Regulations applied in this case and relied on two European Court of Justice cases *Landsorganisationen I Danmark* v. *Ny Molle Kro* [1987] ECR 5465 and *Berg* v. *Besselsen* [1988] ECR 2559. The Tribunal considered that it was an unfair dismissal and she was awarded compensation. It is still important to ask the question "Is there a change in the identity of the employer and is there a transfer of a business as a 'going concern'?", for example, is there a transfer of customer lists, debtors lists and so forth?

A recent Irish decision concerned the application of the regulations to the "contracting out" of services by an employer. In this case the employer, a shopping centre, had employed security staff but decided to contract out the work to a security firm instead. The security firm offered a position to the claimant, who had been employed by the shopping centre, but he refused because he was told he would be working in another location on a lower salary. He brought to the Employment Appeals Tribunal a claim for unfair dismissal which was rejected. He referred the matter to the High Court for review. The key point in this case was whether "the contracting out of the services" was a "legal transfer" within the meaning of the regulations. Relying on European Court of Justice judgments, Blayney, J. considered that there was a transfer of a business and that the Directive is applicable if the business retains its identity or if there is a change in the legal or natural person who is responsible for carrying on the business, regardless of whether ownership is transferred or not. It was considered that the business was the same as before, as exactly the same security services were being provided by five security guards. There had also been a change in the legal or natural person who was responsible for carrying out the business (*Bannon* v. *Employment Appeals Tribunal and Drogheda Town Centre* [1993] IR 500).

This case is a watershed because now employees who are not offered employment in such circumstances may successfully claim unfair dismissal based on these regulations. Heretofore, such persons were invariably in receipt of redundancy and there were usually no further claims.

The sale of a company by a receiver may also come within the scope of the regulations. In *Mythen* v. *the Employment Appeals Tribunal (EAT), Butterkrust Ltd. and Joseph Downes & Sons Limited (in receivership)* ([1990] ELR 1), the claimant had been employed by Joseph Downes & Sons Ltd. which went into receivership. He received a statutory redundancy payment and was successful in obtaining minimum notice monies from the EAT. However, 40 of the Downes employees received offers of employment from Butterkrust, but Mr Mythen did not. He considered that he was unfairly selected for redundancy and brought an unfair dismissals claim against both companies. The Tribunal considered that he could not bring a claim under the regulations and the Unfair Dismissals Act as the regulations had not amended that Act (or indeed any of the other protective legislation). He applied to the High Court for a review of the determination and the High Court quashed the Tribunal decision. Accordingly, an employee who has lost his job as a result of a transfer could bring a claim under the relevant employment protection legislation as well as relying on the transfer of a business regulations against either (or both) the transferor or transferee of the business (see Chapter 21 — Employer Insolvency).

In summary, the regulations provide that all the rights and obligations of the selling company arising from contracts of employment or employment relationships (this includes collective agreements/union management agreements) existing on the date of transfer shall be transferred to the purchaser. If the employee is employed on the date of transfer there shall be no break in service, or in continuity of service, and all entitlements under the employee's contract of employment are automatically transferred. This would include not only wages/salary, but also statutory obligations, such as, service under the redundancy, minimum notice and unfair dismissals legislation, as well as matters like seniority.

One possible grey area regarding the transfer of business is in relation to pension schemes. This matter is unclear and pensions may be frozen as of the date of transfer. The Pensions Act, 1990 may be of some assistance, as the employees at least may now have transferable pension rights to be brought into a new scheme.

TERMINATION OF EMPLOYMENT ARISING FROM A TRANSFER

The primary purpose of these regulations is to prohibit a purchaser from dismissing employees because of the transfer of a business. However, if dismissals arise for economic, technical or organisational reasons, they may be permitted. If redundancies take place following the transfer of a business there should be no difficulty as long as there is no unfair selection. This is extremely important as the staff in the two businesses would have to be looked at together to consider the issue of selection. If employees consider that they have been dismissed because of a transfer, they may well have a cause of action against both their original employer and the purchaser under the Unfair Dismissals Acts, 1977 to 1993.

However, redundancies prior to the proposed transfer of a business may not be genuine within the meaning of the Redundancy Payments Acts. This is a technical point but it is worth considering. Of course, the reality of many redundancies that take place prior to the transfer of the business is that the employee receives not only his statutory entitlements, such as minimum notice, holidays and statutory redundancy, but also an ex-gratia lump sum. One of the provisions of receiving that lump sum would be that the employee would sign a discharge form provided that they had received the sums in full and final settlement of all claims. The Unfair Dismissals (Amendment) Act, 1993 amending the rules for continuity of service provides that the transfer of a business does not break continuity of service for the purpose of unfair dismissal and minimum notice unless the employee received and retained a redundancy payment from the transferor (the employer) at the time of the transfer and by reason of the transfer. This new Act has not been adjudicated by the courts yet but it effectively means that continuity of service is broken by the receipt of a redundancy payment, and if the employee then goes and works for the new owner of the business and is dismissed within one year, they may not have sufficient service to bring an unfair dismissals claim. The ECJ has also concluded that an employee cannot waive their rights in relation to the Directive on the Transfer of a Business so that they would be less well off with the new employer (*Foreningen af Arbejdsledere i Danmark* v. *Daddy's Dance Hall A/S* [1988] IRLR 315, however, note critique of this judgment in *McMullen*, below pages 211/212). Section 13 of the Unfair Dismissals Act, however, provides that an employer may bring a claim if they feel that they have been denied representation or had to sign the agreement under duress (see Chapter 17 — Unfair Dismissal).

CHANGE OF WORKING CONDITIONS

If, following on the transfer of employment, there is a change in working conditions — reduction in salary, change in seniority and so forth — it would be possible for the employee to resign and claim constructive dismissal. However, such an approach without advice would be most imprudent. Such employees would be well advised to have recourse to the grievance procedure (if any), or failing that to refer the dispute to a Rights Commissioner/Labour Relations Commission to try and resolve the matter through negotiation.

DUTY TO INFORM AND CONSULT EMPLOYEES

The vendor and the purchaser are required to inform the employees or their representatives in good time of the:

(1) Reasons for the transfer;

(2) Legal, economic and social implications of the transfer for the employees, and

(3) Measures envisaged in relation to the employees.

These provisions are very general and there is no provision that employees have to receive the full details of the proposed transfer and all the legal and financial arrangements or that they have to be involved in them. Thus, both vendor and purchaser only have to give the most general of information.

The employers do not have to state whether or not there will be redundancies, only what measures are envisaged in the organisation, for example, changing duties, changing seniority and other terms and conditions of employment.

As noted above, there is provision that the vendor/purchaser shall "consult" with the employee representative "in good time" if there are measures envisaged in relation to the employees. Unfortunately "in good time" is not defined and employees are usually advised at the last moment about the proposed transfer. This is not necessarily the employers' fault because during delicate negotiations it may be imprudent for persons other than those negotiating the deal to be aware of it.

If the employees have no representatives, the vendor or the purchaser must give the employees a written statement outlining the above particulars, and notices containing these particulars must be displayed in the work place where the employees can read them.

Employees who feel that their employer has not complied with the regulations can refer the matter to the Department of Enterprise and Employment for investigation. If an officer from the Department is of the opinion that a transaction constituted a transfer, that officer may request the parties to provide all relevant information, books or documents. An authorised officer shall be furnished by the Minister with a certificate authorising the exercise of the officer's powers, for example, for entry on to an employer's premises. If a person fails to respond and provide such information, that person shall be guilty of an offence and shall be liable on summary conviction for a fine not exceeding £300.

GENERAL OFFENCES UNDER THE REGULATIONS

If a person contravenes a provision of these regulations (other than non-provision of information as stated above), that person shall be guilty of an offence and shall be liable to a fine not exceeding £500 on summary conviction. The Minister may bring proceedings under the regulations but they must be instituted within 12 months of the date of the alleged offence.

PROCEDURES

If an employee considers that their job has been lost arising from a transfer of a business, that employee may bring a claim under the unfair dismissals legislation and any other relevant legislation.

GENERAL REFERENCES

Byrne, Gary, "Transfer of a Business and Protection of Employees' Rights"   *Gazette of the Incorporated Law Society of Ireland* — reprinted as a supplement April 1984.

Irish Centre for European Law — Acquired Rights for Employees — Papers from Conference, November, 1988 — Kerr, Tony, "Implementation of Directive 77/187 into Irish Law and Case Law of the Court of Justice".

McMullen, J., *Business Transfers and Employees' Rights*, 2nd ed., Butterworths, 1992.

LETTER TO EMPLOYEE REPRESENTATIVE
FROM THE TRANSFEROR (VENDOR) WHICH SHOULD BE IN
"GOOD TIME"

XYZ Limited
123 New St.
Dublin 40

[date]

Ms Joan Smith
A Union
Old Street
Dublin 1

Dear Ms Smith,

On behalf of the company, I am writing to you as my employees' union
official to inform you that the company is being transferred to A
Limited on [date]. I am obliged to write to you further to the Transfer
of Undertakings Regulations.

The reason for the transfer of our business to A Limited is because
both I and the other Directors are going to retire. A Limited will be
carrying on the business of XYZ Limited as a going concern.

It is envisaged that there should be no legal, economic or social
implications resulting from the transfer affecting your members at
the date of transfer. The continuity of employment of your members
shall not be affected. Furthermore, A Limited shall recognise the
rights connected with the contract of employment and collective
agreements on such transfer.

There are no further measures contemplated at this time in relation
to your members other than a change in identity of their employer.

Yours sincerely,

FOR AND ON BEHALF OF XYZ LIMITED

CHAPTER TWELVE

Employee Participation

The 1970s saw a major interest in employee participation at both board and sub-board level. The Worker Participation (State Enterprises) Act, 1977 was enacted, which provided for employee participation at board level in certain semi-state companies. In 1985 the Minister for Labour set up an Advisory Committee on Worker Participation which included members from both sides of industry. The following were the terms of reference (see Morrissey, below):

(1) To advise the Minister for Labour on the scope for the development of employee participation at sub-board level in different types of work organisation;

(2) To promote interest in practical experimentation in work-place participation;

(3) To identify research needs and make recommendations.

The Advisory Committee reported in 1986. There was apparent agreement as regards increased participation, and the majority considered that legislation should be introduced with reference to organisations in the private sector employing more than 100 people. Employer members of the Committee considered that there should be a purely voluntary approach. The Committee also considered that participation at sub-board level should be reinforced and developed.

Subsequently, the Worker Participation (State Enterprises) Amendment Act, 1988 provided for sub-board level participation in certain semi-state companies and organisations. More recently, the Worker Protection (Regular Part-Time Employees) Act, 1991 extended the benefit of worker participation in the 1977 and 1988 Acts to include regular part-time employees, that is, employees who have 13 weeks continuous service and who are normally expected to work at least eight hours per week.

BOARD PARTICIPATION

The following semi-state companies include board participation:

> Bord na Móna, Córas Iompair Éireann, Electricity Supply Board, Aer Lingus (employees of TEAM Aer Lingus Ltd. may elect persons to the board of Aer Lingus plc), Aer Rianta, An Post, Bord Telecom Éireann and NET (Nitrigín Éireann Teo — employees of Irish Fertilizer Industries Limited may elect persons to the board of NET at one-third worker participation) and the National Rehabilitation Board (the Minister may vary the number of worker directors below the one third arrangement but the number of worker directors cannot be less than two).

This list of companies may be extended by the appropriate Minister (depending on what government department controls the company) by regulation. Sub-board participation applies to all the above companies as well as the following list:

> ACOT, An Foras Talúntais, FÁS, Blood Transfusion Services Board, Board for the Employment of the Blind, Bord Fáilte Éireann, Bord Gáis Éireann, Bord Iascaigh Mhara, Bus Éireann, Bus Átha Cliath, Central Fisheries Board, CERT Limited, An Bord Tráchtála, Dublin District Milk Board, Eolas, General Medical Services (Payments) Board, Great Southern Hotels Limited, Hospitals Joint Services Board, Iarnród Éireann, Industrial Development Authority, Irish National Stud Company Limited, Irish Steel Limited, Kilkenny Design Workshops, Racing Board, RTE, Shannon Free Airport Development Company Limited, Údarás na Gaeltachta, VHI.

Two other companies with provision for board and sub-board participation have been subsequently privatised, B & I and Siúcre Éireann.

BOARD LEVEL PARTICIPATION — WORKER DIRECTOR

Initially, the appropriate Minister determines an election year for each particular semi-state body and also decides on the size of the board with the appropriate number of worker directors. For voting purposes, an employee must be over 18 years of age and be employed for at least one year. All full-time and regular part-time employees are eligible to vote.

There are extremely detailed regulations under the Acts which provide for voting procedures to ascertain whether a majority of employees wish to proceed and vote for worker-directors. There are also detailed regulations for the conduct of a ballot and provision for postal voting.

A candidate for worker-director must be an employee who is aged between 18 and 65 years. Each candidate must be employed in a full-time capacity or as a regular part-time employee within the company for at least three years' continuous service. The candidate must be nominated by a "qualified body", which may be a trade union or any other body recognised for collective bargaining within the particular company.

Following the election, the Minister shall be informed of the successful candidates who must then be appointed to the particular board. A worker-director is entitled to the same fees and expenses as other directors and it should not affect their normal remuneration.

A worker-director may resign their membership of the board by letter addressed to the appropriate Minister. Equally, a Minister may remove such worker-director from office.

Each particular company must take the appropriate steps to amend the memorandum and articles of association to conform with the legislation. Furthermore, each employer may be required by the Minister to bring the Act to the attention of their employees.

SUB-BOARD PARTICIPATION

The Worker Participation (State Enterprises) Act, 1988 provided for the introduction of sub-board participation arrangements in the state enterprises listed above. There is provision for the appointment of an "appropriate officer" who will have responsibility for the procedures in relation to sub-board participation. In summary, the appropriate officer is the company secretary (or whoever performs those functions) or the officer in the company who is acceptable to the trade union(s) or other groups recognised for collective bargaining purposes.

The consultative arrangements may be requested as follows:

(1) A trade union(s) or any other recognised body within the company which represents a majority of employees (or an application signed by the majority of employees) may apply in writing to the appropriate officer of the company requesting sub-board participation; and

(2) The appropriate officer must be satisfied that at least 15 per cent of employees sign the application. That officer must then take a poll of all employees to see if the majority is in favour of the establishment of main or sub-board participation. There are certain time limits within which the poll must be taken. If more than 50 per cent of employees are in favour, arrangements will be made to introduce sub-board participation. If 50 per cent or less are in favour, no further poll may be taken for four years from the date of the result.

The decision of the appropriate officer will be final and cannot be appealed in the event of a dispute concerning eligibility to sign applications for the original request, eligibility to vote at a poll and the clarity of meaning of the question on the ballot paper.

When sub-board participation is requested, the nature of the consultative arrangements by the employee representatives would include the following:

(1) A regular exchange of views and clear and reliable information between management and employees on matters which are specified in the agreement.

(2) Relevant information from management about certain decisions which are liable to have an effect on employees' interests.

(3) Dissemination of information and views arising from the participation.

(4) Provision for review and termination of the consultative arrangement.

(5) Other factors which management and employees may decide between them.

ANNUAL REPORTS

Since 1 January 1989, state enterprises to whom the legislation applies must describe in their annual reports any action taken during the year to introduce sub-board participation as well as any new participation agreement or alterations made to an existing agreement.

State enterprises must carry the costs of all consultative arrangements.

DUTIES AND PROTECTION OF EMPLOYEE REPRESENTATIVES

In June 1993, the Minister for Enterprise and Employment introduced a Code of Practice under the Industrial Relations Act, 1990 on the duties and responsibilities, as well as the protection and facilities, to be afforded to employee representatives by their employers (SI No. 169 of 1993). This Code of Practice is admissible in any court or tribunal and may be extremely important should an employee be dismissed for trade union activities, provided that that employer is a properly elected employee/union representative.

Employee representatives are formally designated by a trade union and normally participate in negotiations about terms and conditions of employment, including any discussions about disputes or grievances. Representatives should normally have one year's service and be elected in accordance with the union rules or the union/management agreement. Their appointment should be confirmed in writing to the employer by the union, and the employer should advise the representative of the procedures for communicating with management. The number of representatives in any employment should have regard to the size of the employment and the number of trade unions/members.

The duties and responsibilities of employee representatives include

(1) Representing their members fairly and effectively;

(2) Participating in negotiation and grievance procedures in accordance with the union/management agreement or the custom and practice of the employment;

(3) Co-operating with management in ensuring that there is proper implementation and observance of trade union/management agreements;

(4) Using agreed dispute and grievance procedures and the avoidance of action — in particular, unofficial action — which would be contrary to the agreements in place and which would affect the continuity of business;

(5) Acting in accordance with the law and the rules of the union and liaising with the full-time union official.

In addition, the representatives should continue to do their own work in the normal way.

Employee representatives who carry out their duties in line with this Code of Practice should not be dismissed or suffer any unfavourable advantage as a result. If an employer considers that a representative is acting beyond that representative's usual authority, or in a manner which is damaging to the employer, the employer should raise the matter first with the representative and, if still dissatisfied, the matter should be referred to the trade union. There is nothing prohibiting the employer from dismissing the representative, for example, if there were a genuine redundancy, as long as there is fair selection for redundancy.

The employer must afford the representative reasonable facilities so that the representative can carry out their duties, for example, reasonable time-off (but there must be employer permission) for trade union meetings and training courses. The representative should be given reasonable access to union members and, if there is a problem, reasonable access to management as well. The representative should also be allowed to collect union dues and distribute union information. The payment of wages/salary during time-off for training courses and representation should be discussed in advance with management.

FINANCIAL PARTICIPATION AND INFORMATION

There are many different forms of financial participation to include profit-sharing, share ownership and share options. It may be defined as a share of the profit or wealth of an enterprise, distributed by employers in addition to wages and direct incentives. During the 1980s there was considerable interest in the concept of profit-sharing. "Building on Reality", the National Plan, 1984–87 stated:

> if, through profit-sharing or employee shareholding, employees share in profits, or own part of their own company, they have a strong incentive to take a more enlightened attitude to industrial change. By having a stake in the business in which they work, employees have a greater incentive to promote increased efficiency and profitability in their companies.

There was provision at that time for certain tax advantages for approved profit-sharing schemes but these benefits have now been repealed by successive Finance Acts. Nonetheless, many employees do own shares in the company in which they work and there are many arrangements where they receive benefits where the employer is in profit.

Publication of Accounts

The Companies (Amendment) Act, 1986 translates the provisions of the 4th EC Company Law Directive, which dealt with the content and publication of the annual accounts of public and private limited companies, into Irish law (excluding companies not trading for profit or companies not having a share capital for charitable/religious purposes). The relevant accounts are the balance sheets, profit and loss accounts and notes to these accounts. The format of such accounts is specified and there are certain rules concerning items to be declared in the accounts, valuation rules of assets and liabilities and the information to be provided by way of notes to the accounts. The Directive also provides regulations regarding the company's annual report and the auditors' report on the company's accounts. In essence, a true and fair view of the company's operations must be given and the Directive provides that there may be a departure from the Directive's provisions in order to give such a true and fair view.

The Act's provisions in relation to specific technical accounting and presentation of accounts does not apply to banks, other financial institutions, certain named companies (e.g. the ACC, ICC) and insurance companies because the technicalities of presentation are not appropriate for such bodies. However, such bodies must file accounts with the Companies Office under other legislation providing details of directors' reports and information on subsidiary and associated companies.

GENERAL REFERENCES

Brennan, N., O'Brien, F.J., and Pierce, A., *Financial Accounting and Reporting in Ireland*, Oak Tree Press, 1991.

Brennan, N., O'Brien, F.J., and Pierce, A., *A Survey of Irish Published Accounts*, 2nd ed., Oak Tree Press, 1992.

Department of Industrial Relations, UCD, *Industrial Relations in Ireland, Contemporary Issues and Developments, 1989*, "Employee Participation at Sub-Board Level", Thomas Morrissey and "The Worker Director in Irish Industrial Relations", Aidan Kelly.

Kerr, A., *Worker Participation (State Enterprises) Act, 1988, Irish Law Statutes Annotated*, Sweet and Maxwell.

Kerr, A. and Whyte, G., *Irish Trade Union Law*, Professional Books, 1985.

Meenan, F., "Profit Sharing", *Gazette of the Incorporated Law Society of Ireland*, July/August 1986.

CHAPTER THIRTEEN

Conditions of Employment in Industry and Services

There are several Acts which provide limits for the hours of work including overtime for employees in industry and in the retail and (certain) services sector. Some of these Acts, though over 50 years old, are still the regulating legislation in Irish industry.

CONDITIONS OF EMPLOYMENT ACTS, 1936 AND 1944

These particular Acts cover conditions of employment in industrial work as defined in the Acts. There are various forms of work which are excluded, namely, non-industrial work such as agriculture, fishing, domestic work and provision of services.

Normal Hours of Work

The legal limits (excluding overtime) for an adult day worker are up to 8.00 p.m. on any ordinary working day and up to 1.00 p.m. on any short day.

An adult worker may not do more than nine hours work in any day and not more than 48 hours in any week. There are, however, certain restrictions in specific industries where these do not apply, for example in printing and the publishing of newspapers, construction, maintenance and repair of telephone installations or broadcasting.

Shift Work

Shift work is only lawful on a continuous process, which is defined as one which is normally required to be carried on without a break or to be carried on for periods of at least 15 hours without a break. The Act provides that the Minister for Enterprise and Employment must grant a licence for such shift work, and it is only given where there is a maximum hourly working day. Controls are also imposed on the amount of overtime.

The Minister may impose certain conditions in the granting of a licence, such as:

(1) There must be agreement at local level on the working of shifts;

(2) There must be access for night-shift employees to facilities for heating food;

(3) There must be access during the day for any medical or similar facilities provided by the employer and normally available to day-shift employees; and

(4) There must be an option for pregnant women to do day work for the duration of their pregnancy.

The Acts specify the following details for adult shift-workers:

(1) A shift may not exceed nine hours

(2) A worker may not work on two consecutive shifts

(3) Eight hours must have elapsed since the worker worked on the previous shift

(4) The weekly number of hours worked may not exceed 48 hours, i.e. averaged over a three-week period

(5) In the case of continuous shift-work, a worker may not work for more than 56 hours in any week.

In some situations, these provisions may be varied.

A female worker may now do night work, although there should be provision for a female employee to do day work if she is pregnant (see Employment Equality (Employment of Women) Order, 1986, SI No. 112 of 1986).

Overtime

There are certain limits in respect of overtime for adults, namely two hours in any day, 12 hours in any week, 36 hours in any period of four consecutive weeks, or 240 hours in any year. There is a specific provision for overtime pay, which must be paid at time plus a quarter for any time in which an employee works overtime on any day.

Breaks

A worker may not work for over five hours without a rest period of at least 30 minutes within this period. Anyone working overtime for a period of more than an hour and a half beyond the normal limits for day work must have a rest period of 30 minutes before starting overtime work.

Shift-workers must be allowed a rest period of at least 15 minutes in each shift, which must be given in the fourth hour of the shift. Furthermore, the worker must remain on the premises during the rest break unless permitted to leave by the employer. There is no legal requirement for breaks to be paid.

Displaying a Summary of the Acts

There is an obligation on employers to display a summary of the terms of the Conditions of Employment Acts at every place where industrial work is carried out. A summary may be obtained from the Government Publications Office.

As stated earlier, these Acts are rather antiquated. Accordingly, the maximum working week of 48 hours (excluding overtime) is beyond the normal hours of employment today. However, these statutory provisions still stand. Nowadays, employees may well receive overtime payment commencing once the 39-hour week has been concluded.

SHOPS (CONDITIONS OF EMPLOYMENT) ACTS, 1938 AND 1942

The Shops (Conditions of Employment) Acts, 1938 and 1942 provide certain terms and conditions of employment in relation to working hours, time off, breaks, Sunday work (which is allowed) for retail and wholesale shops and warehouses, hairdressers, auction rooms, the reception areas of certain industrial works, licensed premises, restaurants, cafés and hotels (for the county borough of Dublin only).

It is not necessary to go into specific details of the statutory provisions of these Acts because there are various Joint Labour Committees which have Employment Regulation Orders in relation to such employments, as stated in Chapter 8. However, it is worth mentioning that these Acts provide that there must be suitable conditions — such as lighting and heating — for persons who work in shops. Also, there is a requirement that shop-owners must provide one seat for every three female staff members, though this sounds rather old-fashioned in this day and age.

PROTECTION OF YOUNG PERSONS (EMPLOYMENT) ACT,
1977

The employment of young persons is governed by the Protection of Young Persons (Employment) Act, 1977, which has very strict provisions.

Under the Act "child" is defined as a person aged between 14 and 15 years. "Young person" is defined as a person aged between 15 and 18 years. A young person may not be employed full-time until the age of 15 years which is the school leaving age. Children under 14 years of age cannot be employed at all. Before employing a child aged between 14 and 15 years, the employer must obtain the written consent of the child's guardian.

Children under 15 years may only be employed to do light non-industrial work provided that the work does not interfere with their school attendance or their health. Furthermore, they cannot be employed during the school term unless it is part of a work experience programme which is approved by the Departments of Education or Enterprise and Employment.

Holiday work cannot exceed seven hours per day or 35 hours per week, and a child must have at least 14 days of holidays free from work. A child cannot do night work between 8.00 p.m. and 8.00 a.m. and there must be 14 hours between shifts.

There are also detailed limitations concerning the normal and maximum working hours for young persons. Furthermore, to employ a person under the age of 18, an employer must obtain a birth certificate.

A young person aged between 15 and 16 years may have a normal working day of eight hours or 37 and a half hours (with a maximum of 40 hours) in any week. A young person between 16 and 18 years may do eight hours per day or 40 hours per week (with the maximum hours being nine hours per day, 45 hours per week, 172 hours in any two consecutive weeks and 2,000 hours in any year). There are certain work breaks, namely 30 minutes after every five hours worked, and there are restrictions on night work, namely that young persons cannot work between 10.00 p.m. and 6.00 a.m. Young persons are not allowed to do industrial work between 8.00 p.m. and 8.00 a.m. The usual provisions for overtime pay apply and the rest breaks are unpaid. However, there must be a 24-hour unpaid day off every seven days.

Records

It is important that an employer keep a register of names, ages, daily starting and finishing times of work, rates of pay and total pay in respect of every child and young person employed. Again, as with the Conditions of Employment Acts, there must be a summary of the Act at the entrance to the employer's premises. Furthermore, there are penalties for being in breach of this Act to include a fine of up to £100 plus £10 for every day the offence continues. There is provision that the fines can be doubled for subsequent offences.

EQUAL TREATMENT

The Employment Equality Act, 1977 provides that an employer is not in breach of the equality provisions in that Act if they are complying with the Conditions of Employment Acts, the Shop Acts, and various other listed Acts. However, this provision is increasingly becoming superfluous, for example, as female employees are now allowed to do night work. However, there are still certain exclusions for women working underground in mines, etc.

HOURS OF WORK BILL AND FUTURE DEVELOPMENTS

In 1984, an Hours of Work Bill was published which provided for a major overhaul of the Conditions of Employment Acts, essentially to bring those Acts more up to date. That Bill was never passed and there have been no enactments to date. The Acts discussed above are required minimum conditions only in normal industrial and commercial practice and are excessively complicated. Nonetheless, there must be provision that such workers have legislation for their protection. The recent EU Council Directive concerning certain aspects of the organisation of working time (93/104/EC) must be legislated in Irish law by November 1996. There are detailed provisions for daily rest periods, breaks, weekly rest periods and a maximum weekly working time. The Directive applies generally but there are numerous exclusions for various categories or workers.

GENERAL REFERENCES

von Prondzynski, F. and McCarthy, C., *Employment Law, Irish Law Texts*, 2nd ed., Sweet and Maxwell, 1989.

CHAPTER FOURTEEN

Pensions

A good pensionable job may be everybody's dream, especially in the public service or in "safe" private employment. Generally speaking, pension schemes in the public service were considered to be a major benefit and indeed nowadays more and more employers in the private sector are providing pension schemes for their employees. Recent years have shown that no job is "safe" or protected from the ravages of recession, as has been reflected in the number of persons made redundant. Thus, in the last number of years there has been considerable focus on pension schemes. However, employees who are fortunate in belonging to a company pension scheme as part of their terms and conditions of employment frequently do not understand the intricacies of pensions.

There is no obligation on an employer to provide a pension scheme for employees. Indeed, up to the enactment of the Pensions Act, 1990, there was little regulation of pension schemes. This Act has come some way in regulating pension schemes and also in implementing the EC Directive 86/378 on equal treatment for men and women in occupational pension schemes.

As previously considered, the Minimum Notice and Terms of Employment Act, 1973 provides that if there is a pension scheme, the employer must provide an employee with details describing it. This is usually done by way of a summary booklet which is given to employees (see Chapter 2 — The Contract of Employment).

Pension schemes are set up by an employer for employees (the beneficiaries) by means of a trust. A trust may be summarised as an obligation where a person (the trustee) holds property (trust property) for the benefit of others (the beneficiaries). Employees are members of the pension scheme, though technically this is quite distinct from their contract of employment.

Pension schemes — voluntary schemes set up by an employer — are invariably called occupational pension schemes because the scheme has been "approved" (or the employer is in the process of seeking "approval") under the Finance Act, 1972 (as amended).

"Approved" pension schemes receive special tax advantages, namely that an employer's contributions (at present up to 15 per cent of gross salary) are tax deductible. A pension scheme may or may not be a contributory one where the employee also contributes. An employee may make additional voluntary contributions if the scheme allows for same. The pension scheme must provide for benefits to the employee or to the surviving spouse, children, dependants and personal representatives, as the case may be.

The maximum benefit a retiring employee can receive is two-thirds of their final salary (i.e. as denoted for pension purposes), though an employee who does not have the full 40 years' service could be entitled to less. There should also be provisions in relation to the age of retirement and what benefits are paid to an employee's widow/widower and dependants. A scheme may allow the employee to take a lump sum up to one and a half times of final salary upon retirement. Again, this is reduced if there are less than 40 years' service.

THE PENSIONS BOARD

The 1990 Act provided for the establishment of the Pensions Board. The Board comprises a chairperson and 12 members who represent the pensions industry, the Ministers for Finance and Social Welfare, employers, trade unions and the various relevant professions.

At the time the Pensions Bill, 1990 was introduced, the Minister for Social Welfare, Dr Michael Woods, TD, stated

> this Bill is an historic step forward in protecting and safeguarding the pension rights of over half a million workers who are members of occupational pensions schemes. . . . Until now, the operation of pension schemes has mainly been governed by nineteenth century trust law. This new legislation will provide the most up-to-date standards for the regulation of pensions as we approach the twenty-first century.

The Pensions Board has been entrusted to carry out the following functions:

(1) To monitor and supervise the operation of the Act and pensions developments

(2) To advise the Minister for Social Welfare on pension matters and on standards for schemes

(3) To issue guidelines on the duties of pension scheme trustees and to encourage the provision of appropriate training facilities for trustees

(4) To publish reports

(5) To perform such other tasks at the Minister's request.

The trustees of a pension scheme are required to register the scheme with the Board.

PRESERVATION OF PENSION ENTITLEMENTS

Until the preservation of benefits provisions in the Act came into force, there was a major difficulty for employees who were members of occupational pension schemes. Upon their departure from the company, these employees frequently left behind their years of pensionable service. Again, at the time the Bill was published, Dr Woods stated

> at present 90% of workers who change jobs cash in their pension contributions. As a result they find themselves with little or no occupational pension. The [Act] provides for the preservation and subsequent revaluation of the pension entitlements of workers who change employments and thus gives greater long term, pension security to individuals and their families.

> This is essential today in view of people living much longer in old age and the rising costs of maintaining a decent standard of living after retirement. Today's 30-year-olds must plan realistically for some 15 years of retirement.

> People should also be free to move employment where their skills are most needed and best rewarded. Artificial barriers to job mobility which can arise from the operation of occupational pension schemes must therefore be removed. The [Act] removes those barriers in providing that a member who leaves, leaves with his/her benefits preserved in a scheme and their purchasing power maintained in line with inflation.

The preservation provisions came into force on 1 January 1993 and apply to persons wtih five or more years' service in a particular pension scheme. However, in order to benefit from this provision, two out of the five years must be after 1 January 1991.

This in effect will mean that schemes will be required to preserve the pension entitlements of its members if they leave their employment after 1 January 1993 but before pensionable age. In other words, such persons will have a pension entitlement preserved for them until they reach normal pensionable age in respect of that particular scheme.

The alternative forms of preservation are for employees to have the choice of having a transfer payment, equivalent to the actuarial value of their preserved benefit entitlement, transferred to the scheme of their new employer, or else the trustee may purchase an approved annuity bond underwritten by a life assurance office.

From 1 January 1996, there must also be an annual revaluation of any preserved benefits in the pension scheme at the annual rate of the consumer price index or by 4 per cent, whichever is the lesser. All additional voluntary contributions which an employee has added to the scheme shall be treated in the same manner.

The downside of this legislation is that employees leaving their jobs, especially younger employees, who would have preferred to have their pension contributions returned to them (if it was a contributory scheme) no longer can, if they have more than five years' service.

Disputes on these issues may be referred to the Pensions Board. There is a right of appeal from a decision of the Board to the High Court on a point of law only.

FUNDING STANDARD

Pension schemes (as long as they are not defined as contribution schemes, see explanation in Lynch and Kelly, below at page 25–32) are now required to have a minimum funding standard and an actuary must provide an actuarial funding certificate for all schemes currently in existence. The first certificate must be provided within a period of three and a half years after the date of the previous certificate. If it is a new scheme, there must be a funding certificate submitted within three and a half years of commencement of the scheme.

There are detailed provisions in the Act setting out the funding standards. The key objective is to ensure that there are sufficient assets within the scheme to secure the pensions for existing beneficiaries, and following a period of 10 years, the benefit expectations of active members relating to their periods of scheme membership. In other words, there must be complete cover for all liabilities of the scheme and if there is not, the scheme must have full cover within a period of 10 years.

The initial actuarial certificate must certify that sufficient assets exist to cover 100 per cent of the following benefits:

(1) Pensions in the course of payment

(2) Additional benefits which were provided by way of additional voluntary contributions or in respect of transfer rights from another scheme (i.e. where a new employee comes into the scheme with transfer rights from another pension scheme)

(3) Any remaining benefits accrued under the scheme in respect of service after 1 January 1991.

DISCLOSURE OF INFORMATION IN RELATION TO SCHEMES

The trustees of a pension scheme must now provide financial and other information about the scheme to members, prospective members, their spouses and authorised trade unions. The information should include the rules of the scheme, its administration and financial basis, and any individual rights and obligations arising under it.

There must also be annual reports in respect of each scheme year after 1 January 1991. The information required includes a trustee's report, an investment report, audited accounts in respect of the scheme year, a copy of the auditor's report and a copy of the latest actuarial funding certificate. There is an exclusion from this provision in respect of certain schemes.

TRUSTEES OF PENSION SCHEMES

The Act outlines the general statutory duties of trustees of occupational pension schemes. Such duties are:

(1) To ensure that the contributions due to the scheme are paid into the fund and are properly invested

(2) To ensure that the benefits of the scheme are paid as they become due

(3) To ensure that proper membership and financial records are kept

(4) To register both the scheme and the names of trustees to the scheme with the Pensions Board. All existing schemes had to register by 1 January 1991.

The duties of a trustee are onerous with a considerable degree of responsibility. Briefly, the general duties of a trustee are to:

(1) Inspect the trust deed

(2) Ensure that all the property is vested in the names of the trustees

(3) Carry out strictly the terms of the trust

(4) Exercise a duty of care

(5) Ensure that there is no delegation of the trustee's duties

(6) Be sure there is no conflict of interest

(7) Act in good faith

(8) Provide information on the pension scheme

(9) Invest trust monies properly

(10) Apply to the High Court where there is doubt as to the interpretation of a trust deed.

From 1 January 1994 there are provisions that employee members of pension schemes may elect member trustees provided that the election process is initiated by at least 15 per cent of the members or by trade unions representing at least 50 per cent of the members. This is applicable to schemes where there are at least 50 members, or in directly invested schemes of not less than 12 members (SI No. 216 of 1993).

EQUALITY

Women are no longer "birds of passage . . . who come for a short time and then fly off to get married and bring up their children" (Lord Denning in *Worringham* v. *Lloyds Bank Ltd.* ([1981] ECR 767 and Curtin, below). Article 119 of the EEC Treaty provides that there must be equal pay between men and women. Over the years it has evolved from case law that pension benefits fall within the scope of equal pay. The European Court judgment in *Bilka-Kaufhaus* (Case 170/84) has confirmed that in EU law, occupational pension schemes and the rules governing them fall within the scope of Article 119. The rules governing pension schemes were considered an integral part of the contract of employment and the benefits paid under the scheme constituted remuneration. Prior to this case the issue was unclear because the European Court held that statutory pension schemes (i.e. state schemes) did not fall within Article 119 (*Defrenne* v. *Sabena*, Case 80/70).

The relevant pieces of Irish legislation are:

(1) The Anti-Discrimination (Pay) Act, 1974 deals with all matters relating to pay including occupational pension schemes. Equality Officers and the Labour Court have given wide latitude to the definition of remuneration, including contributions to pension schemes, survivors' benefits and access to schemes.

(2) The Employment Equality Act, 1977 deals with equal treatment in employment. However, this Act specifically excludes matters dealing with occupational pension schemes.

(3) The Pensions Act, 1990 provides that there must be equal treatment between men and women in relation to occupational pension schemes.

There have been several Irish cases which may be summarised as follows:

(1) *ASTMS* v. *Linson* (EP 1/1977, DEP 2/1977), where there were both different entry and retirement ages to and from the scheme. The Labour Court determined that there should be equal pension benefits for men and women.

(2) *Department of the Public Service* v. *Robinson* (EP 36/1978, DEP 7/1979), considered equality of survivors' benefits, namely that Senator Mary Robinson maintained that the non-provision of a widowers' pension was discriminatory. It was held that the provision of benefits to dependants was part of an employee's remuneration.

(3) In *University College, Dublin* v. *IFUT* (EP 7/1979, DEP 17/79), the Labour Court considered that the provision of a Contributory Widows' and Children's Plan for men only was discriminatory.

These Irish cases have targeted the root of the problems in equal treatment in pension schemes. However, they do not assist in finding solutions.

The EC Directive 86/378 provides that occupational pension

schemes must comply with the principle of equal treatment between men and women. The Directive provides that discriminatory provisions must be removed from pension schemes by January 1993.

The Directive applies to group occupational pension schemes not individual/one member schemes. The principle of the Directive is to exclude discrimination based on sex or marital status connected with:

(1) Scope and access to the scheme,

(2) Obligation and calculation of contributions to the scheme,

(3) Calculation and duration of benefits to the member and their spouse and dependants, and

(4) Retirement from the scheme.

The intent of the Pensions Act is to provide that there cannot be discrimination, either direct or indirect, on the basis of sex in respect of any matter relating to an occupational benefit scheme to include occupational pensions. Occupational benefits from the definition in the Act include ex-gratia redundancy payments, permanent health insurance schemes and other sickness or injury payments (see Lynch and Kelly, below).

There are certain exceptions to this rule, however, such as defined contribution schemes with different treatment which may be explained on actuarial grounds. For example, there is a presumption that women live longer than men, therefore they will receive benefits for longer. The problem then arises that if the pension payment is the same, then women must either make higher contributions or retire later from their job. This problem will have to be addressed in the near future in relation to equality and pension schemes. There must also be equal retirement ages, though this has not caused a major problem in Ireland, as relatively few schemes provided for a lower retirement age for women, and furthermore, Ireland's social welfare code does not discriminate on ages for retirement or receipt of old age pensions.

These issues were considered in the case of *Barber* v. *Guardian Royal Exchange Assurance Group* ([1990] ECR 1889). When Mr Barber was made redundant, the company rules allowed that members of the pension scheme were entitled to an immediate pension at 55 years for men and 50 for women. All other staff received cash benefits and a deferred pension at age 62 for men and 57 for women.

Mr Barber was aged 52 when he was made redundant and thus was not in receipt of a pension. The Court held that such pension benefits fall within the scope of Article 119; an age condition which varies in relation to a person's sex is contrary to Article 119. Article 119 cannot be relied upon prior to the date of this judgment, however, unless legal proceedings had already been instituted. The effect of this judgment is still awaited but as it rules that the principle of equal pay applies to each aspect of remuneration, there may well be a real question to be answered in respect of apparent discrimination where there are defined contribution schemes which have been excluded from the equality principles of the 1990 Act.

An employee who is absent from work because of pregnancy, maternity leave or for family reasons does not lose pension entitlements for that period provided that the pensions scheme allows for same. This is a major step forward because under the Maternity Protection of Employees Act, women who were on maternity leave were not entitled to any remuneration and their employer did not have to make any contribution to the pension scheme for that period.

Disputes on alleged discrimination in relation to access to occupational pension schemes may be referred to an equality officer, the Labour Court and the High Court as laid down in the 1990 Act, which is the same as under the 1974 Act (see section 4). The Labour Court may:

(1) Determine whether a rule in a scheme complies with the principle of equal treatment;

(2) Determine whether any such rule is null and void;

(3) Determine whether the terms of a collective agreement, employment regulation order or contract of employment comply with the principle of equal treatment;

(4) Determine whether an employer has provided equal access to a scheme; and

(5) Recommend a specific course of action to resolve any of the above breaches of the legislation.

DEATH BENEFIT

Frequently a pension scheme will include a death benefit plan should the employee die in service before the normal pension age. Obviously, the provisions and monies payable depend on the scheme itself, but usually the deceased's dependants receive a defined amount of monies in respect of the employee's pensionable service.

INCOME CONTINUANCE PLAN

Frequently, as an addition to a pension arrangement, there is provision for an income continuance plan, whereby an employee who is continuously disabled for over 26 weeks would be entitled to an income continuance payment. This payment only lasts as long as the person is ill and can only continue up to pension age.

Finally, it is strongly recommended that a person should get professional advice from an expert on pensions should that person have any questions in relation to their pension scheme.

GENERAL REFERENCES

Callender, R. and Meenan, F., *Equality in Law between Men and Women in the European Community — Collection of Texts and Commentary on Irish Law*, Martinus Nijhoff Publishers and The Office for Official Publications of the Commission of European Communities, 1994.

Curtin, D., *Irish Employment Equality Law*, The Round Hall Press, 1989

Forde, M., *Employment Law*, The Round Hall Press, 1992.

Kenny, P., "The Pension Act, 1990 — Preservation Regulations", *Industrial Relations News*, IRN 6, 1993.

Lynch, C., and Kelly, R., *Pensions Act, 1990, Law Statutes Annotated*, Sweet and Maxwell.

CHAPTER FIFTEEN

Health and Safety in the Work Place

The key piece of legislation covering health, safety and welfare at work is the Safety, Health and Welfare at Work Act, 1989. There have been numerous other Acts over the years to include the Factories Act, 1955 and the Safety in Industry Act, 1980. There are also other Acts covering working in mines and quarries (Mines and Quarries Act, 1965), the handling of dangerous substances (Dangerous Substances Acts, 1972 and 1989), matters concerning fire safety (Fire Services Act, 1981) and numerous regulations covering various aspects of health and safety, such as the lifting of weights.

The original Acts covered safety in industry and thus all employments were not covered. The 1989 Act provided a major reform of health and safety in the work place. The Act contains many of the key recommendations from the Barrington Report which resulted from the Commission of Inquiry on Safety, Health and Welfare at Work. In summary, the Barrington Report recommended that framework legislation be put in place covering all work places (i.e. to include agriculture, fishing, forestry, transport, laboratories and hospitals) and not merely to cover industry (some 20 per cent of the workforce). The Report stated:

> Our Report is characterised by a certain distrust of legalism. We doubt if safety and health can be advanced by an excessive reliance on detailed and increasingly complex regulations imposed on workplaces from outside. Rather, we see the problem in terms of reform within the workplace based on clearer ideas about the responsibilities of employers, workers, the self-employed and others. The law has a role to play . . . [in] setting a framework within which managers and workers operate, but it is no substitute for a sense of commitment based on responsibilities which are clearly defined and understood.

One major recommendation was that the system must be preventative, and the Report stated:

> It is not merely that prevention is better than cure. Once an accident has happened there is often no cure. If the system is to be preventative, safety must be a feature in the planning of factories and systems of work. This idea governs all our recommendations.

Arising from these views, the 1989 Act was enacted as a framework Act and contains the key principles of health and safety in the work place. The Act contains the statutory duties of employers and employees in comprehensible language. Such duties are based on the common law duties of care. There are additional obligations on manufacturers, suppliers, designers and builders, and all persons are required to consider the impact that their place of work or articles used at work have on the public or visitors to the premises, including independent contractors.

It should be noted that the 1989 Act did not repeal all of the earlier legislation, much of which is still in force with the various regulations made thereunder. Thus the legislative arrangements are somewhat complicated, though they should be streamlined over time.

NATIONAL AUTHORITY FOR OCCUPATIONAL SAFETY AND HEALTH

This independent Authority was set up under the Act and it took over the functions of the industrial inspectorate at the Department of Labour. The Authority comprises a chairperson and 10 ordinary members appointed by the Minister for Enterprise and Employment.

The functions of the Authority are to:

(1) Make adequate arrangements for the enforcement of the 1989 Act and all other statutory provisions

(2) Promote, encourage and foster the prevention of accidents and injury to health at work in accordance with the provisions in the 1989 Act

(3) Encourage and foster activities and measures which are directed towards the promotion of safety, health and welfare of persons at work

(4) Make arrangements as it considers necessary in order to provide information and advice on health and safety matters

(5) Make all the necessary arrangements to undertake, promote, sponsor, evaluate and publish the results of research, surveys and studies relating to hazards and risks to the safety and health of persons at work or arising from work activities

(6) Draw up codes of practice.

The Authority has considerable powers of enforcement and its inspectors may enter premises and inspect all documents and the actual work place itself. The inspector may be accompanied by a member of the Garda Síochána if there is reasonable belief that there will be a serious obstruction to the inspector in the course of their duties.

An inspector may issue an improvement notice if the inspector is "of the opinion" that there has been a breach of the "relevant statutory provisions" or if an improvement plan has not been submitted. A person who is aggrieved by an improvement notice may apply to the District Court within 14 days of the notice being served. The District judge may confirm the notice, cancel it or make any necessary modification. If matters are not resolved, the inspector may issue a prohibition notice. Failure to comply with a prohibition notice may lead to imprisonment or a fine of up to £1,000. Application may be made to the District Court within seven days of its service to have it cancelled or modified. Finally, if matters are still unresolved application may be made to the High Court for an order restricting or prohibiting the use of a place of work. This can be done by way of ex parte application, in other words, the other side does not have to be notified. The significance of a failure to remedy matters is increased at each stage in the process.

GENERAL DUTIES OF EMPLOYERS

The Act sets out the statutory duties of care, but these provisions are only recognisable by the courts in respect of criminal proceedings (as outlined above). The breach of any of these provisions does not give a cause of action in civil proceedings. Thus one has to fall back on the common law duties of care, namely, the rules that have been built up by the courts over the years. Nonetheless such duties as described in the Act may be used as a good summary of the general duties of care. It is worthwhile stating the exact provisions of such duties:

6(1) It shall be the duty of every employer to ensure, so far as is reasonably practicable, the safety, health and welfare at work of all his employees.

(2) Without prejudice to the generality of an employer's duty under subsection (1) the matters to which that duty extends include in particular:

(a) as regards any place of work under the employer's control, the design, the provision and the maintenance of it in a condition that is, so far as is reasonably practicable, safe and without risk to health;

(b) so far as is reasonably practicable, as regards any place of work under the employer's control, the design, the provision and the maintenance of same means of access to and egress from it;

(c) the design, the provision and the maintenance of plant and machinery that are, so far as is reasonably practicable, safe and without risk to health;

(d) the provision of systems of work that are planned, organised, performed and maintained so as to be, so far as is reasonably practicable, safe and without risk to health;

(e) the provision of such information, instruction, training and supervision as is necessary to ensure, so far as is reasonably practicable, the safety and health at work of his employees;

(f) in circumstances in which it is not reasonably practicable for an employer to control or eliminate hazards in a place of work under his control, or in such circumstances as may be prescribed, the provision and maintenance of such suitable protective clothing or equipment, as appropriate, that are necessary to ensure the safety and health at work of his employers;

(g) the preparation and revision as necessary of adequate plans to be followed in emergencies;

(h) to ensure, so far as is reasonably practicable, safety and the prevention of risk to health at work in connection with the use of any article or substance;

(i) the provision and the maintenance of facilities and arrangements for the welfare of his employees at work; and

(j) the obtaining, where necessary, of the services of a competent person (whether under a contract of employment or otherwise) for the purpose of ensuring, so far as is reasonably practicable, the safety and health at work of his employees.

Employers and self-employed persons also have a duty towards persons who are not employees — visitors or independent contractors, for example.

GENERAL DUTIES OF EMPLOYEES

The 1989 Act also sets out the statutory duties for employees and the same provision applies that these are enacted for the purpose of criminal proceedings. However, they are of more importance within the context of discipline and dismissal for the purposes of the Unfair Dismissals Acts, 1977 to 1993, that is, if there is a breach of one of these provisions it may prove reasonable grounds for dismissal.

Again the provisions of the Act are worth noting:

9(1) It shall be the duty of every employee, while at work:

(a) to take reasonable care for his own safety, health and welfare and that of any other person who may be affected by his acts or omissions while at work;

(b) to co-operate with his employer and any other person to such extent as will enable his employer or the other person to comply with any of the relevant statutory provisions;

(c) to use in such manner so as to provide the protection intended any suitable appliance, protective clothing, convenience, equipment or other means or thing provided (whether for his use alone or for use by him in common with others) for securing his safety, health or welfare while at work; and

(d) to report to his employer or his immediate supervisor, without unreasonable delay, any defects in plant, equipment, place of work or systems of work, which might endanger safety, health or welfare of which he becomes aware.

(2) No person shall intentionally or recklessly interfere with or

misuse any appliance, protective clothing, convenience, equipment or other means or thing provided in pursuance of any of
the relevant statutory provisions or otherwise, for securing the
safety, health or welfare of persons arising out of work activities.

SAFETY STATEMENT

All employers have a general obligation to provide a safety statement
which must specify the manner in which safety, health and welfare
at work is to be adhered to. The safety statement may be used in
evidence in any criminal or civil proceedings (e.g. for personal injury
arising from an accident). The safety statement must identify hazards and provide an assessment of the risks to safety and health.

The statement must specify:

(1) The arrangements and the resources provided for safeguarding
the safety, health and welfare of persons employed at a place of work
to which the safety statement relates;

(2) The co-operation required from employees as regards safety,
health and welfare; and

(3) The names and job titles where applicable of the persons responsible for the performance of tasks assigned to them by the said
statement.

If an inspector considers that a safety statement is inadequate, he
may direct that it be revised and the employer must so comply within
30 days.

The company director's report must provide an evaluation on
safety in the company for the period covered by the report.

SAFETY REPRESENTATIVE

Every employer must consult with their employees to ensure their
health, safety and welfare at work and to take into account any
representation that they may have. Employees may select their own
safety representative. A safety representative shall have a right to
information in so far as it is reasonably practical to ensure employees'
safety and health in the work place. An employer must inform the
safety representative when an inspector enters the work place for an
inspection.

A safety representative has the following powers:

(1) To make representations to an employer on any aspects of safety, health and welfare at the place of work.

(2) To investigate accidents and dangerous occurrences provided that the representative shall not interfere with or obstruct the performance of any statutory obligation required to be performed by any person under any of the relevant statutory provisions — for example, a safety representative cannot prevent a safety inspector from investigating an accident.

(3) To make oral or written representations to inspectors on matters of safety, health and welfare at work.

(4) To receive advice and information from inspectors on matters of safety, health and welfare at work.

(5) To carry out inspections subject to prior notice to the employer and to agreement between the safety representative and the employer as to frequency. The parties shall consider the nature and the extent of the hazards in the place of work in determining the frequency of inspections.

(6) To investigate potential hazards and complaints made by any employee whom the representative represents relating to that employee's health, safety and welfare at the place of work, subject to prior notice to the employer, and in circumstances in which it is reasonable to assume that risk of personal injury exists.

(7) To accompany an inspector on any tour of inspection other than one made for the purpose of investigating an accident.

GENERAL DUTIES OF DESIGNERS, MANUFACTURERS AND OTHERS

Again, these duties contained in the Act are only referable in the context of criminal proceedings. Thus, there are duties on the manufacturers, designers, importers and suppliers of goods such as adequate testing, updating of information, the necessary research to eliminate hazards and so forth.

REGULATIONS

The Safety, Health and Welfare at Work (General Application)

Regulations, 1993 (SI No. 44 of 1993) came into effect on 18 February 1993. The regulations are extremely lengthy and detailed but all persons are advised to read them. These regulations extend the requirements of the 1989 Act, which as previously stated is a framework Act, and also implement EC Directive 89/391/EEC on the introduction of measures to encourage improvements in the health and safety of workers in the work place. The regulations also implement various other related EC Directives.

In summary, the regulations impose general and specific obligations on employers with regard to the evaluation and reduction of exposure of employees to occupational risks and hazards in the work place. Equally, employees have to co-operate with their employers on their health and safety in the work place. Existing legal obligations relating to the safe use of electricity, the provision of first-aid facilities and notification of accidents and dangerous occurrences to the Authority are revised and updated. The cost of any measures relating to health and safety shall be borne by the employer alone, including the cost of all safety clothing etc. The regulations have detailed provisions concerning:

(1) Requirements for all work places, for example, temperature, lighting rest rooms, washrooms and so forth, with specific regulations for older and newer premises with a cutoff date of 31 December 1992;

(2) Work equipment requirements for equipment used for the first time before and after 31 December 1992;

(3) Listing of work activities which require personal protective equipment;

(4) Listing of safety equipment for various parts of the body, such as head or feet, with requirements for various different types of work;

(5) Matters that have to be considered for the manual handling of loads;

(6) Minimum requirements for all display screen equipment and work stations; and

(7) Listing of dangerous occurrences, such as flammable substances.

SAFETY IN INDUSTRY ACTS, 1955 AND 1980

Many of the provisions in these Acts are still law and provide for safety (e.g. danger arising from machinery and the lifting of weights), health (e.g. temperature), and welfare (e.g. washing facilities). However, the regulations (SI No. 44 of 1993) also apply. There are also provisions in respect of certain processes such as asbestos and chemicals. The Acts provide that all accidents resulting in somebody being absent and injured from work for more than three days must be notified to the Authority. There are numerous regulations under these Acts, but eventually all regulations will be covered under the 1989 Act.

OFFICE PREMISES ACT, 1958

This Act covers offices where more than five persons are employed. However, the safety legislation under the 1989 Act now covers all work places so its requirements must be complied with. The key points in the Act are: (a) that a minimum temperature of 63° F must be arrived at within one hour of commencement of work; (b) each employee must have 50 square feet of space, effective ventilation, sufficient light and clean sanitary conveniences; (c) there should be adequate drinking water, seating, and a first-aid box; and so forth.

COMMON LAW

General Duty of Care

The common law duty of care runs alongside the health and safety legislation. As stated above, the various statutory duties of employers and employees are not admissible in a civil action for damages (though the safety statement is) and thus it is important to consider the common law duties.

It is settled law that "the duty of an employer towards a servant is to take reasonable care for the servant's safety in all the circumstances of the case". This principle was further clarified by Mr Justice Henchy in *Bradley* v. *CIE* [1976] IR 217 at page 223, where he stated:

> The law does not require an employer to ensure in all circumstances the safety of his workmen. He will have discharged his duty of care if he does what a reasonable and prudent employer would have done in the circumstances.

In that case the claimant was a signalman whose duties included servicing lamps on certain signals at the top of vertical signposts. He reached each lamp by climbing the half-inch round steel rungs of an almost vertical steel ladder which was attached to each signal post. While descending the ladder, his right foot slipped on a rung; he fell to the ground and was injured. He claimed damages and the High Court jury found CIE had been negligent in failing to provide a safe place of work. He was awarded damages.

Evidence was given that Mr Bradley's fall would have been prevented if an elliptical steel cage had been attached to the ladder so that he could go up and down in the cage. On appeal to the Supreme Court it was held that the suggested steel cage had not been shown either to have been one which was commonly used by other railway operators or one a reasonably prudent employer would think was necessary for the protection of his employees. The High Court award was overruled.

In *Brady* v. *Beckman Instruments (Galway) Inc.* [1986] ILRM 361, at page 363, the plaintiff contracted a form of dermatitis as a result of inhaling certain fumes. It was considered that the plaintiff had very little exposure, and his injury was "unique and improbable as not to be one which could be said to have been reasonably foreseeable by his employers". Therefore, it is not sufficient for the injured employee merely to seek damages on a bare allegation of negligence. An employee must make sure to state how and why the employer was in breach of their duty of care. Equally, the duty varies according to the employee's circumstances. Accordingly, an employee's lack of work experience, expertise, youth or physical disability may be taken into account in assessing the duty of care owed by the employer.

The duty of care is further considered under the following headings:

Competent Staff

An employer owes a duty to use due care to select proper and competent staff. However, before an employer is liable, the employer must be aware of their incompetence. In the case of *Hough* v. *Irish Base Metals Ltd.* (8 December 1967 and page 323, McMahon and Binchy, below) the Supreme Court held that certain "larking" for a bit of fun did not constitute a breach of the duty of care. In this case an employee was injured when jumping away from a gas fire which had been placed near him for "a bit of devilment" by another employee. As no evidence was given of lack of supervision, there was no liability.

This duty is to be distinguished from vicarious liability where the employer will be responsible for the torts (wrongs) of fellow-employees of the injured employee in the course of their employment.

Safe Place of Work

The employer must ensure that a reasonable safe place of work is provided and maintained for employees. It is not sufficient to show that the employee was aware of the danger on the premises. The test that is applied is that of reasonable foresight on the part of the employer. However, an employer is not entitled to expect employees to act in the interests of their own safety. Premises which are not under the employer's control may cause problems, for example, delivering goods to customers' premises. There is no definite answer to this problem but the general principle that where there is no liability on the customers' part, that freedom from liability will also extend to the employer.

Proper Equipment

An employer has the duty to take "reasonable care to provide proper appliances and to maintain them in a proper condition and so to carry on his/her operations as not to subject those employed by him/her to unnecessary risk". Equally, an employer may be liable for the failure to provide equipment essential to the safety of the employee or the failure to maintain equipment in a safe condition.

Safe System of Work

Once again "safe" means what is reasonable under the circumstances. "System" may be loosely defined as a method of doing work. Therefore, "If an accident causes injury to a workman and the accident results from a risk of an unsafe system of work, against which the employer should have, but did not, take reasonable precautions to guard, then the employer is liable for damages" (*Kinsella* v. *Hammond Lane Industries Ltd.* 96 ILTR 1 at page 4). Examples of failure to provide a safe system would include unstable scaffolding or failure to provide adequate assistance.

CONTRIBUTORY NEGLIGENCE

In any civil proceedings for damages, the employer must have some evidence that the employee contributed to the accident, otherwise this contention will not be accepted by the court. However, the courts are aware that the employer sets standards of care and that the employee, in the employee's own economic interests, may be obliged to accept a less than adequate level of safety. In *Stewart* v. *Killeen Paper Mills Ltd.* ([1959] IR 436 at page 450), an employer customarily failed to keep in its correct place a protective guard on a dangerous machine in a paper mill and thus caused the employee operating the machine to take a chance in grabbing at paper and injuring himself. He was not found to have contributed to his accident. Kingsmill-Moore J. stated that "Where it can be shown that a regular practice exists unchecked it is difficult to convict of contributory negligence a workman who follows such practice".

Other matters such as an employee's failure to wear protective clothing or to comply with safety requirements would cause contributory action on the employee's part.

CONTRACT OF INSURANCE

When an employer takes out employer liability insurance, that employer is entering into a contract with the insurance company. From the employer liability point of view, certain aspects of the standard contract are worth noting:

(1) The employer subrogates the right to conduct or control on their own behalf any claim made under the policy. In effect this means handing over the running of the insurance claim to the insurers' solicitors, and that the insurance company will be the decision-maker as regards the substance or otherwise of the claim.

(2) It will ensure that employees other than those working under a contract of service are covered, for example, independent contractors. If they are not so covered there could well be a claim against the company's public liability policy.

CLAIMS FOR PERSONAL INJURY AND TIME LIMITS

The Statutes of Limitation, 1957 and 1991 provide that a claim for personal injury as a result of negligence, nuisance or breach of duty must be brought within three years from the date of the cause of action accrued or the date of knowledge (if later) of the person injured. Personal injuries include any disease and any impairment of a person's physical or mental condition.

The "date of knowledge" refers to the date on which the individual first had knowledge of the following facts:

(1) That the individual actually had been injured;

(2) That the injury in question was significant;

(3) That the injury was attributable in whole or in part to the act or omission which is alleged to constitute negligence, nuisance or breach of duty;

(4) The identity of the defendant; and

(5) If it is alleged that the act or omission was by another person, then the identity of that person and the facts supporting the bringing of an action against that person.

The "knowledge" includes what the injured person should know from facts which are observable or ascertainable to that person with medical or other expert advice. A person has to take all reasonable steps to get that knowledge.

Normally in personal injury cases little time elapses between a prospective plaintiff suffering an injury and appreciating that they have a cause of action in respect of it. Occasionally, however, a person may contract a disease which is slow to manifest itself, or a comparatively trivial incident may lead after many years to epilepsy or some cancerous condition. For example, in cases of pneumoconiosis and asbestosis, substantial injury to the lungs may be in existence for years before it is actually discovered. The time limit would run from the date of discovery of the alleged injury. In these situations, a person would have to take all reasonable steps to obtain medical advice. In the case of failure to do so, then the time limit would run from the date the person suspects the condition.

If a person dies within the three-year limitation period, such proceedings for alleged injury must be brought within three years from the date of death, or from the date that the personal representative became aware of the facts of the case, whichever is the later.

COURT PRACTICE AND PROCEDURE

Frequently a notice of claim will commence with the employer receiving a letter from the employee's solicitor referring to the incident, asking for an admission of liability and agreement to pay substantial damages within seven days, otherwise proceedings will be issued and served on the employer. At this point an employer should notify the insurers and send them a copy of the letter. Furthermore, records (if any) should be searched to check the date of the accident.

Assuming that the employer has not admitted liability and the employee wishes to proceed with a claim, the employee must decide in what court to commence proceedings, which is determined by the financial jurisdiction of each court:

(1) District Court — up to £5,000

(2) Circuit Court — between £5,000 and £30,000

(3) High Court — any amount over £30,000

At this stage there are certain court documents which must be served on each party before the case is ready to go into court. The real purpose of these documents is for both parties to find out about the circumstances of the alleged accident and loss.

Briefly, the necessary documents for each court are:

(1) District Court — (a) Civil Process, (b) Notice of Intention to Defend, (c) Counterclaim. These pleadings are usually not complicated and can be dealt with expeditiously.

(2) Circuit Court — (a) Civil Bill, (b) Notice of Appearance, (c) Notice for Particulars, (d) Defence, (e) Notice for Trial. These pleadings take approximately six months if done expeditiously. The timing of the hearing will depend on the circuit, that is, the length of the lists of cases awaiting hearing.

(3) High Court — (a) Plenary Summons, (b) Notice of Appearance, (c) Statement of Claim, (d) Notice for Particulars, (e) Reply to Particulars, (f) Defence, (g) Reply, (h) Notice of set-down for trial. These pleadings take about six to eight months if done expeditiously. The case then goes into the list and it takes nine to twelve months before the matter comes up for hearing, but there can be very long delays.

It might be noted that all the above are routine court documents. In many cases there may also be third party proceedings, that is, a second defendant. This would necessitate further documentation.

EMPLOYER POSITION

The insurance company's solicitor and counsel will act on the employer's behalf and handle all court documentation. However, it is important that an employer request that all court pleadings be conducted as speedily as possible, the reason being that if damages are awarded or if the case is settled, such monies will be computed on the basis of loss. Thus, the shorter the time, the less loss will be incurred. Loss will comprise not only lost earnings but account will also be taken of the physical condition of the employee, the state of the labour market, and non-pecuniary loss, such as payment for suffering, loss of amenities, loss of life expectation. Employers should ensure that they are fully informed of all documents which are exchanged between the parties. Many cases do not go to full hearing as they may either be settled at the initial stages of the pleadings or else at the door of the court.

COSTS

Costs are also a major item in any of these cases as there are legal costs and witness costs. Both sides may retain (depending on the circumstances) solicitors, one senior counsel and one junior counsel and expert witnesses including medical consultants, engineers and actuaries.

DISMISSAL DURING PROCEEDINGS AGAINST EMPLOYER

It is a common occurrence that an employee alleges involvement in an accident at work and then goes out sick for a considerable time. During their absence they brings proceedings against their employer for negligence, claiming damages. Faced with such circumstances employers frequently leave employees "on the books" and do not apply normal procedure for long-term absenteeism. The result is that when the employee's injury claim is completed (either goes to court or is settled) they will look for their job back. From an employer viewpoint, such position is unenviable because the employer is not in a good position to dismiss since fair procedures have not been applied. In such situation, the employee usually claims they are fit to return. On balance, the most practical thing for the employer to do is to get the employee medically examined, taking them back only if they are certified fit to return. An assessment about future employment can be made at that stage. In any event the insurance company may increase the company premium or indeed refuse to cover the particular employee. If the employee is certified unfit to return, the employer may have no option but to terminate the employment. There is no obligation on the employer to find alternative work or "light work". However, if there is custom and practice in the employment to provide alternative work, the employer should do everything reasonable to find other suitable work for the employee.

Thus, when an employee goes out sick following an alleged accident an employer is advised to follow and apply normal absenteeism procedures. The employer may then be in a position to dismiss the employee and successfully defend an unfair dismissal claim. It can be argued that the act of dismissal can lead to further problems insofar as the employee may receive more in damages because of the loss of their job. Of course, the company premium could also be affected. From an employment law viewpoint, however, it is more prudent to follow normal absenteeism/dismissal procedures should a dismissal arise. Employers should make clear the reason for dismissal, that is, by reason of incapability to perform the job, as opposed to dismissal due to the employee taking legal proceedings against the employer.

GENERAL REFERENCES

Barrington Report, *Report of the Commission of Inquiry on Safety Health and Welfare at Work*, Stationery Office, 1983.

Byrne, R., Health, Safety and Welfare at Work Act, 1989, *Irish Law Statutes Annotated*, Sweet and Maxwell.

Forde, M., *Employment Law*, The Round Hall Press, 1992.

Kerr, T., *Statute of Limitations (Amendment) Act, 1991, Irish Law Statutes Annotated*, Sweet and Maxwell.

McMahon and Binchy, *Irish Law of Torts*, 2nd ed., Butterworths (note in particular Chapter 18 on Employers' Liability).

White, J.P.M., *Irish Law of Damages for Personal Injuries and Death*, Butterworths, 1989.

SECTION THREE

TERMINATION OF EMPLOYMENT

CHAPTER SIXTEEN

Notice

An employer or an employee who wishes to terminate the contract of employment must give the requisite notice unless agreed otherwise. Prior to the enactment of the Minimum Notice and Terms of Employment Act, 1973, it was the common law which decided what was the acceptable period of notice to terminate the contract of employment. That period was decided on the basis of the position that the employee held and the time periods between payments, for example, monthly, weekly, or hourly. Thus, if an employee were paid weekly, the notice period would be one week, though an employee who was an executive may be entitled to a few months' notice. More recently, in the case of *Tierney* v. *Irish Meat Packers* (High Court, unreported, Lardner, J. 1989 and noted at ((1989) 8 JISLL 59) an employee with nine years' service as group Credit Controller was given the statutory minimum notice of six weeks. The High Court considered that this was not reasonable so he was awarded six months' notice.

The Minimum Notice and Terms of Employment Act, 1973 provides basic notice periods, based on the length of service, which an employer must give unless, of course, the employee is dismissed for misconduct. The Act also provides the period of notice which an employee who is resigning must give an employer. Furthermore, it provides that an employee is entitled to a written statement of the terms and conditions of employment (see Chapter 2 — The Contract of Employment).

STATUTORY MINIMUM NOTICE

The Act covers all employers and all employees who are normally expected to work over eight hours per week (the 1973 Act was amended in 1984 to bring the weekly hourly threshold down from 21 to 18 hours, and then in 1991 to include regular part-time employees thus reducing the threshold to eight hours). There are certain exclusions to include the employer's immediate family if living with the employer and employed in the same house or farm; civil servants;

members of the permanent Defence Forces and the Garda Síochána; and seamen signing on under the Merchant Shipping Act, 1894.

NOTICE TO EMPLOYEES

To dismiss an employee who has been in continuous service for 13 weeks or more, the employer must give a minimum period of notice based on the employee's length of service, as follows:

(1) 13 weeks' to 2 years' service — 1 week

(2) 2 to 5 years' service — 2 weeks

(3) 5 to 10 years' service — 4 weeks

(4) 10 to 15 years' service — 6 weeks

(5) 15 or more years' service — 8 weeks.

Service is continuous unless an employee is dismissed or leaves voluntarily. It is not usually affected by strikes, lockouts, lay-offs or dismissal followed by immediate re-employment. These rules have been further amended by the Unfair Dismissals (Amendment) Act, 1993, namely that if an employee receives and accepts a statutory redundancy payment, then service is broken. A series of fixed term (or specified-purpose contracts) with renewals may constitute continuous service (see Chapter 3 — Temporary Employment and Chapter 16 — Unfair Dismissal for the new provisions in the Unfair Dismissals (Amendment) Act, 1993 in respect of renewal of fixed term and specified-purpose contracts). Transfer of ownership of a firm or part of a firm does not break continuity of service (see Chapter 11 — Transfer of a Business). The rules of continuity of service are contained in a schedule to the Act (which has been amended by the Unfair Dismissals Acts, 1977 to 1993). It might also be noted that the 1993 Act provides that continuity of service is not broken if an employee has been re-employed within 26 weeks after dismissal, if it was for the purpose of avoiding liability under the unfair dismissals legislation.

There are also rules for computable service contained in the Act. These are the actual periods of service which are used to assess an employee's entitlement to the various periods of notice. This should not be confused with continuous service, as if an employee's service is broken, the period of computable service has to start over again. Periods of service which are not computable include (a) any week in which an employee is not normally expected to work eight hours; (b) any period of lay-off; sickness or injury; (c) any agreed absence over 26 weeks; or (d) any absence due to a strike in his employment.

CONTRACTUAL NOTICE

The law provides that an employee is entitled to the longer of contractual notice or statutory minimum notice. The 1973 Act provides the statutory minimum notice to which an employee is entitled. However, if the contract of employment provides for a longer period of notice, then that is the notice period to which the employee is entitled. Similarly, if the contract of employment provides for one month's notice and an employee has over 10 years' service, the Act will apply, thereby giving the employee an entitlement to six weeks' notice.

NOTICE TO EMPLOYER

An employer is entitled to one week's notice from an employee who has been in continuous employment for 13 or more weeks and wishes to end a contract of employment.

LAY-OFF OF EMPLOYEE

An employee who has been put on lay-off and is subsequently made redundant by the employer is still entitled to notice monies. In other words, lay-off cannot be used as a mechanism to avoid paying statutory notice (*Industrial Yarns* v. *Greene* [1984] ILRM 15). However, an employee on lay-off who then claims redundancy may not be entitled to monies in lieu of notice unless the lay-off was seen as a method of avoiding the payment of notice monies.

MISCONDUCT

If an employee is dismissed for "misconduct", the employer does not have to give any notice or monies in lieu of notice. The term "misconduct" has led to confusion because it is not defined in the Act and we must look to the common law for a suitable definition. The High Court in *Brewster* v. *Burke and the Minister for Labour* ((1985) 4 JISLL 98) accepted a UK definition of "misconduct":

It has long been part of our law that a person repudiates the contract of service if he wilfully disobeys the lawful and reasonable orders of his master. Such a refusal fully justifies an employer in dismissing an employee summarily.

In this case the employee maintained that he was entitled to compensation for notice based on his length of service, but the employer stated that he was not so entitled as he had failed to comply with a reasonable order. The Employment Appeals Tribunal decided that the employee was entitled to compensation for notice and the High Court, in considering the UK precedent, agreed with the EAT determination.

The Tribunal has generally taken a narrow view of the meaning of the term "misconduct". It would include violence and theft, but may not include refusal by an employee to accept reasonable instructions, being late, dismissal arising from conflict of interest, and so forth.

WAIVER OF NOTICE OR PAYMENT IN LIEU OF NOTICE

On termination of employment, an employer or an employee may waive their right to notice or an employee may accept payment in lieu of notice. However, both parties must be in agreement to such an arrangement. Failing that, an employee is entitled to stay on and work during the notice period, though the practicalities are that there may be no work for the employee and indeed it is usually beneficial for the employee to receive payment in lieu of notice as notice monies (up to £6,000 plus £500 for each complete year of service) may be paid without any reduction of income tax or PRSI (see Chapter 20 — Taxation of Termination Payments).

RIGHTS OF EMPLOYEE DURING NOTICE

During the notice period, the employee is entitled to normal pay and any other rights, such as sick leave, pension contributions, or company car on the basis that the employee is available and willing to work even though work may not be provided. An employee is entitled to the benefit of monies in lieu of notice even if that employee is on lay-off during the notice period (*Irish Leathers Ltd.* v. *Minister for Labour* (1986) 5 JISLL 211). In *Irish Shipping Ltd.* v. *Byrne, the Minster for Labour and Others* ((1987) 6 JISLL 177), Lardner, J. considered that the employees were not entitled to compensation for loss of minimum notice. Following a winding up order and the appointment of a liquidator, the employees were re-employed on a day to day basis and worked for a longer period than their statutory entitlement and received their usual pay. They were not considered to have had any loss and thus no compensation was awarded.

HOLIDAYS

Holidays may run concurrently with the notice period provided that the employee is still in employment. The reason being is that under the Holidays (Employees) Acts, 1973 and 1991 the employer may decide when holidays may be taken.

NOTICE AND REDUNDANCY

All periods of notice under the Minimum Notice and Terms of Employment Act, 1973, the Redundancy Payments Acts, 1967 to 1991, the Protection of Employment Act, 1977 and contractual notice run concurrently. For example, a company letting go a large number of staff must give the Minister for Enterprise and Employment at least 30 days' notice under the Protection of Employment Act, 1977 (collective redundancies). An employee with between five and ten years' service would be entitled to two weeks' notice under the Redundancy Acts and would also be entitled to four weeks' notice under the Minimum Notice and Terms of Employment Act. In this situation, however, the employee would be entitled to four weeks' notice as all the periods of notice run together, plus an additional two days' notice under the Protection of Employment Act.

Another example would be an employee who had three months' notice in the contract of employment and over 15 years service. The employee may have eight weeks' statutory minimum notice plus two weeks' redundancy notice, but in this situation should be given three months' notice and need only receive the RP1 (Notice of Redundancy) two weeks before the actual termination. If a person is entitled to contractual notice, it is considered that the statutory part of his notice is that period prior to the termination of employment. Thus an employee who receives the contractual period of notice and is let go prior to its completion (presuming that it is longer than the statutory period of notice) is entitled to the balance under the Minimum Notice and Terms of Employment Act (*Jameson* v. *MCW Ltd.* M 878/1983).

NOTICE MUST BE CERTAIN

While notice does not have to be in writing, it must be specific and certain. It is not sufficient for an employer to tell an employee that the employee is going to be dismissed, without giving the actual date.

The High Court has clarified this point by confirming that notice must be certain. In *Bolands Ltd. (in receivership)* v. *Josephine Ward and Others* ([1988] ILRM 382), the receiver informed employees that their employment was terminating on a specific date with a notice period complying with statutory minimum notice. However, the receiver decided to continue trading in the hope that he would be able to obtain a purchaser and the original notice was extended week by week for some time. When the employees were terminated they maintained that they had not received their statutory minimum notice. They appealed to the EAT and were successful (and were awarded full monies in lieu of notice less one week) and the High Court accepted the EAT decision. However, the receiver appealed to the Supreme Court which considered that they had been in receipt of their minimum notice as the receiver had acted in good faith in granting the extensions; it was clear that the employees knew that they were under notice and that they were benefiting from the notice extensions.

CONSTRUCTIVE DISMISSAL

An employee who resigns and claims constructive dismissal under the Unfair Dismissals Acts, 1977 to 1993, even if successful, is not entitled to statutory minimum notice.

NOTICE CANNOT BE WITHDRAWN

Notice of termination of employment cannot be withdrawn except by agreement between the parties.

REMEDIES

If either party is disputing their right to notice, the length of notice or the calculation of continuous service, the issue may be referred to the Employment Appeals Tribunal for determination. Any person who is dissatisfied with the Tribunal's decision — or the Minister for Enterprise and Employment at the request of the Tribunal — may refer an issue to the High Court on a point of law (see Chapter 23 — Employment Appeals Tribunal).

The vast majority of cases that are brought to the Employment Appeals Tribunal under this Act are in relation to a person's entitlement to notice, for example, an employee given four weeks when they should have been entitled to six, or not getting the necessary amount of pay during the notice period, and so forth. Invariably, these cases under the Minimum Notice Act go hand in hand with a claim under the Unfair Dismissals Acts and the Redundancy Payments Acts at the same time.

The Employment Appeals Tribunal only has authority to grant statutory minimum notice, and thus an employee who has an entitlement to more than statutory notice will have to bring their claim to the appropriate court, namely, the District Court for sums up to £5,000, the Circuit Court for sums up to £30,000 and the High Court for larger amounts.

COMPENSATION

The Tribunal may dismiss a claim by an employee, or it may award compensation for any loss arising from the employer not giving notice. Social welfare receipts — unemployment benefit or assistance — are not deducted from such an award (*Irish Leathers Ltd.* v. *Minister for Labour* (1986) 5 JISLL 211). However, an employee who is ill and not available for work during the notice period is not entitled to any compensation as that employee is deemed unavailable for work. For the same reason, an employee on strike during the notice period has no entitlement to compensation.

An employee who is working during the notice period and in receipt of at least the same earnings as they would have received from their previous employer has no entitlement. However, if the employee receives less monies they would be entitled to the difference, as compensation in this Act is based on "loss".

SETTLEMENTS

If there is a settlement on termination of employment which includes notice monies, it is extremely important to state that fact fully in the settlement agreement, and the amount of monies the employee received. Furthermore, such an arrangement must be fully explained to an employee so that they understand that they cannot subsequently claim that they are entitled to statutory notice monies. If such an agreement was not explained to the employee and there was

no specific provision for notice monies, the employee could successfully bring a minimum notice claim to the Employment Appeals
Tribunal.

GENERAL REFERENCE

Kerr, T., "The Year in Review" in *Journal of the Irish Society of Labour
    Law*, Vols. 1–8.

CHAPTER SEVENTEEN

Unfair Dismissal

The Unfair Dismissals Act came into force on 15 April 1977 and was a major watershed in Irish employment law. For the first time an employee claiming unfair dismissal was entitled to a statutory remedy, namely, reinstatement, re-engagement or a maximum of 104 weeks' remuneration. Since then there have been several Acts which have amended the 1977 Act, namely the Protection of Employees (Employers' Insolvency) Act, 1984, which reduced the hourly threshold; the Worker Protection (Regular Part-Time Employees) Act, 1991, which extended the scope of the unfair dismissals legislation to cover regular part-time employees; and finally the Unfair Dismissals (Amendment) Act, 1993, which made a number of key amendments. The 1993 Act applies to all dismissals on or after 1 October 1993.

Prior to the enactment of this legislation, an employee who considered that they were unfairly dismissed could only pursue an action through the courts for wrongful dismissal, a lengthy and expensive remedy. Furthermore, the employee would technically only be entitled to damages in respect of their lost notice as provided under their contract of employment if they did not get the requisite notice. They may also be entitled to other damages, for example, relocation expenses. However, this remedy was quite impractical for the ordinary working person, as the costs of the case may well be greater than the amount that they succeeded in being awarded. Actions for wrongful dismissal or breach of contract may be taken by executives with long notice periods. This action may also be used by employees who have less than the required service under the Act, but such cases are infrequent.

The 1977 Act provided that a claimant had to decide whether to bring proceedings for statutory unfair dismissal or wrongful dismissal at common law. The 1993 Act has amended this provision somewhat by providing that if a rights commissioner has issued a recommendation under the Act, or if a Tribunal hearing has commenced, the employee cannot obtain damages at common law for wrongful dismissal. Alternatively, if a court hearing has commenced for wrongful dismissal, the employee will not be entitled to redress under the unfair dismissals legislation.

The only alternative for employees was to bring a claim under the Industrial Relations Acts to a rights commissioner or the Labour Court. The wording in the 1977 Act often led to confusion. The Act provided that an unfair dismissal should not be referred to a rights commissioner under the Industrial Relations Act, 1969. In the case of *Sutcliffe* v. *Pat Russell Haulage Ltd.* ([1991] ELR 42), the claimant referred his claim to a rights commissioner under the 1969 Act and was awarded "exemplary compensation" of £2,500. The claimant was not satisfied with this and brought a claim under the Unfair Dismissals Act to the Tribunal. The Tribunal considered that it had no jurisdiction. However, the High Court disagreed with this determination and referred the case back to the Tribunal for processing as the Tribunal should have considered the rights commissioner recommendation as a nullity (*Sutcliffe* v. *McCarthy and Ors.* [1993] ELR 53).

This was by far the more popular route taken by employees prior to the enactment of the unfair dismissals legislation. However, it had the major drawback that the employers did not have to attend such hearings and even if they did, the recommendations were not enforceable and the employee had no statutory entitlement to be reinstated. This route is still taken by employees who consider that they have been unfairly dismissed but do not have the necessary service under the Act.

In order to avoid this form of procedural confusion, the 1993 Act provides that if a rights commissioner has issued a recommendation or has commenced a hearing in respect of a dismissal, the dispute cannot also be referred to a rights commissioner or the Labour Court under the Industrial Relations Acts, 1946 to 1990. Alternatively, if a rights commissioner has made a recommendation or if a hearing has commenced before the Labour Court under the Industrial Relations Acts, then the employee is not entitled to redress under the unfair dismissal legislation.

APPLICATION OF THE ACT

Obviously, there must be a dismissal before a claimant can obtain redress under the Act. Dismissal may occur where:

(1) The contract of employment was terminated by the employer, whether notice was given or not;

(2) The employee had no option but to resign because of the conduct of the employer (constructive dismissal — see below); or

(3) A fixed-term or specified-purpose contract was not renewed (see Chapter 3 — Temporary Employment).

If a former employee does not come within the scope of the Unfair Dismissals Acts a claim for redress cannot be pursued. Accordingly, the substantive facts or the reason for dismissal cannot be determined by the adjudicating body which may be the rights commissioner, the EAT, the Circuit Court or High Court.

CONTRACT OF EMPLOYMENT

A claimant must have been an employee under a contract of service, whether written or oral. This has already been discussed in Chapter 2 — The Contract of Employment and Chapter 3 — Temporary Employment. If the employee died subsequent to the dismissal, the claim may be brought by the personal representative of the deceased employee.

Invariably, there is no difficulty in deciding who the employer was (see also Chapter 23 — Employment Appeals Tribunal) as one merely has to look at the contract of employment or some other document, for example, an "offer of employment" letter or pay-slip. However, in a few cases the identity of the employer was not clear, as transpired in *Allison* v. *Incorporated Law Society of Ireland and Laurence Cullen, President* (UD 492/1986). In summary, the claimant acted as secretary to the president for his term of office which lasted for one year. She had worked for two successive presidents and was paid directly by the presidents' professional offices, yet worked on the Law Society premises. The presidents were reimbursed 85 per cent of her salary by the Law Society and she received a P45 from the president at the end of each term of office. The president for 1986, Laurence Cullen, entered into negotiation with her but decided not to employ her. The Tribunal considered that she was not an employee of Mr Cullen and stated that "it appears to us that the true employer was and remained until termination, the Society, and . . . that succeeding Presidents acted as agents of the Society." The case shows that the Tribunal is likely to take the "fairest" view as to who the employer was.

The 1993 Act has extended the scope of who may be considered an employee, namely that for the purposes of the unfair dismissals legislation "agency temps" will now be considered to be employees of the hiring employee if they are placed by an employment agency. Of course such employees will have to have worked the necessary service and hours.

CONTINUITY OF SERVICE

An employee who does not have the requisite one year's continuous service cannot fall within the scope of the Act. The unfair dismissals legislation provides that the rules for assessing and computing periods of service are contained in the First Schedule of the Minimum Notice and Terms of Employment Acts, 1973 to 1991. These rules have already been discussed in Chapter 16 — Notice. The 1993 Act provides that the dismissal of an employee followed by their re-employment by the same employer within 26 weeks will not break their continuity of service if the dismissal was connected with the avoidance of liability under the Act.

However, an employee who maintains that she was unfairly dismissed by reason of trade union membership or activities, pregnancy or was denied her entitlement under the maternity legislation does not have to have one year's service.

The Worker Protection (Regular Part-Time Employees) Act, 1991 has caused further complexity to issues of continuity. First, a regular part-time employee must have one year's service under the Act to bring an unfair dismissals claim. However, if she maintains that she was dismissed by reason of trade union membership or activities, pregnancy, or being denied her maternity rights, she must have 13 weeks' service.

AGE

The Act does not apply to persons who were under 16 years of age on the date of their dismissal. An employee who has reached 66 years, or normal retirement age, on the date of their dismissal also may not bring a claim under the Act. The normal retirement age is usually the 65th birthday. However, if the employer's specified retirement age was 60 years and an employee was dismissed on their 60th birthday, they would not fall within the scope of the Act. Arising from this provision it is important that the contract of employment states clearly the retirement age. If, for example, the retirement age was specified as 67 years, then equally the employee could not bring a claim under the Act because that employee had exceeded the 66-year limit. (In one unusual case the Tribunal accepted that the age of 20 years was the normal retirement age for the category of employment that the employee was in (*Humphries* v. *Iarnród Éireann,* UD 1099/1988).

Retirement age was considered in the recent High Court case of *Donegal County Council* v. *Porter and Ors.* ([1993] ELR 101) where a number of firefighters with long service were dismissed on the ground that they had reached 55 years. There were no written contracts and there was no reference to a specific date of retirement. Their expectation was that they would work until they reached 60 years, presuming that they were capable of performing their duties. The Department of the Environment issued a circular letter recommending a retirement age of 55 years and the Council decided to implement its terms. Flood, J. stated that the attempt to force them into retirement at 55 years was an attempt to alter unilaterally the contractual situation and would be a breach of contract unless it could be lawfully sustained. As there were no substantial grounds justifying the dismissal, reinstatement was ordered.

HOURS

In summary, a person is normally expected to work at least 18 hours per week, or eight hours per week in the case of a regular part-time employee. This is as a result of the Worker Protection (Regular Part-Time Employees) Act, 1991, which brought regular part-time employees within the application of the Unfair Dismissals Acts, provided they have the necessary service.

The law does not specifically provide for averaging the hours over a period of time (*McFadden* v. *Ryan t/a Zodiac Apparel*, M 294/1981). The only practical way of determining the hours is to look at the hours actually worked and the custom and practice associated with the duties, for example, regular compulsory overtime. As a rule of thumb, an employee who more often than not worked over eight hours per week would fall within the scope of the Act even though there was the odd week where fewer hours were worked.

In *Edwards* v. *Aerials and Electronics (Irl) Ltd.* (UD 302/1985), it was held that as neither employer nor employee could provide evidence as to hours worked, the hours were deemed indeterminable and the claim failed. However, this was an extremely unusual situation.

Where an employee actually works a limited number of hours but is "on-call" for a number of hours, then "on-call" hours are deemed to be working hours. Accordingly, such employees as nurses, firefighters, etc. may fall within the scope of the legislation (*Bartlett* v. *Kerry County Council*, UD 178/1978) and more recently the High Court decision of *Donegal County Council* v. *Porter and Ors.*, above).

ILLEGALITY

There are certain types of contract which are forbidden at common law and are therefore illegal, for example, contracts to defraud the Revenue. The first such case was *Lewis* v. *Squash (Irl) Ltd.* (UD 146/1982 and [1983] ILRM 363), where the claimant received in addition to his salary of £14,000 the sum of £2,000 for "expenses". The Tribunal found that the £2,000 was in fact a salary increase though it was not returned to the Revenue by the company or the employee as part of his salary. The Tribunal found that the contract of employment was tainted by an illegality and therefore unenforceable.

A valid and enforceable contract of employment thus must exist upon which the claim under the Act is founded. In *Morris* v. *Peter Keogh (Upholsterers) Ltd.* (UD 947/1984) there was a perfectly valid and enforceable contract. In that case, the employee while in employment claimed unemployment benefits. The Tribunal considered that the employee's wrongful declarations made his contract of employment unenforceable and the claim failed.

In *Wosser* v. *Dublin Corporation* (UD 42/1989) the Tribunal considered that social welfare fraud, even where admitted, was a matter for the Department of Social Welfare. In the last number of years there has been a number of these cases as employers have become increasingly concerned about social welfare fraud in relation to the claiming of disability benefit while at work. Spot checks and the tightening up of social welfare payments by the Department of Social Welfare have also been responsible.

The 1993 Act now provides that if an employee has been unfairly dismissed and if there was a term or a condition of the contract of employment which breached the Income Tax Acts or the Social Welfare Acts, then the employee will be entitled to redress for dismissal. The adjudicating bodies shall send the file to the Revenue and/or the Department of Social Welfare. Previously if there was such a breach the employee was not entitled to any redress.

TIME LIMITS

In summary, the claim for unfair dismissal must be brought to a rights commissioner or the Employment Appeals Tribunal within six months of the date of dismissal. The 1993 Act provides that the time limit may be extended up to 12 months from the date of dismissal as long as a rights commissioner or the Tribunal is satisfied that there were exceptional circumstances preventing the service of the claim within the first six months of the date of dismissal. This is considered in detail in Chapter 23 — Employment Appeals Tribunal.

SETTLEMENT

Section 13 of the Unfair Dismissals Act states that:

> a provision in an agreement (whether a contract of employment or not and whether made before or after the commencement of this Act) shall be void in so far as it purports to exclude or limit the application of, or is inconsistent with, any provisions of this Act.

In effect, this means that there cannot be an agreement between an employer and employee to contract out of this legislation. Such agreement would be rendered void and unenforceable under the Act.

Such attempted "contracting out" could be contained in a contract of employment or in an agreement on termination of employment. The exceptions as provided by the Act are fixed term or specified-purpose contracts, though there may not be a series of such contracts.

This appears to be a straightforward provision (a similar one is contained in the Redundancy Payments Acts) yet such agreements have raised key legal issues. The first is the equitable principle of promissory estoppel. To put this simply, if a termination agreement is entered into prior to any statutory proceedings, and the employee then brings a claim under the Act, the employee is estopped from denying the agreement and its validity. Thus the claimant should not be able to pursue a claim under the Act.

The Tribunal has taken many different approaches to such agreements. In *Kehoe* v. *Memorex Media Products Ltd.* (UD 222/1987), the estoppel argument was accepted by the Tribunal. In this case the claimant had received statutory redundancy and an ex gratia sum "in full and final settlement of all matters on termination of employment". The claimant argued that she entered into the agreement under duress. There was no evidence of duress and the claim fell on the issue of estoppel. However, in *Dempsey* v. *Memorex Media Products Ltd.* (UD 306/1987) which had similar facts to the Kehoe case, the Tribunal side-stepped the legal theory of estoppel and appeared to be more pragmatic as to how they approached the claim. The Tribunal heard all the evidence and held that there was a genuine redundancy, thus a "fair" dismissal.

One interpretation of this section has meant that if a settlement is arrived at, the Tribunal may rely on this section and hear the substantive part of the case and rule thereon.

In practical terms, this issue can arise where an employee's contract is about to be terminated for any reason, although it more usually happens in a redundancy situation where monies are offered to the employee on the basis of a "full and final settlement". This situation is commonplace. It can be generally stated that such an agreement would stand up as long as the employee is fully advised of their rights by a solicitor or their union official. An employee can still bring a claim under the Act, but the chances of success are slim if the employee was fully advised prior to the signing of the agreement.

The early case of *Eate* v. *Semperit (Ireland) Ltd.* (UD 46/1977) was most interesting. Prior to his dismissal, the claimant accepted a sum of money which was to be in full and final settlement of all outstanding claims he may have had against the company. The Tribunal did not accept this agreement as valid and, relying on Section 13, held that the claimant was unfairly dismissed though he was not entitled to additional compensation.

However, if such an agreement is entered into following the initiation of proceedings or after a rights commissioner's hearing, the Tribunal would more than likely hold that the agreement did not exclude or limit the application of the Act (*Doyle* v. *Pierce (Wexford) Ltd.*, UD 50/1979).

Another option, invariably unpopular because of the preference of the parties to have such agreements shrouded in secrecy (e.g. the employer may not wish to create a precedent), is after the initiation of proceedings to "register" the agreement with the Tribunal. The Tribunal would not register such an agreement and issue a determination thereon unless it was satisfied that the employee, in particular, was fully represented and was satisfied as to its terms. Such an arrangement would not be considered to limit the operation of the Act.

In the early years of the operation of the Act, where there was a settlement of a claim prior to a hearing, the Tribunal invariably issued a determination stating that there was a settlement to the satisfaction of the parties, sometimes including the details. From the early 1980s onwards, the practice of issuing such determinations stopped, probably as a result of the requested secrecy of the parties (usually the employer).

The key term of the settlement agreement is that the claimant withdraws proceedings under all the Acts they have claimed under and that the agreement be kept confidential to the parties. It is normal to have a settlement agreement which would provide, for example, that the former employee signs an agreement with the following wording:

> I.............accept the sum of £xxx in full and final settlement of all statutory, contractual and any other claims arising from my employment with ....Ltd.

However, the Tribunal has taken the opposite view in a number of cases even where it has been satisfied that the employee agreed to the settlement. Further, the employee must have had full knowledge that such sum was final settlement of, in particular, all statutory claims arising from the employment and that the employee could not then bring a claim under the 1977 Act. The employee should have been in receipt of legal or trade union advice so that there would be no element of duress. These points were considered in *Kehoe* v. *Memorex Media Products Ltd.* (UD 222/1987) where the employer raised the estoppel argument in the context of a claim for selection for redundancy. The employee did not deny that she had signed a document "in full and final settlement of all claims" when she was in receipt of a statutory lump-sum plus an ex gratia severance payment, but maintained that she signed it under duress. Her argument was defeated on the basis that she had full knowledge of the document she was signing. Accordingly, the issue of selection for redundancy was not fully considered.

EXCLUSIONS

Certain categories of employees are excluded under the Act, including members of the defence forces and the Garda Síochána, civil servants, officers of local authorities, vocational education committees and health boards, FÁS trainees and apprentices (if employed by FÁS) and close relatives of an employer who reside in the same house or farm with the employer. Temporary officers of health boards now fall within the scope of the Act.

DISMISSAL DURING PROBATION OR TRAINING

The Act does not apply to the dismissal of an employee during a period of probation or training if the contract is in writing and the duration of the probation or training is one year or less and is so stated in the contract.

The Act does not apply in relation to the dismissal of an employee during the period of employment when the employee is undergoing training for the purpose of becoming qualified or registered as a nurse, pharmacist, health inspector, medical laboratory technician, occupational therapist, physiotherapist, speech therapist, radiographer or social worker.

DISMISSAL DURING APPRENTICESHIP

If an employee is employed as a statutory apprentice (under the Industrial Training Act, 1967) the Act will not apply to their dismissal if the dismissal takes place during the first six months of the apprenticeship or within one month after the completion of the apprenticeship.

In *MacNamara* v. *Castlelock Construction & Development Ltd.* (UD 808/1984), it was contended that the claimant, employed as a third year apprentice, fell outside the scope of the Act because he had between six months' and one year's service. It was held that he had a viable claim.

PERSONS WHO WORK OUTSIDE THE STATE

The Act does not apply to the dismissal of an employee who (a) ordinarily worked outside the State unless the employee was ordinarily resident within the State during the term of the contract or, (b) was domiciled in the State during the term of the contract and the employer (if an individual) was ordinarily resident in the State during the term of the contract, or if it is a company which had its principal place of business in the State during the term of the contract.

In *Dignam* v. *Sisk Nigeria Ltd. and John Sisk and Son Ltd.* (UD 125/1983), the claimant originally worked for John Sisk and Sons Ltd. and then applied for the position of contracts manager with Sisk Nigeria Ltd., a company incorporated in Nigeria with its sole area of business there. The claimant was not dismissed by John Sisk and Sons Ltd. but by Sisk Nigeria Ltd. Accordingly, the Tribunal had no jurisdiction and the claimant did not fall within the scope of the Act.

DIPLOMATIC IMMUNITY

This issue was considered by the Supreme Court in the case of the *Government of Canada* v. *Employment Appeals Tribunal and Brian Burke* ([1992] ELR 29). In this case the employee was employed as a driver with the Canadian Embassy in Dublin between June 1986 and May 1988 when he was dismissed. He brought proceedings under the Minimum Notice and Terms of Employment Act, 1973 and also the Unfair Dismissals Act, 1977 before the Employment Appeals Tribunal. The Canadian Government submitted that the Tribunal had no jurisdiction to hear the claims which were rejected and the Tribunal went on to award the claimant compensation in the sum of £10,200. This determination was referred to the High Court by the Canadian Government for judicial review. In the High Court ([1991] ELR 57), McKenzie J. considered that the Tribunal was justified in proceeding to hear the claims since the doctrine of absolute sovereign immunity had no application in the modern world. However, the Supreme Court thought otherwise and considered that the employment of an embassy chauffeur is within the sphere of governmental or sovereign activity and that the doctrine of restrictive immunity applied. Accordingly, because of this doctrine such an employee has no cause of action against his employer.

CONSTRUCTIVE DISMISSAL

In summary, constructive dismissal arises where an employee is left with no option but to resign because of the employer's breach of contract. It is defined in the Act as:

the termination by the employee of his contract of employment with his employer whether prior notice of the termination was or was not given to the employer, in circumstances, in which, because of the conduct of the employer, the employee was or would have been entitled, or it was or would have been reasonable for the employee, to terminate the contract of employment without giving prior notice of the termination to the employer.

In strict legal terms the concept of "constructive dismissal" is difficult. However, the tests applied to "constructive dismissal" may be summarised as the contract test and the reasonableness test (see Redmond — Dismissal Law in the Republic of Ireland.)

The contract test was summarised by Lord Denning, M.R. in *Western Excavating (E.C.C.) Ltd.* v. *Sharp* [1978] ICR 121).

If the employer is guilty of conduct which is a significant breach going to the root of the contract of employment, or which shows that the employer no longer intends to be bound by one or more of the essential terms of the contract then the employee is entitled to treat himself as discharged from any further performance.

The alternative reasonableness test asks whether the employer "conducts himself or his affairs so unreasonably that the employee cannot fairly be expected to put up with any longer, [if so] the employee is justified in leaving".

The Tribunal has not detailed which test it has applied in constructive dismissal cases. However, examples would be where employers have changed the employee's terms and conditions, for example, demotion, or where "life at work" has become so intolerable that the employee feels that there is no other option but to resign their employment.

In these cases, the onus is first on the employee to prove that they were dismissed, and then on the employer to show that it was a fair dismissal.

The first key case, which is still the classic example of constructive dismissal, was *Byrne* v. *RHM Foods (I) Ltd.* (UD 69/1979). The claimant was employed as a secretary working for a marketing manager. The marketing manager was suspended, but the managing director assured the claimant that her own job was safe. Subsequently, however, the keys of the marketing manager's filing cabinet were taken away and the claimant was given no work and had no contact with her colleagues. When her telephone was disconnected she felt that she had no other option but to resign. The Tribunal in upholding her claim that this was not a genuine resignation commented that the

> [claimant's] continuous isolation without knowledge of what was going on or contact by any person [made it] reasonable and understandable her confidence and trust in her employer should be undermined to the extent that she could tolerate it no longer.

A more recent case is *Gallery* v. *Blarney Woollen Mills Ltd.* ([1990] ELR 143). In this case the claimant was employed as a manager at the Kilkenny shop at the time of the takeover by Blarney Woollen Mills Ltd. Prior to the transfer, she maintained that she was totally responsible for the operation of the Dublin shop. Following on the takeover, she considered that her position and duties had become unclear and her authority was being undermined by decisions taken by the new head of retail in the Blarney Group. She was advised after a number of weeks that the new management was not happy with her performance. She wrote to the head of retail asking for a written confirmation of the terms and conditions in her contract and also asked for an indication that the company placed full trust and confidence in her. The reply was unsatisfactory and the claimant wrote again saying that if she did not receive a written reply dealing with the various points raised she would be forced to take steps to protect her position. She then received a reply requesting a meeting to discuss the matter with her. She responded by stating that the company's conduct amounted to constructive dismissal and she resigned.

The company referred the Tribunal to the cases of *Conway* v. *Ulster Bank* (UD 474/1981) and *Beatty* v. *Bayside Supermarket* (UD 142/1987). Both these cases clearly established that, where there is a union/management agreement containing a grievance procedure, such procedure should be substantially followed by employees when they consider that there is a breach of contract by their employer.

The Tribunal, however, considered that this was a constructive dismissal and stated that "the respondent company acted unreasonably in its dealings with the claimant and she became frustrated leaving her with no option but to resign".

There is a considerable number of cases where an employee resigns and then claims constructive dismissal. In such situations, the Tribunal can hold there was a clear resignation and therefore there was no dismissal. However, in certain cases, for example, if an employee just "walks off" the job, the Tribunal could hold that there was no dismissal and no resignation. Accordingly, it could be argued that the employee is still employed.

It should be noted that there is no provision for "self dismissal". In other words, an employer cannot state to an employee that if that employee does not do something or does not come in to work that it is deemed to be a "self dismissal". There is no such thing; either the employer or the employee must actually terminate the contract of employment.

Finally, an employee who is aware that there is a breach of contract should not live with such a breach for too long because it could then be considered to be an acquiescence to the breach of contract.

DISMISSAL ARISING FROM LOCKOUT OR STRIKE

The 1993 Act has amended the 1977 Act by providing that the lockout of an employee shall be deemed to be a dismissal. If at the end of the lockout the employee was not reinstated or re-engaged (the meaning of which was extended by the 1993 Act and considered below under Redress) and one (or more) were reinstated or re-engaged, it would be considered an unfair dismissal.

The 1993 Act provides that the dismissal of an employee for taking part in a strike or industrial action is an unfair dismissal if at least one other employee was not dismissed for the same action, or if another employee was reinstated or re-engaged.

The date of reinstatement or re-engagement is the date as agreed between the employer and employees, or if there is no agreement the date on which reinstatement or re-engagement was offered to the majority of the workforce.

If a particular employee is dismissed for taking part in a strike and other employees are not so dismissed, it would be an automatically unfair dismissal. However, if during the course of a strike or other industrial action there was abusive behaviour from an employee, it could be a fair dismissal.

If one looks at this section of the Act, it is arguable that if an employer dismissed all employees who were on strike or taking part in an industrial action it could be considered a fair dismissal. However, this is obviously problematic and not advisable.

UNFAIR DISMISSAL

The substantive part of the Act provides that all dismissals are deemed "unfair" unless there were substantial grounds justifying the dismissal. There are certain grounds which constitute "fair" dismissal, namely dismissal arising from the employee's capability, competence, qualifications, conduct, redundancy and where the employee's ongoing employment was in contravention of statutory provisions. The Act contains a number of grounds where a dismissal is deemed unfair as listed below.

Membership of a Trade Union or Involvement in Trade Union Activities

An employee cannot be dismissed because of trade union membership or because of a proposal that they or another employee become a member of a trade union. However, this only applies if the activity is engaged in outside normal hours of work or during the hours at work when it is allowed. The employee does not have to have one year's continuous service to bring a claim for this reason, and the age limits also do not apply for this form of claim.

The burden of proof would be on the claimant to show that the employer was aware that they were a member of a trade union or engaged in such activities.

In the case of *Wixted* v. *Sang Mann* ([1991] ELR 208), the claimant joined a trade union because of poor working conditions. Subsequently, the union wrote to management requesting a meeting to discuss the wages and conditions of employment of their members. The claimant was dismissed and at the Tribunal the employer maintained that he was dismissed for poor work performance. The Tribunal did not accept this and considered that he was dismissed wholly or mainly because of his trade union activities.

In a similar case, *White* v. *Simon Betson* ([1992] ELR 120), the claimant was only employed for one month when his employment was terminated. The claimant maintained that his weekly wage was agreed when he started work, but that he was then paid irregular amounts at regular intervals. He was out sick for a few days (having provided a medical certificate) and he was given his wages and told not to come into work any more. The claimant advised the Tribunal that some three days prior to his termination he had become a member of SIPTU. SIPTU had written to the employer requesting a discussion on the claimant's conditions of employment. The employer again maintained that there was poor work performance and that he had made up his mind to terminate the employment on the first day that the employee was out sick. Furthermore, he maintained that he had received no letter from SIPTU until after the termination of the employment. The Tribunal considered that the correspondence had been received prior to the termination of the employment and that the decision to dismiss was as a result of his trade union membership and was therefore unfair.

Again, one has to say generally that the Tribunal is very conscious of the constitutional right to be a member of a trade union.

Religious or Political Views

It would be an automatically unfair dismissal if an employee were dismissed because of their religion or politics. The dismissal of an employee because of their religion is problematical, however. In the case of *Merriman* v. *St James' Hospital* (Circuit Court, Clarke, J., 24 November 1986), the claimant, a hospital attendant, was dismissed because she refused to bring a crucifix and candle to a dying patient. When subsequently asked why by the nurse in charge, the claimant replied that she was a Christian and that it was not the Word of God to do so, and that she did not adore false gods. There were subsequently meetings and correspondence between the parties and finally she was asked to resume duty as long as she was prepared to bring a crucifix and candle to a patient's bedside if so instructed. After additional discussion, however, she was dismissed.

The judgment notes that it is the practice to bring a crucifix and candles to the bedside of a Catholic patient who is dying and to assist in various other religious rites and services which are made available for patients in the hospital. The attendant does not have to participate personally but only to assist. Clarke, J. ordered her re-engagement and that she did not have to participate in a religious rite or ceremony and that in her case the carrying of the crucifix and candle be dispensed with. She advised the Court that she was unwilling to attend patients at their religious services. In effect, this meant that her terms and conditions would be different from the other hospital attendants. She was awarded £800 compensation.

Civil or Criminal Proceedings

It would be deemed an unfair dismissal if an employee were dismissed because they might threaten or institute civil proceedings against the employer, or if the employee were likely to be a witness in such proceedings. Equally, in relation to criminal proceedings against the employer, if the employee were dismissed after making statements to the prosecuting authority it would be an unfair dismissal.

An example would be if an employee has been out ill for some considerable time because of a work accident and subsequently institutes proceedings against the employer. The employer may have decided that the employee is no longer capable of performing the job and dismiss the employee. If so, the employer can only dismiss by reason of absenteeism and not because the employee has proceeded to take action for damages.

Race, Colour or Sexual Orientation

An employee cannot be dismissed by reason of their race or colour. It should be noted that there may be some future developments on this point as was envisaged under the Equal Status Bill, 1991, namely that there can be no discrimination against persons on any grounds. The 1993 Act also provides that an employee cannot be dismissed because of their sexual orientation.

Age

The 1993 Act provides that an employee cannot be dismissed because of age. This in no way affects the provision that an employee must be aged between 16 years and normal retiring age or 66 years before they can fall within the scope of the Act. This amendment may have far-reaching effect, particularly in cases where employees maintain that the reason that they were selected for redundancy was because of their age.

Membership of the Travelling Community

The 1993 Act provides that an employee cannot be dismissed because they are a member of the travelling community.

Pregnancy and Maternity

An employee cannot be dismissed by reason of her pregnancy or related matters. Also, an employee cannot be dismissed for pursuing her entitlement to maternity leave under the Maternity Protection of Employees Acts, 1981 and 1991.

However, it may be a fair dismissal if (a) an employee is unable to do the work for which she was employed by reason of her pregnancy (or related matters) or (b) if there was no other suitable employment for her, or if she has been offered suitable alternative employment and refused.

Again, the burden of proof is on the employee to prove that she was dismissed by reason of her pregnancy. However, if she is incapable of performing her job the burden of proof is on the employer.

In the case of *Matthews* v. *Ophardt Products Ltd.* (UD 550/1983), the claimant was unable to do contractual overtime work because of her pregnancy. The claimant maintained that she was dismissed by reason of her pregnancy and claimed that there was only an occasional requirement for overtime. However, the Tribunal considered that she was not dismissed by reason of her pregnancy, but that because of her pregnancy she was unable to perform the work for which she was employed.

Another case highlights the issue of absenteeism during pregnancy. In *Hallissey* v. *Pretty Polly (Killarney) Ltd.* (UD 362/1984), the claimant was employed as a factory worker and out sick for a pregnancy-related illness. She submitted medical certificates which only stated that she was unfit for work. She was advised that her employment would be terminated if she did not return to work by a particular date. Her employment was terminated and during the course of the hearing the company advised the Tribunal that the company doctor had been kept informed of the claimant's progress — both verbally and by way of medical reports by her doctor. The Tribunal considered that the employer made all reasonable efforts to inform itself of the true state of the employee's health and that the decision to dismiss was reasonable in all the circumstances.

As stated above, an employee cannot be denied maternity rights. In the case of *Maxwell* v. *English Language Institute* ([1990] ELR 226), the claimant had been employed as a secretary for a short time, though there was a conflict of evidence as to whether she was employed on a probationary or on a permanent basis. Nonetheless, she submitted a maternity allowance claim form to her employer who failed to complete it. She subsequently advised her employer that she intended taking maternity leave and was dismissed. The employer maintained that her work was unsatisfactory but he had never disciplined her. It was considered that she was dismissed by reason of her pregnancy.

In the case of *Flynn* v. *Sister Mary Anna Power and the Sisters of the Holy Faith* ([1985] ILRM 336), the claimant considered that she was dismissed by reason of pregnancy. She was a secondary school teacher in a New Ross convent school living with a married man in the town and was pregnant by him. The school manager wrote to her (following a meeting some months earlier) requesting her resignation because of the children's parents complaining about her "lifestyle" and her "open rejection of the norms of behaviour and the ideals which our school exists to promote". Mr Justice Costello considered (in summary) that it was a fair dismissal and that her pregnancy was not the cause (since her work had deteriorated and there were also complaints about her living with a married man). Also, the claimant knew that there were certain obligations on teachers in religious schools even though there was no written statement to that effect in her contract of employment. Furthermore, an employee's conduct in sexual matters outside the place of employment may justify dismissal if it is capable of damaging the employer's business, and in this case her lifestyle might damage the school's efforts to foster certain norms of behaviour and religious tenets that the school was established to promote.

The issue of dismissal following on maternity leave was considered in Chapter 5 — Maternity Leave, as are future developments, with particular reference to the provision of "leave" during pregnancy if the employee is not able to perform her range of duties.

BURDEN OF PROOF

There is a presumption under the Act that all dismissals are deemed unfair, except (a) where dismissal is not in dispute, for example, where the claimant has resigned and is claiming constructive dismissal, and (b) where there are jurisdictional points at issue, for example, the employee's continuity of service or time limits. In cases where the employee proves that neither of the above applies, however, the burden of proof shifts on to the employer to prove that the dismissal was fair.

FAIR PROCEDURES

An employer must be reasonable in regard to all the circumstances, and thus the constitutional right to fair procedures must be applied.

In other words, the employee is entitled to be aware of all the evidence against them and to respond to such allegations.

The 1993 Act has attached even greater statutory importance to fair procedures as it provides that the adjudicating body may consider the "reasonableness . . . of the conduct of the employer (whether by act or omission) . . . in relation to the dismissal. . . ." Account will also be taken of any union/management agreement or custom and practice in the employment concerned, or to a Code of Practice relating to dismissals approved by the Minister for Enterprise and Employment. The net effect of these provisions is that the Tribunal (and other bodies) will be even more strict and there will be greater compensation or a higher likelihood of re-employment being awarded to an unfairly dismissed employee.

The Act does not state that a specific disciplinary procedure should be applied, but a standard procedure would be as follows:

(1) counselling

(2) verbal warning

(3) written warning

(4) final written warning

(5) suspension with/without pay

(6) dismissal.

The purpose of a disciplinary procedure is not to terminate an employee's employment but rather to assist the employee in their performance. Where there is a serious issue such as alleged theft, the employer should suspend the employee with pay, pending a full and thorough investigation. The employee should have the opportunity to be represented. An employer does not have to decide the guilt or innocence of an employee, but can make the decision to dismiss on the balance of probabilities that the person "committed an offence". In cases of poor performance, an employee should be brought through the whole disciplinary process making sure that the employee is given every opportunity to improve with adequate training.

It is also absolutely vital that an employee brought through the disciplinary process be clearly advised of the next stage in the process if there is no improvement. If a final written warning is given, an employee should be clearly told that if they do not improve within a certain period of time, they will be dismissed.

FAIR DISMISSAL

The Act provides a number of grounds which may constitute a fair dismissal. This section of the Act is important so it is quoted in full.

> 6(1) Subject to the provisions of this section, the dismissal of an employee shall be deemed for the purposes of this Act, to be an unfair dismissal unless, having regard to all the circumstances, there were substantial grounds justifying the dismissal. . . .

> 6(4) Without prejudice to the generality of subsection (1) of this section, the dismissal of an employee shall be deemed, for the purposes of this Act, not to be an unfair dismissal, if it results wholly or mainly from one or more of the following:

>> (a) the capability, competence or qualifications of the employee for performing work of the kind which he was employed by the employer to do,

>> (b) the conduct of the employee,

>> (c) the redundancy of the employee, and

>> (d) the employee being unable to work or continue to work in the position which he held without contravention (by him or by his employer) of a duty or restriction imposed by or under any statute or instrument made under statute. . . .

Incapability

Incapability was defined by the Employment Appeals Tribunal in the case of *Reardon* v. *St Vincent's Hospital* (UD 74/1979): "Incapability may be generally defined as long-term illness." Generally speaking, there is nothing prohibiting an employer dismissing an employee for long-term absenteeism when it can be established that there is no reasonable return date to work.

In the case of *Bolger* v. *Showerings (Ireland) Ltd.* [1990] ELR 184, Mr Justice Lardner set out the key requirements (in summary) that an employer will have to comply with in order to have a fair dismissal, namely:

(1) It was the ill-health which was the reason for his dismissal;

(2) That this was substantial reason;

(3) That the employee received fair notices that the question of his dismissal for incapacity was being considered; and

(4) That the employee was afforded the opportunity of being heard.

This case also established that where there is no dispute between the parties as to the incapacity of the employee, it is not necessary to await medical tests before the decision to dismiss. A note of caution must be added to this last statement as one obviously has to look at each case on its own merits. However, if the employee has been out from work for an unreasonable length of time and cannot give a return date, dismissal may be reasonable.

One myth that still prevails is that an employee who is out sick and has handed in medical certificates cannot be dismissed. This is a total fallacy. Equally, employers may well ask, after what period of absenteeism may the employee be dismissed? There is no answer to this either, but an employer must be reasonable and have carried out all necessary enquiries to see when the employee can return to work. If there is no reasonable return date and if the employee has been out for a lengthy period, then dismissal may be permissible. Extreme caution should be exercised at all times, however.

It is well established that for an employee who is no longer capable of performing their duties, there is no obligation on the employer to provide "light work" or alternative duties (*Gurr* v. *The Office of Public Works* [1990] ELR 42).

There are many other forms of absenteeism besides long-term, such as intermittent absenteeism with a variety of illnesses or a pattern of being absent on Fridays and Mondays or on a Tuesday after a long weekend. Employers do not have to tolerate this either, but again all fair procedures and warnings must be exhausted. For example, a pattern as discussed above may be as a result of alcoholism, and if so the employer should ensure that the employee is referred to necessary treatment centres to try and combat this illness. Still, if attendance does not improve an employer may terminate the employment following appropriate warning procedures.

Employers have lost many cases by not complying with reasonable procedures, for example, not asking the employee for a reasonable return date or not sending the employee to a company doctor in order to establish the true medical position and a prognosis for a return date to work.

If an employer has a sick pay scheme, an employee may not abuse it, for example, by working while on sick leave. Again, it is well established that this may be a fair ground for dismissal.

Competence

A person's lack of competence as a ground for dismissal may be extremely hard to prove, especially where one is dealing with employees whose duties are in "grey" areas, such as executive staff. Invariably, decisions on competence may be subjective rather than objective.

The case of *O'Donoghue* v. *Emerson Electric (Ireland) Ltd. t/a Thermodisc Ireland* (UD 177/1986) highlights the issue of competence. The claimant had been a managing director of the US subsidiary since 1984. His summary dismissal arose from the company's performance compared with projected targets supplied to the IDA. The claimant was not aware of these targets, though he was deemed responsible for not achieving them. His production goals were based on his own targets supplied to the US parent, which were exceeded. There was alleged poor performance in the 1986 financial year. However, the Tribunal considered that no reasonable decision to dismiss could be based on the information available before the expiry of the first quarter of the company's financial year. It was also considered that the employee had no clear warning of dissatisfaction or an opportunity to improve the performance of the company. The claimant was held to have been unfairly dismissed and was awarded compensation in the sum of £52,542. This award includes a deduction as the Tribunal considered that the claimant contributed 30 per cent to his dismissal because he had failed to resolve friction between two managers in the Irish operation. This shows that the Tribunal accepts that a manager must apply certain managerial skills.

This decision highlighted the requirement for fair procedures and warnings where one is dealing with alleged poor company performance, and in particular that an employee with responsibility for reaching certain targets must have full knowledge of such targets. This decision counteracts the view that one cannot use the same procedures when dealing with management.

The Tribunal observed that:

> we are satisfied that the respondent, far from giving the claimant any clear warning or proper opportunity to improve the performance at the Irish plant to the satisfaction of the American management did not express its dissatisfaction to him in clear terms. Isolated passing comments on some details cannot be construed as warnings, or indeed expressions of dissatisfac-

tion, especially against a background of sometimes fulsome praise.

In the case of *Richardson* v. *H. Williams & Co. Ltd.* (UD 17/1979), the claimant was dismissed because the company had been dissatisfied with his work performance over a period, in particular in relation to his authorising payment of accounts by cheque while not following the company procedure. He was also lacking in carrying out freshness checks (i.e. on perishable items). The Tribunal noted that the claimant was not given an opportunity to defend himself and the Tribunal applied the following principles:

(a) where an employee has been given a justified warning, that unless his work improved in a specific area, that his job would be in jeopardy, then it follows that such employee must be given

(i) a reasonable time within which to effect such improvement;

(ii) a reasonable work situation within which to concentrate on such defects;

(b) if an employee improves in the complained of area to the reasonable satisfaction of the employer, and such defect is not repeated, then such a warning cannot be solely relied on in relation to a dismissal for other reasons.

In the case of *O'Neill* v. *Bus Éireann* ([1990] ELR 135), Judge O'Malley in the Circuit Court stated that he was referred to the case of *Alidair Ltd.* v. *Taylor* ([1978] ICR 445), where Lord Denning, MR made a statement which is appropriate:

whenever a man is dismissed for incapacity or incompetence, it is sufficient that the employer honestly believes on reasonable grounds that the man is incapable or incompetent. It is not necessary for the employer to prove that he is in fact, incapable or incompetent.

Judge O'Malley considered that:

this is a very wide statement and I do not entirely agree with it; but it does lay down the grounds for a proper approach for a

Court which is considering the results of the deliberation of an Industrial Tribunal. It also indicates that it is irrelevant whether or not fair procedures were adopted in arriving at the decision that the party in question was incompetent.

The Employment Appeals Tribunal did look into whether there was a fair enquiry or not, and Judge O'Malley considered that it was more for the High Court to assess whether their decision was correct. Once a court is satisfied that there were grounds for the belief that an employee was incompetent, the procedures adopted in arriving at that belief are only relevant to justify that belief.

Qualifications

An employee may be fairly dismissed if he does not have the requisite qualifications for performing the work for which he was employed. This issue arises rarely because more than likely it would be a redundancy situation if an employer wanted to obtain a person with the necessary higher skills.

In *Ryder and Byrne* v. *Commissioners of Irish Lights* (High Court, Costello, J., 16 April 1980, unreported), the employer had a requirement for two of its staff to obtain higher technical qualifications within a reasonable time. They failed to comply with this requirement and it was considered a fair dismissal.

Conduct

An employee may be dismissed by reason of their conduct or "misconduct", though the term "misconduct" is not contained in the Act. Misconduct is a very broad term and may include the following:

- abuse of sick pay schemes
- clocking offences
- conflict of interest
- theft/irregularities
- refusal to obey reasonable instructions
- violence.

This is obviously not a comprehensive list but provides a good indication of what may be construed as misconduct.

In the case of *Dunne* v. *Harrington* (UD 166/1979), the Tribunal clearly set out its reasoning in cases of dishonesty, and this approach should be carried out by employers in all situations which may lead to a conduct dismissal:

1. We do not consider our function to be the establishment of guilt or innocence;

2. We do not seek to impose on an employer or employee a standard of behaviour so high as of itself to be unfair;

3. Faced with a problem requiring investigation, an employer may investigate it:

(a) personally in a fair and reasonable manner i.e. as fully as is reasonably possible, confronting the "suspected" employee with "evidence", checking on and giving fair value to the employee's explanations or comments and allowing the employee to be represented at all such meetings/confrontations if the employee requests it or a union/management agreement requires it and to produce "counter evidence" ... or

(b) to rely on the reports of others. If he does so without confronting the accused employee with the contents of same, without hearing, investigating and giving value to his replies, giving him reasonable opportunity to produce rebutting "evidence" and to be represented if the employee feels this to be desirable, then such employer breaches a fundamental rule of natural justice, viz that the other party (i.e. the employee in these circumstances) should be heard.

In short, an employer acting on the reports of third parties and not acquainting the employee of same does so at his peril if it results in the dismissal of that employee. We wish to make it clear that we are basing our comments on an internal inquiry of an industrial or business nature. . . .

4. Faced with the information amassed by a fair and reasonable investigation an employer should apply himself to it in a fair and reasonable way (as a prudent and concerned employer would) and reach his conclusion as to the appropriate disciplinary measure which should of course relate reasonably to the "offence"

Some areas of misconduct will now be considered:

Abuse of sick pay schemes. As stated above, it is established that an employee cannot abuse the sick pay scheme. A typical example would be an employee who maintains that they are sick and then works for somebody else. In the case of *Hardy* v. *Cadbury Ireland Ltd.* (UD 727/1983), the claimant was out sick yet was allegedly collecting clothes for friends and bringing them to the dry cleaners for a charge. The employee was dismissed for being in breach of the sick pay scheme and the Tribunal upheld the dismissal.

Clocking offences. An example of this would be clocking another employee's card to give the impression that the latter had worked overtime. This is clear misconduct and may be dismissible as it is a breach of the trust the employer had in the employee. Equally, the completion of overtime sheets when the overtime was not actually worked would be in breach of trust (*Grimes* v. *Otis Elevator Group Ireland* UD 292/1988).

Conflict of interest. An employee may not act in conflict of their employer's interests. An employee has a duty not to compete with their employer and not to divulge confidential information or trade secrets. In *Shortt* v. *Smurfit Corrugated Ireland Ltd.* (UD 540/1986), the claimant was employed as a specialist designer of rubber stereos which are used in the printing on cardboard boxes. It was established that he was providing a similar service to the company's competitors and the Tribunal upheld his dismissal. The Tribunal also took a dim view of a claimant who worked as a butcher in a co-op store and then established his own butcher's shop only yards away from his employer (*Whitty* v. *Waterford Co-Operative Ltd.*, UD 192/1986 and UD 764/1986 — there were procedural difficulties in this case hence two claims).

Theft/irregularities. Generally speaking, in a dismissal arising from an alleged theft, the value of the goods taken is immaterial because if the employer has reasonable belief that goods were taken at all, there is a clear breach of trust.

If there are criminal proceedings pending, an employer should nonetheless carry out a full investigation, and not await the outcome of those proceedings. An employer can terminate employment on the reasonable belief that an employee committed the offence and does not decide the guilt of the employee. Of course, if an employee is acquitted by the courts the employer may be in a difficult situation.

A recent case highlights these problems. In *Sheehan* v. *H. M. Keating & Son Ltd.* ([1993] ELR 12), the claimant was dismissed for allegedly stealing tyres which were the property of the company. It was submitted on behalf of the claimant that the dismissal had been delayed and the company stated that this was at the request of the Garda Síochána so that they could facilitate their investigation. In fact, the Garda investigation was not completed until November 1991, yet the employee was dismissed in July of that year and the company had completed its investigation the month before. The Tribunal considered that in June there were grounds to justify dismissal by reason of gross misconduct, but as fair procedures were not applied it was an unfair dismissal. However, since the claimant contributed 100 per cent to his dismissal he received a nil award.

In *Hestor* v. *Dunnes Stores Ltd.* ([1990] ELR 12), on the other hand, the employer applied fair procedures and it was shown that if an employee cannot offer a reasonable explanation there may be a justifiable dismissal. Employees in this company were entitled to purchase goods subject to certain procedures and supervision from management. The claimant took a packet of ham, as well as packets of chips and burger buns from stock. The chips and buns were paid for but the packet of ham was allegedly concealed under the claimant's arm. She was confronted by a security officer and presented the items that had been paid for, then the ham fell to the floor. The claimant was questioned and she gave no reasonable explanation other than that she forgot about the ham. The Tribunal considered that it was a fair dismissal and this was upheld by Clarke, J. in the Circuit Court where he considered the issue was not whether or not she stole the ham, but whether it was reasonable or not to dismiss her having regard to her conduct.

REDUNDANCY

The redundancy of an employee may be a good defence to an unfair dismissals claim. In order for an employee to bring a claim under the Unfair Dismissals Acts the employee must have one year's service. However, an employee who has been made redundant does not necessarily have to fall within the application of the Redundancy Payments Acts, 1967 to 1991. In other words, even though an employee has not been in receipt of statutory redundancy payment, that employee can still bring a claim for unfair dismissal on the basis that it was not a genuine redundancy, in other words, that the dismissal was for some other reason. The Unfair Dismissals Act does not state that it has to be a redundancy within the meaning of the Redundancy Payments Acts, though the definition of redundancy in those Acts would be applied (see Chapter 18 — Redundancy). Redundancy is defined in Section 7(2) of the Redundancy Payments Act, 1967 as amended by the Redundancy Payments Act, 1971 as:

> an employee who is dismissed shall be taken to be dismissed by reason of redundancy if the dismissal is attributable wholly or mainly to —
>
> (a) the fact that his employer has ceased, or intends to cease, to carry on the business for the purposes of which the employee was employed by him, or has ceased or intends to cease, to carry on that business in the place where the employee was so employed, or
>
> (b) the fact that the requirements of that business for employees to carry out work of a particular kind in the place where he was so employed have ceased or diminished or are expected to cease or diminish, or
>
> (c) the fact that his employer has decided to carry on the business with fewer or no employees, whether by requiring the work for which the employee had been employed (or had been doing before his dismissal to be done by other employees or otherwise, or
>
> (d) the fact that his employer has decided that the work for which the employee had been employed (or had been doing before his dismissal) should henceforward be done in a different manner for which the employee is not sufficiently qualified or trained, or
>
> (e) the fact that his employer has decided that the work for which the employee had been employed (or had been doing before his dismissal) should henceforward be done by a person who is also capable of doing other work for which the employee is not sufficiently qualified or trained.

In a number of cases the employee has successfully maintained that statutory redundancy as a reason for dismissal was a "sham" or a "cloak". One particular case, *Edwards* v. *Aerials and Electronics*

(Ireland) Ltd. (UD 236/1985), highlights this issue. This case shows
the problem of making an employee redundant within the context of
a reorganisation. The claimant was managing director of the Irish
subsidiary of a company based in Belfast. It was decided to cut the
overheads of the Dublin company, which was losing money, by re-
moving a tier of management and running the company from Belfast.
The claimant contended that he was not dismissed by reason of
redundancy but for some other reason, maintaining that there had
been a change in attitude towards him. He gave evidence that there
had been disagreements at board level and that more recently he was
not allowed to visit suppliers and that decisions were being made
about the company with which he as managing director did not agree.
    The Tribunal was of the view that:

> the claimant has raised major doubts as to whether the redun-
> dancy was genuine. We recognise that the function of a full time
> managing director no longer exists but we must direct our
> minds to the cause and effect relationship between redundancy
> and dismissal. The issue was whether he was dismissed because
> the employee had decided to reorganise the structure of the
> company, or whether a decision was taken to dismiss him for
> some other reason. In other words, was the reorganisation a
> cause or a consequence? On balance we are inclined to the latter
> view.

This decision demonstrates that if an employee is made redundant it must be based on genuine grounds for redundancy and not as
a "cloak" for some other reason. In other words, if a company wishes
to have a reorganisation it must show the requirements for same and
not use it as a vehicle for dismissal for any other reason, such as
incompetence.

UNFAIR SELECTION FOR REDUNDANCY

A person bringing a claim maintaining that it was not a genuine
redundancy may also claim that they were unfairly selected for
redundancy. The Act states as follows:

> [where] if an employee was dismissed due to redundancy but
> the circumstances constituting the redundancy applied equally
> to one or more other employees in similar employment with the
> same employer who have not been dismissed, and either

(a) the selection of that employee for dismissal resulted wholly or mainly from one or more of the matters specified in sub-section 2 [clarified below] of this section or another matter that would not be a ground justifying dismissal, or

(b) ho was selected for dismissal in contravention of a procedure (being a procedure that has been agreed upon by or on behalf of the employee and by the employee or a trade union, or an excepted body under the Trade Union Acts, 1941 to [1990], representing him or has been established by the custom and practice of the employment concerned) relating to redundancy and there were no special reasons justifying a departure from that procedure,

then the dismissal shall be deemed, for the purposes of this Act, to be an unfair dismissal.

This means that if an employee is selected for redundancy because of trade union membership or activities, religious or political opinions, involvement in civil or criminal proceedings against an employer, race or colour, pregnancy, or the denial of maternity rights, sexual orientation, age or membership of the travelling community, it will be an unfair selection. Such grounds for selection are rare and in most cases an employee may not have the necessary proof to substantiate the claim.

We will now look at the issue of the actual selection for redundancy. An employer must comply with the custom and practice or the procedure agreed in a union or management agreement unless there were special reasons to depart from it.

Again, the best way of considering this issue is to paraphrase the wording in the Act:

(1) The employee must have been dismissed because of redundancy;

(2) The circumstances constituting the redundancy must have applied equally to one or more other employees;

(3) Those other employees must have been employed in employment similar to that of the claimant and with the same employer;

(4) The selection of the dismissed employee must have resulted wholly or mainly from one or more of the grounds for unfair dismissal (see above);

(5) Alternatively, the employee must have been selected for dismissal in contravention of a procedure agreed upon by or on behalf of the employer and the employee or a trade union, or established by custom or practice in the employment concerned relating to redundancy and where there were no special reasons to depart from the said procedure.

An employer will have to show that a redundancy situation existed at the date of dismissal. Therefore, if an employee is made redundant as a result of a downturn in business, management accounts will be needed for the period concerned to prove that fact, for example, balance sheets, sales reports and so forth.

The employer should also have full details of all other relevant employees and their job duties. Also, there should be copies of the employee's RP1, RP2 and any other relevant documentation. There should also be evidence of the actual selection process, for example, copies of procedural agreements and if there are none there should be details of the normal custom and practice in the particular employment. In other words, the employer should have looked at previous redundancies within the particular employment.

As in all dismissal cases, each case stands on its own merits but it is worthwhile illustrating a few examples. A good example of the "last in — first out" approach to redundancy selection is seen in the case of *O'Connor* v. *S.S.I.H (Ireland) Ltd.* (UD 50/1983). Here the Employment Appeals Tribunal held that in the absence of any union/management agreement the custom and practice of "last in — first out" should be adhered to. In this particular case, the company contended that the claimant who had six years' service was made redundant. The claimant stated that she had been employed as a clerk typist and had been promoted to receptionist and then promoted to stock control. There were three other women employed. Another employee with two years' service was employed as a receptionist, did stock control, typing, book-keeping and answered the telephone. The book-keeper had 12 years' service. The company stated that there was a redundancy situation and that there was no custom and practice of "last in — first out". The decision to keep the employee with two years' service was because she was particularly good. However, the company agreed that the claimant could have done her work and therefore was unfairly selected for redundancy and was awarded compensation.

On the other hand, it may be permissible to "keep the best". In

Cassidy v. *Smith and Nephew Southalls (Ireland) Ltd.* (UD 35/1983), the Tribunal considered the company was entitled to select the claimant for redundancy rather than a particularly good employee.

The union and management agreement may contain various criteria for choosing somebody for redundancy, but the key issue is that there must be objective criteria, for example, the employee's level of attendance, competence, skills and flexibility.

However, in the case of *Kirwan* v. *Iona National Airways Ltd.* (UD 156/1987) a pilot who was selected for redundancy on the basis of his productivity was considered to have been unfairly selected as he was never informed that his low productivity was imperilling his position with the company.

REDRESS

An employee who is unfairly dismissed is entitled to redress consisting of whatever the rights commissioner, the Employment Appeals Tribunal or the Circuit Court considers appropriate "having regard to all the circumstances". Although not stated in the Act, in practice this extends to the High Court which hears appeals from the Circuit Court. Such appeals are full hearings of the case (not just appeals on a point of law). However, it should be noted that in the *State (Irish Pharmaceutical Union)* v. *Employment Appeals Tribunal* ([1987] ILRM 36), it was considered that the views of both sides should be considered before redress is awarded. Such redress may be reinstatement, re-engagement, or compensation. The 1993 Act provides that where redress is being awarded, the rights commissioner, the Tribunal or the Circuit Court has to give reasons in the written order as to why either of the other two forms of redress was not awarded to the employee, for example, if compensation is being awarded, as to why reinstatement or re-engagement has not been awarded.

Re-employment

Over the last few years, and in particular from 1984, it has become apparent that in a high number of cases the remedy of re-employment has been awarded, the reasoning being that more than likely the employee will not yet have found alternative employment. Between 1989 and 1991, re-employment was awarded in approximately 30 per cent of cases where an employee was considered to have been unfairly dismissed. Undoubtedly, this is due to current economic circumstances for the most part. Further, there has been consistent criticism over the last number years that the Tribunal is awarding low amounts of compensation. Taking these two points into account the Tribunal has become more likely to award re-employment. However, this remedy is more often applied to unskilled, semi-skilled or skilled workers in large employments rather than members of management or those in small employments.

Reinstatement

Section 7(1)(a) of the Act states:

> Reinstatement by the employer of the employee in the position which he held immediately before his dismissal on the terms and conditions on which he was employed immediately before his dismissal together with a term that the reinstatement shall be deemed to have commenced on the day of the dismissal.

In effect, reinstatement means that an employee who has been unfairly dismissed is awarded their old position back immediately as if they were never dismissed. It is usually awarded where there is no blame attributable to the employee. This means that loss of earnings (net pay, i.e. gross weekly pay less income tax, PRSI and social welfare) has also to be paid to the former employee. This would also include loss of pension contributions, if appropriate. Thus, the employee should be at no loss whatsoever and their continuity of employment is retained. The application of reinstatement has been further extended by the 1993 Act and provides that if an employee is reinstated and if the terms and conditions are more favourable, then the new terms and conditions apply. The purpose of this extension would be so that the reinstated employee may receive the benefits of any favourable changes in terms and conditions of employment which applied to other employees.

In *McCrum* v. *Initial Services Ireland Ltd.* (UD 693/1984), the company contended that the claimant's record of absence and late attendance were appalling. The claimant was given several warnings culminating in a week's suspension. In the week prior to dismissal she was absent for a number of days and was also late on two occasions. Finally, she was absent on a particular day and the company was informed by telephone that she was suffering from a toothache and would be consulting her dentist. The following day the claimant handed in her certificate from her dentist covering her absence for 10 days, that is, from the date she telephoned in. When she met the plant manager she was informed that the company had already decided to dismiss her in view of her attendance records. The claimant was awarded reinstatement based on the fact that the company did not consider her excuse reasonable and had, in fact, already decided to dismiss her prior to such explanation. Furthermore, as the facts were not in dispute, the Tribunal decided that the claimant need not give evidence as the employer had not discharged the burden of proof.

In *Reilly* v. *Smurfit Cartons Ltd.* (UD 722/1983), the claimant was dismissed for being absent from work without permission and for falsification of clock cards. Two employees were involved in this incident; one was suspended for eight weeks, without pay, while the claimant was dismissed. It was contended that the claimant had a previous warning but this was not available in evidence before the Tribunal.

The Tribunal considered that the claimant's conduct was of a serious nature but the fact that he was dismissed while the other employee, who was guilty of the same conduct, was only suspended was not satisfactory to the mind of the Tribunal. Accordingly, the claimant was also awarded reinstatement but was given the same period of suspension without pay as the other employee, that is, eight weeks. Thus, he was not to receive the full financial loss.

In considering these cases, both employees were unskilled workers who did not have alternative employment prior to the Tribunal hearing. Further, the Tribunal considered there was not a fair application of reasonableness by the employer and, accordingly, the employees were awarded reinstatement.

Re-engagement

Section 7(1)(b) states:

> Re-engagement by the employer of the employee either in the position which he held immediately before his dismissal or in a different position which would be reasonably suitable for him on such terms and conditions as are reasonable having regard to all the circumstances.

In effect, this means that an employee either gets their old position back or else a different position which would be reasonably suitable for them on such terms and conditions as are reasonable.

The remedy of re-engagement is less clear than reinstatement and therefore the Tribunal in most cases explains what it means by it. The normal situation is that re-engagement of an employee does not break their continuity of service. However, in *Scott* v. *Yeates & Sons Limited, Opticians* ([1992] ELR 83) the Tribunal clearly stated that there was a break in continuity. An employee who is re-engaged is not entitled to any loss of monies between the date of dismissal and the date of re-engagement. This remedy, which is applied more frequently than reinstatement, is usually awarded where the employee has contributed somewhat to their own dismissal. From the employee's point of view, it is obviously less satisfactory and, of course, it is less costly to the employer than having to reinstate the employee.

This re-employment remedy has been consistently applied by the Tribunal in relation to dismissals where an employer has been in breach of procedure or natural justice in a "conduct" dismissal. It can also be applied in absenteeism dismissals where there is a breach of fairness, for example, not getting the up-to-date medical position of the employee before making a decision to dismiss. Again, the remedy is more usually applied in large employments.

Examples of where re-engagement was awarded, and the circumstances of such an award, will now be considered.

Procedures. In *Bolger* v. *Dublin Sport Hotel Ltd.* (UD 45/1985), the claimant was dismissed from his position of assistant head waiter because he failed to report to work and was, in fact, working for another employer on that particular day. The Tribunal stated that in this case the company should have considered alternative options, namely, a period of suspension without pay and/or a final written warning. Though the Tribunal did note that the claimant's conduct was serious, it determined that the claimant be re-engaged.

This remedy may also be used where it is clear that the employee has committed serious misconduct yet the employer failed to use proper procedures to investigate the issue. The employer should consider the range of responses to such conduct, for example, suspension without pay/final written warning. The purpose of applying this remedy in such situations is to hold the status quo; in other words, the employee is re-employed and, depending upon the circumstances, fair procedures are applied to a further investigation and the employee could then be dismissed for a second time (*Whitty* v. *Waterford*

Co-Operative Society Ltd. — UD 192/1986 and UD 764/1986).

Absenteeism. This remedy has been applied in a number of absenteeism cases. Indeed, the use of the re-engagement remedy is quite a normal approach to find an equitable solution. More than likely, the reason the Tribunal awards re-engagement to an employee who has been dismissed because of long term absence is that the employee would not be entitled to compensation since they may have been unavailable for work following on the dismissal and for the foreseeable future. Furthermore, if there was not sufficient up-to-date medical information at the date of dismissal, the employer may now have an opportunity of obtaining such information and, equally, the employee has a further chance of becoming medically fit in the intervening period.

In *McLoughlin* v. *Celmac (I) Ltd.* (UD 799/1984), the claimant was dismissed because of illness-related absenteeism. The Tribunal noted that the company made the decision to dismiss without having up-to-date medical opinion with regard to his future availability for work. The Tribunal considered the claimant should have been medically examined and there is an onus on an employer to get up-to-date medical evidence prior to making the decision to dismiss. In this case the claimant was awarded re-engagement and he was to receive no monies from the date of dismissal to the date of re-engagement.

In *Walsh* v. *A. Guinness Son & Co. (Dublin) Ltd.* (UD 871/1985), the claimant, a storeman, had a very unsatisfactory attendance record and could give no firm indication as to when he would be fit for work. A decision was made to dismiss the claimant and subsequently a meeting was held with the union at which the claimant said he had been informed by his doctor that he would be fully fit to resume work. The company decided that the dismissal should stand. However, the Tribunal took the view that, in or about the time of the dismissal, there was a clear indication that the claimant would be fully fit within a short period. The Tribunal further considered that it was unreasonable to terminate his employment at that time in the light of the information then available. On reading the determination, it would appear that no up-to-date medical evidence was sought by the company on the claimant's medical condition. Accordingly, the Tribunal considered that re-engagement was the most appropriate remedy.

In some cases where absenteeism has been the reason for dismissal, the Tribunal has taken a different approach to re-engagement. In *McGrane* v. *Mater Private Nursing Home* (UD 369/1985), for example, the claimant was also dismissed by reason of absenteeism. Noting that there was no definite pressure placed on the nursing home to replace the claimant, the Tribunal considered that she was unfairly dismissed. The Tribunal ordered re-engagement from such date as the claimant was certified fit to resume work, provided that she be so certified not later than 31 December 1985 (the determination was dated 9 October 1985). However, in the event of the claimant not being so certified within that period, the determination fails. This means that re-engagement was awarded but the claimant must be fit to resume work by a particular date to have any entitlement to return.

In *Heneghan* v. *El Company Ltd.* (UD 253/1985), the Tribunal took the view that the claimant should be re-engaged. Part of the reasoning in this case was that the claimant — a machine operator — was not a key employee and that in a company which employed about 400 people it was not necessary or reasonable to terminate her employment. The claimant submitted to an examination by the company doctor but there was a conflict of evidence between her own and the company doctor (the company/union agreement provided for steps to be taken in these circumstances — presumably an independent medical examination). Shortly after her employment was terminated, she claimed she was fit to resume work.

COMPENSATION

From a review of the Annual Reports of the Employment Appeals Tribunal it appears that compensation amounts awarded under the Act are relatively low. For example, in 1991 the average compensation figure was £2,660 and in 1985 the average figure was £2,460. It should be borne in mind that each case rests on its own merits and that compensation is based on the employee's salary and the employee's "loss". So if an employee has been unfairly dismissed and obtains a job on the same rate of pay soon after their dismissal, their "loss" may be relatively low. Under the 1977 Act, the Tribunal (and the other adjudicating bodies) had to deduct social welfare receipts, earnings and tax rebates from the employee's net wage loss. The 1993 Act has remedied this situation and provides that social welfare receipts and tax rebates shall no longer be deducted from an employee's loss. Accordingly, in the future the compensation awards may be higher.

Section 7 (1)(c) of the Act defines compensation as:

> payment by the employer to the employee of such compensation (not exceeding in amount 104 weeks remuneration in respect of the employment from which he was dismissed calculated in accordance with regulations . . .) in respect of any financial loss incurred by him and attributable to the dismissal as is just and equitable having regard to all the circumstances.

The maximum an unfairly dismissed employee may be awarded is 104 weeks' gross remuneration. Remuneration includes "allowances in the nature of pay and benefits in lieu of or in addition to pay". There are specific regulations to work out weekly wage and overtime, commissions etc. There are also specific provisions in the Act for the calculation of loss.

When an award of compensation is being made, account must be taken of the extent to which the financial loss was attributable to an act, omission or conduct on the part of the employer. The 1993 Act has extended this to include the extent to which the employer applied fair procedures in the union/management agreement or custom and practice in the employment concerned (or the provisions of any future Code of Practice on dismissals) and if there was a failure by the employer to set out the grounds for dismissal if requested by the employee. The effect of these provisions is that if an employer breaches fair procedures there will more than likely be a higher award for the unfairly dismissed employee.

Loss

"Financial loss", in relation to the dismissal of an employee includes

> any actual loss and any estimated prospective loss of income attributable to the dismissal and the value of any loss or diminution, attributable to the dismissal, of the rights of the employee under the Redundancy Payments Acts, 1967 to [1991], or in relation to superannuation.

Financial loss may be considered under the following headings:

(1) Actual loss. This is the employee's loss from date of dismissal to the date of the Tribunal hearing, that is, gross weekly pay less income tax, PRSI, income tax rebate received, unemployment benefit/assistance.

(2) Future loss. This is loss attributable to future loss of earnings. In considering such loss, the Tribunal has to take into account factors such as the employee's future employment prospects, skill and age.

Note: All awards for compensation arising from dismissals as and from 1 October 1993 will not have social welfare receipts and tax rebates deducted.

(3) Loss of rights under protective legislation and superannuation. The employee, particularly one with long service, is awarded monies for the loss of protection under the Redundancy Payments Acts, 1967 to 1991, Unfair Dismissals Acts, 1977 to 1993 and the Minimum Notice and Terms of Employment Acts, 1973 to 1991. Such monies are frequently low but the dismissed employee will have to build up service in any new employment in order to fall within the scope of these Acts once again. For example, should a redundancy situation arise, the loss may be considerable as the employee may be the "last-in" in a new employment, therefore, the "last in — first out" principle would more than likely militate against that employee.

Although not specifically mentioned in the Act, the Tribunal has awarded nominal compensation for loss of statutory rights under the unfair dismissals and minimum notice legislation. Pension loss may be the main contributor towards high awards as the loss of pension rights is an extremely important factor in the assessment of compensation for unfair dismissal. The assessment of the loss is very difficult. The return of the employee's own contributions (less tax plus interest) is not sufficient to compensate for the loss of future pension rights. This has now changed because an employee is entitled to a transfer value of the pension benefits or deferred pension built up from 1 January 1991. Thus, they may not lose out on past benefits but would still lose out on future benefits. One must also consider that it may take the employee approximately two years to belong to the pension scheme operated by their employer, or indeed the new employer may not operate a pension scheme (there is no requirement on an employer to provide one). A further basis for compensation would be if the previous employer operated a non-contributory pension scheme and the new employment operates a contributory scheme. Therefore, the additional cost of the new scheme would have to be considered.

It might be noted that there are very few cases where pension loss was awarded.

Maximum Award

An unfairly dismissed employee may be awarded a maximum of 104 weeks' gross remuneration. However, loss is actually computed on a net basis. A clear example of how the maximum may be awarded is as follows using the main headings in *Bunyan* v. *United Dominions Trust (Ireland) Ltd.* (UD 66/1980):

Calculation of annual remuneration:

		£
1.	Salary	15,826
2.	Annual bonus	500
3.	Company contribution to pension scheme	3,000
4.	Private use of company car	2,000
5.	Value of lunches and subscriptions	200
6.	Employer's PRSI	701
	Total Remuneration	22,227

In this case a pension was part of the employee's remuneration. Calculation of the employee's loss and pension loss was as follows:

	£
Pension loss	44,800
Actual loss, i.e. net remuneration less social welfare*	19,558
Future loss* (arising from dismissal measured over 5 years x £8,000)	40,000
Diminution of rights under protective legislation	160
Total Actual Loss	104,518
Claimant's contribution to the dismissal:	
Less 45%	47,033
Net Loss	57,485
Statutory Maximum (2 x £22,227)	44,454
Total Compensatory Award	44,454

[Note that such deductions will not be made in the future]

The key point is that the deduction for contribution to the dismissal is taken from the total loss rather than from the maximum award.

A similar calculation was also used in *Moriarty* v. *F.W. Woolworth plc* (UD 672/1984) where the claimant, dismissed for alleged irregularities, was awarded the maximum. The reason he was awarded the maximum (£34,840) was that the Tribunal considered he would not find suitable alternative work between then and retirement age.

The maximum was also awarded in the case of *Maughan* v. *Janssen Pharmaceuticals BV* (UD 1127/1984) where the Tribunal considered in detail its reasoning for such award. The claimant, an administration manager with the company, was dismissed for alleged non-performance following the installation of a computer. In such cases the Tribunal must consider the claimant's age, skills, length of service and the general employment market and likely rates of pay should she find alternative employment. It considered that she would be unlikely to get as good a job again and that, as a career woman, she would likely seek and be available for employment until normal retirement age. She was awarded £38,722.

Deduction of Social Welfare

The deduction of such monies and tax rebates will not apply to any dismissal where compensation is awarded arising from a dismissal which takes place on or after 1 October 1993. The Tribunal has generally adopted the practice of deducting unemployment benefit or unemployment assistance from the net weekly pay. However, the first Tribunal award which failed to deduct social welfare receipts from the loss was *Keenan* v. *Clarke Oil Products Ltd.* (UD 46/1987). The practice of the Tribunal before that date was to deduct social welfare from compensation, and in some cases if the social welfare deduction exceeded loss, the employee received a nil award.

Such approach by the Tribunal was controversial and the Tribunal has stated in only a small number of cases that it was not deducting social welfare receipts. However, in many cases the Tribunal has only shown the amount awarded, with no clarification as to whether social welfare was deducted or not.

Employee Contribution to Dismissal

Section 7 of the Act refers to "compensation in respect of any financial loss incurred by him and attributable to the dismissal as is just and equitable having regard to all the circumstances". The Tribunal thus has discretion in its award of compensation, for example, it can deduct a percentage contribution if the employee has failed to mitigate their loss or if the employee has contributed to their dismissal.

Section 7 (2) provides:

> Without prejudice to the generality of subsection (1) of this section, in determining the amount of compensation payable under that subsection referred shall be had to . . .
>
> (b) the extent (if any) to which the said financial loss was attributable to an action, omission or conduct by or on behalf of the employee,
>
> (c) the measures (if any) adopted by the employee or, as the case may be, his failure to adopt measures, to mitigate the loss aforesaid . . .

and

> (f) the extent (if any) to which the conduct of the employee (whether by act or omission) contributed to the dismissal. [(f) from 1993 Act].

In *Shiels* v. *Williams Transport Group (Ireland) Ltd.* (UD 191/1984) the claimant, an export manager, was dismissed for allegedly having drugs on his employer's premises. The claimant admitted having such illegal drugs and admitted using them at work. The company procedures were faulty, however, as he was not interviewed by management. The Tribunal considered he was unfairly dismissed but he contributed to his dismissal by 100 per cent. No redress was awarded.

This case shows that it is virtually impossible for an employer to succeed in a case where there is a breach of fair procedure. The Tribunal repeated this approach in many other cases and in *Sheehan* v. *H.M. Keating & Sons Ltd.* ([1993] ELR 12) where the claimant had been convicted of theft of company property after his dismissal. Prior to the dismissal, the Tribunal considered that fair procedures were not applied, but since he contributed 100 per cent to his dismissal, he received a nil award. However, the Tribunal awarded minimum notice even though he was dismissed for alleged misconduct.

However, in *O'Loughlin* v. *Climatic Building Systems Ltd.* (UD

600/1984), the general manager was dismissed for allegedly acting in conflict with the interest of his employer. No proper investigatory procedures — which would have taken two months — were applied by the employer. The claimant was awarded only two months' net pay because if the company had carried out a proper investigation there may have been reasonable grounds for dismissal.

Mitigation of Loss

If an employee fails to mitigate their loss — for example, if an employee fails to look for another job — the Tribunal may take that into account and deduct a small percentage from the total award. Also, an employee who fails to register and collect unemployment benefit or assistance for a period of time after their dismissal cannot claim the full loss for that period. In other words, the Tribunal will only give that employee loss less the social welfare to which they would have been entitled (see non-deduction of social welfare above).

Basic Award

The 1993 Act provides that if an employee has been unfairly dismissed but incurs no loss, then a basic award may be given. An example would be where an employee finds a similar job immediately after their dismissal and thereby incurs no loss. There would be provision for a basic award of up to four weeks' remuneration in such situations.

Reduction in Award — Redundancy

Frequently a compensation award may be reduced because the employee would have been dismissed in any event by reason of redundancy. Such a factor was taken into account by the EAT in *Ryan* v. *Noel & Francis O'Kelly t/a O'Kelly Bros.* (UD 1030/1983). The Tribunal found the claimant, a contracts manager/surveyor, to have been unfairly dismissed. He was awarded compensation from the date of dismissal to the date when he would have been made redundant in any event.

The ex-gratia aspect of redundancy payment was considered in *O'Connor* v. *Premier Dairies Ltd.* (UD 614/1984). Here, the claimant was dismissed by reason of redundancy, but the company broke an agreement with him to keep him on for temporary work. If he had been employed for one extra week, he would have been entitled to statutory redundancy pay and an ex-gratia payment. The loss attributable to his unfair dismissal was one week's pay plus the ex-gratia lump sum.

Taxation

The normal taxation rules on termination payments apply for Tribunal awards under the Unfair Dismissals Acts, 1977 to 1993 and the Minimum Notice and Terms of Employment Acts, 1973 to 1991 (see Chapter 20 — Taxation of Termination Payments).

Costs

In the EAT case of *Conway* v. *Westair Aviation Ltd.* (UD 652/1983), the Tribunal awarded witness costs to the claimant as it considered that the company acted "frivolously or vexatiously". Such ruling was further to paragraph 19 (2) of the Redundancy (Redundancy Appeals Tribunal) Regulations 1968, (S.I. No. 24 of 1968) incorporated into the Unfair Dismissal (Claims and Appeals) Regulations, 1977. Such costs may only be for travelling expenses or any other costs associated with the hearing. Legal costs are not included.

Procedures

The procedures applicable to bringing a case under the Unfair Dismissals Acts, 1977 to 1993 are considered in section 4.

GENERAL REFERENCES

Department of Industrial Relations, UCD, *Industrial Relations in Ireland: Contemporary Issues and Development*, Murphy, T., "The Impact of the Unfair Dismissals Act, 1977, on Workplace Industrial Relations", December, 1989.

Employment Appeals Tribunal, *Annual Reports*, Stationery Office, Dublin.

Kerr, T. and Madden, D., *Unfair Dismissal Cases and Commentary*, Federation of Irish Employers, 1990.

Meenan, F., *A Survey of Unfair Dismissals Cases, 1977–1984*, Supplement to FUE Bulletin, June, 1985.

Murphy, T., "Restoring Management Prerogative; the Unfair Dismissals Act in Practice", *Journal of Irish Business and Administrative Research*, Vol. 6, No. 1, April, 1984 and reply Meenan, F., "Restoring Management Prerogative", *IBAR*, Vol. 6, No. 2, October, 1984.

Redmond, M., *Dismissal Law in the Republic of Ireland*, Incorporated Law Society of Ireland, 1982.

CHAPTER EIGHTEEN

Redundancy

Statutory redundancy payments under the Redundancy Payments Acts, 1967 to 1991 are meant to compensate for the loss of security, seniority and other benefits which have built up in employment, an employee whose position has become redundant. The statutory payment is relatively low, especially as it is calculated on an earnings ceiling of £250 per week (or £13,000 per year). Therefore, many employees negotiate a severance payment that is higher than the statutory award, usually based on an employee's length of service.

The principal Redundancy Payments Act is the 1967 Act which was amended by the 1971, 1973 and 1979 Acts. The Acts were also amended by the Protection of Employees (Employers' Insolvency) Act, 1984 and the Worker Protection (Regular Part-Time Employees) Act, 1991. The Redundancy Payments Acts are complicated and the purpose of this chapter is to look at their key provisions.

If an employer is making a number of employees redundant, the Protection of Employment Act, 1977 may apply. This Act provides for consultation between the parties beforehand and that certain notice must be given to the Minister for Enterprise and Employment (see Chapter 19 — Collective Redundancies).

DEFINITIONS OF STATUTORY REDUNDANCY

Redundancy is defined as meaning one of the grounds of statutory redundancy in Section 7(2) of the Redundancy Payments Act, 1967 (as amended) of the Redundancy Payments Act, 1971.

> ... an employee who is dismissed shall be taken to be dismissed by reason of redundancy if the dismissal is attributable wholly or mainly to:
>
> (a) the fact that his employer has ceased, or intends to cease, to carry on the business for the purposes of which the employee was employed by him, or has ceased or intends to

cease, to carry on that business in the place where the employee was so employed, or

(b) the fact that the requirements of that business for employees to carry out work of a particular kind in the place where he was so employed have ceased or diminished or are expected to cease or diminish, or

(c) the fact that his employer has decided to carry on the business with fewer or no employees, whether by requiring the work for which the employee had been employed (or had been doing before his dismissal) — to be done by other employees or otherwise, or

(d) the fact that his employer has decided that the work for which the employee has been employed (or had been doing before his dismissal) — should henceforward be done in a different manner for which the employee is not sufficiently qualified or trained, or

(e) the fact that his employer has decided that the work for which the employee had been employed (or had been doing before his dismissal) should henceforward be done by a person who is also capable of doing other work for which the employee is not sufficiently qualified or trained.

A redundancy situation must arise at the date of dismissal. If it does not, a redundant employee may successfully bring a claim for unfair dismissal (e.g. *Glynn* v. *Pepe (Irl) Ltd.* [1993] ELR 39).

APPLICATION OF ACT

There are certain provisions which an employee must fulfil before being entitled to a statutory redundancy payment:

(1) The employee must work or have worked under a contract of service or apprenticeship; however the Acts do not apply to an apprentice who is being made redundant within one month of the completion of apprenticeship. The Acts also apply to a person who had worked under a fixed-term contract and the contract has expired, provided that there is a redundancy situation.

(2) The employee was in employment which was insurable for all Social Welfare Benefits, and since 6 April 1991, the employee must have earned at least £25 per week.

(3) The employee must be aged between 16 and 66 years.

(4) The employee must normally have been expected to work at least eight hours per week (this includes regular part-time employees).

(5) The employee must have been continuously employed for 104 weeks between the ages of 16 and 66 years. This does not necessarily mean that an employee actually has to work the 104 weeks.

(6) The employee must have been dismissed within the statutory definition of dismissal.

CONTINUITY OF SERVICE

The Acts have complicated rules which establish whether an employee has continuity of service and how to compute reckonable service in order to calculate redundancy payments. Nonetheless, there is a presumption in the Acts that all service is continuous unless proven otherwise, for example, if the employee had resigned or had previously received a redundancy payment from the same employer. This means that the burden of proof is on the employer to prove that service was broken. The Act states that "a person's employment during any period shall, unless the contrary is proved, be presumed to have been continuous".

The Tribunal is very reluctant to determine that there is a break in continuity of service. The continuity rules are difficult but they may be summarised as follows, noting the overriding provision in paragraph 4 of the Second Schedule to the Act: "For the purposes of this Schedule employment shall be taken to be continuous unless terminated by dismissal or by the employee's voluntarily leaving the employment".

Continuity is not broken by (a) sickness or injury of less than 78 weeks, or (b) lay-off, holidays, or authorised leave of less than 26 weeks

In *Irish Shipping* v. *Adams and Ors.* ((1987) 6 JISLL 186), the High Court (on appeal from the EAT) considered continuity of employment in respect of seamen with periods of service at sea followed by periods when they were not actually working. The facts were that at the end of a tour of duty at sea it was understood that the seamen would return to service again with Irish Shipping only, as soon as a suitable vacancy arose. It was common to spend six months at sea and four months on shore. The first few weeks on shore were paid leave (holidays). Earlier, the Employment Appeals Tribunal relied on the statutory presumption that there was continuity of employment and the various interruptions in service did not break continuity. It was concluded that the periods spent on shore comprised holidays and the balance being lay-off or agreed absence with the employer, presuming the employee sought further service. Thus there was continuity of service and an entitlement to statutory redundancy.

As stated above, the Tribunal is reluctant to consider that there was a break in an employee's continuity of service. There have been enormous difficulties in understanding the true meaning of these rules, in particular. They may be best highlighted by the claims brought under the Redundancy Payments Acts by former employees of Gateaux who were terminated as a result of the closedown of the company in autumn 1990. In this case, there was a large number of employees with "casual" service who were on a recall list. They only worked for varying parts of the year depending on their seniority on the list. Their employment usually came to an end before Christmas and they were given notice of termination. They were given a new contract for every period that they worked. The Tribunal relied on the presumption that service was continuous. In their decision the Tribunal did not refer to the stipulation that a break of over 26 weeks lay-off meant that continuity would be broken. The Tribunal instead appears to have relied on Rule 4 referred to previously — that "employment shall be taken to be continuous unless terminated by dismissal or by the employee's voluntarily leaving the employment".

Thus Rule 4 was overriding and there was never any termination by either employer or employee and continuity was not broken (*Farrell* v. *Gateaux Ltd.* 547/1990).

Continuity is also not broken by:

(1) Service in the Reserve Defence Force

(2) Absence from work because of a lock-out by the employer or for taking part in a strike

(3) Transfer of a business

(4) Maternity leave, additional maternity leave or time off under the Maternity Protection of Employees Acts, 1981 and 1991

(5) Reinstatement, and generally re-engagement, under the Unfair Dismissals Acts, 1977 to 1993

(6) Delayed receipt of the full statutory minimum notice

(7) Dismissal due to redundancy before reaching 104 weeks' continuous service and if there is a resumption of work within 26 weeks of the original termination.

RECKONABLE SERVICE

The rules for reckonable service are used actually to compute the period of service, which is then used to reach the statutory redundancy entitlement. The following periods of service are excluded:

(1) Lay-off

(2) Absence from work due to a strike in the employer's business

(3) Absence from work due to strike or lockout in a business or industry other than that in which the employee is employed since 1 January 1968

(4) Authorised absence in excess of 13 weeks in a 52 week period

(5) Absence due to illness in excess of 26 weeks

(6) Absence in excess of 52 weeks due to occupational injury.

NO DISMISSAL

There are certain circumstances where there is not a dismissal and thus no entitlement to a redundancy payment within the meaning of the Acts:

> if the employee's contract is renewed or if the employee is re-engaged under a new contract by the same employer and the new arrangement is to take effect immediately (i.e. the old contract is finished on a Friday and the next contract commences on the Monday); or

> the renewal or re-engagement follows an offer in writing made by the employer before the ending of the current contract. The new contract must take effect immediately or not later than 4 weeks from the end of the previous contract.

Also, if there is a re-engagement by a different employer and the employment commences immediately upon the agreement of the parties confirming the terms and conditions of employment (with a written statement that service is continuous), then there is no entitlement to redundancy as there is no dismissal.

An employee who unreasonably refuses an offer of re-employment may not be entitled to a redundancy payment. If the employee was offered re-employment on different terms and conditions within two weeks after the service of the Redundancy Notice (to take effect within four weeks), and if the employee unreasonably refuses the offer, then there is no entitlement to redundancy. An example of "different terms and conditions" would be a change in location. If the employee claims redundancy then, the employee's individual circumstances are taken into account as regards the physical practicalities of going to work in the new location; for example, if the employee had a car it may be considered that it was an unreasonable refusal.

REDUNDANCY DUE TO LAY-OFF OR SHORT-TIME

Lay-off is defined in the Acts as where an employee's employment ceases because the employer is not able to provide the employee with work and

> it is reasonable in the circumstances for the employer to believe that the cessation of employment will not be permanent and . . . the employer gives such notice to the employee prior to the cessation.

There is no specific period of notice laid down in the Act.

Short-time arises where there is a decrease in the employee's work so that the employee's pay is less than 50 per cent of their normal weekly remuneration. If an employee has been laid off or kept on short-time for four or more consecutive weeks, or for a series of six or more weeks (of which not more than three were consecutive) within a period of 13 weeks, then the employee may be entitled to a redundancy payment. The employee must give the employer notice of intention to claim redundancy payment (see the RP9 form on pages 265-66) after the expiry of either period, or not later than four weeks after the end of the lay-off or short-time.

Alternatively, the employee may give notice in writing to the employer (i.e. whatever notice is required under the contract, or else one week's notice) of the intention to terminate the contract. In this situation, the employee will not be entitled to notice because the employer is terminating the contract of employment (provided that the lay-off or short-time is genuine and is not to avoid the payment of notice).

The employer may issue a counter-notice stating that they will be able to provide at least 13 weeks' work within a period of four weeks from the date of receipt of the claim. The employee must receive the counter-notice within seven days of the employee's intention to claim a redundancy payment. If the employer does not fulfil the counternotice, the employee is entitled to redundancy.

REDUNDANCY PROCEDURE

Redundancy Notice

An employer who proposes to dismiss an employee must give their employee the RP1 form, i.e. Notice of Redundancy (see pages 257-58). The employer must also send a copy of this form to the Minister for Enterprise and Employment.

This issue of notice is extremely important because the employee's entitlement to notice can be decided by the Minimum Notice and Terms of Employment Acts, 1973 to 1991 or the contract of employment. An employee is entitled to the benefit of the longest period of notice — that is, statutory notice or contractual notice — but, nevertheless, the RP1 form must be given at least two weeks before the date of redundancy dismissal (See Chapter 16 — Notice). For example, if the employee is entitled to at least eight weeks' notice, the most practical thing for an employer to do is to give the employee the RP1 form at least eight weeks before the proposed date of redundancy.

The employer must complete the following details on the RP1 form:

- Employer's PAYE number

- Business name and address of the employer

- Nature of the employer's business, e.g. retail, shoe manufacturing and so forth

- Employee's RSI number

- Employee's name and address

- Sex of employee

- Social welfare insurance number

- Occupation of the employee

- Address of place of employment

- Reason for the redundancy, e.g. company closedown, market conditions, requirements for employees with higher skills

- Date of commencement of employment

- Number of hours that the employee is normally expected to work

- Date of termination of employment

- Signature of the employer/officer in employing company with job title and date.

If an employee will not accept the notice, the employer should send it by registered post to the employee and advise the Department of Enterprise and Employment that the employee would not accept it and that it was sent by registered post.

Time off

An employee who is being made redundant (i.e. who has 104 weeks' continuous service) is entitled to paid time off in order to look for a new job or to make arrangements for training for further employment. This time off is paid time off, but it must be reasonable.

Leaving Before Notice Expires

If an employee who has been given notice of dismissal wishes to leave before the notice has expired, they may terminate their employment in writing beforehand. This may be done by way of the RP6 form. However, this may only be done during the period of the notice to which the employee is entitled, called the "obligatory period" in the Act. If the employer has given notice over and above the employee's entitlement, the employee cannot give such a notice during that extra period, otherwise the employee would lose the redundancy payment. Of course, the employer may agree to bring forward the obligatory period of notice so that the employee can get the redundancy payment (see pages 263-64).

Redundancy Certificate

The employer must give the employee the Certificate of Redundancy (the RP2 form — see pages 259-60) on the date of dismissal. This form requires the following details:

- Employer's PAYE number
- Business name and address of the employer
- Employee's RSI number
- Employee's surname and first name
- Sex of the employee
- Social welfare insurance number (if applicable)
- Date of birth
- Occupation
- Date of commencement of employment
- Number of hours normally expected to work per week
- Periods of non-reckonable service with the reason why they are so non-reckonable e.g. periods of lay-offs.

PART I

- Calculation of statutory lump sum payment
- Total years of reckonable service
- Number of week's pay due
- Amount of normal weeks' pay which will include gross weekly wage; average regular overtime; and benefits in kind which will give a total
- Ceiling of earnings applicable, if the earnings are lower than a normal week's pay (the present ceiling on statutory redundancy is £250.00 per week)
- Amount of lump sum payable.

PART II

- Employee's receipt for lump-sum payment.

It should be noted that this part of the form is only in respect of the statutory lump-sum payment. In other words, if an employee were receiving an ex-gratia amount over and above the statutory lump sum, it should not be included on this form.

It is important that the employee actually receives the redundancy payment because this form is deemed to be an acknowledgement thereof.

PART III

• Declaration by employer.

This is the part of the form where the employer declares that the employee was dismissed by reason of redundancy and that the employee is entitled to the lump sum which is set out on the form. Indeed, even if an employee is entitled to no lump sum at all, this should be so stated. The employer must sign this part of the form stating the position held in the company and the date.

Statutory Redundancy Payment

An employee who has been dismissed (or who terminates their own employment as a result of lay-off or short time) is entitled to a statutory redundancy payment as follows:

(1) A half-week's normal weekly remuneration for each year of continuous and reckonable service between 16 years and their forty-first birthday; plus

(2) A week's normal weekly remuneration for each year of continuous and reckonable year of service between 41 and 66 years; plus

(3) The equivalent of one week's normal weekly remuneration.

In simple terms, the formula is a one-half week's pay per year of service up to forty-first birthday, plus one week's pay per year of service from 41 years to 66 years, plus one week's pay.

There are various complex rules for the calculation of the statutory redundancy payment which is based on normal weekly remuneration to take into account commission and other varied payments. The weekly wage which is to be used for the calculation of statutory redundancy is the wage applying on the date that the employee is declared redundant, that is, the date on which the employee is given the RP1 form (*Minister for Labour* v. *Nokia Ltd.*, High Court, Costello, J., unreported, 30 March 1983 and noted ((1984)) 3 JISLL at page 49).

The statutory redundancy payment is subject to a ceiling of £13,000 per annum or £250 per week. Statutory redundancy payments are tax free (see Chapter 20 — Taxation of Termination Payments).

Refusal of Employee to Accept Redundancy

As mentioned earlier, if an employee refuses to accept the redundancy notice an employer may send such notice to the employee's home by registered post. The employer should simultaneously send a copy to the Minister. Equally, if an employee does not accept (and sign) the RP2 form and the redundancy monies, the employer should send same to the employee by registered post. The employer can still apply for the rebate (see below) by sending copies of all documentation and a copy of the cheque for redundancy monies to the Minister explaining that the employee would not accept redundancy and that all forms and payments were sent to the employee's home by registered post.

Employer's Rebate from the Social Insurance Fund

The employer applies to the Minister for Enterprise and Employment for the rebate from the Social Insurance Fund. This amounts to 60 per cent of the statutory redundancy payment paid to an employee (the rebate is only concerned with the statutory aspect of a redundancy payment). The employer completes the RP3 form (see pages 261-62).

If an employer fails to comply with the above provisions (i.e. the serving of the RP1 form), the Minister may reduce the amount of rebate payable to the employer to 40 per cent. The RP3 form must be sent to the Minister within six months of the date of payment of the redundancy lump sum, with a copy of the Redundancy Certificate.

RP3 form. The following details for the RP3 form should be included:

- Employee's PAYE number
- Business name and address of the employer
- Amount of rebate that the employer is claiming
- Signature of the employer, stating the position held in the company and the date.

Employers should note in claiming the rebate that the Department of Enterprise and Employment may check with the Revenue Commissioners and any other Government Department (e.g. Social Welfare) to see that everything is in order. For example, they may ensure that the employee got the appropriate period of notice which shall be included in the P45 form.

SEVERANCE

Frequently an employer will pay an employee monies over and above statutory redundancy. In unionised employments, the employee's trade union may negotiate with the employer for a higher redundancy payment. There are many different formulae, for example, two weeks' pay per year of service plus statutory, or four weeks' pay per year of service plus statutory, or a lump sum based on a certain number of years' service, etc. Section 51 of the 1967 Act provides that "any provision in an agreement (whether a contract of employment or not) shall be void in so far as it purports to exclude or limit the operation of any provision of this Act".

Therefore, caution must be exercised in redundancy negotiations either to pay the statutory lump sum separately, or to specify that amount separately in any agreement so that the employee knows what the statutory payment is. In the *Minister for Labour* v. *O'Connor and Irish Dunlop Company Ltd.* ((1985) 4 JISLL 72), Kenny, J. in his High Court judgment stated:

> When an employer has failed to issue a redundancy certificate to an employee when dismissing him by reason of redundancy, compensation paid to the employee on dismissal for redundancy can be treated as payment by the employer of the statutory lump sum only when the employer proves to the satisfaction of the Tribunal (i) that the employee at the time of payment knew the amount of the statutory lump sum to which he was entitled at the date of the dismissal and (ii) that the employee agreed to accept the sum paid in discharge of his claim for the statutory lump sum.

In this case the employee was made redundant and should have received £500, but he was not given an RP2 form. The employee did not know the exact amount of his statutory entitlement during the course of negotiations on his lump sum or when it was paid. It was held that he was entitled to the statutory lump sum in addition to the £500.

The ruling in *Talbot (Ireland) Limited* v. *the Minister for Labour and Ors.* ((1985) 4 JISLL 87) by Barron, J. is also of importance. It concerned the closing down of the Talbot car assembly plant. Arising from a strike, there were negotiations between the company, the unions, the government and various State agencies, which resulted in letters of resignation from the employees and acknowledged payment of monies "in full and final settlement of any claim". The employees successfully brought claims for statutory redundancy to the EAT. The company appealed this decision to the High Court, and Barron J., in referring the matter back to the Tribunal for rehearing, stated that the Tribunal had to answer the following question:

> Was the claim to statutory redundancy payment discussed in the course of the negotiations leading up to the making of the agreement and the signing of the letters of negotiation?

The Tribunal reheard the whole case and determined that Talbot had discharged its liability under the Act and that the employees were in full knowledge of their legal position. There was no evidence that either the employees or their advisers were unaware of the manner in which statutory lump sums were calculated under the Acts. The document they signed was also important as it was acknowledgement of payment by Talbot of a stated sum

> as final settlement of any claim I have against the Company other than any payment outlined in 3 [training payment made during an extended notice period] of the above agreement or payments available to me as a member of the Talbot Works Pension Scheme.

Therefore there was no additional entitlement to statutory redundancy payments.

TAXATION

As stated above, statutory redundancy payments are tax-free. The Finance Acts provide certain further allowances for employees on termination of employment. The first £6,000 of a termination payment, together with £500 for each complete year of service (Finance Act, 1993), may be paid tax free. There is a further allowance of £4,000, making a total of £10,000 tax free provided that the employee has never claimed that extra relief before.

There is also the Standard Capital Superannuation Benefit Relief and Top Slicing Relief (see Chapter 20 — Taxation of Termination Payments).

CLAIMS PROCEDURES

The Act provides for Deciding Officers who are officials in the Department of Enterprise and Employment (Redundancy Section) who make decisions in relation to redundancy, for example, whether the redundancy payment was correct, who the employer was and any other matter under the Act. More usually, the deciding officers decide on the rebate to which an employee is entitled.

Invariably, all claims under the Act are referred to the Employment Appeals Tribunal for determination. Less frequently, appeals against a deciding officer's decision, usually in respect of non payment of the rebate by the Social Insurance Fund, may be referred to the Tribunal. Deciding officers may also refer matters to the Tribunal if they are in doubt in a particular case.

An employee must refer a redundancy claim to the Tribunal within 52 weeks of the date of dismissal or termination of employment after lay-off or short-time. The 52-week time-limit may be extended to 104 weeks if reasonable cause can be shown for the delay.

This is considered in more detail in Chapter 23 — Employment Appeals Tribunal.

NON-PAYMENT BY THE EMPLOYER

If an employee has not been paid statutory redundancy after taking all reasonable steps (excluding legal proceedings), or if the employer is insolvent or has died, an application may be made to the Social Insurance Fund for payment. The RP77 form and the RP14 form (see pages 267-70) may be used. However, the more usual step is for the employee to bring a claim to the Tribunal and to send the Determination to the Fund to request payment.

FORM RP1

NOTICE OF PROPOSED
DISMISSAL FOR REDUNDANCY

REDUNDANCY PAYMENTS ACTS, 1967 TO 1991

AN ROINN FIONTAR AGUS FOSTAÍOCHTA – DEPARTMENT OF ENTERPRISE AND EMPLOYMENT

Note for Employer: On the date that this notice is given by an employer to the employee a copy of it must be sent to the Minister for Enterprise and Employment at Davitt House, 65A Adelaide Road, Dublin 2. Failure to do this may lead to a reduction in rebate payable.

PLEASE COMPLETE THIS FORM IN BLOCK CAPITALS

EMPLOYER'S PAYE REGISTERED NUMBER

Figures   Letter

BUSINESS NAME OF EMPLOYER

BUSINESS ADDRESS

GIVE DETAILS OF TYPE OF BUSINESS IN WHICH REDUNDANCY ARISES

For Official Use

NACE

Figures   Letters

EMPLOYEE'S REVENUE AND SOCIAL INSURANCE (RSI) NO.

To: SURNAME

FIRST NAME

ADDRESS

SEX	Male		Tick
Female		Appropriate Box

SOCIAL WELFARE INSURANCE NUMBER
(If any)
Figures

DATE OF BIRTH OF EMPLOYEE | Day | Month | Year

OCCUPATION _____

ADDRESS OF PLACE OF EMPLOYMENT

_____

_____

GIVE DETAILS OF THE REASON FOR REDUNDANCY

_____

_____

For Office Use

MANCO

AREA

REASON

DATE OF COMMENCEMENT
OF EMPLOYEE'S EMPLOYMENT | Day | Month | Year

NUMBER OF HOURS NORMALLY
EXPECTED TO WORK PER WEEK

It is necessary to terminate your employment by reason of redundancy. In accordance with the provisions of the **Redundancy Payments Acts, 1967** to **1991**, I hereby give you notice that your employment will terminate on

Day | Month | Year

SIGNATURE OF EMPLOYER _____

POSITION HELD IN COMPANY _____

DATE OF NOTICE | Day | Month | Year

FORM RP2

REDUNDANCY CERTIFICATE

REDUNDANCY PAYMENTS ACTS, 1967 TO 1991

AN ROINN FIONTAR AGUS FOSTAÍOCHTA – DEPARTMENT OF ENTERPRISE AND EMPLOYMENT

Note: Before completing this form please refer to explanatory booklet.

PLEASE COMPLETE THIS FORM IN BLOCK CAPITALS

EMPLOYER'S PAYE REGISTERED NUMBER

Figures   Letter

BUSINESS NAME OF EMPLOYER _____

BUSINESS ADDRESS _____

_____

EMPLOYEE'S REVENUE AND SOCIAL INSURANCE (RSI)
NUMBER

Figures   Letters

To: SURNAME _____   FIRST NAME _____

SEX
| Male | | Tick |
| Female | | Appropriate Box |

SOCIAL WELFARE INSURANCE NUMBER
(If Any)
Figures

DATE OF BIRTH
Day   Month   Year

OCCUPATION

For Official Use
MANCO

DATE OF COMMENCEMENT
Day   Month   Year

DATE OF TERMINATION
Day   Month   Year

NUMBER OF HOURS NORMALLY
EXPECTED TO WORK PER WEEK

PERIODS OF NON RECKONABLE SERVICE

	DAY	MONTH	YEAR		DAY	MONTH	YEAR	REASON
From				To				_____
From				To				_____
From				To				_____

1. CALCULATION OF STATUTORY LUMP SUM PAYMENT

Note: Regard should be had to ceiling on normal weekly remuneration.

(i)   Total Reckonable Service _____ Years

      (excluding service before age of 16 and other non-reckonable service)

(ii) Number of weeks pay due _____ Weeks

(iii) Amount of Normal Week's Pay:

Gross Weekly Wage	Average Regular Overtime	Benefits In Kind	Total
£	£	£	£

(iv) State ceiling on earnings applied for purposes of calculation if the statutory ceiling is lower than normal week's pay _____ £

(v) Amount of Statutory lump sum payment to which employee is entitled _____ £

---

2. EMPLOYEE'S RECEIPT FOR LUMP PAYMENT

Note: In no circumstances should this receipt be used for any payment other than the statutory redundancy lump sum or part thereof. This receipt will not be accepted as valid unless the sum paid is inserted.

WARNING: DO NOT SIGN THIS RECEIPT UNTIL YOU ACTUALLY RECEIVE PAYMENT OF THE SUM BEING ACKNOWLEDGED.

I acknowledge receipt of a lump sum redundancy payment amounting to _____ £

	DAY	MONTH	YEAR

Signature of Employee _____

---

3. DECLARATION BY EMPLOYER

I declare that the employee was dismissed by reason of redundancy, that the employee is entitled to a lump sum of the amount set out in Part 1(v) of this certificate, and that the employee was paid a lump sum of _____ £

(If no payment was made, please insert NIL)

Signature of Employer _____

Position held in Company _____ Date

FORM RP3

AN ROINN FIONTAR AGUS FOSTAÍOCHTA	DEPARTMENT OF ENTERPRISE AND EMPLOYMENT

EMPLOYER'S CLAIM FOR REBATE FROM THE SOCIAL INSURANCE FUND

REDUNDANCY PAYMENTS ACTS 1967 TO 1991

NOTES

Before completing this form please refer to explanatory booklet. A claim for rebate must be sent to the Minister for Enterprise and Employment addressed to his office in Dublin within six months of the date of payment of the redundancy lump sum. It must be accompanied by the copy of the Redundancy Certificate on which the employee has signed the receipt for the lump sum.

Please complete this form in BLOCK CAPITALS

Employer's PAYE Registered Number [_____]
FIGURES   LETTER

Business Name of Employer [_____]

Business Address [_____]

To the Minister for Enterprise and Employment:—

I certify that the employees whose names are listed overleaf (and on continuation sheets numbered   to   ):—

(i) ceased employment on the dates on the attached Redundancy Certificates,

(ii) in accordance with the terms of the Redundancy Payments Acts, 1967 to 1991, were paid lump sums for which they have signed receipts on the attached copies of redundancy certificates and that these redundancy certificates are true copies of the certificates given to the employees concerned.

I understand that in order to establish my right to any rebate it may be necessary for you to refer to information given by me to the Revenue Commissioners and other Government Departments, and I hereby give my consent to the disclosure of such information for this purpose only. I also certify that none of the redundancy payments to which this claim refers is awaiting the decision of an Appeals Tribunal.

I claim rebate amounting to [£   ] and declare that no other claim for rebate has been made in respect of the service of these employees between the dates of commencement and termination on the attached redundancy certificates.

Signature of Employer _____

Position held in Company _____ **Date** _____

RP3

CLAIM FOR REBATE FROM THE SOCIAL INSURANCE FUND

EMPLOYEE'S REVENUE AND SOCIAL INSURANCE (RSI) NUMBER	EMPLOYEE'S		AMOUNT OF REBATE CLAIMED £
	SURNAME	FIRST NAME	

FDU 5/93

FORM RP6
(Obligatory Period)

LEAVING BEFORE REDUNDANCY NOTICE EXPIRES

It may be that when you get form RP1 - Notice of proposed dismissal for Redundancy - you might wish to leave your employment sooner than the date of termination notified to you, e.g., to take up alternative employment. If you decide to leave, there is a risk that you may lose any entitlement to redundancy payments unless you notify your employer in writing and also comply with the general conditions on the back of this form. You may use this form for writing to your employer.

If after receipt of this notice your employer objects to your leaving your employment and you leave notwithstanding, you may have to prove to the satisfaction of the Employment Appeals Tribunal that your grounds for leaving were reasonable.

PART 1:
NOTICE TO AN EMPLOYER BY AN EMPLOYEE TO TERMINATE EMPLOYMENT
(SECTION 10 OF THE REDUNDANCY PAYMENTS ACT, 1967 AS AMENDED BY
SECTION 9 OF THE REDUNDANCY PAYMENTS ACT, 1979)

To: ....

....
(Name and Address of Employer)

With reference to your Notice of Redundancy (RP 1) dated.................proposing to terminate my employment on.................(date of termination notified), I hereby give you notice of my intention to anticipate dismissal by leaving on.....................(insert date on which you propose to leave). Note that *the date on which you give this notice and the date on which it expires must be within the obligatory period of notice*. Your employer's consent may be necessary to ensure this, see Part 3 of this form).

Revenue & Social Insurance No:........................   Signed: ....(Employee)

Social Welfare Insurance No:.............................   Date: ....

PART 2:
COUNTER-NOTICE BY EMPLOYER

To: ....
Name of Employee

I request you to withdraw your notice and to continue in my employment until the date on which my notice expires. If you do not withdraw your notice I will contest any liability to pay you a redundancy payment. My reason for objection is ....

....

Signed: ....(Employer)

Date: ....

PART 3:
CONSENT BY EMPLOYER TO ALTER DATE OF HIS DISMISSAL NOTICE SO AS TO
BRING EMPLOYEE'S ANTICIPATORY NOTICE WITHIN THE OBLIGATORY PERIOD.
(SECTION 9 OF THE REDUNDANCY PAYMENTS ACT 1979).

I agree that the date of termination notified on my notice of proposed dismissal (RP1) be altered to.................so that the giving of employee's notice to anticipate dismissal and the expiration date of his anticipating notice shall be within the obligatory period of notice.

Signed: ....(Employer)

Date: ....

EMPLOYEES PROPOSING TO ANTICIPATE THEIR REDUNDANCY NOTICE BY LEAVING SOONER THAN THE DATE OF TERMINATION NOTIFIED TO THEM ON FORM RP1 SHOULD READ THESE NOTES CAREFULLY BEFORE COMPLETING THE FORM OVERLEAF. *(This is not a statutory form and it is open to you to use an alternative means of communication with your employer, provided it is in writing).*

If you have been given Notice of proposed dismissal for Redundancy (Form RP1) and you wish to leave your job sooner than the date you are to become redundant *(as set out on the redundancy notice)* you should, if you want to preserve your entitlement to redundancy payment, fill in the form overleaf and send it or give it to your employer.

This must be done within (not before) your obligatory period of notice. Normally this period is the two weeks immediately before the date you are to become redundant but if you have been in the job for between 5 and 10 years, this period is extended to 4 weeks; if you have been in the job 10 to 15 years the period is 6 weeks and if you have been more than 15 years the period is 8 weeks. If your contract of employment lays down a longer period of notice, this longer period is the obligatory period of notice in your case.

You may leave your job before the date specified in your redundancy notice and still preserve your redundancy entitlement only if the dates on which you give notice and *on which you leave are within your obligatory period* of notice as set out in the previous paragraph. Furthermore if your employer give you a counter-notice in form similar to the "counter-notice by employer" overleaf you will not be entitled to redundancy payment if you unreasonably refuse to comply with his request. *(Any disputes on this matter may be referred to the Appeals Tribunal).*

If the date on which you wish to give notice is outside the obligatory period your employer may bring it within that period by agreement in writing to an alteration of the date of termination shown on his notice of dismissal (RP1). Part 3 of this form may be used for this purpose. You should obtain written agreement to alteration of termination date on employer's notice *prior to giving your anticipation notice,* and if your employer refuses to agree to such alteration you must wait until a date within the obligatory period before giving anticipatory notice.

NOTE FOR EMPLOYERS

IF an employee under notice of redundancy leaves by his own decision before the date set out in his notice (RP1) without complying with all of the conditions set out above, he may not be entitled to a lump sum under the Redundancy Payments Acts. Should you pay an employee a lump sum to which he is not entitled because he has not complied with the procedures outlined on this form, you will not get a rebate from the Department of Labour unless the Employment Appeals Tribunal decides otherwise.

If you agree to an employee leaving before the date set out in his notice of redundancy (RP1), though within his obligatory period of notice, you must attach completed form RP6, or whatever written notice you have received from him, to your claim for rebate, as evidence of compliance with these procedures, otherwise you will not be paid rebate.

If the date on which an employee wishes to give you anticipatory notice is outside the obligatory period you may (though you are not obliged to) bring it within such period by alteration of the termination date on your dismissal notice. Your agreement to do so must be in writing. Part 3 of this form may be used for this purpose.

If you do *not* agree to your employee's leaving before the date set out in his notice of redundancy (RP1), though within his obligatory period of notice, you should, *before the expiration date of his anticipatory notice* give him counter-notice in writing. Part 2 of this form may be used for that purpose.

The redundancy lump sum will be based on the period: date on which service commenced to date of actual termination.

Issued by the Department of Labour
(available from Employment Exchanges and FAS Offices)

A1 900.5.   P27651 SPL. 30M 3/91 Mount Salus 500193 - Labour

FORM RP9

AN ROINN SAOTHAIR	DEPARTMENT OF LABOUR

LAY OFF AND SHORT TIME PROCEDURES

NOTES

An employer may use Part A overleaf of this form to notify an employee of temporary lay off or temporary short time (lay off and short time are defined at the end of this page).

An employee may use Part B overleaf of this form to notify his / her employer of intention to claim a redundancy lump sum payment in a lay off or short time situation.

An employer may use Part C overleaf of this form to give counter notice to an employee who claims payment of a redundancy lump sum in a lay off / short time situation.

EMPLOYER'S PAYE REGISTERED NUMBER

Figures   Letter

BUSINESS NAME AND ADDRESS OF EMPLOYER

DESCRIPTION OF BUSINESS IN WHICH REDUNDANCY ARISES

FOR OFFICIAL USE ONLY — NACE CODE

EMPLOYEE'S REVENUE AND SOCIAL INSURANCE (R.S.I.) NUMBER

Figures   Letters

EMPLOYEE'S SURNAME

EMPLOYEE'S FIRST NAME

ADDRESS OF EMPLOYEE

SEX (TICK ✔ APPROPRIATE BOX)

☐ MALE   ☐ FEMALE

DATE OF BIRTH OF EMPLOYEE

Day   Month   Year

DATE OF COMMENCEMENT OF EMPLOYEE'S EMPLOYMENT

Day   Month   Year

ADDRESS OF PLACE OF EMPLOYMENT

FOR OFFICIAL USE ONLY — AREA CODE

DEFINITION OF LAY OFF AND SHORT TIME

A lay off situation exists when an employer suspends an employee's employment because there is no work available, when the employer expects the cessation of work to be temporary and when the employer notifies the employee to this effect.

A short time working situation exists when an employer, because he has less work available for an employee than is normal, reduces that employee's earnings to less than half the normal week's earnings or reduces the number of hours of work to less than half the normal weekly hours, when the employer expects this reduction to be temporary and when the employer notifies the employee to this effect.

PART A : Notification to employee of TEMPORARY LAY OFF or TEMPORARY SHORT TIME

Notification in respect of this part need not be in writing

It is necessary to place you on   ☐ **TEMPORARY LAY OFF**   ☐ **TEMPORARY SHORT TIME**
(Please tick ✔)

as and from   Day   Month   Year

by reason of _____

_____

I expect the LAY OFF / SHORT TIME to be temporary.

Signature of Employer _____ Date _____

PART B : Notice of Intention to claim Redundancy Lump Sum Payment in a LAY OFF / SHORT TIME situation

An employee who wishes to claim a redundancy lump sum because of lay off / short time must serve notice of intention to claim in writing within four weeks after the lay off / short time ceases. In order to become entitled to claim a redundancy lump sum on foot of a period of lay off, short time or a mixture of both, that period must be at least four consecutive weeks or a broken series of six weeks where all six fall within a thirteen-week period. An employee who wishes to terminate his contract of employment by reason of lay off or short time must give his employer the notice required by his contract or if none is required, at least one week's notice.

An employee who claims and receives redundancy payment in respect of lay off or short time is deemed to have voluntarily left his employment and therefore not entitled to notice under the Minimum Notice and Terms of Employment Act, 1973.

To *(Business Name of Employer)* : _____

I give you notice of my intention to claim a redundancy lump sum in respect of LAY OFF / SHORT TIME *(Delete whichever does not apply)*

From   Day Month Year   To   Day Month Year

Signature of Employee _____ Date _____

PART C : Counter Notice to Employee's Notice of Intention to claim a Redundancy Lump Sum

Notification in respect of this part must be in writing and must be given to the employee within seven days of service of the employee's notice.

I contest any liability to pay you a Redundancy Lump Sum on the grounds that it is reasonable to expect that

Day   Month   Year

within four weeks of the date of service of your notice, namely [   ] **(Date of Service),**

you will enter upon a period of employment of not less than thirteen weeks during which you will not be on lay off or short time any week.

Signature of Employer _____ Date _____

FDU91/120

FORM RP14

AN ROINN SAOTHAIR	DEPARTMENT OF LABOUR

EMPLOYEE'S APPLICATION FOR LUMP SUM
FROM THE SOCIAL INSURANCE FUND

NOTES FOR EMPLOYEE

This form is to be used when applying to the Minister for Labour for payment of a redundancy lump sum from the Social Insurance Fund. You should only use this form if you have applied in writing to your employer for payment (Form RP77 may be used) and he has failed to pay the redundancy lump sum.

This Form must be accompanied by either a Redundancy Certificate or a favourable decision from the Employment Appeals Tribunal.

If you have applied in writing and your employer refuses to give you a Redundancy Certificate or ignores your application and you consider that you are entitled to a redundancy payment, you may appeal to the Employment Appeals Tribunal. If the Appeals Tribunal decides that you are entitled to a redundancy lump sum they will issue a decision which should be sent to the Minister for Labour with this form.

Please complete this form in BLOCK CAPITALS

Employer's PAYE Registered Number ⌊_|_|_|_|_|_|_|_|_⌋
FIGURES   LETTER

(Available on Notice of Dismissal (RP1), Redundancy Certificate (RP2) and P45)

Business Name of Employer

Business Address

If the employer is deceased, give the name and address of his representative. If the business is in liquidation or receivership, please supply the name and address of the liquidator or receiver. If the business has ceased trading but has not gone into liquidation or receivership, and the employer is no longer available at the business address, please supply the address at which he may be contacted.

Name

Address

Employee's Revenue and Social Insurance (R.S.I.) Number

FIGURES   LETTERS

Surname

First Name

Address*

NON PAYMENT BY MY EMPLOYER DUE TO	TICK ✔
LIQUIDATION	
RECEIVERSHIP	
BANKRUPTCY	
CLAIMS INSOLVENCY	
EMPLOYER DECEASED	
REFUSES TO PAY	
IGNORES MY APPLICATION	
OTHER REASON (GIVE DETAILS)	

PLEASE ATTACH: Notice of Dismissal (RP1) and Redundancy Certificate (RP2), or state Employment Appeals Tribunal Case Number:_____ Decision Date: _____

I claim payment of a lump sum / part of a lump sum from the Redundancy Fund by reason of default on the part of my employer. I applied in writing to my employer for payment on _____ (Date).

SIGNATURE OF EMPLOYEE _____ **DATE** _____

A person who fraudulently applies to the Minister for a lump sum shall be guilty of an offence and shall be liable on summery conviction to a fine of up to £300.

*Please ensure that the employee's correct address is given on this form as the cheque in respect of the lump sum entitlement shall be posted to that address. Any changes of address must be notified immediately to the Redundancy Payments Section of the Department of Labour.

FDU91/120

FORM RP77

EXPLANATORY NOTE FOR EMPLOYEE WHEN APPLYING TO AN EMPLOYER FOR A LUMP SUM

This form may be used by an employee

A.   who considers that he is entitled to redundancy payments and his employer has not acknowledged his entitlement by giving him

   (i)   Notice of proposed dismissal for Redundancy (Form RP1)

   (ii)   Redundancy Certificate (Form RP2)

   (iii) Lump sum payment

   If an employee has received (i) and (ii), or (ii) only but not (iii), he should apply in writing to his employer for payment.

B.   who considers that he has received an incorrect lump sum

C.   who has received a favourable decision from the Appeals Tribunal on his redundancy appeal and who wishes to pursue the matter of payment of the lump sum, or an unpaid part of it, with his employer's representative.

   Should a payment or a balance of payment be refused or this application be ignored by an employer, the following options are open to the employee:

   If he has not received a Redundancy Certificate (Form RP2): he may apply to the Appeals Tribunal for a declaration of redundancy or a declaration of the facts of redundancy. Form RP51A* should be consulted and used for this purpose.

   If he holds a Redundancy Certificate or alternatively has received a favourable decision from the Appeals Tribunal on his redundancy appeal: he may refer the matter to the Department of Labour for further attention. Form RP14* should be consulted and used for this purpose.

   IMPORTANT

1.   Record the date on which you apply for payment to your employer.

2.   Allow a reasonable time, say 14 days, for the employer to deal with the matter before proceeding further.

3.   Do not use this Form for purposes other than applying to an employer for payment of a statutory Redundancy lump sum or balance of a lump sum.

4.   If dismissal arises in a lay-off or short-time situation consult Form RP9* in the first instance.

NOTE FOR EMPLOYERS AND EMPLOYEES

The following informational leaflets in particular on the Redundancy Payments Scheme may be of interest in connection with disputes.

   Checking of qualifications for Redundancy Lump Sum.

   Explanatory leaflet for employers who claim inability to pay lump sums.

   Explanatory leaflet on the Appeals Tribunal which deals with disputes.

Issued by
Department of Labour
Davitt House,
*Available from any Employment Exchange   65A Adelaide Road,
or from the Department of Labour   Dublin 2.

P.27651 SPL. 30m 3/91 Mount Salus 500193 - Labour

FORM RP77

REDUNDANCY PAYMENTS ACTS, 1967 TO 1990

A claim by an employee against an employer for a lump sum or part of a lump sum.

An employee who is in doubt about whether he has a valid claim or not can check against an informational leaflet on the qualifications - (see the footnote overleaf).

To: ....

....

....

Name and Address of Employer

I claim a lump sum payment/s balance of lump sum payment* from you in respect of my dismissal. My claim is based on the following grounds (tick whichever applies):

The grounds of my dismissal constitute redundancy but I have not received a redundancy notice/redundancy certificate* nor a lump sum payment. I request these. ☐

I have received a redundancy notice/redundancy certificate* but no lump sum payment. ☐

The lump sum which I received is incorrect. Particulars of the error are: ☐

....

....

I have received a favourable decision from the Appeals Tribunal in regard to my redundancy appeal and I now request to pay the lump sum due to me. ☐

Insurance No. ....   Signed..

Date:...   Address:...

....

....

....

*Strike out whichever is not applicable.

CHAPTER NINETEEN

Collective Redundancies

The Protection of Employment Act, 1977 provides for certain procedural requirements which an employer must follow in the event of collective redundancies. The 1977 Act came into force pursuant to EC Directive 75/129/EEC, though there is now an amending Directive, 92/56/EEC, which shall come into force in Irish law by June 1994 (see below). The 1977 Act does not apply to establishments employing less than 21 people.

Collective redundancies mean dismissals arising from redundancy during any period of 30 consecutive days where the numbers being made redundant are:

(1) Five employees in an establishment employing 21 to 49 employees;

(2) Ten employees in an establishment normally employing 50 to 99 employees;

(3) Ten per cent of employees in an establishment normally employing 100 to 299 employees; or

(4) Thirty employees in an establishment normally employing 300 or more employees.

An establishment is defined as a location where an employer carries on business, and that location may be defined as a work place, factory, quay, warehouse, building site, wholesale or retail shop, hotel or office. Therefore, if an employer has a number of establishments, each location has to be considered. One also has to consider the total number of employees employed in each location, including those who also perform some of their duties elsewhere.

The number of employees normally employed (including temporary ones) in a location shall be the average of the numbers employed in each of the 12 months preceding the date on which the first dismissal takes effect.

It is important to note that this Act does not apply to the

dismissal or termination of employees who were employed under a fixed-term or specified purpose contract, persons employed by the State, officers of local authorities and persons employed under the Merchant Shipping Act, and employees in an establishment where business is being terminated following bankruptcy or winding-up proceedings.

CONSULTATION

This Act provides that an employer proposing to create collective redundancies shall initiate consultations with employee representatives with a view to reaching an agreement. An employee representative means a union official, or a staff association official (including shop stewards) with whom it has been the employer's practice to conduct collective bargaining negotiations.

The consultations should take place at the earliest opportunity and at least 30 days before the first dismissal takes effect. The subject matter of the consultation shall include the possibility of avoiding the proposed redundancies by reducing the number of employees to be dismissed, and the basis on which particular employees will be made redundant.

The employer is obliged to provide the employee representatives with all information in writing in relation to the proposed redundancies:

(1) The reasons for the proposed redundancies;

(2) The number and descriptions or categories of employees whom it is proposed to make redundant;

(3) The number of employees normally employed; and

(4) The period in which it is proposed to effect the redundancies.

An employer who does not comply with this consultation process shall be guilty of an offence and shall be liable to a fine of £500.

OBLIGATION ON EMPLOYER

There is an obligation on the employer to notify the Minister for Enterprise and Employment of the proposed redundancies at the earliest opportunity but at least 30 days before the first dismissal takes effect. An employer who breaches this requirement may be guilty of an offence.

Statutory regulations (SI No. 140 of 1977) provide that certain particulars must be included in the notification to the Minister:

(1) The name and address of the employer, indicating whether the employer is a sole trader, a partnership or a company;

(2) Address of the establishment where the collective redundancies are proposed;

(3) Total number of persons normally employed at that establishment;

(4) Numbers and description or categories of employees whom it is proposed to make redundant;

(5) Period within which the collective redundancies are proposed to be effected, stating the dates on which the first and final dismissals are expected to take effect;

(6) Reasons for the proposed collective redundancies;

(7) Names and addresses of the trade unions or staff associations representing employees affected by the proposed redundancies, and with which it has been the practice of the employer to conduct collective bargaining negotiations; and

(8) The date on which consultations with each trade union or staff association commenced and the progress achieved in those consultations to the date of notification.

The employee representatives may forward, in writing, to the Minister for Enterprise and Employment any observations relating to this Notification. It is important to note that collective redundancies shall not take effect before the expiry of the 30-day period beginning on the date of the Notification to the Minister. If the collective redundancies are effected by an employer before the expiry of the 30-day period, the employer shall be guilty of an offence and shall be liable to a fine not exceeding £3,000. However, where an employer is convicted of an offence in relation to a failure to supply employee representatives with certain information, or if collective redundancies take place before the 30-day notice expires, the employer may argue that there were substantial reasons relating to the business which made it impracticable to comply with these statutory requirements. Records of collective redundancies should be retained by the employer for three years.

FURTHER CONSULTATIONS WITH THE MINISTER

The Minister may request the employer to enter into consultations with the Minister or with an authorised officer in order to seek solutions to the problems caused by the proposed redundancies. Authorised officers are invariably civil servants of the Department of Enterprise and Employment, and they may enter the employer's premises and make enquiries to be satisfied that the Act is being complied with.

FUTURE DEVELOPMENTS

The amending Directive 92/56/EEC must come into Irish law by June 1994 at the latest. Employers will have to provide the criteria for selection for redundancy and the method of calculating redundancy payments other than statutory ones, presumably referring to certain ex-gratia payments. The Directive also provides that workers and their representatives have access to judicial/administrative bodies, such as the Employment Appeals Tribunal, for enforcement of these procedures.

CHAPTER TWENTY

Taxation of Termination Payments

Unlike monies which are received as damages in a personal injury action, monies received on termination of employment are taxable. These payments are frequently called ex-gratia payments or redundancy payments (excluding statutory redundancy payments). However, there are certain exceptions or allowances. Such payments also include notice monies and awards under the Unfair Dismissals Acts, 1977 to 1993.

The tax provisions shall be considered first and then some practical examples are used to explain this taxation.

INCOME TAX

The provisions dealing with income tax are contained in Section 114 and 115 and Schedule III of the Income Tax Act, 1967 (as amended by later Finance Acts and in particular the Finance Act, 1993). Section 114 brings within the tax charge any payments on retirement or removal from office or employment. The payment:

(1) Must not be otherwise chargeable to income tax (e.g. salary, holiday pay)

(2) Must be made directly or indirectly in consideration of the termination of employment or any change in its functions or emoluments, including payments in commutation of annual or periodic payments, whether chargeable to tax or not

(3) May or may not be in pursuance of a legal obligation

(4) May be for remuneration other than money (e.g. receipt of company car).

The individual receiving the monies or goods (e.g. company car) must be the holder or past holder of the employment.

In the following situations the payment will be treated as being to the employee:

(1) Payment given to the employee's executor or administrator (i.e. if the employee is deceased), or

(2) To the employee's spouse or any relative or dependant, or

(3) To any person to whom the payment is made on behalf of the holder or past holder of the employment.

Section 115 provides for certain further exemptions in respect of foreign employment, or payments made on termination of employment due to the employee's death, injury or disability. There is also relief in respect of certain approved pension schemes where the contribution by the employer was assessed as payments by the employee.

RELIEF

Certain tax reliefs are available:

(1) Statutory redundancy payments — that is, payments under the Redundancy Payments Acts, 1967 to 1991 — are tax free;

(2) The first £6,000 of a termination payment is tax free. However, if an employee receives two or more payments from the same employer or an associated employer, the total exemption is still £6,000. The Finance Act, 1993 provides that the basic amount of £6,000 is increased by £500 for each year of service. The total figure of £6,000 plus £500 per year of complete service is the basic exemption.

The basic exemption may be increased by £4,000 provided that:

(1) The employee must not have claimed and received this increased amount before, and

(2) The £4,000 increase is reduced in an equal amount by any tax-free lump sum, for example, commutation monies received from a pension fund either at the time of termination or receivable in the future under an approved pension scheme relating to the employment.

The practical application of all of this is that £6,000 (plus the additional benefit of £500 per year of service) can be paid directly to the employee. However, if the termination is for any sum above £6,000 plus the additional allowances in a termination situation (excluding statutory redundancy), approval must be granted by the Revenue Commissioners.

The letter sent by the employer to the Revenue would contain the following:

- Name and PRSI number of employee

- Name, address and RSI number of employer

- Date of termination

- Amount of termination payment excluding statutory redundancy

- Amount of notice monies paid if not included in the above

- Pension details to include

- Copy of the pension booklet

- Monies to be paid arising from vested rights under the pension scheme.

Presuming no difficulties arise, the Revenue send an approval letter for payment within a few weeks.

If the necessary approval is not granted or if there is not sufficient time, the employer must deduct tax (on the basis of the employee's allowances) from the part of the lump sum over £6,000 (plus the additional £500 per year of service). If the employer does not deduct the tax, the employer will be liable for the amount not correctly withheld.

OTHER ALLOWANCES

Where a former employee has long service or is receiving a large severance sum, the simpler way of looking at taxation is to consider the tax exempt amount as being (a) £6,000 (plus £500 per year of service) or (b) Standard Capital Superannuation Benefit (SCSB). SCSB may be computed as:

$$\frac{A \times B}{15} - C$$

where

A = average remuneration for the last three years of service

B = number of complete years of service

C = any tax-free sum received or receivable under an approved superannuation scheme

EXAMPLE

An employee has worked for 20 years at an average salary for the last three years of £18,000 and has received £4,000 commutation from his pension scheme. He is to receive a termination payment of £20,000, excluding statutory redundancy but including monies in lieu of notice.

$$\frac{£18,000 \times 20}{15} - 4,000 = £20,000$$

Therefore the termination payment will be exempt from tax. (Under the normal relief the employee would only have got £16,000, i.e. £6,000 plus £10,000 (£500 per year of service) plus £4,000 minus £4,000 (pension)).

However if the employee had only 18 years service the calculation would work out at:

$$\frac{£18,000 \times 18}{15} - £4,000 = £17,600$$

The employee would have to pay tax on the balance of £2,400 (i.e. £20,000 – £17,600). In order to work out the tax on £2,400, the next relief shall be considered.

TOP SLICING RELIEF

When the taxable amount is arrived at, the employee will be taxed at their standard rate of tax which may be even higher than the rate they normally pay because of the lump sum. However, the Top Slicing Relief ensures that the employee will be taxed at an average rate over the previous three years of assessment rather than their current rate of tax. This should have the benefit of reducing the amount of tax payable.

Top Slicing Relief may be computed as:

$$\frac{A - (P \times T)}{I}$$

where

A = the additional tax which would be payable if the taxable lump sum were treated as income earned in the year of assessment, i.e. at the date of termination, over the amount which would be payable if the lump sum were not taxable.

P = the taxable lump sum.

T = the total amount of tax chargeable in respect of the total income of the employee for the five preceding years of assessment.

I = the total taxable income for five preceding years of assessment

The figure arrived at by applying this formula is deducted from the tax chargeable for the year of assessment to which the payment relates, i.e. at the beginning of the next tax year.

PRSI

A Class K contribution is payable by the employee on the amount of a lump-sum payment which is subject to tax. This is approximately 3.25 per cent.

SOCIAL WELFARE

A person who is unemployed and available for work is entitled to unemployment benefit or assistance. Since 20 July 1992 persons under 55 years who receives redundancy payments in excess of £12,000 are disqualified from unemployment benefit for nine weeks from the date of termination.

GENERAL REFERENCES

Corrigan, K., *Taxation on Termination of Employment* (1983) 2 JISLL 37.

Kerr, T., *Taxation on Termination of Employment — The Commonwealth Perspective* (1984) 3 JISLL 23.

CHAPTER TWENTY-ONE

Employer Insolvency

The financial position of employees who lose their jobs as a result of employer insolvency is substantially protected as a result of the Protection of Employees (Employers' Insolvency) Act, 1984. The Act results from an EC Directive (80/087/EEC) relating to the protection of employees in the event of the insolvency of their employer. The Directive came into force in Ireland on 22 October 1983 and applies to insolvencies after that date.

State guarantees for employees if their employer becomes insolvent are provided for in the Act in relation to the non-payment of wages or salary, holiday pay, sick pay, monies in lieu of notice and any recommendation, determination or order in respect of unfair dismissal, wrongful dismissal, equal pay and equal treatment claims. Pension matters are also covered, subject to a ceiling and time limits.

BANKRUPTCY

If an individual becomes bankrupt, all that individual's property vests in the Official Assignee in Bankruptcy. This is provided for in the Bankruptcy Act, 1988 which contains procedures for the administration of estates in bankruptcy cases.

LIQUIDATION

There are several different forms of liquidation, such as a creditors' voluntary winding-up or a members' voluntary winding-up (i.e. where there are not sufficient monies to pay debts), or a compulsory liquidation by the High Court. When such a liquidation arises, the business is no longer operating, so the contract of employment comes to an end. In some cases the liquidator may carry on the business for some time and the employees may continue working for the liquidator under their contracts. In other cases, before there is a final order for liquidation, a provisional liquidator is appointed, and, presuming that person is running the business, the employees will work for him.

RECEIVERSHIP

If a creditor is not being paid, there is usually provision in the loan agreement for the appointment of a receiver. For example, a bank appoints a receiver whose duty it is to safeguard sufficient assets to protect the monies owing. The whole company may not be insolvent. A receiver goes in and runs the business as a going concern and it may have no effect on the employees, although invariably a receivership is a forerunner to an insolvency.

COURT EXAMINER

The Companies (Amendment) Act, 1990 made provision for the High Court to appoint an examiner when a company is in financial difficulties (e.g. as happened in 1990 with the Goodman companies) to see if the company can be saved and to enter into arrangements with creditors. Again, however, the examiner may consider that the company cannot be saved, and then there may eventually be a liquidation.

PREFERRED CREDITORS

An employee may be ranked as a preferred creditor on the insolvency of an individual or a company by virtue of the bankruptcy and companies legislation. Such legislation applies to certain named or preferred debts owed to employees.

Ranking before all other creditors, the liquidator's expenses must be paid as well as the Revenue Commissioners', if certain taxes are owed. For the other creditors, a preferred creditor ranks behind the holder of a fixed charge (e.g. on land) but in front of debenture holders secured by a floating charge (e.g. book debts) or unsecured creditors. Commercial agreements may have retention of title clauses by virtue of which the ownership of goods is held by the seller until the purchase price has been paid. Such a clause may confer a "super preferential" status on the seller, as they are not now part of the winding-up proceedings. Accordingly, if the purchaser becomes insolvent, there are less assets to realise for the benefit of employees.

The Bankruptcy Act, 1988 (individual employers) provides preferential status for the wages/salary of an employee for four months before the date the employer is adjudged to be bankrupt, subject to a maximum of £2,500. Holiday pay, sick pay and pension contributions are also covered and there are particular rules in the case of farm labourers.

The Companies Acts have similar provisions in respect of wages up to a maximum of £2,500. The Acts also cover arrears for holiday pay, sick pay and for the provision of superannuation benefits, compensation and redundancy payments payable under the Unfair Dismissals Acts, 1977 to 1993, the Minimum Notice and Terms of Employments Acts, 1973 to 1991 and the Redundancy Payments Acts, 1967 to 1991 as preferred debts under the above legislation. However, it might be noted that an employee will receive their statutory redundancy lump sum from the Social Insurance Fund.

Prior to the enactment of the 1984 Act, if there were insufficient funds to pay an award made by the Tribunal to an employee before the commencement of the winding-up, the employee would not be paid in full. If the award was made after the date of the winding-up, the employee would be an unsecured creditor and there would be no guarantee of sufficient funds to pay them. The payment of such sums is now guaranteed.

The above is a general explanation of a very technical area of law. However, the Act as regards employees' rights is a considerable improvement on the original position as it guarantees employees' entitlements, subject to certain conditions.

DEFINITIONS

The 1984 Act has a number of definitions:

Employee

The definition of an employee is the same as in the Redundancy Payments Acts, 1967 to 1991 and now covers regular part-time employees.

Insolvent

An employer is deemed to become insolvent if the employer is an individual (i.e. as opposed to a company) and has been adjudicated bankrupt, or has filed a petition for or has executed a deed of arrangement with their creditors, or if they have died and the estate is insolvent.

Date of Insolvency

The date of insolvency in the case of an individual is the date of adjudication, the date of filing the petition, or the date of executing the deed of arrangement, or the date of death (as the case may be).

If it is a company (as defined by the Companies Act, 1963, as amended), the date of insolvency is the date a winding-up order is made, or a resolution for voluntary winding-up is made, or if a receiver or manager has been appointed under a debenture secured by floating charge, or of the appointment of a provisional liquidator or the date the receiver or manager is appointed. A co-operative is regarded as being insolvent on the day the manager or receiver is appointed.

The Minister for Enterprise and Employment may also specify by regulation the circumstances and date in which a specified class or description of employer is deemed to be insolvent. This is usually to cover a situation where an employer has ceased trading and no formal bankruptcy or winding-up proceedings have been initiated.

EMPLOYEES' RIGHTS

An employee (the applicant) may apply to the Minister on the prescribed form and the Minister shall pay the debts owed. However, the Minister must be satisfied that:

(1) The applicant falls within the scope of the Act and the employer has become insolvent;

(2) The date of insolvency is not earlier than 22 October 1983; and

(3) On the "relevant date" the applicant was entitled to be paid the whole or part of any debt. In respect of an unfair dismissal, equality or notice claim, it is the date of the Order awarding the compensation, or the date of the employer's insolvency, whichever is the later. In relation to the other debts, it is the date of termination of employment or the date of the employer's insolvency.

The payments are paid out of the Social Insurance Fund which is funded by employer PRSI payments.

DEBTS

Where appropriate, the Social Insurance Fund pays debts under this Act. The amount payable to an employee in relation to a debt is based on £250 per week (if less than one week, it is on a proportional basis). If the debt results from an award under the unfair dismissals or equality legislation, there cannot be a payment unless the time limit for bringing the appeal has expired or an appeal was made and withdrawn. Legal costs are not paid by the Fund.

The debts include:

Normal Weekly Remuneration

This has the same meaning as in the Redundancy Payments Acts, 1967 to 1991. The applicant shall only be entitled to an amount in arrears for a period, or aggregate of periods, of not more than eight weeks.

Sick Pay

Any arrears due for a period or periods not exceeding in total eight weeks under a sick-pay scheme which forms part of an employee's contract of employment. These payments are only applicable for periods in which the employee was unable to fulfil the contract because of ill-health and for sick pay to which the employee became entitled. Only the difference between disability or injury benefit and normal weekly remuneration is payable.

Court awards for arrears of wages and sick pay are also covered.

Holiday Pay

Holiday pay is defined as pay in respect of a holiday actually taken or any holiday pay which has accrued at the date of termination of the employee's employment. Such debt shall not exceed payment, in respect of a period of eight weeks, to which the employee became entitled during the relevant period. It also includes court awards for holiday pay.

The relevant period in all these cases means the 18 months before the date of insolvency or termination of employment.

Notice

An amount which an employer is required to pay under an award by the Employment Appeals Tribunal under the Minimum Notice and Terms of Employment Acts, 1973 to 1991.

Recommendation, Determination or Order under the Unfair Dismissal Acts, 1977 to 1993

Any amount which an employer is required to pay further to a recommendation of a rights commissioner, determination of the Tribunal or a Circuit Court order.

Wrongful Dismissal (claim for damages for breach of contract)

A court award for damages is also covered provided the employee was so entitled on the relevant date. However, the maximum amount payable will be limited to what the employee would have obtained as redress under the Unfair Dismissals Acts.

Employment Regulation Order

Any amount which an employer is required to pay under an employment regulation order within the meaning of the Industrial Relations Acts and, in relation to which, proceedings have been instituted against the employer for an offence under section 45 (as amended) of the Act.

Equal Pay or Equality

Any amount specified in a recommendation, determination or order under the Anti-Discrimination (Pay) Act, 1974 or the Employment Equality Act, 1977 which an employer is required to pay further to an equality officer's recommendation, or a determination by the Labour Court or a decision of the High Court. Also included are damages awarded under the 1977 Act, fines imposed under either the 1974 or 1977 Acts and compensation directed to be paid under the 1974 or 1977 Acts. Any amount, damages, fine or compensation under this heading is a debt only if the recommendation, decision, determination, award or order was made during or after the expiration of the relevant period.

RIGHTS OF MINISTER

When the employee receives payment in respect of a debt, all rights and remedies in respect of that debt which the employee may have under the relevant company or bankruptcy legislation will be transferred to the Minister.

RELEVANT OFFICER

Payment will not normally be made from the Fund in respect of any debt until a statement of the amount of debt owed has been received from the relevant officer. The officer must furnish such statement when requested by the Minister.

A relevant officer may be an executor, an administrator, the official assignee or a trustee under an arrangement between an employer and their creditors under a trust deed executed by an employer, or a person designated by regulations under the Act for certain classes of employer. The Act provides that the Minister may appoint a person to be a relevant officer in circumstances where no formal bankruptcy or winding-up proceedings have been initiated.

PROCEDURE

The Protection of Employees (Employers' Insolvency) (Forms and Procedure) Regulations, 1984 provide statutory forms which may be used to make a claim under the Act. Certain forms are to be completed by the employee and given to the employer's representative (e.g. receiver, liquidator, etc.) The representative then makes application on behalf of the employee for such payments.

Employee Forms

These forms are for the most part self-explanatory.

Form IP1. Employee's application for a payment of arrears of wages, sick pay, and holiday pay owed by an insolvent employer (pages 291-94).

Form IP2. Employee's application for payment of a Tribunal award under the Minimum Notice and Terms of Employment Acts, 1973 to 1991 (pages 295-96).

Form IP4. Employee's application for payment of arrears of statutory minimum wages, entitlements under the Anti-Discrimination (Pay) Act, 1974, Employment Equality Act, 1977, Unfair Dismissals Acts, 1977 to 1993, or court awards in respect of unfair/wrongful dismissal (pages 299-302).

The employee on signing these forms must:

(1) Declare they have made no other applications;

(2) State they are aware that their rights and remedies as a preferential creditor against the employer will be transferred to the Minister when paid (see below); and

(3) State upon payment that there is no appeal pending and that they are not subject to appeal by anyone else.

Employer Forms

The relevant officer or employment representative completes the following forms:

Form IP3. Application by an employer's representative for funds in respect of wages, sick pay, holiday pay and minimum notice awards (pages 297-98).

Form IP5. Application by an employer's representative for funds to pay entitlements under an Employment Regulation Order, Unfair Dismissals Acts, 1977 to 1993, Anti-Discrimination (Pay) Act, 1974 and Employment Equality Act, 1977 (pages 303-4).

The employer's representative must:

(1) Declare that to the best of their information the entitlements are correct;

(2) Consent to disclose such information as may be necessary;

(3) Undertake to distribute to employee(s) concerned the appropriate amounts which they receive as a result of this application;

(4) Declare that they have not appealed or are not aware of any such appeal (on Form IP5);

(5) Attach copies of IP1, IP2, and IP4 (as appropriate) signed by the employee;

(6) State in whose favour the instrument of payment (e.g. cheque) should be drawn; and

(7) Sign the Form IP3 or IP5.

The Minister, on receipt of the application, will pay such monies to the relevant officer (employer representative) unless there are particular reasons for making payment direct to the employee. Once the relevant officer has made payment to the employee, the Minister must be informed in writing, including details of any deductions made in relation to income tax, PRSI, pensions scheme contributions.

The Act provides that the payment may be made by the Minister even though no statement has been supplied where:

(1) A period of six months has elapsed since application but no payment has been made;

(2) The Minister is satisfied that the payment should be made; or

(3) It appears to the Minister that there is going to be a further delay before a statement is received in relation to the debt.

The Minister may refuse an application completely or part thereof if there is collusion between the employee and the employer that such debt would be the subject of the application and the employer has the means to pay the debts or part thereof.

Information

The Minister may by notice in writing require the employer to provide relevant information including records kept pursuant to Section 10 of the Holidays (Employees) Act, 1973, that is, registers, wage sheets and so forth.

PENSIONS SCHEMES

There is provision for the payment of unpaid contributions to an occupational pension scheme which forms part of the contract of employment. Unpaid relevant contributions shall be paid out of the Fund. Relevant contributions are defined as contributions which were not paid by an employer in accordance with an occupational pension scheme either on the employer's own account or on behalf of an employee. An employee's contribution is only payable when that sum has been deducted from their pay.

The sum payable in respect of unpaid employer contributions shall be the lesser of:

(1) The balance of contributions remaining unpaid for the period of 12 months ending on the day prior to the date of insolvency, or

(2) The amount certified by an actuary to be necessary for the purpose of meeting the liability of the scheme to pay the benefits provided by the scheme.

Unpaid contributions on behalf of an employee shall not exceed the amount prior to insolvency.

Procedure

The Protection of Employees (Employers' Insolvency) (Occupational Pension Scheme) (Forms and Procedure) Regulations, 1990 provide statutory forms for making such claims:

Form IP6. This form is to be used in case of application for payment of (a) amounts deducted from pay of an employee in respect of contributions to the scheme which were not paid into the scheme and (b) unpaid contributions of an employer on the employer's own account to an occupational pension scheme. Part 1 must be completed by a trustee, administrator or other person competent to act on behalf of the occupational pension scheme. Part 2 must be completed by the insolvent employer's representative (pages 305-10).

Form IP7. This is the Actuarial Certificate, which must be completed by the actuary. This Certificate must accompany the IP6 when a claim in respect of unpaid pension scheme contributions is being made. The actuary must sign the form giving details of their professional qualification and business name and address. The terms of the scheme must be attached to this Certificate (pages 311-12).

EMPLOYMENT APPEALS TRIBUNAL

Complaints may be made to the Employment Appeals Tribunal by (a) a person to whom the Minister has failed to make any payment or (b) by one who claims that any such payment is less than the amount which should have been paid.

Complaints (under this Act) shall only be heard in relation to the following debts.

- Remuneration

- Monies owing under sick-pay schemes

- Holiday pay

- Unpaid pension contributions

The complaint must be made within six weeks of the decision of the Minister further to an application for payment, or, if this time period is not practicable, within such period as the Tribunal considers reasonable. If the Employment Appeals Tribunal finds that the Minister is liable, a declaration shall be made to that effect.

Procedure

There are no statutory forms for making such complaints to the Tribunal except the normal form (RP51A) for minimum notice claims (see Chapter 23 — Employment Appeals Tribunal).

Appeal

Decisions of the Employment Appeals Tribunal may be appealed to the High Court on a point of law within 21 days of the decision.

Offences

Proceedings for an offence may only be instituted with the consent of the Minister. If a person making an application under the Act, whether for themselves or another person, knowingly makes a false statement, false representation or conceals a material fact, furnishes false documents or refuses or wilfully neglects to provide information, *inter alia*, such person shall be liable on summary conviction to a fine not exceeding £500. If an offence is committed by a body corporate, both the company and certain officers may also be liable.

GENERAL REFERENCES

Forde, M., *Employment Law in Ireland*, The Round Hall Press, 1991.
Keane, R., *Company Law in the Republic of Ireland*, 2nd ed., Butterworths, 1991.

SCHEDULE

FORM IP 1

| AN ROINN SAOTHAIR | DEPARTMENT OF LABOUR |

EMPLOYEE'S APPLICATION FOR PAYMENT OF ARREARS OF WAGES, SICK PAY AND HOLIDAY PAY OWED BY AN INSOLVENT EMPLOYER

PROTECTION OF EMPLOYEES (EMPLOYERS' INSOLVENCY) ACTS, 1984 TO 1991

IMPORTANT   PLEASE READ THESE NOTES BEFORE COMPLETING THIS FORM

1 After completion, this form should be sent or returned to the insolvent employer's representative.

2 The insolvent employer's representative is the person appointed in connection with an employer's insolvency (e.g. receiver, liquidator, person appointed by Minister for Labour).

3 Deductions for income tax, pay-related social insurance and occupational pension scheme contributions, etc., will be made by the employer's representative from payments due to the employees where appropriate.

4 (A separate) Form IP2 should be completed where payment is being claimed in respect of minimum notice and Form IP4 should be used for claims in respect of arrears of statutory minimum wages or entitlements arising under the Unfair Dismissals Act, 1977, the Anti-Discrimination (Pay) Act, 1974 or the Employment Equality Act, 1977.

5 The maximum period for which arrears are payable for each individual item is eight weeks. In the case of sick pay, payment will not exceed the difference between any social welfare benefit payable and normal pay.

6 The amount of the gross weekly wage to be inserted in Part 2 (a) should include an average of regular overtime and any other regular commission/bonus, etc., calculated in accordance with the Redundancy Payments Acts. If rates given in Part 2 and Part 4 differ, please explain. Date of commencement of employment, number of hours normally expected to be worked per week, are required to establish entitlement and status of employees under the Worker Protection (Regular Part-Time Employees) Act, 1991. For the purposes of calculating arrears a statutory ceiling on gross weekly wages is applied. The current ceiling is £250 per week.

7 Deductions for union dues, V.H.I., etc., which were made from gross wages and not paid over to the relevant authority should be inserted in Part 2 (b).

PART 1	COMPLETE THIS FORM IN BLOCK CAPITALS

EMPLOYEE'S SURNAME

EMPLOYEE'S FIRST NAME

ADDRESS OF EMPLOYEE

EMPLOYEE'S REVENUE AND SOCIAL INSURANCE (R.S.I.) NUMBER

Figures | Letters | Class of Ins. Letter No.

IF OVER 66 YEARS OF AGE OR UNDER 16 YEARS OF AGE, PLEASE GIVE DATE OF BIRTH

Day   Month   Year

BUSINESS NAME AND ADDRESS OF INSOLVENT EMPLOYER

OCCUPATION (If you are a Director or Shareholder please indicate)

DATE OF COMMENCEMENT OF EMPLOYMENT
Day   Month   Year

DATE OF TERMINATION OF EMPLOYMENT
Day   Month   Year

PART 2	ARREARS OF WAGES

Number of days normally expected to be worked per week ☐

(a) From   Day Month Year   To   Day Month Year   **Total Number of Weeks Due**

From   Day Month Year   To   Day Month Year

Gross Weekly Pay (See Note 8)   £

Number of Hours Normally Expected to be Worked per Week

Total Arrears of Wages Claimed (See Note 5)   £

(b) Deductions from Wages: I.e. Union Dues, V.H.I. etc.

	WEEKLY AMOUNT DEDUCTED IN EACH CASE	RELEVANT PERIOD		TOTAL NO. OF WEEKS DUE IN EACH CASE	TOTAL AMOUNT DEDUCTED IN EACH CASE
(i) Union Dues	£	From Day Month Year	To Day Month Year		£
(ii) V.H.I.	£	From Day Month Year	To Day Month Year		£
(iii) Any other Deductions (Specify)	£	From Day Month Year	To Day Month Year		£
			Total Arrears of Deductions Due		£

PART 3   ARREARS DUE UNDER A COMPANY SICK PAY SCHEME

	Day	Month	Year		Day	Month	Year	Total Number of Weeks Due
From				To				

Total Amount of Social Welfare Benefit Payable during the Period   £ _____

Weekly Payment by Employer under Sick Pay Scheme
(Exclusive of Social Welfare Payments)   £ _____

Gross Weekly Pay *(See Note 6)*   £ _____

Total Arrears of Sick Pay Claimed *(See Note 5)*   £ _____

PART 4   ARREARS OF HOLIDAY PAY

(State only your gross basic wage)

	Day	Month	Year		Day	Month	Year	Total Number of Weeks Due
From				To				

(This refers to period in which holiday entitlement arose)

Annual Leave Entitlement   No. of Days _____

Gross Weekly Pay *(See Note 6)*   £ _____

Total Arrears of Holiday Pay Claimed *(See Note 5)*   £ _____

I apply for payment due to me under the Protection of Employees (Employers' Insolvency) Acts, 1984 to 1991 and declare that I have made no other applications in respect of the amounts shown above. I am aware that my rights and remedies against my employer in respect of this amount will be transferred to the Minister for Labour when payment has been made.

Signature ——————————————————————————————   Date ——————————————————————————

EMPLOYEE'S APPLICATION FOR PAYMENT OF AN
EMPLOYMENT APPEALS TRIBUNAL AWARD UNDER THE
MINIMUM NOTICE AND TERMS OF EMPLOYMENT ACT,1973

An Roinn Saothair - Department of Labour

Protection of Employees (Employers' Insolvency) Act, 1984

IMPORTANT: PLEASE READ THESE NOTES BEFORE COMPLETING THIS FORM

1. After completion, this form should be sent or returned to the insolvent
    employer's representative.

2. The insolvent employer's representative is the person appointed in
    connection with an employer's insolvency (e.g. receiver, liquidator,
    person appointed by the Minister for Labour).

3. This form should be used only for a claim in respect of an unpaid minimum
    notice award.   A separate form IP1 should be completed where payment
    is being claimed in respect of unpaid wages, sick pay entitlements
    or holiday pay and form IP4 should be used for claims in respect of
    arrears of statutory minimum wages or entitlements arising under the
    Unfair Dismissals Act, 1977, the Anti Discrimination (Pay) Act, 1974 or
    the Employment Equality Act, 1977.

4. There is a ceiling on gross wages for the purpose of making payments
    from the Fund.   You should refer to the explanatory booklet for the
    ceiling applicable.

PART 1 COMPLETE THIS FORM IN BLOCK CAPITALS	
Employee's Surname:	Employee's Revenue and Social Insurance (R.S.I.) Number:
Employee's First name:	Figures · Letters
Address of Employee	Business name and address of insolvent Employer:-
Occupation · Date of Termination of employment · Day Month Year	Address of place of employment

PART 2: AWARD BY THE EMPLOYMENT APPEALS TRIBUNAL UNDER SECTION 12
OF THE MINIMUM NOTICE AND TERMS OF EMPLOYMENT ACT, 1973

	Day	Month	Year

Date of Employment Appeals Tribunal Award

Reference number of award

Gross weekly Wage ———————————————— £

Total Amount Claimed/due ——————————————— £

PLEASE ATTACH A COPY OF THE TRIBUNAL AWARD

I apply for payment due to me under the Protection of Employees (Employers'
Insolvency) Act, 1984 and declare that I have made no other applications in
respect of the amount shown above.   I am aware that my rights and remedies against
my employer in respect of this amount will be transferred to the Minister for
Labour when payment has been made.

Signature _____   Date _____

WARNING: Legal proceedings may be taken against anyone making a false statement
on this form.

FORM IP 3

APPLICATION BY AN EMPLOYER'S REPRESENTATIVE FOR FUNDS IN RESPECT OF WAGES, SICK PAY, HOLIDAY PAY AND MINIMUM NOTICE AWARDS .

An Roinn Saothair - Department of Labour
Protection of Employees (Employers' Insolvency) Act, 1984

PLEASE COMPLETE THIS FORM IN BLOCK CAPITALS

Figures   Letter

EMPLOYER'S PAYE REGISTERED NUMBER

BUSINESS NAME OF
INSOLVENT EMPLOYER

BUSINESS ADDRESS

NATURE OF BUSINESS

FOR OFFICIAL USE

NACE

Date of Insolvency	Day	Month	Year	TYPE OF INSOLVENCY (e.g. liquidation, receivership, bankruptcy etc.)
(e.g. date of appointment of liquidator receiver etc.)				

To: Minister for Labour, Davitt House, Mespil Road, Dublin 4.

In connection with the provisions of the Protection of Employees (Employers' Insolvency) Act, 1984, I have accepted, based on the best information available to me, the entitlement of the employees as shown overleaf.   No other notification has been made by me in respect of these entitlements.   I understand that it may be necessary for you to refer information on the entitlements to the Revenue Commissioners and Government Departments. I hereby give my consent to the disclosure of such information as may be necessary.   I also agree to make available to you such records as may be required for examination. I undertake to distribute the appropriate amounts to the employees concerned from the funds received pursuant to this application.
Copies of forms IP1 and IP2 as appropriate signed by the employees involved are attached.

The Instrument of payment
should be drawn in favour of ———

Address ———

Signature of Employer's Representative _____

Date _____   Telephone _____

(1) Employee's Name	(2) Revenue & Social Insurance Number	(3) Total arrears of Wages £	(4) Net Total Arrears of Sick Pay	(5) Total Arrears of Holiday Pay £	(6) Total Arrears Amount of Minimum Notice Award by EAT £	(7) Total of Columns (3), (4), (5) & (6) £

GRAND TOTAL £

EMPLOYEE'S APPLICATION FOR PAYMENT OF ARREARS OF STATUTORY MINIMUM WAGES, ENTITLEMENTS UNDER THE ANTI - DISCRIMINATION (PAY) ACT, 1974, EMPLOYMENT EQUALITY ACT, 1977, UNFAIR DISMISSALS ACT, 1977 OR COURT AWARDS IN RESPECT OF UNFAIR DISMISSAL.

AN ROINN SAOTHAIR - DEPARTMENT OF LABOUR

Protection of Employees (Employers' Insolvency) Act, 1984

IMPORTANT: Please read these notes before completing this form.

1. After completion, this form should be sent or returned to the insolvent employer's representative.

2. The insolvent employer's representative is the person appointed in connection with an employer's insolvency (e.g. receiver, liquidator, person appointed by Minister for Labour).

3. A separate form IP1 should be completed where payment is being claimed in respect of arrears of wages, sick pay and holiday pay and form IP2 should be used for claims in respect of Minimum Notice awards by the Employment Appeals Tribunal.

4. Claims in respect of statutory minimum wages can only be made in respect of employments covered by an Employment Regulation Order. In case of doubt, about the application of an Employment Regulation Order, claimants should contact the General Inspectorate Section of this Department.

5. Please attach a copy of Recommendation, determination or order as appropriate, if available.

6. Warning: Legal Proceedings may be taken against anyone making a false statement on this form.

PART 1   COMPLETE THIS FORM IN BLOCK CAPITALS

Employee's Surname :	Employee's Revenue and Social Insurance (R.S.I.) Number:
Employee's First Name:	Figures Letters
Address of Employee:	Business Name and Address of Insolvent Employer:
Occupation: Date of Termination of Employment Day Month Year	
	Address of Place of Employment:
Gross Weekly Pay £	

PART 2 : ANTI-DISCRIMINATION (PAY) ACT 1974

(1) Equality Officer Recommendation (Note: attach copy of recommendation).

Day Month Year

Date of Recommendation: [| |]   Reference Number: [   ]

Amount of Recommendation_____ [£   ]

Has an appeal been lodged with the Labour Court?—[Yes |]   tick   ✓ appropriate
                                                 [No |]   box

(Note: If an appeal has been lodged, no payment can be made unless it is
       withdrawn, or is determined by the Labour Court. If it has been
       determined by the Labour Court, please complete section 2 following).

(2) Labour Court Determination (Note: attach copy of determination).

Day Month Year

Date of Determination—[| |]   Reference Number: [   ]

Amount of Award_____ [£   ]

Has an appeal been lodged with the High Court?——[Yes |]   tick   ✓ appropriate
                                                [No |]   box

(3) Fine arising out of Civil Court decision (note: attach copy of decision if available)

Day Month Year

Date of Decision——[| |]   Amount of Award: [£   ]

Location of Sitting——[   ]

(4) Compensation awarded by Labour Court or Civil Court (note: attach copy of award).

Who awarded the compensation———[Labour Court |]   tick ✓
                               [Civil Court |]   appropriate box

Day Month Year

Date of Decision——[| |]   Amount of Award: [£   ]

Reference Number——[   ]   Location of Sitting——[   ]
(if any)   (if heard in Civil Court)

(5) High Court Judgement (note: attach copy of judgement).

Day Month Year

Date of Judgement——[| |]   Amount of Award: [£   ]

PART 3 : EMPLOYMENT EQUALITY ACT, 1977

(1) Equality Officer Recommendation (Note: attach copy of recommendation).

Day   Month   Year

Date of Recommendation—☐☐☐   Reference Number: ☐

Amount of Recommendation _____ £ ☐

Has an appeal been lodged with the Labour Court?—Yes ☐ tick ✓
                                                 No ☐   appropriate box

(Note: If an appeal has been lodged, no payment can be made unless it is withdrawn
or is determined by the Labour Court. If it has been determined by the
Labour Court, please complete section 2 following).

(2) Labour Court Determination (Note: attach copy of determination).

Day   Month   Year

Date of Determination—☐☐☐   Reference Number: ☐

Amount of Award_____ £ ☐

Has an appeal been lodged with the High Court?—Yes ☐ tick ✓
                                               No ☐   appropriate box

(3) Damages/Fine awarded by the Civil Court (Note: attach copy of fine/award, if
available).

What did the Civil Court award?—Damages ☐ tick ✓
                                Fine ☐   appropriate box

Day   Month   Year

Date of Award —☐☐☐   Amount of Award: £ ☐

Location of Sitting—☐

(4) Compensation awarded by Labour Court (Note: attach copy of award).

Day   Month   Year

Date of award of
compensation—☐☐☐   Reference Number: ☐

Amount of Award_____ £ ☐

Has an appeal been lodged with the High Court?—Yes ☐ tick ✓
                                               No ☐   as appropriate

(5) High court Judgement (Note: attach copy of judgement, if available).

Day   Month   Year

Date of Judgement —☐☐☐   Amount of Award: £ ☐

**PART 4: STATUTORY MINIMUM WAGES UNDER AN
EMPLOYMENT REGULATION ORDER**

Note: A claim under this part is not payable unless proceedings against the employer,
under section 45(1) of the Industrial Relations Act, 1946, for the amount involved
have been instituted.

State title of Employment
Regulation Order

Have proceedings been instituted against the employer — | Yes | | tick ✓
                                                          | No | | appropriate box

If yes, by whom

In which Court (if applicable)

State period in respect of which the claim is being made:

From: | Day | Month | Year | To: | Day | Month | Year | Total number
                                                                          of weeks

Total Arrears Claimed — £

PART 5 : UNFAIR DISMISSALS ACT, 1977

(1) Rights Commissioner Recommendation (Note: Attach copy of Recommendation).

Date of Recommendation — | Day | Month | Year | Amount of Award — £

Has an appeal been lodged with the Employment Appeals Tribunal? — | Yes | | tick ✓
                                                                   | No | | appropriate box

(2) Employment Appeals Tribunal Determination (Note: Attach copy of determination).

Date of Determination — | Day | Month | Year | Reference Number:

Amount of Award — £

Has an appeal been lodged with the Circuit Court? — | Yes | | tick ✓
                                                     | No | | appropriate box

(3) Court Order (See note below)

Date of Order — | Day | Month | Year | Amount of Award — £

I apply for payment due to me under the Protection of Employees (Employers' Insolvency)
Act, 1984 and declare that I have made no other applications in respect of the amounts
shown above. I am aware that my rights and remedies against my employer in respect of
this amount will be transferred to the Minister for Labour when payment has been made.
I also declare in respect of the amounts claimed above that I have made no appeal in
respect of these amounts and I am not aware, to the best of my knowledge, that these
amounts are the subject of appeal by anybody else.

Signature: _____   Date: _____

Note: This part should also be used to claim payment of court awards for damages at
common law for wrongful dismissal.

APPLICATION BY AN EMPLOYER'S REPRESENTATIVE FOR FUNDS TO PAY ENTITLEMENTS UNDER AN EMPLOYMENT REGULATION ORDER, UNFAIR DISMISSALS ACT, 1977 , ANTI-DISCRIMINATION (PAY) ACT,1974 AND EMPLOYMENT EQUALITY ACT,1977.

An Roinn Saothair - Department of Labour
Protection of Employees (Employers' Insolvency) Act, 1984.

PLEASE COMPLETE THIS FORM IN BLOCK CAPITALS

Business Name of Insolvent Employer	Employer's P.A.Y.E Registered Number Figures Letter
Business address of Insolvent Employer	Date of Insolvency (eg date of appointment of Liquidator, Receiver etc.) Day Month Year
Nature of Business	For Office Use Nace	Type of Insolvency (e.g. liquidation, receivership, bankruptcy, etc)

To: Minister for Labour, Davitt House, Mespil Road, Dublin 4.

In connection with the provisions of the Protection of Employees (Employers' Insolvency) Act, 1984, I have accepted, to the best of my knowledge, the entitlement of the employees as shown in this form. No other notification has been made by me in respect of these entitlements. I understand that it may be necessary for you to refer information on the entitlements to the Revenue Commissioners and Government Departments. I hereby give my consent to the disclosure of such information as may be necessary. I also agree to make available to you such records as may be required for examination. I undertake to distribute the appropriate amounts to the employees concerned from the funds received pursuant to this applicatic

I declare in respect of the amounts shown on this form for the employees concerned that I have made no appeal in relation to the amounts shown and I am not aware, to the best of my knowledge, that these amounts are the subject of appeal by the employees concerned or anybody else.

The instrument of payment should be drawn in favour of

Address

Signature of Employer's Representative

Date: Telephone:

1	2	3	4	5	6	7
Employer's Name	Revenue and Social Insurance Number	Amount under the Anti-Discrimination(Pay) Act, 1974. £	Amount under the Employment Equality Act, 1977. £	Amount under Unfair Dismissals Act, 1977 or Court Order for wrongful dismissal	Amount under the Industrial Relations Act, 1946 (Employment Regulation Order)	Total of columns (3), (4), (5) & (6). £
					GRAND TOTAL	£

SCHEDULE

PART I   FORM IP6

| AN ROINN SAOTHAIR | | DEPARTMENT OF LABOUR |

APPLICATION FOR PAYMENT OF UNPAID OCCUPATIONAL PENSION SCHEME CONTRIBUTIONS

PROTECTION OF EMPLOYEES (EMPLOYERS' INSOLVENCY) ACTS, 1984 AND 1990.

> **IMPORTANT: PLEASE READ THESE NOTES**
> **BEFORE COMPLETING THIS FORM**

1. Part 1 of this form and the schedule should be completed by a trustee, administrator or other person competent to act on behalf of the occupational pension scheme.

2. After completion of Part 1 and the schedule, this form should be sent or returned to the insolvent employer's representative.

3. The insolvent employer's representative is the person appointed in connection with an employer's insolvency (e.g., receiver, liquidator or a person appointed by the Minister for Labour under Section 5 of the Protection of Employees (Employers' Insolvency) Act, 1984).

4. Part 2 of this form should be completed by the insolvent employer's representative.

5. Where a claim is being made for unpaid contributions payable by an employer on his own account, a completed actuarial certificate, Form IP7, must be obtained by the insolvent employer's representative and attached to the claim.

6. A copy of the terms of occupational pension scheme should be attached to this application, if not already furnished to the Department of Labour.

7. Documentation confirming the existence of the occupational pension scheme should accompany this application, e.g. a Trust Deed and a Deed of Adherence in the case of an industry-wide scheme and a Trust Deed in the case of an individual scheme.

8. The annual subscription rate together with a breakdown of the unpaid contributions in respect of the 12 months prior to the date of insolvency should be attached.

9. The date of insolvency for the purpose of payments under the above Act is defined in Section 4 of the Protection of Employees (Employers' Insolvency) Act, 1984.

> **PART 1   TO BE COMPLETED BY A PERSON COMPETENT TO**
> **ACT FOR THE OCCUPATIONAL PENSION SCHEME**
> *(See Note 1)*

To   ...   .

NAME OF INSOLVENT EMPLOYER'S REPRESENTATIVE

I am/we are authorised to
act on behalf of ...   ...

NAME OF OCCUPATIONAL PENSION SCHEME

In respect of employee(s) of

NAME OF INSOLVENT EMPLOYER

TYPE OF OCCUPATIONAL PENSION SCHEME
(e.g., Contributory, Non-contributory)

I/We certify that the provisions of the occupational pension scheme, which
was in operation for the 12 months prior to the date of the insolvency,
provided for contributions as follows:—

Total amount of contributions payable on the
employer's own account for the 12 months
prior to the date of insolvency   ...   ...   £

Total amount of contributions payable by the
employee(s) for the 12 months prior to the
date of insolvency ...   .   £

I/We apply for payment from the Social Insurance Fund, in accordance with
the terms of the Protection of Employees (Employers' Insolvency) Acts,
1984 and 1990, of relevant unpaid contributions to the occupational pension
scheme.

I/We declare that any money received by me/us as a result of this application
will be paid into the resources of the occupational pension scheme.

I/We understand that where payment is made from the Fund in respect of pension contributions, any rights and remedies in respect of those contributions belonging to the persons competent to act in respect of the scheme shall become rights and remedies of the Minister for Labour.

Signature(s) _____

_____

_____ Date_____

Designation (Trustee/Administrator, etc.) _____

_____

Name(s)

Address

PART 2   TO BE COMPLETED BY THE INSOLVENT
         EMPLOYER'S REPRESENTATIVE

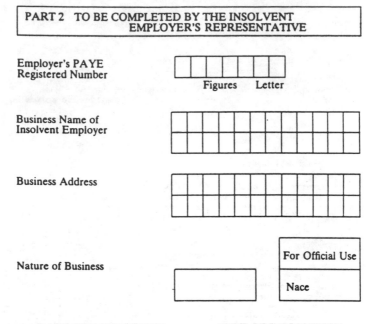

Employer's PAYE
Registered Number

Figures   Letter

Business Name of
Insolvent Employer

Business Address

Nature of Business

For Official Use

Nace

DATE OF INSOLVENCY   TYPE OF INSOLVENCY

(As defined in Section 4 of the Pro-   (e.g. Liquidation, Receivership,
tection of Employees (Employers'   Bankruptcy, etc.)
Insolvency) Act, 1984)

Day   Month   Year

I have examined the claim set out in Part 1 on this form and in the attached
schedule. I certify, based on the best information available to me, that the
amount of contributions which were not paid into the occupational pension
scheme in respect of the 12 months prior to the date of insolvency are:—

Amount unpaid by the insolvent employer on
his own account   ...   .   £

Amount deducted from the employees' wages
in respect of contributions to the occupational   £
pension scheme but which was not paid into
the said scheme   ...   .

Did sickness/disability   Did Life Assurance form
form part of the scheme   part of the scheme
                    Yes   No   Yes   No

If "yes" state element of   If "yes" state element of

contribution_____   contribution_____

An Actuarial Certificate (Form IP 7) Is attached   Is not   (*Tick*
(*See Note 5*)   attached   *appropriate*
                                                                 box)

☐   ☐

To: Minister for Labour,
Davitt House,
Mespil Road,
Dublin 4.

In accordance with the provisions of the Protection of Employees
(Employers' Insolvency) Acts, 1984 and 1990, I have accepted, based on
the best information available to me, the amounts outstanding to the
occupational pension scheme as shown in this application. I confirm that
all employees in the scheme were insurable at the date of termination of
employment for all benefits under the Social Welfare Acts, 1981 to 1990
in accordance with section 3 of the Protection of Employees (Employers'
Insolvency) Act, 1984. I understand that it may be necessary for you to
verify information on the application with other Government Departments. I hereby give my consent to the disclosure of such information as
may be necessary. I also agree to make available to you such records as
may be required for examination. I undertake to pay to the applicant
for payment into the occupational pension scheme concerned any funds
received pursuant to this application.

Name of Employer's
Representative

Address

Signature of Employer's Representative_____

Date_____ Telephone Number_____

WARNING LEGAL PROCEEDINGS MAY BE TAKEN
AGAINST ANYONE MAKING A FALSE STATE-
MENT ON THIS FORM

SCHEDULE

Schedule of deductions made from employees' wages (Contributory Pension Scheme) and on behalf of employees (Non-contributory Pension Scheme) in respect of contributions to the Occupational Pension Scheme which were not paid into the Scheme.

NAME OF OCCUPATIONAL PENSION SCHEME

(Attach continuation sheets to this schedule if necessary)

Name of Employee*	R.S.I. Number	Period of Debt		Amount Deducted but not paid into Scheme†
		From	To	£
		Grand Total		£

* State if any of the employees were directors of the company by placing "D" after the name above.

† Contributions are payable only in respect of periods of paid employment during the period of debt.

PART II   FORM IP7

ACTUARIAL CERTIFICATE

UNPAID OCCUPATIONAL PENSION SCHEME CONTRIBUTIONS

AN ROINN SAOTHAIR — DEPARTMENT OF LABOUR

PROTECTION OF EMPLOYEES (EMPLOYERS' INSOLVENCY) ACTS,
1984 AND 1990.

IMPORTANT: PLEASE READ THESE NOTES
             BEFORE COMPLETING THIS CERTIFICATE

1. This certificate should be completed by an actuary.

2. This certificate must accompany Form IP 6 when a claim in respect
    of unpaid pension scheme contributions, payable by an Employer
    on his own account, is being made.

NAME OF OCCUPATIONAL PENSION SCHEME

BUSINESS NAME OF INSOLVENT   DATE OF INSOLVENCY
        EMPLOYER

[As defined in Section 4 of the Act]

Day   Month   Year

(*a*) The dissolution provisions of the above occupational pension scheme
are as set out in the attached copy of the terms of the occupational
pension scheme.

(*b*) I certify, in accordance with Section 7 (3) (*b*) of
the Protection of Employees (Employers' Insol-   £
vency) Act, 1984, that the amount necessary for the
purposes of meeting the liability of the scheme on
dissolution to pay the benefits provided by the scheme
to or in respect of the employees of the employer is

SIGNATURE OF ACTUARY   DATE

PROFESSIONAL QUALIFICATION

BUSINESS NAME AND ADDRESS OF ACTUARY		
Last Name		First Name

SECTION FOUR

INDUSTRIAL RELATIONS AND ADJUDICATING BODIES

This section explains the operation of the various industrial relations and adjudicating bodies, namely the Labour Relations Commission and its various services, in particular Rights Commissioners and Equality Officers. The Labour Court in its role of hearing both industrial relations and equality claims is considered, as is the operation of the Employment Appeals Tribunal.

The practice and procedure for bringing claims and appeals under each piece of employment legislation is considered with the use of the relevant statutory forms (which are printed at the end of each chapter) and the actual procedure of the bodies at hearing. Irish legislation has a battery of forms and different bodies to whom claims are brought and this section aims to explain and simplify these procedures.

CHAPTER TWENTY-TWO

Labour Relations Commission

The Industrial Relations Act, 1990 established the Labour Relations Commission, which formally came into operation on 21 January 1991. The purpose of the Labour Relations Commission is to promote better industrial relations. One of the main reasons for its establishment was to enhance the appellate function of the Labour Court, which was hearing too many matters that could and should have been resolved at a lower level or between the parties themselves.

The Labour Relations Commission comprises:

(1) A chairperson, who is appointed by the Minister for Enterprise and Employment after consultation with both employer and employee organisations;

(2) Two employee and two employer members who are nominated by the Minister following consultation with their relevant organisations, namely, the Irish Business and Employers' Confederation (formerly the Federation of Irish Employers) and the Irish Congress of Trade Unions; and

(3) Two independent members also nominated by the Minister.

The Labour Relations Commission also has a chief executive. The first chief executive was appointed by the then Minister for Labour and each subsequent one will be appointed by the Minister, after consultation with the Commission.

FUNCTIONS OF THE COMMISSION

The Commission has general responsibility for promoting the improvement of industrial relations, including the following functions:

(1) To provide a conciliation service

(2) To provide an industrial relations advisory service

(3) To prepare codes of practice relevant to industrial relations, after consultation with unions and employer organisations

(4) To offer guidance and help to resolve disputes concerning their implementation

(5) To appoint Equality Officers of the Commission and provide staff and facilities for the equality officer service

(6) To nominate persons for appointment as Rights Commissioners and provide staff and facilities for the rights commissioner service

(7) To conduct or commission research into matters relevant to industrial relations

(8) To review and monitor developments in the area of industrial relations

(9) To assist joint labour committees and joint industrial councils in the exercise of their functions.

INDUSTRIAL RELATIONS

The primary purpose of the Labour Relations Commission is to resolve trade disputes through conciliation without reference to the Labour Court. The Labour Relations Commission investigates each dispute and the Labour Court only becomes involved once the Commission reports that no further efforts will advance resolution, or if it waives its conciliation function. Of course, if there are "exceptional circumstances", the Labour Court may intervene in a dispute, provided it has first consulted the Labour Relations Commission.

The Commission may, at the request of one or more parties to a trade dispute or on its own initiative, offer its appropriate services with a view to bringing about a settlement.

Unless there is provision within a procedure for direct reference to the Labour Court, trade disputes shall be first referred to the Commission, generally to the conciliation service. Previously, Industrial Relations Officers (more usually called Conciliation Officers) were part of the Labour Court, but they are now incorporated within the Labour Relations Commission.

The Labour Relations Commission has assisted in the drawing up of Codes of Practice under the Industrial Relations Act, namely the Code of Practice on Dispute Procedures, 1992. It has also been involved in the resolution of the many disputes since its establishment.

REFERENCE OF A DISPUTE BY MINISTER

Where the Minister for Enterprise and Employment is of the opinion that a trade dispute has either occurred or may occur in the future, and if it affects the public interest, the Minister may refer the matter to the Commission or the Court which shall endeavour to resolve the dispute.

If the Minister is of the opinion that the trade dispute is of special importance, the Commission or the Court or others may be requested to conduct an inquiry into the dispute and to furnish a report to the Minister on the findings.

EQUALITY SERVICE

The equality service, which comprises Equality Officers who hear claims under the equality legislation, was originally part of the Labour Court and is now part of the Labour Relations Commission. Equality officers are independent in their function and a person who is dissatisfied with a recommendation may appeal to the Labour Court (see below on equality claims).

RIGHTS COMMISSIONER SERVICE

A Rights Commissioner can hear individual grievances/disputes under the Industrial Relations Act, 1969, the Unfair Dismissals Acts, 1977 to 1993, the Maternity Protection of Employees Acts, 1981 and 1991 and the Payment of Wages Act, 1991.* A rights commissioner shall be independent in the performance of their functions and is now also part of the Labour Relations Commission.

With respect to an individual grievance under the Industrial Relations Act, 1969, a party to a trade dispute may object to a rights commissioner hearing the matter, but must do so within three weeks after notice has been sent by post to that party. Otherwise, the objection shall have no effect. An appeal of a rights commissioner's recommendation to the Labour Court must be notified in writing to the Court within six weeks after the recommendation. A rights commissioner must notify the Court, the Minister for Enterprise and Employment and the Commission of every recommendation made by the rights commissioner.

*It is also proposed that the rights commissioner will hear initial claims under the Adoptive Leave Bill, 1993 and the Terms of Employment (Information) Bill, 1993.

Rights commissioner hearings are heard in private and are relatively informal. Invariably both parties have a short written submission setting out the facts of the matter with their respective arguments. The rights commissioner commences proceedings by confirming the Act under which the claim is brought and then hears the respective arguments. At this stage the rights commissioner may wish to see each party on its own to find out further information and to see if there is a basis for a resolution to the dispute. If the rights commissioner does not see a resolution the parties will be called back together, asked if there are further arguments and then advised that a written recommendation will be issued in due course. If there is a resolution to the dispute the rights commissioner will act as a mediator to try and effect a settlement. When a settlement is reached, the rights commissioner may draft the settlement agreement and have it signed by both parties. This settlement agreement may then be issued in the form of a recommendation. All recommendations are private to the parties.

If there is no settlement of the dispute, the recommendation may be appealed to the Labour Court.

There are no specific forms to refer a dispute to the rights commissioner services or to appeal a recommendation to the Labour Court.

UNFAIR DISMISSALS ACTS, 1977 TO 1993 AND MATERNITY PROTECTION OF EMPLOYEES ACTS, 1981 AND 1991

An individual who considers that they were unfairly dismissed may refer their claim under the Unfair Dismissals Acts to a rights commissioner. The claim (in writing) must be served on the rights commissioner within six months of the date of dismissal (see page 324). The Unfair Dismissals (Amendment) Act, 1993 provides that, in exceptional circumstances, the claim may be served within 12 months of the date of dismissal (see Chapter 23). The employer may within 21 days of receipt of the notice object to a rights commissioner hearing the case. The objection must be in writing to the rights commissioner's office. If there is an objection, the employee may refer the matter to the Employment Appeals Tribunal. Once the unfair dismissals claim has been properly served on both the employer and the rights commissioner, there is no problem on time limits. Thus, where there is an objection to the rights commissioner hearing, the claim does not have to be referred to the EAT within the six-month time limit (*The State (Hywel J. John)* v. *the Employment Appeals Tribunal, Imbucon Management Consultants Ltd., and Imbucon Management Consultants (Ireland) Ltd.* ((1984) 3 JISLL 143) (note: the amendments on time limits in the 1993 Act should avoid such a situation occurring).

An employee who considers that she was dismissed or claims constructive dismissal for a maternity related reason may claim under both the Unfair Dismissals Acts and the Maternity Acts within the same time limits. The same procedures as above apply. A claimant who was denied some benefit under the Maternity Acts (e.g. annual leave) must bring her claim within 156 weeks of the occurrence of the dispute (see page 325).

If the matter goes to hearing by a rights commissioner and is not settled, the recommendation may be appealed to the Employment Appeals Tribunal within six weeks of the receipt of the recommendation. The appeal must be served on the Employment Appeals Tribunal (and advisedly on the other party as soon as possible after service on the Tribunal). (For a maternity appeal see page 330). Notwithstanding this provision in the 1993 Act, it is advisable to serve the notice to the other side within the six-week limit. The appeal must be in writing (the RP51A form (see Chapter 23 — Employment Appeals Tribunal) may be used) and contain the following details:

- Name of the case, e.g. *X* (employee) v. *Y Ltd.* (employer)
- Reference number
- Name of employer with address
- Name of employee with address
- Date of commencement of employment
- Date of notice of dismissal
- Date of termination
- Weekly pay — gross and net
- Statement that appellant wishes to appeal the recommendation to the Employment Appeals Tribunal
- Name of representative.

The appeal must be signed by the appellant or the appellant's representative.

PAYMENT OF WAGES ACT, 1991

Complaints Procedure

An employee may complain to a rights commissioner in writing (see page 326) that their employer has made an unlawful deduction or required an unlawful payment from his wages. A complaint must be made within six months of the date of the alleged breach of the Act. However, the rights commissioner has discretion if they are satisfied that exceptional circumstances prevented the making of the complaint in time. Thus, the six-month period can be extended by a further six months as is considered reasonable.

The rights commissioner will send a copy of the Notice of Complaint to the employer. The parties will then be given an opportunity to be heard and to present any evidence relating to the complaint. After the hearing, the rights commissioner will give a decision in writing (unless the matter is settled). Proceedings before the rights commissioner will be in public unless a party makes a successful application to the rights commissioner to have the matter heard in private.

Compensation for Illegal Deductions

If a rights commissioner considers a complaint to be well-founded, the employer will be ordered to pay the employee compensation. The rights commissioner may award twice the amount of deduction or payment (by the employee) or else one week's net wages — whichever is the greater.

A rights commissioner cannot issue a decision at any time after the employee has commenced proceedings in the civil courts for the recovery of the deduction or payment. Equally, an employee cannot recover monies for the payment or deduction if the rights commissioner has given a decision.

The rights commissioner must send a copy of the decision to the Employment Appeals Tribunal.

Appeal to Employment Appeals Tribunal

Either party may appeal the decision of the rights commissioner in writing to the Employment Appeals Tribunal. Such an appeal must be made within six weeks of the date of the communication of the rights commissioner recommendation. The Payment of Wages (Appeals) Regulations, 1991, SI 351 of 1991 governs appeals to the Tribunal. An appeal shall contain the following information:

(1) The names, addresses and descriptions of the parties to the proceedings;

(2) The date of the decision to which the appeal relates and the name of the rights commissioner who made the decision; and

(3) A brief outline of the grounds of appeal.

The RP51A Form (see Chapter 23) may be used for the appeal.

Time Limits for Implementation

A rights commissioner's decision or a Tribunal determination may give a date by which the decision or determination will be implemented, in other words, the date by which the monies must be paid to the employee. If no such date is given, the implementation (payment) date is deemed to be six weeks from the date on which the decision/determination was communicated to the parties concerned.

Enforcement of Decisions and Determinations

A rights commissioner's decision or a Tribunal determination may be enforced as if it were an order of the Circuit Court made by a judge of that court.

TERMS OF EMPLOYMENT (INFORMATION) BILL, 1993

It is proposed that an employee may claim in writing that an employer has breached the Bill within six months of the date of commencement of employment. The rights commissioner may:

(1) Declare that the claim was or was not well founded;

(2) Confirm the particulars in the statement or alter or add to the statement;

(3) Require the employer to give the employee a written statement containing the particulars as specified by the rights commissioner;

(4) Order the employer to pay the employee compensation up to four weeks' remuneration.

The rights commissioner recommendation may be appealed to the

Employment Appeals Tribunal within six weeks of the date of com-munication. It is recommended that the Notice of Appeal be served on the employer also. The Tribunal may also enforce the recommen-dation.

ADOPTIVE LEAVE BILL, 1993

It is proposed that a dispute under this Bill may be referred to a rights commissioner within six months from the date the employer receives first notification of the adopting parent's intention to take leave (or additional leave) under the Bill. In exceptional circum-stances the time limit may be extended to 12 months. It is recom-mended that the employer be served with a copy of the claim.

The rights commissioner recommendation may be appealed to the Employment Appeals Tribunal within four weeks of the date of the recommendation. The Tribunal shall copy the appeal to the employer within five weeks.

If there was a dismissal arising from adoptive leave, a claim should be brought under the unfair dismissal legislation.

LABOUR COURT

The Labour Court was established under the Industrial Relations Act, 1946 to assist in the resolution of industrial disputes and to uphold good standards in industrial relations.

The Court consists of a chairperson and, currently, two deputy chairpersons. There are six members of the Court who are appointed by the Minister for Enterprise and Employment on the nomination of the Irish Business and Employers' Confederation and the Irish Congress of Trade Unions. Those members of the Court are known as employer or employee members. The persons appointed are ex-perienced union and employer organisation officials or former indus-trial relations specialists. The Court works in divisions with each division comprising the chairperson, or vice-chairperson, and an employer and employee member. The members of the Court are not lawyers but the Court has a legally qualified registrar who advises on legal issues. The Court can appoint technical assessors (usually specialist advisors) if it so wishes, as long as the advice is put to the parties to the dispute for their comment (see *The State (Cole)* v. *The Labour Court* (1984) 3 JISLL 128).

Industrial relations matters are first referred to the Labour

Relations Commission and, if matters are not settled at this stage and if the Commission is satisfied that no further efforts on its part will advance the resolution of the dispute, then the matter may be referred to the Labour Court. Both sides have to agree to the Labour Court hearing the dispute. The Court will then hear the matter and issue a non-binding recommendation, which may not be appealed to a court of law. If either party to a dispute does not agree to go to conciliation, the matter may be referred by one party to the Court for adjudication. This is under Section 20 of the Industrial Relations Act, 1969. The Court's recommendation is binding on the parties.

A rights commissioner's recommendation (individual grievances under the 1969 Act) may be appealed to the Court and the Court's recommendation is binding on the parties.

Under the equality legislation, the Court acts as a quasi-judicial body, akin to the Employment Appeals Tribunal (see Chapter 24 — Equal Pay and Equal Treatment Claims).

Labour Court hearings are normally held in private but either side may make application to have the hearing in public. The Labour Court hears cases in its premises in Dublin (Beggars Bush, Haddington Road) and sits around the country as is convenient to the parties. Both parties provide written submissions to the Court, and evidence is not heard by the Court as in a court of law. The Court also has power to summon witnesses who may be obliged to bring documents to a hearing. An application has to be made personally to the Court. The Court can also hear evidence on oath, but this is unusual.

```
┌─────────────────────────────────────────────────────────┐
│ ┌───────────────────────────────────────────────────────┤
│ │        Unfair Dismissals Act 1977 - 1993              │
│ │       APPLICATION  TO  RIGHTS  COMMISSIONER           │
└─┴───────────────────────────────────────────────────────┘
```

NAME: _____   EMPLOYER'S NAME _____
                                (Full legal name
                                 if in doubt consult
                                 your P60 OR P45)

ADDRESS: _____   ADDRESS _____

_____   _____

_____   _____

                                (Location of employment)_____

                                   _____

TEL NO _____   TEL NO _____

Date on which Employment began: _____/ /_____

Date of Dismissal: _____/ /_____

Pay (including Benefits and Regular Overtime) per week: £_____

Have you made an appeal to the Employment Appeals Tribunal under
this Act.

The grounds of my claim are as follows:_____

_____

_____

_____

_____

Employee's Signature:_____Date:_____

L.R.C. Tom Johnson House, Haddington Road, Dublin 4.

DEPARTMENT OF LABOUR
MATERNITY PROTECTION OF EMPLOYEES ACT 1981
APPLICATION to RIGHTS COMMISSIONER

EMPLOYEE DETAILS

Name: I_____I

Address: I_____I

I_____I

I_____I

Tel.: _____

EMPLOYER DETAILS

Name: I_____I

Address: I_____I

I_____I

I_____I

Tel.: _____

EMPLOYMENT DETAILS

Employment began: _____/_____/_____

Employment ended: _____/_____/_____ [if applicable]

Pay (including benefits and regular overtime)
per week: £_____

ADDITIONAL INFORMATION

Have you made an appeal to the Employment Appeals Tribunal
under:

REDUNDANCY PAYMENTS ACTS?	YESI__INOI__I
MINIMUM NOTICE ACT?	YESI__INOI__I
MATERNITY ACT?	YESI__INOI__I

(please tick)

GROUNDS OF THE CLAIM: _____

_____

_____

_____

EMPLOYEES SIGNATURE_____ **DATE:** _____

THE LABOUR RELATIONS COMMISSION
An Coimisiún um Chaidreamh Oibreachais

TOM JOHNSON HOUSE, HADDINGTON ROAD, DUBLIN 4. TEL: 01-660 9662 FAX: 01-668 5069
Teach Thomás Mac Seáin, Bóthar Haddington, Baile Átha Cliath 4. Tel: 01-660 9662 Fax: 01-668 5069

NOTICE OF COMPLAINT TO RIGHTS COMMISSIONER
PAYMENT OF WAGES ACT 1991

NAME: _____ : EMPLOYER'S NAME _____
                                 : (Full legal name)
                                 : (if in doubt consult_____
                                 : (your P60 or P45)_____
ADDRESS_____ : ADDRESS _____
        _____ :   _____
                                 :   _____
TEL NO _____ : TEL NO _____

I wish to present a complaint to a Rights Commissioner that my
employer contravened the above Act in relation to A OR B below.
(Please complete appropriate section).

(A) DEDUCTION FROM PAY   DATE OF DEDUCTION_____

     AMOUNT OF DEDUCTION £ _____   DID YOU RECEIVE NOTICE
                                           INTENT TO MAKE THE
                                           DEDUCTION

     WHAT WAS THE REASON FOR THE   YES   NO
     DEDUCTION? please specify
     _____   IF YES HOW MUCH NOTICE?

     _____

                                  OR

(B) ARE YOU MAKING A CLAIM FOR   DATE PAYMENT SHOULD HAVE
     NON PAYMENT OF   BEEN RECEIVED

     (Please calculate monies due)   _____/_____/_____

     1. WAGES/PAY   AMOUNT £_____
     2. MINIMUM NOTICE   AMOUNT £_____
     3. HOLIDAY PAY   AMOUNT £_____
     4. OTHER   AMOUNT £_____
     If 4 please specify   _____

     TOTAL AMOUNT   £_____

SIGNATURE: _____

DATE: _____

Commission Members: D. J. McAuley (Chairman), K. Duffy, F. Flood, P. Flynn, M. Keegan, Prof. J. O'Connor, T. O'Sullivan

---

Chief Executive: Kieran Mulvey

CHAPTER TWENTY-THREE

Employment Appeals Tribunal

The Employment Appeals Tribunal (the Tribunal) was formerly named the Redundancy Appeals Tribunal and was renamed by the Unfair Dismissals Act, 1977. The Tribunal hears claims and appeals under:

- Redundancy Payments Acts, 1967 to 1991
- Minimum Notice and Terms of Employment Acts, 1973 to 1991
- Unfair Dismissals Acts, 1977 to 1993
- Maternity Protection of Employees Act, 1981 and 1991
- Protection of Employees (Employers' Insolvency) Acts, 1984 and 1991
- Worker Protection (Regular Part-time Employees) Act, 1991
- Payment of Wages Act, 1991.

It is proposed that the Tribunal will hear appeals under the Adoptive Leave Bill, 1993 and the Terms of Employment (Information) Bill, 1993, when enacted.

The Tribunal consists of:

(1) A chairperson who must be a solicitor or a barrister of not less than seven years' standing;

(2) Twelve vice-chairpersons, all of whom are solicitors or barristers; and

(3) Thirty-eight ordinary members who are representative in equal numbers of employers and employees. The employer members are nominated by employer organisations and the employee members by ICTU.

All members are appointed by the Minister for Enterprise and Employment, usually for a three-year term.

The Tribunal sits by division, each division comprising the chair-person or a vice-chairperson, an employer and an employee member. A secretary from the Tribunal secretariat is also in attendance.

This chapter describes the operation of the Tribunal and the various requirements to bring claims under the Acts listed above. The text is arranged in the appropriate procedural sequence, as opposed to considering each Act separately, in order to avoid unnecessary repetition.

WRITTEN REASON FOR DISMISSAL

A person who has been dismissed should write to their employer and ask for the written reasons for the dismissal as provided for in section 14 of the Unfair Dismissals Acts. An employer must respond in writing within 14 days of this request. An employer does not have to go into detail but must give a statement of the principal grounds for dismissal. The next stage is for the former employee to consider whether to bring a claim under the Unfair Dismissals Acts. At this stage it would be prudent for an employee to seek advice from a solicitor or trade union official.

There may be another option to bringing a statutory unfair dismissal claim, that is, the case could be brought to the civil courts for wrongful dismissal. The Unfair Dismissals (Amendment) Act, 1993 provides that once either a rights commissioner has issued a recommendation or the Tribunal hearing has commenced, an employee cannot bring a claim for wrongful dismissal. Alternatively, once a court hearing has commenced for wrongful dismissal, an employee cannot bring a claim for unfair dismissal.

HOW TO BRING A CLAIM

In order to bring a claim, an employee must get a copy of the RP51A form (see page 354) which is available from the Tribunal offices or from employment exchanges. As stated above, there are various Acts — as listed below — under which a claimant (an employee or a former employee) can claim.

Unfair Dismissals Acts

A claimant must have the requisite service, have worked the appro-priate hours and six months must not have elapsed since the date of dismissal (see service of RP51A below). The "date of dismissal" may be summarised as:

> where prior notice has been given under the contract of employment and the Minimum Notice and Terms of Employment Acts, the date the notice expires. . . .
>
> where either notice was not given or the notice did not comply with the notice as provided for in the contract of employment or the Minimum Notice and Terms of Employment Acts, then the date of dismissal is the later of the dates to comply with the notice in the contract or the Acts *or* if there is not a renewal of a fixed-term or specified-purpose contract, the date of the expiry or the cesser.

The 1993 Act provides that the time limit may be extended to 12 months from the date of dismissal if the rights commissioner or the Tribunal considers that there are exceptional circumstances which prevented the service of the claim within the six months.

An appeal of a rights commissioner recommendation must be in writing (the RP51A form may be used) and must be filed with the Tribunal within six weeks of the recommendation being given to the parties. The 1977 Act provided that the appeal had to be served on the other side within the six-week period, but the 1993 Act provides that the Tribunal will copy the other side. Nonetheless, it is still recommended to copy the other side within six weeks. The 1993 Act provides that the claim may be served directly on the Tribunal.

Minimum Notice and Terms of Employment Acts

A claimant must have the necessary service, have worked the appropriate hours, and six years must not have elapsed since the notice monies were due.

Redundancy Payments Acts

The claimant must have the necessary service, have worked the appropriate hours, and one year must not have elapsed since the date of dismissal. However, the one-year time limit may be extended by a further year if the Tribunal considers that there is reasonable cause for the delay in bringing the claim.

A proposed claimant may bring a claim under each of these Acts separately or at the same time. It is important to tick off the relevant box or boxes in the claim form (RP51A).

For example, a former employee who considers that they have been unfairly dismissed may bring a claim under the Unfair Dismissals Acts, but they may also consider that they did not receive appropriate notice or did not receive all the notice monies due to them. Thus, it is important that the employer ticks off both these boxes on the claim form; if the boxes are not ticked off the employer technically has not brought a claim under the Acts.

Maternity Protection of Employees Acts

As long as an employee pays Class A PRSI and earns over £25.00 per week, she may claim under this Act. If an employee considers that she was denied (for example) annual leave for the period while she was on maternity leave, she must bring a claim within 156 weeks of the occurrence of the dispute. If an employee considers that she was dismissed because she took maternity leave, or she resigned because the work that she was given upon return from maternity leave was unsuitable, she should bring a claim under this Act. It is also important, however, that she bring a claim under the Unfair Dismissals Acts because it is under that legislation that she may get the necessary redress should she succeed with her claim. If there is an appeal of a rights commissioner's recommendation, it must be filed with the Tribunal and copied to the other side within six weeks of the date of receipt of the recommendation.

Worker Protection (Regular Part-Time Employees) Act

Claims under this Act are usually in respect of a request to the Tribunal to determine whether an employee has the necessary continuous service under the Act. If there is another claim, such as unfair dismissal, redundancy, minimum notice or maternity, a claim should be made under the other appropriate Act(s) (as outlined above) at the same time.

Protection of Employees (Employers' Insolvency) Act

A person claiming under any of the above named Acts in an insolvency situation should claim under this Act as well and the appropriate forms (see Chapter 23 — Employer Insolvency) should be sent to the liquidator at the same time. Before an employee can be in receipt of minimum notice, the Tribunal has to hear the claim and issue a written determination granting such compensation.

Payment of Wages Act

Claims under this Act are by way of appeal from the rights commissioner and must be appealed within six weeks of the date of receipt of the rights commissioner's recommendation.

Adoptive Leave Bill

Claims under this Bill will be by way of appeal from the rights commissioner and must be appealed within four weeks of the date of receipt of the recommendation.

Terms of Employment (Information) Bill

Claims under this Bill will be by way of appeal from a rights commissioner's recommendation and must be appealed within six weeks of the date of receipt of the recommendation.

COMPLETION OF FORM RP51A

We shall now consider the completion of Form RP51A (see page 354) which is the document that actually commences proceedings before the Tribunal. It is extremely important that the employee (prospective claimant) fills it out correctly and that the employer checks all the relevant details on receipt of this form.

An employee may complete this form themselves, though it is more usual to contact a solicitor or union official for assistance. That same representative would represent the employer at the hearing of the case and deal with all the paperwork in the preparation of it.

If a former employee is unable to obtain a blank Form RP51A their claim may be brought by way of letter to the Tribunal clearly stating under what Act(s) the claim is being made, and all the details as given below. It should be noted that this is not recommended but in exceptional circumstances it may be allowed.

Part I

Box 1. What Act(s) are being claimed under? As stated above, it is vital that the appropriate box(es) are ticked off on this form.

Box 2. Name and Address of the person making the claim (or appeal). This is straightforward. However, if the claimant changes address and/or telephone number after completing this form they should advise the Secretary of the Tribunal immediately.

The claimant's occupation, sex and RSI number should also be specified.

Box 3. Name and Address of Employer. The correct and complete title of the employer must be given, for example, ABC Limited, with the appropriate address, that is, registered office or business address. The correct name of the employer can be obtained on the contract of employment, pay slips, P45 or some other company documentation that the employee has received.

It is vital that the correct title of the employer is provided; otherwise, it may be argued before the Tribunal that, as the correct employer is not stated, there is no claim. In an unfair dismissals case, for example, if the correct name of the employer is not given and if six months have elapsed since the date of dismissal, the employee may not be able to bring a claim because technically the claim would be out of time. The claimant would then have to plead that there were exceptional circumstances which prevented the claim being served within the six months, and ask for an extension of up to 12 months from the date of dismissal to serve the claim. Therefore, if an employee or their representative is in any doubt as to the true name of the employer, they should do a search in the Companies Office in Dublin Castle to ascertain the correct name of the employer or, if there is sufficient time, write to the employer for the correct title of the company.

The form also asks for details of the employer's telephone number and the registered PAYE number of the employer. The latter can be ascertained from the pay slip.

Box 4. Name and Address of Employee Representative. The claimant must put in the name and address of the person who will be representing them. This is important because the Tribunal will automatically send to the representative as well as to the employee all documentation regarding the claim. The representative may be a trade union official, a solicitor or some other person. It is important that the claimant not put the name of a representative without notifying that person first and giving them a copy of the claim form.

Box 5. Town or Nearest Town to Place of Employment. The Tribunal hears claims all around the country. However, if the employee states a large town on the form, they might get a speedier hearing because the Tribunal sits more frequently in large centres.

All the Dublin hearings take place in the Tribunal premises in the Department of Enterprise and Employment (Adelaide Road). Country sittings usually take place in courthouses, county council chambers or hotels.

Box 6. Dates. **Date of birth:** though this is generally only relevant in redundancy claims, employees should complete this and employers should check it.

Date employment began: employees should have no difficulty in completing this as all they have to do is refer to their contract of employment. If there is no written contract, however, employees may have difficulty in remembering the exact date of commencement. This frequently happens where the employee commenced employment as a seasonal or casual employee. Usually, they will remember the month and the year when they commenced employment. This detail is extremely important for redundancy and minimum notices cases, less so for unfair dismissal cases as long as the employee has over one year's service. Employers should always check this date from their records and, if incomplete, they should provide the information for the Tribunal at the hearing.

Date dismissal notice was received by the employee: employees usually remember this date, except in some cases where dismissal is in dispute. Nonetheless, it should be completed. Employers should always check this date, especially where there is a claim for minimum notice as well, because an employee could put in a later date and they may pay more notice monies than are actually due. Also, the employee may put in a later date which would give them sufficient service within the relevant legislation.

Date employment ended: this may be the same date as the date notice was given by the employer where, for example, the employee was not given notice or monies in lieu of notice. If an employee was given one month's notice and worked the notice period, then the date that they actually left employment should be given. If the employee was in receipt of monies in lieu of notice then the date that employment ended should be the date that the employee was paid up to, that is, if four weeks' notice was given on 1 March, then the date employment ended is 29 March.

If an employee resigns and claims constructive dismissal, then the date they left employment is the date that should be put in. Employers should ensure that this date is correct, especially where monies in lieu of notice was paid.

Date or expected date of confinement: this date is only necessary where there is a claim under the Maternity Protection of Employees Acts.

Box 7. Normal Weekly Pay. For the purposes of all the above mentioned legislation, it is important to list the weekly pay as opposed to the monthly pay or yearly salary. For example, under the Unfair Dismissals Acts maximum compensation is 104 weeks' remuneration while the Redundancy Acts base statutory redundancy pay on a weekly basis, as do the Minimum Notice and Terms of Employment Acts.

An employee claiming under the Unfair Dismissals Acts should furnish details in net terms, that is, pay less income tax and PRSI. There are specific regulations under the Acts for the computation of weekly pay (Unfair Dismissals (Calculation of Weekly Remuneration) Regulations, 1977 — S.I. No. 287/1977). These regulations are complicated, and standard practice for overtime payments, commissions, shift premia etc. is to average pay received over the six-month period prior to the date of dismissal. If there is any dispute, however, the regulations may be strictly adhered to. These may be summarised as follows:

(1) The weekly earnings of an employee paid at an hourly rate or on a fixed wage or salary shall include any regular bonuses or allowances or payment in kind. For the purposes of the Act, the earnings to be taken are those in the last week of employment prior to the date of dismissal. Overtime may be determined by taking an average of the 26 weeks' worked ending 13 weeks prior to the date of dismissal. If an employee did not work one (or more) of those 26 weeks, a further week(s) prior to then shall be taken into account.

(2) If an employee is paid by piece rate or commission, then the

average is taken by dividing the pay in the 26 weeks (ending 13 weeks prior to the date of dismissal) by the number of hours worked by the employee, and multiplying that amount by the number of hours an employee in similar employment would have worked.

(3) Where there are no normal weekly working hours, the average pay shall be computed over the 52-week period prior to the date of dismissal.

(4) If an employee has less than one year's continuous service, the Tribunal shall calculate the remuneration as near as it can to these regulations.

The Minimum Notice and Terms of Employment Act, 1973 provides details in the Second Schedule for the calculation of pay during the notice period. It may be summarised as follows:

(1) An employee is entitled to be paid in respect of normal working hours when ready and willing to work, even if the employer had no work available. If the employee usually works overtime, it should be included in the term "normal working hours".

(2) If an employee's pay is not calculated with reference to time, or if an employee has no normal working hours (for example, they may be paid by salary and commission or by commission only), then the rate of pay shall be calculated by averaging the pay in the 13 preceding weeks prior to the giving of the notice.

The Redundancy Payments Act, 1967 (as amended) provides rules for the calculation of normal weekly remuneration (subject to a ceiling of £250 per week). It is calculated from the date the employee was declared redundant, that is, the date on which they received notice. It may be summarised as follows:

(1) An employee on a fixed wage, or salary which does not vary in relation to work done, receives the normal weekly earnings (including any regular bonus or payment in kind) at the date of the declaration of the redundancy.

(2) Overtime earnings are calculated by ascertaining the total amount of such earnings in the 26-week period which ended 13 weeks before the date on which the employee was declared redundant, and dividing that amount by 26.

(3) The weekly remuneration of an employee paid by a piece rate or commission (i.e. where remuneration varies in relation to work done),

is calculated by averaging remuneration paid in the 26-week period which ended 13 weeks prior to the declaration of the redundancy.

(4) Any period within the 26 weeks in which the employee did not work should be disregarded and the most recent weeks in which the employee worked prior to the declaration of redundancy are the weeks to be taken into account.

For claims under the minimum notice and redundancy legislation, details should be furnished in gross terms, that is, pay with no deductions of income tax and PRSI. However, for a claim made under the unfair dismissals or minimum notice legislation, details should be available on a gross and net basis.

Basic weekly pay: this is just the basic pay before overtime, shift premia etc. If a person is on a straight salary with no other payment, then the weekly salary should be included here.

Regular bonuses or allowances: this could include shift premia, commission payments and so forth. As these payments may be sporadic and uneven, the pay should be averaged out over 26 weeks ending 13 weeks prior to the date of dismissal or declaration of redundancy.

Average weekly overtime: this should be calculated in the same way as bonuses or allowances.

Any other payments including payments in kind: these would include VHI, company car (the personal element should be included, i.e. non-business mileage), the employer's portion of a pension contribution (this may be found by checking the pension booklet, telephone rental (the personal element, which is usually assessed as one-third of the total).

The weekly total should then be filled in.

An employee who does not know the exact details of the above should put on this section that "details will be supplied". However, the Tribunal should be reverted to as soon as possible with such details.

Employers should check this section in great detail because otherwise compensation (under any heading) awarded by the Tribunal may cost them more than it should. Employers should always go to the Tribunal with all pay details for the employee for at least the nine months prior to dismissal.

Normal weekly working hours: this should be completed by the employee but it is not significant as long as the employee is normally expected to work the requisite eight hours per week.

Box 8. Basis of Employment and Type of Business. Employees should state whether they were permanent, temporary, seasonal or whether they were working under fixed-term or specified purpose contracts. Details of the expiry of contracts should be given. This can be very important where there is a series of fixed term contracts or where the employee has been working as a seasonal employee. Employers should check this as well in case any difficulties arise under the above points. It should be noted once more that "permanent" and "temporary" have no legal meaning as long as the employee has worked for the requisite period to be covered under the relevant legislation.

Details of the type of business should be very brief, for example, shop or engineering works.

Box 9. Grounds of Application. It is important that this be accurately completed — for example, "dismissed for alleged theft without explanation and there was no warning" or "redundancy lump sum wrongly calculated" or "I received two weeks' notice monies instead of four weeks' monies" — because this is all the Tribunal may see before the hearing and if it is incomplete or inaccurate they may get the wrong impression of the case.

Employers should read this section as well because if there are any inaccuracies (even if the claim is going to be defended) the employer should be aware of them when they are completing the defence, known as the Form T2 (see below).

Box 10. Redress Sought. This is obviously important, especially under the unfair dismissals legislation. Does the employee want their job back? If so, they should put in "reinstatement". If they want compensation they should state so on the form. The Tribunal will check as to what redress the employee wants at the end of the hearing, but nonetheless it should be accurately completed.

An employee claiming under the redundancy legislation should put in "redundancy lump sum" and/or "added years of service". If an employee is claiming under the minimum notice legislation, they should put in "monies in lieu of notice" and/or "additional notice monies based on correct length of service".

Employers should read this section to find out what redress the employee is seeking. For example, if the employee is looking for compensation for an unfair dismissals claim, the employer may decide to enter into negotiations if the employee is willing. There is no obligation on the employee or the employee's representative to enter into any discussions at any stage.

Box 11. Signature and Date. The employee should sign and date the form.

Part 2

This part of the RP51A only has to be completed by employees bringing claims under the Unfair Dismissals Acts or the Maternity Protection of Employees Acts.

Under the Unfair Dismissals Acts, the questions are as follows:

Have you sued your employer under Common Law procedures in the matter of your claim on unfair dismissal? The answer to this question should be "No" because an employee should only commence proceedings under the Act or at common law for wrongful dismissal but not both. If proceedings are commenced under one heading, you are precluded from proceedings under the other, although note the provisions of the 1993 Act.

Have you a claim currently with a rights commissioner on unfair dismissal? An employee can initially bring their claim to a rights commissioner and appeal that recommendation to the Tribunal, but they cannot have initial applications in both adjudicating bodies.

Do you object to a claim on unfair dismissal being heard by a rights commissioner? If the claim is to be heard by the Tribunal (except on appeal from a rights commissioner's recommendation) the answer to this should be "Yes" since the Tribunal cannot hear a claim unless the rights commissioner hearing has been objected to within 21 days of receipt of the claim. If an initial claim was sent to a rights commissioner by the employee and the employer has objected to it being heard by the rights commissioner, then this should be so stated.

Are you appealing a recommendation of a rights commissioner in regard to your claim on unfair dismissal? As the same form is used for an appeal of a rights commissioner recommendation to the Tribunal, the answer to this should be "Yes". The name of the rights commissioner and the date of the recommendation should be given.

An appeal of such a recommendation must be served on the Tribunal and the other side (i.e. the employer or the employee) within six weeks of the date of receipt of the recommendation.

If this is not an appeal of a rights commissioner's recommendation, the answer should be "No".

Are you referring your claim to the Tribunal following the failure of your employer to implement (within six weeks) a recommendation of a rights commissioner on unfair dismissal? A rights commissioner recommendation should be implemented within six weeks, that is, compensation should be paid to the employee or the reinstatement or re-engagement should take place with payment of "back monies" as appropriate. Again, this is important because the Tribunal should be aware of this occurrence, although technically the reference to the Tribunal for implementation does not have to take place within six weeks of the recommendation. The name of the rights commissioner and the date of the recommendation should be provided.

Under the Maternity Protection of Employees Act the questions are as follows:

Have you a dispute currently with a rights commissioner about maternity entitlement (other than unfair dismissal)? The purpose of this question is to ascertain whether the employee has another claim under the Maternity Acts, for example, provision of company car during maternity leave. Such claims are rare, as invariably the claims under the Acts go hand in hand with an unfair dismissal claim.

Do you object to a dispute under the Maternity Protection of Employees Act being heard by a Rights Commissioner? The same points as under the Unfair Dismissals Acts apply.

Are you appealing a recommendation of a Rights Commissioner in regard to a dispute about maternity entitlement? The same points as under the Unfair Dismissals Acts apply.

Are you referring your case to the Tribunal following the failure of your employer to implement a recommendation of a rights commissioner on maternity entitlement? The same points as under the Unfair Dismissals Acts apply.

SERVICE OF RP51A

Once the RP51A has been completed it should be sent by registered post or delivered personally to the Tribunal in Dublin. A copy of the RP51A should be sent to the employer either by registered post or by hand. Service must be within the six-month limitation period unless it has been extended because of exceptional circumstances. The 1993 Act provides that a copy of the RP51A shall be given to the employer as soon as possible after receipt by the Tribunal of the claim. This new provision suggests that the employer does not have to be served within the limitation period. As there is no interpretation of this section yet, it would be prudent to ensure that both the Tribunal and the employer are served within the limitation period.

There is a form RP51B which may be used by either an employer or an employee when appealing against a decision of the Minister for Enterprise and Employment in a redundancy matter. In practice, this form is normally used by employers appealing to the Tribunal contending that the deciding officer in the redundancy section of the Department did not allow them a full redundancy rebate (see Chapter 18 — Redundancy).

APPEALS FROM RIGHTS COMMISSIONER RECOMMENDATION

The RP51A form may be used as the form to appeal a rights commissioner's recommendation under the Unfair Dismissals Acts or the Maternity Protection of Employees Acts. The RP51A should be served on the Tribunal in exactly the same way as above within six weeks from the date the rights commissioner's recommendation was given to the parties.

IMPLEMENTATION OF RIGHTS COMMISSIONER'S RECOMMENDATION

The Unfair Dismissals (Amendment) Act, 1993 provides that if a recommendation has not been carried out by an employer and the time limit for an appeal has expired, then it may be referred to the Tribunal for a determination to implement it. The Tribunal will not have to rehear the case.

TITLES OF THE PARTIES

Once the claim form has been served, the former employee and the employer are now party to legal proceedings. Thus they shall be called the claimant (the former employee) and the respondent (the employer). When there is an appeal of a rights commissioner's recommendation the party bringing the appeal is the appellant and the other party is the respondent. However, for simplicity, the parties shall be called the claimant and the respondent.

DEFENCE — NOTICE OF APPEARANCE — FORM T2

Once the employer has been served with an RP51A, a defence must be filed with the Tribunal. The regulations (Unfair Dismissals (Claims and Appeals) Regulations, 1977 — SI No. 286 of 1977) provide that the Notice of Appearance — see page 356 — must be filed with the Tribunal within 14 days.

When the RP51A is served on the employer by the claimant, there is no "blank" T2 form attached. Thus the practice has arisen where on receipt of the RP51A, the Tribunal copies it to the employer attaching a blank T2 and allots a reference number to the case — for example, UD 1/1993 — which is shown on the T2. The Acts under which the claimant is claiming are also marked by the Secretariat of the Tribunal. There is no obligation on the Tribunal to send the T2 to the respondent/employer, however, and to avoid difficulties with the 14-day limit, the practice has arisen of the employer/respondent writing a letter to the Tribunal on receipt of the RP51A, advising that it intends to defend the claim(s) and briefly stating the grounds of defence. It is acceptable to file the defence by way of such letter.

The 1977 regulations (as amended) state that:

> a party to a claim or appeal who does not enter an appearance to the claim or appeal . . . shall not be entitled to take part in or be present or be represented at any proceedings before the Tribunal in relation to the claim or appeal unless the Tribunal at its discretion otherwise decides.

While the Tribunal has discretion in relation to the non-entry of a Notice of Appearance, the Supreme Court in *Halal Meat Packers (Ballyhaunis) Ltd.* v. *Employment Appeals Tribunal* ([1990] ILRM 293) held that it was the duty of all courts and tribunals to administer justice and that justice required both parties to be heard. Thus, one may conclude that generally the Tribunal must hear both parties. Nonetheless, it is advisable to enter a Notice of Appearance in good time.

The grounds of defence may be stated very simply, for example:

(1) The claimant was dismissed for consistent lateness following warnings;

(2) The claimant was dismissed for absenteeism;

(3) The claimant was dismissed after a full and thorough investigation for allegedly taking company products;

(4) The claimant is not entitled to a statutory redundancy payment as there is no redundancy situation;

(5) The claimant is not entitled to notice monies as he was dismissed for gross misconduct.

Respondents may complete this form themselves but it is recommended that they obtain advice before doing so.

The respondent should also state the name of the person who will represent them at the hearing. It is advisable to have a solicitor, an employer organisation representative or an industrial relations expert handle all the paperwork and the preparation of the case from this point on.

The Notice of Appearance should be served on the Tribunal by registered post or by hand and the Tribunal will acknowledge its receipt. It is also good practice to copy it to the claimant's representative or the claimant if they are not represented. If the respondent considers that the hearing of the claim will take more than a half day, the Tribunal should be so advised at this time. Such a request should not be taken lightly as the Tribunal allots specific dates and times for hearings. The Tribunal will (as with all documents) copy the other side.

In the rare circumstances where the respondent is conceding the claim(s) the appropriate section of the form may just be signed by the employer.

NOTICE OF HEARING

The next stage in the process is that the Tribunal secretariat will send out a Notice of Hearing — see page 358. This is an important document as it states the date, time and place of the hearing of the claim(s). Even though neither party has to be formally represented by lawyers or by their respective trade union or employer representatives at the hearing, they may still obtain representation at this time. There is no requirement to notify the Tribunal of such change but if there is correspondence or if there are any difficulties, the Tribunal will contact the claimant or the respondent directly if there is no stated representative on record. If there is representation, the Tribunal will notify both the parties themselves and also the representatives.

ADJOURNMENTS

If the date of hearing does not suit either party, it may, after the receipt of the Notice of Hearing, make application to the Tribunal for an adjournment. Application must be made to the Tribunal in person. It is not permissible to write a letter, send a facsimile or telephone the Tribunal. Only a sitting division of the Tribunal can grant an adjournment of a case.

As the dates of hearings are fixed and the intent is to have a hearing as soon as possible, the Tribunal is very reluctant to grant adjournments. The Tribunal is even less likely to grant adjournments when the case is listed for hearing outside a major city as the Tribunal may not visit that particular town very often and the claimant may have to wait a few months before the case is listed for hearing again. Adjournments are only given when the person applying has a good reason. They should also notify the other side and have a letter of consent (from the other side) to the application for the adjournment. It should be remembered that, if a party to the hearing or a necessary witness will not be available, the representative (claimant or respondent) must write to the Tribunal at an early stage of the proceedings so that the Tribunal knows what dates not to hear the case.

NOTICE TO ATTEND AND GIVE EVIDENCE

If either party needs a particular witness to give evidence, it may have to make application to a sitting division of the Tribunal for a Notice to Attend and Give Evidence — see page 359. This is commonly called a subpoena, translated from Latin meaning "under penalty". An individual who has been served with a subpoena and fails to turn up at the Tribunal to give evidence is committing an offence and is liable to a criminal conviction and a fine. The Tribunal may refer the matter to the Director of Public Prosecutions if the individual does not attend, unless there is a very good reason, for example, serious illness. The fine for not attending to give evidence is £1,000 and the chairperson or vice-chairperson of the Tribunal may issue a document to use in a prosecution to confirm that the person did not attend, failed to produce a document or attended but refused to give evidence.

This Notice is a relatively simple procedure. The representative (or each of the parties themselves) has to fill out a form which the Tribunal provides, giving the name and address of the proposed witness and an undertaking to the Tribunal that they shall undertake to discharge all costs and expenses in relation to the witnesses' travel arrangements and compensate them for the loss of a day's pay. Once this form has been completed, the representative makes application to the Tribunal and advises as to why the particular witness is required. In the majority of cases the Tribunal will accept the submission and ask the representative if they undertake to serve the subpoena, which should be served personally or by registered post.

In some cases a party to the claim may want an individual not only to attend and give evidence but to bring certain documents as well. This application can be done in the same way as an application for a subpoena by simply listing the specific documents. It is not sufficient to request unnamed documents, for example, all letters in respect of Mr X. The request must be specific and there must be a good reason for such documents to be brought to the hearing.

REPRESENTATION OF PARTIES AT HEARING

As stated previously, the claimant may represent themselves at the hearing or have legal or trade union representation. Employers may be represented by the owner or by a member of management, have legal representation or representation by their employer organisation. More usually, both parties have representation.

PREPARATION FOR THE HEARING

There is a considerable volume of work in the preparation for the hearing. Each side should check all the Tribunal documents:

- RP51A form
- T2 form
- Notice of Hearing
- Any other Tribunal documents and letters, e.g. subpoenas.

Each side should fully prepare its case by going through the facts and then applying the relevant legislation to those facts. If there is any doubt as regards the application of the law, they should consult their solicitor.

The next stage is that all documents should be fully checked. The following is a useful checklist:

- Contract of employment or letter of appointment

- Letter of promotion

- Union management agreement; grievance, disciplinary and dismissal procedures

- All correspondence and memoranda relating to the reason for dismissal and other related employment issues (for an employer it is a good idea to bring along the complete personnel file)

- Written warnings

- Dismissal letter

- Minutes of meetings, e.g. disciplinary and dismissal meetings

- Medical certificates and medical reports

- Sales figures, budgets, etc. (where applicable)

- Pension booklet

- All pay details (including calculations)

- P45 form

- Redundancy notices (where applicable)

- Details of previous redundancies and the method of selection

- Details of all social welfare receipts, including the type of social welfare — for example, unemployment benefit, details of tax rebates (for all dismissals taking place after 1 October 1993 these will not be necessary as the Tribunal and other adjudicating bodies will no longer be deducting social welfare receipts or income tax rebates).

- Copies of letters applying for jobs.

There should be at least six copies of every document that will be presented before the Tribunal: three for the Tribunal, one for the secretary of the division of the Tribunal, one for the other side and one for the representative.

WITNESSES

As the Tribunal hears a case by the direct evidence of the parties, both sides need witnesses. There is usually no difficulty in deciding who the necessary witnesses are.

The employer should have present the manager who dismissed the employee and all other relevant management and supervisory personnel, for example, the persons who gave warnings to the employee. Depending on the size of the respondent company, the employer side usually has more witnesses than the claimant/employee side.

All potential witnesses should be advised that evidence is given on oath and that they will be subject to cross-examination by the other side as well as to questions from the members of the Tribunal. They should also be advised that the evidence they give is privileged. In other words, they cannot be sued for defamation though this does not mean that they can perjure themselves or tell untruths on oath. Since many potential witnesses have not given evidence before, it is useful to explain to them the procedure at the Tribunal.

It is important to remind witnesses that they can only give evidence as to what they know or what they saw; their opinions and what they heard from other people are not relevant. If a person is uneasy about giving evidence a subpoena may be considered, but generally it is better if people give evidence of their own free will. People should not be harassed into giving evidence as that serves nobody's interest.

It is important to go through the facts of the case with the potential witness and point out the flaws in the case and the type of questions that they may be asked in cross-examination. A witness should not be made to change their story, however, as they will be giving evidence on oath.

All persons should be advised that the Tribunal hearing is public and that the media are quite free to go along. It is rare that the Tribunal hearing is in private. This only happens when one side makes application that it be heard in private and the Tribunal rarely grants such application. An "in camera" hearing — from the Latin "in the chamber" — only happens when there are matters of a confidential nature involved, such as sensitive company documents. The application to have the hearing heard in private is usually considered at the beginning of the hearing and such application is invariably made in public and a decision given in public.

SETTLEMENTS

Sometimes the representatives of the parties may get together before the Tribunal hearing and have "off the record" discussions in an attempt to agree a settlement of the case. They may ask the Tribunal for a few minutes in order to settle the case — to which the Tribunal usually agrees. When the parties do reach agreement, they can advise the Tribunal that there is no necessity to hear the case. The representatives should not withdraw the actual claim(s) at once, though if they do they can re-enter within a specified period of time, usually four weeks. If the settlement does not then take place, they can re-enter the claim(s) and the case will be listed in the normal way again. Where there is a settlement, the Tribunal usually makes no order because the settlement is confidential to the parties.

A settlement can also take place some days before the hearing. If the representatives are satisfied that there is a settlement, it is advisable to notify the Tribunal some days prior to the actual listing of the case so that the Tribunal's time is not wasted and the same procedure as above can apply.

THE HEARING

The purpose of the Tribunal is to provide a speedy, inexpensive and informal method of adjudication. It should be noted that if either party is not represented, the members of the Tribunal invariably assist that person with their case.

While the hearings are relatively informal in comparison to a court of law, one must still bear in mind that there is a certain formality and procedure as is evidenced by the usual arrangement of the parties at the hearing.

At the beginning of the hearing the chairperson of the Tribunal checks all details on the RP51A form, in particular, the correct names/titles of the claimant and of the respondent. If the claimant does not have the correct name of the employer, this is usually amended at the hearing. This will only cause a difficulty, for example, if there is an unfair dismissals claim and six months have expired after the date of dismissal. The employer may well argue that it is now too late to amend the claim where it is clearly out of time. Other details concerning date of birth, date of commencement, date of notice and date of dismissal are also confirmed with the parties. If there is any dispute regarding these dates, the Tribunal hears evidence and then decides on the correctness of these dates. In maternity cases, the date of confinement is also considered.

Details of pay to include gross weekly pay and details as regards overtime, commissions, pensions etc., are also considered. If there is disagreement between the parties on these figures, various pieces of documentary evidence will be considered to include the P45, pay slips, details of pension schemes and so forth. Especially in unfair dismissals cases, the Tribunal notes what the required redress is.

Once these formalities have been completed, the Tribunal asks the representative of either side (or the claimant and employer, as appropriate) to make brief opening statements. It must be noted that these are only opening statements and not evidence within the procedure of the Tribunal. The Tribunal in the normal course does not accept submissions (written or otherwise) on the facts of the case. It makes its decision based on the evidence of the parties, which is why it is vital that both parties have all their witnesses available at the hearing.

The next stage in the procedure is that, for example in an unfair dismissals case, the employer would acknowledge that dismissal is not in dispute and proceed with the employer's witnesses. However, if the dismissal is in dispute (i.e. the employer maintains that there was no dismissal or that the employee resigned) then the employee will have to give evidence first to show that there was a dismissal. The employer (including witnesses) may also have to give evidence. When the Tribunal has heard this evidence, it may give a verbal determination immediately that there was or was not a dismissal. If there was a dismissal, the hearing then follows the normal course and the employer evidence is heard first and then the employee evidence. If there was no dismissal, this is the end of the proceedings as the employer has no case to answer.

If the employer raises jurisdictional issues — for example, that the claim is out of time or that the employee does not have sufficient service — then the evidence is heard and the Tribunal considers whether it has jurisdiction to hear the case. If it does not, that is the end of the matter.

A witness about to give evidence must take evidence on oath which is administered by the secretary of the Tribunal division. If a witness does not wish to take evidence on oath, they may affirm their evidence before the Tribunal.

When the oath is taken, the first employer (respondent) witness gives their direct evidence. Usually the employer representative asks the witness various questions and if there are not many facts in dispute they may lead the witnesses to a certain extent. During the course of the employer's evidence, the employer representative may wish to submit into evidence various documents such as the contract of employment, grievance/disciplinary/dismissal procedures, letters of warning, and final dismissal letter. It is important that all these documents are put into evidence by the employer representative (with the appropriate witness) because if they fail to do so at this stage they may well be barred from introducing such evidence later on. It must be noted that while the Tribunal is informal it generally complies with basic rules of evidence.

When the first employer witness has completed their evidence they are subject to cross-examination by the employee representative. The representative may cross-examine the witness on all aspects of the claimant's employment, but it is important to note that all questions that are in dispute must be put to the employer witnesses prior to the employee and the employee witnesses giving evidence. Otherwise the employee witnesses may not be allowed to give that evidence later on. The employee representative may want to introduce certain documents into evidence at this stage.

Once the formal evidence and cross-examination has been completed, the members of the Tribunal may ask the witness questions. These may be for clarification purposes or to find out further information, especially where both parties have glossed over certain issues. Questions that are asked by the Tribunal members are invariably extremely important and searching.

There is no limit to the number of witnesses that either party can have. Typically an employer may have the evidence of the supervisor, the personnel manager and any other appropriate members of management, whereas the employee has fewer witnesses.

The Tribunal has power to summon vital witnesses should it consider it necessary, though this procedure is adopted very rarely.

Once all the employer evidence has been completed, the employee gives evidence. However, an employee representative may ask the Tribunal for a direction in the case, that is, the employee representative may argue that the employer has not shown a sufficient case to surmount the burden of proof. The Tribunal may withdraw to consider the application, though usually it will direct that it wishes to hear the employee's evidence unless it is clear that the dismissal has been unfair.

The employee would invariably give evidence first, which would be subject to cross-examination by the employer representative and to questioning by the Tribunal. The employee will then call the various employee witnesses who shall also be subject to cross-examination and to questioning by the members of the Tribunal.

At the end of the claimant's evidence they should give evidence as regards loss which will also be subject to cross-examination. For example, the employee should advise the Tribunal what social welfare benefits they have been in receipt of, the type of social welfare benefit — for example, unemployment benefit or disability (which is important in absenteeism cases) — the tax rebate they received and whether they have been looking for work or not. The deduction of unemployment benefit and assistance and tax rebates will not apply to dismissals occurring after 1 October 1993. The employee should have copies of applications for various jobs and should show that they went looking for a job as soon as was reasonably practical after dismissal.

When all the evidence has been heard the Tribunal will ask the parties if they wish to give closing statements. This does not happen in every case but is typical in the more complicated ones. In a closing statement, the representatives invariably give a brief summary of the case and request the Tribunal to hold with their side. The representatives may refer to various previous determinations of the Tribunal and to Irish dismissal cases from the Circuit Court and the High Court. Sometimes the Tribunal is referred to UK cases where there are similar facts and points of law.

The Tribunal will then ask the parties what redress they wish to have. The Tribunal has an obligation to ask this question in claims under the Unfair Dismissals Acts (following the Supreme Court judgment in *State (Irish Pharmaceutical Union)* v. *Employment Appeals Tribunal* [1987] ILRM 36). Usually the claimant will ask for reinstatement and invariably the employer will state that that redress is simply not appropriate. The Tribunal hears both representatives on this particular point.

If the employer's representative considers that the employee did not mitigate or lessen their loss, various submissions can be made. For example, if an employee waited six months before looking for a job, the employer representative may claim that they did not mitigate their loss and thus any unfair dismissals award should be reduced accordingly.

Furthermore, where compensation is requested by the employer representative as being the preferable redress (if the Tribunal holds in favour of the employee), the employer representative can request the Tribunal to hold that there was a contribution on the employee's part to the dismissal. Thus, any award can be reduced.

After the hearing, the Tribunal may state to the parties that they will make their decision at that time, providing that they can come to such a decision, or they can advise the parties that they will receive the determination in writing in approximately six to eight weeks. If the Tribunal awards redress under the unfair dismissals legislation, the Unfair Dismissals Act, 1993 provides that the reason for not awarding the two other forms of redress must be given.

The Tribunal determination is signed by the chairperson of the division who heard the case. The determination will have on it the date of its signature and shall be sent out to both parties at the same time by registered post. Attached to the determination is a dated covering letter which is considered to be the date of communication of the determination. This date is vitally important for time limits as regards appeals.

COSTS

The only costs that the Tribunal can award are travelling expenses. Costs are not awarded to any person who is appearing before the Tribunal in a representative capacity, whether it be the claimant, the respondent, solicitor, barrister, trade union official or an official of an employers' organisation.

However, a witness or a party to a case may be awarded costs if it is considered that it is a frivolous and vexatious claim. In certain other circumstances, the Tribunal may also award costs, but again they only relate to travelling and other expenses such as the loss of a day's pay. It is very rare for the Tribunal to award costs.

APPEAL OF DETERMINATION

A person who is dissatisfied with the Tribunal determination may appeal it in whole or in part. No time should be wasted in seeking legal advice at this stage, as there are strict time limits involved. The time limits are as follows:

Unfair Dismissals

A person has six weeks to appeal the determination, either in whole or in part, to the Circuit Court. The Notice of Appeal must be filed in the Circuit Court office within six weeks of the date of communication of the determination, that is, the date on the covering letter of the Tribunal determination (see page 361). The Notice of Appeal does not have to be served on the other side within the six-week period, though it is advisable to do so (*Morris* v. *Power Supermarkets Ltd.* [1990] IR 296 and see pages 362 and 363).

The Circuit Court will completely rehear the case. The Circuit Court decision may be appealed to the High Court within 10 days for a further rehearing. The High Court decision may be appealed to the Supreme Court on a point of law only.

The 1993 Act has attempted to reinforce considerably the implementation provisions in the 1977 Act. If an employer has failed to carry out the terms of a Tribunal determination within six weeks of the date of communication of the determination, and if there is no appeal, either the employee or the Minister for Enterprise and Employment may make application for its terms to be carried out. If reinstatement or re-engagement were awarded by the Tribunal, the Circuit Court may order compensation instead. The Circuit Court may also order that interest be paid under Section 22 of the Courts Act, and where the original determination ordered re-employment the employee will be entitled to loss of wages suffered by the failure to implement it.

If an employer fails to comply with a Circuit Court order, the Minister may make application to have the order enforced. The Circuit Court will then make the appropriate order.

All costs will be borne by either the Minister or the employer (see Circuit Rules No. 2), 1981 (Unfair Dismissals Act, 1977 SI No. 316 of 1981).

Maternity

The same time limit as under the unfair dismissals legislation applies.

Redundancy and Minimum Notice

The Tribunal determination may only be appealed to the High Court on a point of law. Legal advice should be sought. The summons should be issued within 21 days of the date of communication of the Tribunal determination, though this time may be extended to six weeks.

Payment of Wages Act

The Tribunal determination may be appealed to the High Court on a point of law. It is advised to do so within 21 days. Also, the Tribunal may request the Minister to refer a question of law to the High Court.

Terms of Employment (Information) Bill

The proposals are the same as under the Payment of Wages Act.

Adoptive Leave Bill

The proposals are the same as under the Payment of Wages Act.

GENERAL REFERENCES

Angel, J., "How to Prepare Yourself for an Industrial Tribunal", Institute of Personnel Management, UK.

Department of Enterprise and Employment, Form RP51A and the notes attached thereto.

Department of Enterprise and Employment — An Explanatory Leaflet on the Employment Appeals Tribunal.

FORM RP 51A
(Part II is overleaf)

PART 1

NOTICE OF APPEAL TO EMPLOYMENT APPEALS TRIBUNAL UNDER

FOR OFFICIAL USE
Case No.

1.

TICK APPROPRIATE BOX OR BOXES	
(i) Redundancy Payments Acts, 1967 to 1991	
(ii) Minimum Notice and Terms of Employment Acts, 1973 to 1991	
(iii) Unfair Dismissals Acts, 1977 and 1991 (see Part II)	
(iv) Maternity Protection of Employees Acts, 1981 and 1991 (See Part II)	
(v) Worker Protection (Regular Part-Time Employees) Act, 1991	

IMPORTANT: Please read the notes supplied then complete this form in **BLOCK CAPITALS**

2. NAME AND ADDRESS OF PERSON MAKING APPEAL

Phone No:

Occupation	Sex

RSI No.

3. EMPLOYER'S FULL LEGAL NAME AND ADDRESS (IF IN DOUBT CONSULT YOUR P60 AND/OR P45.)

Phone No:

Registered (PAYE) No.

4. NAME, ADDRESS OF REPRESENTATIVE (UNION OFFICIAL ETC.,) OF PERSON MAKING THIS APPEAL

Phone No:

5. TOWN OR NEAREST TOWN TO PLACE OF EMPLOYMENT

6. GIVE THE FOLLOWING DATES	Day	Month	Year
Birth			
Employment began			
Dismissal notice received			
Employment ended			
Date or expected date of confinement			

7. NORMAL WEEKLY PAY

	£	p
Basic Weekly Pay		
Regular bonus or allowances		
Average Weekly Overtime		
Any other payments including payments in kind—specify		
Weekly Total Gross		
Net		
Number of hours normally expected to work per week	Number	

8. BASIS OF EMPLOYMENT (PERMANENT, PART-TIME, TEMPORARY, ETC.) AND TYPE OF BUSINESS

9. THE GROUNDS OF MY APPLICATION ARE AS FOLLOWS:

10. APPEALS UNDER REDUNDANCY PAYMENTS ACTS

Has your employer issued you with a Redundancy Certificate   Yes/No

Have you applied to your employer or to the Department of Enterprise and Employment for your redundancy payment   Yes/No

11. REDRESS SOUGHT

12.

Signed:

Date:

PART II

IF YOU WISH A CLAIM UNDER THE UNFAIR DISMISSALS ACTS OR A DISPUTE UNDER THE MATERNITY PROTECTION OF EMPLOYEES ACTS TO BE HEARD BY THE EMPLOYMENT APPEALS TRIBUNAL, ANSWER ANY OF THE FOLLOWING QUESTIONS WHICH ARE RELEVANT TO YOU

CLAIM UNDER UNFAIR DISMISSALS ACTS

Insert "Yes" or "No" in each box

Have you sued your employer under Common Law procedures in the matter of your claim on unfair dismissal?

Have you a claim currently with a Rights Commissioner on unfair dismissal?

Do you object to a claim on unfair dismissal being heard by a Rights Commissioner?

(THE TRIBUNAL CANNOT HEAR YOUR CLAIM UNLESS THERE IS AN OBJECTION TO A RIGHTS COMMISSIONER HEARING YOUR CLAIM)

Has your employer objected to a claim on unfair dismissal being heard by a Rights Commissioner?

Are you appealing a recommendation of a Rights Commissioner in regard to your claim on unfair dismissal? If so, state:—

Name of Rights Commissioner _____

Date of the Recommendation _____

Are you referring your claim to the Tribunal following the failure of your employer to implement (within six weeks) a recommendation of a Rights Commissioner on unfair dismissal? If so, state:

Name of Rights Commissioner _____

Date of the Recommendation _____

DISPUTE UNDER THE MATERNITY PROTECTION OF EMPLOYEES ACTS

Have you a dispute currently with a Rights Commissioner about maternity entitlement (other than unfair dismissal)?

Do you object to a dispute under the Maternity Protection of Employees Acts being heard by a Rights Commissioner?

(THE TRIBUNAL CANNOT HEAR YOUR CLAIM UNLESS THERE IS AN OBJECTION TO A RIGHTS COMMISSIONER HEARING YOUR CLAIM)

Has your employer objected to a dispute under the Maternity Protection of Employees Acts being heard by a Rights Commissioner?

Are you appealing a recommendation of a Rights Commissioner in regard to a dispute about maternity entitlement? If so, state:—

Name of Rights Commissioner _____

Date of the Recommendation _____

Are you referring your case to the Tribunal following the failure of your employer to implement a recommendation of a Rights Commissioner on maternity entitlement? If so, state:—

Name of Rights Commissioner _____

Date of the Recommendation. _____

Return this form to: Secretary
Employment Appeals Tribunal,
Davitt House,
65A Adelaide Road,
Dublin 2.

P29878 5pl. 5m 6/93 Fodhla 134581—Labour

FORM T2

Please quote this reference number on all correspondence

1. Redundancy Payments Acts, 1967 to 1991

2. Minimum Notice and Terms of Employment Acts 1973 to 1991

3. Unfair Dismissals Acts, 1977 and 1991

4. Maternity Protection of Employees Acts, 1981 and 1991

5. Protection of Employees (Employers') Insolvency Acts, 1984 to 1991

6. Worker Protection (Regular Part-Time Employees) Act, 1991

7. Payment of Wages Act, 1991

NOTICE OF APPEARANCE

by a respondent against whom an appeal has been lodged under the items of legislation shown ticked above

by _____ Appellant

against _____ Respondent

A.   The appeal under 1, 2, 3, 4, 5, 6 and 7 is not conceded and notice is given that an appearance will be entered before the Tribunal to contest the appeal on the following grounds. (In all cases care should be taken to give sufficient detail of the facts on which you intend to rely in contesting the appeal(s).)

It is proposed to be represented at the hearing of the Tribunal by

_____ who
should be notified of the date of the hearing in due course.

Signed _____

Date _____

B.   The appeal under 1, 2, 3, 4 5, 6 and 7 is conceded. Please request the appellant to withdraw his/her appeal in the matter.

Signed   _____

Date   _____   7mfx3117 pmc

AN BINSE ACHOMHAIRO FOSTAÍOCHTA
65A BÓTHAR ADELAIDE
BAILE ÁTHA CLIATH 2

*All communications should be
addressed to the Secretary.*

Reference No. ....

THE EMPLOYMENT APPEALS TRIBUNAL
65A ADELAIDE ROAD
DUBLIN 2

☎ (01) 765861
FAX (01) 769047

Your ref:

Case No: _____   Date: _____

Appellant: _____ Respondent: _____

1. <u>REDUNDANCY PAYMENTS ACTS, 1967 TO 1991</u>

2. <u>MINIMUM NOTICE AND TERMS OF EMPLOYMENT ACTS, 1973 TO 1991</u>

3. <u>UNFAIR DISMISSALS ACTS, 1977 AND 1991</u>

·4. <u>MATERNITY PROTECTION OF EMPLOYEES ACTS, 1981 AND 1991</u>

5. <u>PROTECTION OF EMPLOYEES (EMPLOYERS' INSOLVENCY ACTS; 1984 TO 1991</u>

6. <u>WORKER PROTECTION (REGULAR PART-TIME EMPLOYEES) ACT, 1991</u>

A Chara/Chairde

I acknowledge receipt of Notice of Appearance under _____ above

dated _____.   A copy of the Notice has been sent to the

appellant(s). A notice of hearing will be sent to you before the date fixed

for the hearing of the appeal.

Mise le meas

_____
Runai

AN BINSE ACHOMHAIRC FOSTAÍOCHTA

65A BÓTHAR ADELAIDE

BAILE ÁTHA CLIATH 2

*All communications should be
addressed to the Secretary*

THE EMPLOYMENT APPEALS TRIBUNAL

65A ADELAIDE ROAD

DUBLIN 2

☎ (01) 676 5861

FAX (01) 676 9047

DATE:

NAME
ADDRESS

APPELLANT -v- RESPONDENT

Hearing No:

Dear Sir/Madam

Notice is hereby given that the appeal(s) under the
MINIMUM NOTICE AND TERMS OF EMPLOYMENT ACTS, 1973 TO 1991 & UNFAIR
DISMISSALS ACTS, 1977 AND 1991
will be heard by the Tribunal at ....
on ....
(or as soon hereafter as may be).

Each party must appear at the hearing with witnesses (if any) at
the above time and place and bring with him all documents on
which he intends to rely. Any documents being submitted to the
Tribunal at the hearing should be copied in advance and four
copies should be provided to the Tribunal.

Each party (other than a respondent who has not entered an
appearance) is entitled to be represented by counsel or solicitor
or by a representative of a trade union or of an employer's
association or, with leave of the Tribunal, by any other person.

Please note that the non-attendance of a party or his representative
or witnesses will not be accepted as reason for the adjournment of
the proceedings except for very grave reasons. Adjournments are
only granted in exceptional circumstances. A party seeking an
adjournment must make a formal application to any sitting division
of the Tribunal. Good cause must be shown and the consent of the
other party sought before any application for an adjournment will
be considered by the Tribunal, but the existence of such consent
alone is never a sufficient reason for granting an adjournment.
Only in the gravest circumstances will the foregoing procedure be
departed from and then only at the discretion of the Tribunal.

Yours sincerely

Secretary

AN BINSE ACHOMHAIRC FOSTAÍOCHTA
65A BÓTHAR ADELAIDE
BAILE ÁTHA CLIATH 2

*All communications should be
addressed to the Secretary.*

Reference No. . . . .

THE EMPLOYMENT APPEALS TRIBUNAL
65A ADELAIDE ROAD
DUBLIN 2

☎ (01) 765881
FAX (01) 769047

(1) REDUNDANCY PAYMENTS ACTS, 1967 TO 1991
(2) MINIMUM NOTICE AND TERMS OF EMPLOYMENT ACT, 1973 AND 1991
(3) UNFAIR DISMISSALS ACT, 1977 AND 1991
(4) MATERNITY PROTECTION OF EMPLOYEES' ACT, 1981 AND 1991
(5) PROTECTION OF EMPLOYEES (EMPLOYERS' INSOLVENCY) ACT, 1984 TO 1991
(6) WORKER PROTECTION (REGULAR PART-TIME EMPLOYEES) ACT, 1991
(7) PAYMENT OF WAGES ACT, 1991

Case Nos.

NOTICE TO ATTEND AND GIVE EVIDENCE

In the matter of a claim by

2 under 2 &
3 above. Please note that you are requested by the above-named Tribunal to
attend a hearing of the above claim at the above address, Room G.14 on
at the hour of 10.30 o'clock in the
forenoon (official time) to give evidence.

Dated this 1st day of September 1992.

RUNAI

To:

Your attention is directed to the extract from Section 39(as amended by
Section 18 of the Unfair Dismissals Act, 1977 and Section 17 of the Redundancy
Payments Act, 1979) of the Redundancy Payments Act, 1967 as set out on the
back of this Notice; Section 1 of the Minimum Notice and Terms of Employment
Act, 1973 and Section 1 of the Unfair Dismissals Act, 1977.

sub12.pl

EXTRACT FROM SECTION 39 (as amended) OF THE REDUNDANCY PAYMENTS ACT, 1967

Section 39(17)
(as amended)

(a) The Tribunal shall, on the hearing of any matter referred to it under this Section, have power to take evidence on oath and for that purpose may cause to be administered oaths to persons attending as witnesses at such hearing.

(b) Any person who, upon examination on oath authorised under this subsection, wilfully and corruptly gives false evidence or wilfully and corruptly swears anything which is false, being convicted thereof, shall be liable to the penalties for wilful and corrupt perjury.

(c) The Tribunal may, by giving notice in that behalf in writing to any person, require such person to attend at such time and place as is specified in the notice to give evidence in relation to any matter referred to the Tribunal under this section or to produce any documents in his possession, custody or control which relate to any such matter.

(d) A notice under paragraph (c) may be given either by delivering it to the person to whom it relates or by sending it by post in a prepaid registered letter addressed to such person at the address at which he ordinarily resides.

(e) A person to whom a notice under paragraph (c) has been given and who refused or wilfully neglects to attend in accordance with the notice or who, having so attended, refuses or wilfully fails to produce any document to which the notice relates shall be guilty of an offence and shall be liable on summary conviction thereof to a fine not exceeding one hundred and fifty pounds.

AN BINSE ACHOMHAIRC FOSTAÍOCHTA
65A BÓTHAR ADELAIDE
BAILE ÁTHA CLIATH 2

*All communications should be
addressed to the Secretary*

THE EMPLOYMENT APPEALS TRIBUNAL
65A ADELAIDE ROAD
DUBLIN 2
☎ (01) 676 5861
FAX (01) 676 9047

Date _____

1. REDUNDANCY PAYMENTS ACTS, 1967 TO 1991

2. MINIMUM NOTICE AND TERMS OF EMPLOYMENT ACTS, 1973 TO 1991

3. UNFAIR DISMISSALS ACTS, 1977 AND 1991

4. MATERNITY PROTECTION OF EMPLOYEES ACTS, 1981 AND 1991

5. PROTECTION OF EMPLOYEES (EMPLOYERS' INSOLVENCY) ACTS, 1984 TO 1991

6. WORKER PROTECTION (REGULAR PART-TIME EMPLOYEES) ACT, 1991

Case No: _____

Appeal of: _____ against the

decision of: _____

under _____ above.

A Chara/Chairde

I am directed by the Employment Appeals Tribunal to enclose a copy of the decision of the Tribunal in the above case.

Mise le meas

_____
Runai

_____
_____
_____
_____
_____

SCHEDULE

FORM No. 1

AN CHUIRT CHUARDA
(THE CIRCUIT COURT)

.... CIRCUIT   COUNTY OF ....

UNFAIR DISMISSALS ACT, 1977, S. 10 (1)

BETWEEN/

THE MINISTER FOR LABOUR

                                                              Applicant
                                    -and-

.... Respondent

TAKE NOTICE that the Minister for Labour having his office at ....
in the County of ....
hereby applies to the Court sitting at ....
in the County of .... pursuant to the provisions of Section 10 (1) of
(a) insert name of   the above Act on behalf of .... *(a)*
employee   for redress under the said Act and for the costs of the Application.

AND TAKE NOTICE that the Minister will rely upon the following matters
in support of the application:

(1) The said ....*(a)*
is the employee of the Respondent for the purposes of the said Act.

(2) The Employment Appeals Tribunal on the ..... day of .... 19... has
determined that the said employee be entitled to redress under the said Act
and accordingly ordered the Respondent to reinstate/re-engage/compensate
(b) Delete where   *(b)* the said employee as by *(b)* ....
necessary   *(c)*
(c) insert brief
details of the   (3) The Respondent has failed to carry out the terms of the said determina-
determination.   tion, which was communicated to the parties on the ....day of ....
                    19....

AND TAKE NOTICE that the application will be listed for hearing by the
Court on the .... day of ....19 ...... or on the first available day
(d) Omit the   thereafter. *(d)*
words "or on the
first available day   Dated the   day of   19
thereafter" where
the application is   SIGNED ....
made in Dublin.
                                                             Solicitor for Applicant

                                                             (Address).................

To   ....

     ....

     ....

      The above named Respondent/Solicitor for Respondent and to the
Secretary Employment Appeals Tribunal, Davitt House, Mespil Road,
Dublin 4.

FORM No. 2

AN CHUIRT CHUARDA
(THE CIRCUIT COURT)

.... CIRCUIT   COUNTY OF ....

UNFAIR DISMISSALS ACT, 1977, S. 10 (4)

BETWEEN

.... Appellant

-and-

.... Respondent

TAKE NOTICE that the above named Appellant of ....
in the County of ....
hereby applies to the Court Sitting at ....
in the County of ....
pursuant to the provisions of Section 10 sub-section (4) of the above Act by
way of Appeal against the determination of the Employment Appeals
Tribunal dated the .... day of ....19..... granting/refusing (*a*) the
claim of the Appellant/Respondent (*a*) herein for redress under the said Act,
and for an Order providing for the costs of this application. The said
determination of the Employment Appeals Tribunal was communicated to
the the Appellant on the ....day of..........19....

(a) delete where
appropriate

AND TAKE NOTICE that the Appellant will rely upon the following
grounds in support of his appeal: (*b*)

(b) here insert
grounds relied
upon. If appeal is
against part only
of the
determination
clearly identify
that part against
which an appeal is
sought.

AND TAKE NOTICE that the application will be listed for hearing on
the.........day of..........19.... or on the first available day thereafter. (*c*)

Dated the   day of   19

SIGNED: ....
Appellant/Solicitor for Appellant

(c) Omit the
words "or on the
first day
thereafter" where
the application is
made in Dublin.

TO:
        ....

of   ....

        ....

the above named Respondent/Solicitor for Respondent and to the
Secretary, Employment Appeals Tribunal, Davitt House, Mespil Road,
Dublin 4.

CHAPTER TWENTY-FOUR

Equal Pay and Equal Treatment Claims

The purpose of this chapter is to describe how to bring an equal pay or an equal treatment claim under the Anti-Discrimination (Pay) Act, 1974 and the Employment Equality Act, 1977. Equality disputes in relation to pension schemes may also be referred through the equality adjudication machinery but technically the procedures are now under the Pensions Act, 1990. However, before the procedures are considered, the adjudicating bodies, namely equality officers and the Labour Court, will be considered.

EQUALITY OFFICERS

Equality officers, although not lawyers, have a specialised knowledge of equality law. They are officers of the Labour Relations Commission (LRC) though they act independently of it. Invariably, they are recruited from the staff of the Department of Enterprise and Employment.

Hearings before equality officers are informal and private. Such hearings are held all around the country although the majority are heard at the LRC premises in Dublin. Equality officers investigate "disputes", which may include carrying out work inspections (see below) and listening to various witnesses. Both parties usually provide detailed written submissions which include all legal issues, details of the work of the claimant and comparator and the comparison of such work under the Act. At the conclusion of the investigation, the equality officer issues a written recommendation.

LABOUR COURT

As stated previously, the Labour Court's main and original function was to resolve industrial conflict and to mediate industrial disputes. The equality legislation added a quasi-judicial and appellate role for the Court, however. The Court sits by division with three members in each division — namely, the chairperson/deputy chairperson and an employer and employee member — and the division must both hear and investigate appeals against the equality officer's recommendations. In equality dismissal cases, the claims are referred directly to the Labour Court. The Court may implement an equality officer's recommendation (i.e. where the employer has not paid) but it must investigate the claim at the same time.

The Labour Court issues written determinations which are binding on the parties unless appealed to the High Court on a point of law. A Labour Court determination may be judicially reviewed by the High Court (if for example there were unfair procedures adopted at the Court hearing), and if quashed the matter is referred back to another division of the Labour Court (or an equality officer) for a new hearing or to decide on certain specific issues.

The Labour Court's hearings are normally held in private unless the Court is requested that the hearing be in public. Both parties provide written submissions on the appeal and, especially in equal pay appeals, the Court may visit the employer's premises and undertake a work inspection.

The Labour Court may hold preliminary hearings about the acceptability of claims under the Employment Equality Act, 1977 in relation to time limits. More usually, it does not and the matter is referred by the Court to an equality officer.

EQUAL PAY CLAIM

Dispute

The Anti-Discrimination (Pay) Act, 1974 provides that an equal pay "dispute" between an employer and an employee may be referred to an equality officer. The term "dispute" is not defined in the Act but it may be considered broadly to be where an employee claims to be doing "like work" as specified by a certain section and subsection of the Act — for example, Section 3 (a), (b), and/or (c) — with a named comparator in the same place, and the employer then rejects the claim.

The Employment Equality Agency (the EEA) can also refer a pay issue to an equality officer where it feels "that an employer had failed to comply with an equal pay clause" even though technically no dispute has arisen, or where it is not feasible for an employee to bring such an action.

Forms

There are no statutory forms or regulations for the bringing of equal pay claims (unlike other legislation). However, the Labour Court has issued a document entitled "Procedures of the Labour Court and equality officers in relation to the Anti-Discrimination (Pay) Act, 1974 and the Employment Equality Act, 1977", which came into use on 1 December 1989 and is continually updated. The Labour Court document is extremely useful and it is recommended that both parties use the forms that are provided. These forms are reproduced at the end of this chapter.

It is recommended that a person referring an equal pay dispute complete the appropriate form (see pages 382-83) and send it to the Head of equality officer Service with the following information:

(1) Confirmation that the claimant(s) is in dispute with the employer and a request that an equality officer investigate it.

(2) The name and address of the employer, which must be correct, as otherwise the employer can argue that the claim is invalid. The claimant would then have to lodge a new claim and could lose out on back-pay. Arrears of pay can only go back three years to the date of reference to an equality officer.

(3) The name of each individual claimant; a claim is invalid unless the claimant(s) is specifically named. If there is a large number of claimants an appendix to the claim form may be useful clearly headed "claimants".

(4) The name of each individual comparator; a claim is invalid unless the comparator(s) is listed. Again, if there is a large number of comparators it may be useful to have an appendix to the claim for clearly headed "comparators".

(5) A statement on what grounds equal pay is being claimed, i.e. (a) same work and/or (b) similar work and/or (c) work of equal value. Unless the claimant(s) is perfectly sure on what grounds equal pay is being claimed, all these boxes should be ticked.

(6) The name and address of the party referring the dispute with their signature and the date. This is invariably a union official, an officer

of the Employment Equality Agency or a solicitor, though it may be the claimant(s) themselves.

It is good practice to copy this to the employer. The Head of Equality Officer Service will also copy it to the employer concerned and set a date for a preliminary hearing to obtain the basic details from both sides and to clarify the names of the claimant(s) and comparator(s) and the basis on which equal pay is claimed.

Once the equality officer is satisfied that there is a valid dispute and that the claim is properly referred, written submissions will be requested from both sides.

Evidence

An equality officer who considers that they are not getting all the evidence that they require has the right of entry on to the employer's premises to inspect employer records and to inspect work-in-progress. Any person who obstructs or impedes an equality officer may commit an offence and be liable to a fine of £100 on summary conviction or on conviction on indictment to a fine of £1,000.

Prior to the hearing, the equality officer normally requests either party to complete a document detailing the work done by both the claimant and comparator. This completed document will be used as a basis for the subsequent work inspection.

During the course of an equal pay investigation, the equality officer will take evidence of the work of both the claimant(s) and the comparator(s). This work inspection is extremely important and is akin to the oral evidence that would be given at any court or Tribunal case. It is important that both parties are represented during the work inspection, in other words that trade union officials, employer representatives and any other representatives be present.

Burden of Proof

Discrimination must be proved by the person alleging it. This is the legal position. In practice a claimant only has to show that they were in some way discriminated against and then the employer must substantiate their action.

Costs and Legal Aid

An equality officer cannot award costs to either party and there is no provision for legal aid. However, the EEA may assist individuals who are bringing a claim where there is a point of principle involved and it is not reasonable for the claimant(s) to bring their own claim.

In many equal pay claims, the claimant(s) is represented by their trade union and thus would have no costs as it would be incorporated in the trade union subscription. Employers in equal pay claims are usually represented by their employer organisation, so again these costs would be associated with membership.

In equal treatment claims the representation is wider and many claimants and employers use legal representation and would thus have to carry their own costs.

Award of Equal Pay

Equal pay may be awarded retrospectively, that is, for up to three years prior to the date of reference of the dispute to the equality officer for investigation, or for such period as the claimant was performing "like work" with the comparator, if shorter. Equal pay is the difference between the claimant's rate of pay and that of the comparator.

The equality officer's recommendation is not legally binding, however. For example, if an award is being made in favour of a claimant and it is not implemented, the claimant should refer the matter to the Labour Court for a determination within the six week appeal period (see pages 384-85). This same form is used for appeals to the Labour Court under both the 1974 Act and 1977 Act (equal treatment). If the employer does not pay during the six-week appeal period and the employee fails to apply for implementation, however, the employee is entitled to nothing.

If there is a reference to the Labour Court under the 1974 Act to implement a recommendation, all references to the 1977 Act should be deleted. The following information should be given:

(1) Name and address of appellant, that is, the successful claimant

(2) Name and address of the respondent, that is, the employer

(3) The date the dispute was referred to the Equality Officer Service

(4) The date the equality officer issued the written recommendation, that is, the date at the end of the recommendation. It would also be prudent, bearing in mind time limits, to give the date of receipt of the recommendation. A copy of the recommendation should be attached to this notice

(5) The extent to which the respondent has failed to implement the recommendation "in full"

(6) The grounds of appeal may be completed by stating that full implementation of the recommendation is required

(7) Date and signature of the appellant or the appellant's representative.

This must be delivered to the Chairperson of the Labour Court within six weeks of the date of the recommendation.

APPEAL OF EQUAL PAY RECOMMENDATION

An equal pay recommendation may be appealed to the Labour Court within six weeks of the date of the equality officer's recommendation. This time limit is very strict. The same form as for implementation of the equality officer's recommendation is used. However, the appellant must list out the grounds for appeal. Thus, the first part of No. 5 must be completed.

Grounds of appeal could be as follows:

(1) It was not within the jurisdiction of the equality officer to issue a recommendation granting equal pay as the claimant and comparator were not working in the same "place"

(2) The equality officer erred in law and in fact in granting equal pay etc.

The listing of the grounds is very important because otherwise the Labour Court will deem the appeal invalid.

Answer to an Appeal

On foot of receiving a Notice of Appeal, the other side (usually called the respondent) should give the grounds for its rejection of the appeal. This may be done by the use of the attached form (pages 386-87). The respondent should provide the following information:

(1) Name of both the appellant and the respondent

(2) Date the appeal was served on the respondent

(3) Grounds on which the appeal is disputed

(4) Relief requested by the respondent (this part of the form is not generally applicable in equal pay cases but may be used, for example,

where the employer is disputing some aspect of the equal pay award or is prepared to accept the award but needs more time to pay the arrears of equal pay)

(5) Date and signature.

This completed form should be sent to the Chairperson of the Labour Court and it is good practice to send a copy to the appellant or their representative as well.

The Labour Court has an obligation to investigate the dispute. It will hear the submissions of both sides and will usually also carry out a work inspection with all the divisions of the Court present. Again, both sides should have representation at the work inspection. If there is job evaluation evidence it will be heard from the job evaluation expert. The Labour Court will then issue its determination which is legally binding. This is a detailed document setting out the facts of the case and the reasoning for the determination.

Complaint of Non-implementation of a Labour Court Determination

An employee alleging that a Labour Court determination has not been implemented should complete the appropriate form (pages 388-89) and send it to the Chairperson of the Labour Court. The form should be completed (deleting the references to the 1977 Act) as follows:

(1) List names and addresses of the employee and the employer respondent;

(2) Include the date of the Labour Court determination;

(3) State details of what the employer has failed or neglected to do, for example, failed to pay arrears of equal pay;

(4) State what the employer is prepared to do (obviously this can only be completed if the employee has had some discussion with the employer).

Answer to Complaint of Non-implementation of a Labour Court Determination.

To respond to a complaint of non-implementation the employer should complete the appropriate form (see pages 390-91), deleting the references to the 1977 Act, and provide the following details:

(1) Name of both claimant and employer respondent

(2) Date the notice of implementation was served on the employer

(3) Why the complaint is being opposed or why the determination cannot be implemented, for example, the employer may request that arrears of equal pay be staggered over a period of time.

The Labour Court will consider the complaint and hear all the relevant parties. If the Court considers that the claim is well-founded it will issue an order that the determination is to be implemented. The determination must then be implemented by the employer within two months of the date of the order, or the employer will be guilty of an offence and shall be liable to a fine not exceeding £100, and, if the offence continues, a fine of £10 per day as long as the determination is not implemented. The court that hears the offence (i.e. the District Court) may impose on the employer a fine in the amount that is owed to the employee under the Labour Court determination. The employee may appeal the amount awarded to them to the court of appropriate jurisdiction (i.e. District Court up to £5,000; Circuit Court up to £30,000 and the High Court for greater amounts). It should be stressed that such a set of circumstances would be very unusual.

Appeal of Equal Pay Determination to High Court

Either party may appeal the determination to the High Court, though only on a point of law. It is effected by way of a Special Summons which must be issued within six weeks of the date of receipt of the determination. There is provision that an application can be made to the High Court for an extension of time for the issuing of the special summons, but such application must be made within six weeks of the receipt of the determination. The High Court judgment may be appealed to the Supreme Court on a point of law. If there are matters of EU law, the High Court may refer the legal issues for judgment to the European Court of Justice.

Judicial Review

If a party feels that they have not received a fair hearing, they may refer the Labour Court determination to the High Court for judicial review. This is a discretionary remedy on the part of the High Court and, unless there is a very good case, such a path is not recommended. If the High Court considers that there is a case for the Labour Court to answer, the determination will be quashed and referred back to another division of the Labour Court for a complete rehearing, or in some cases back to the equality officer.

EQUAL TREATMENT CLAIMS

An employee or a potential employee who considers that there is a dispute under the Employment Equality Act, 1977 should send the Section 28 form (Employment Equality Act, 1977 (section 28) Regulations, 1977 — SI No. 344 of 1977 (see pages 378-79) to the employer. The purpose of this form/questionnaire is for the prospective claimant (or their representative) to outline the grounds of the alleged discrimination and ask the employer to respond. The employer must respond within 21 days of the service of the form. If the prospective claimant is still dissatisfied with the information provided by the employer, the matter can then be referred to the Labour Court outlining the alleged grounds of discrimination (see pages 392-94).

The Labour Court may refer a claim to an industrial relations officer or, more likely, to an equality officer for investigation. The following information is required:

(1) Name and address of the claimant

(2) Name and address of the person who allegedly discriminated against the claimant

(3) Date the alleged discriminatory act took place

(4) Details of the alleged discriminatory act

(5) Whether the claimant was allegedly discriminated on grounds of sex or marital status

(6) Whether there was indirect discrimination.

Prospective claimants are advised to bring claims on the basis that they were discriminated against both directly and indirectly.

Time Limits

The issue of time limits is particularly important in this legislation, and all prospective claimants should be aware of Section 19 (5) which provides:

save only where reasonable cause can be shown . . . a reference under this Section shall be lodged not later than six months from the date of the first occurrence of the act alleged to constitute discrimination.

The Second Commission on the Status of Women recommended that this time limit should run from the most recent act of discrimination, as the current provision is unnecessarily harsh. An example of a case where the employees were not able to bring a claim because of the time limit was *Braun Ireland Ltd.* v. *Six Female Employees* (DEE 8/1992), which concerned an allegation by the employees that they had been treated less favourably than male employees under the company's job evaluation scheme. The issue to be considered was whether or not the incidents described by the claimants constituted the "first occurrence" of that act of discrimination. The Labour Court determined that the claim was out of time and that there was no reasonable cause for the delay, even though the union had attempted to resolve matters by direct negotiation.

Equality Officer

Claims under the Employment Equality Act, 1977 are heard in exactly the same way by equality officers as under the 1974 Act, except that it is less likely that they will do a work inspection. Normally these matters are dealt with by submissions from both parties and two to three hearings in order to hear all the evidence.

An equality officer's recommendation under this Act has exactly the same status as under the 1974 Act and the same forms are used in order to refer the matter to the Labour Court for implementation.

Appeal to Labour Court

The procedure for appealing and implementing the recommendation to the Labour Court is exactly the same as under the 1974 Act (see pages 384-85).

The Labour Court may:

(1) Hold that there was or was not discrimination;

(2) Recommend a specified course of action;

(3) Award compensation up to a maximum of 104 weeks' remuneration;

(4) Hold that a person did or did not procure or attempt to procure discrimination or that a publication was or was not discriminatory.

Answer to an Appeal

The same form (pages 386-87) is used as under the 1974 Act. The section on relief is more important under this Act where, for example, the claimant has been awarded compensation but is appealing the recommendation because the award is too low. Thus, the employer may state that they are prepared so to pay the award.

Complaint of Non-implementation of a Labour Court Determination

There is exactly the same procedure as under the 1974 Act and the same form is used (pages 388-89), though of course all references should be made to the 1977 Act. Arrears of pay are not appropriate to this Act, but there may be reference to a high award that the employer will not pay or, where the Labour Court has determined, a specified course of action which has not been implemented.

Answer to a Complaint of Non-implementation of a Labour Court Determination

Again, the legal procedure and consequence of not implementing a determination is the same as under the 1977 Act. The employer should complete the form (see pages 390-91) and delete references to the 1974 Act.

Appeal to High Court and Judicial Review

This is exactly the same as under the 1974 Act.

DISMISSAL AND EQUALITY

All discriminatory dismissals must be referred directly to the Labour Court. As discussed previously (see section 2), dismissals fall into two categories, namely, a straightforward discriminatory dismissal (e.g. unfair selection for redundancy simply because an employee is a woman) or victimisation or retaliatory dismissals.

Complaint concerning Victimisation or Retaliatory Dismissals

Victimisation or retaliatory dismissals shall be considered first. The same form is used for such claims under both the equal pay and equal treatment legislation. Again it should be noted that the six-month time limit applies unless reasonable cause can be shown. On this form (pages 395-96) the claimant must complete the following:

(1) Whether the claim is under the equal pay legislation (the 1974 Act) or the equal treatment legislation (the 1977 Act);

(2) Name, address and occupation of the claimant;

(3) Name and address of former employer;

(4) Weekly wage or salary;

(5) Date of dismissal;

(6) Reason for the dismissal (there are details on the form and the appropriate section should be marked, e.g. the dismissal occurred because the employee brought an equal pay claim and the date of the claim); and

(7) Brief details of the evidence on which the claimant will rely.

This form should then be sent to the Chairperson of the Labour Court. An updated version of this form is now available.

Answer to Complaint concerning Victimisation or Retaliatory Dismissals

The employer should complete the appropriate form (pages 390-91) and send it to the Chairperson of the Labour Court and a copy to the claimant employee. In completing the form, the key issues are the employer's defence(s), e.g.:

(1) The claimant has brought their claim outside the six-month time limit and no reasonable cause has been shown.

(2) The claimant was not dismissed for discriminatory reasons; it was because of their conduct.

The following redress may be awarded: (a) reinstatement, or (b) re-engagement, or (c) compensation up to a maximum of 104 weeks' remuneration. The recent European Court of Justice judgment in

Marshall v. *Southampton and South-West Area Health Authority (No. 2)* ([1993] IRLR 445) may have an effect on this ceiling of 104 weeks' remuneration. The key principle in this case is that it is contrary to the EC Equal Treatment Directive for national legislation to lay down an upper limit on the amount of compensation recoverable by a victim in respect of loss and damage sustained.

A claimant cannot be in receipt of an award under these Acts as well and under the Unfair Dismissals Acts, 1977 to 1993.

Appeals

The Labour Court determination may be appealed to the High Court on a point of law. The same time limit as above applies. In cases of retaliatory dismissal, an employer may appeal the Labour Court determination to the Circuit Court. Again, the same redress as above applies.

Criminal Offences

An employer may be guilty of an offence if there is retaliatory dismissal of an employee for attempting to enforce their rights under the equality legislation. The employer in such instance will be liable on summary conviction to a fine not exceeding £1,000.

If the Labour Court makes an order in relation to either retaliatory or discriminatory dismissal and the employer fails to carry it out, the employee is guilty of an offence. If an order of the Labour Court (or other Court on appeal) has not been carried out within two months of the date of the order, the employer is liable on summary conviction to a maximum fine of £100 and, where there is a continuing offence, there can be a fine of up to £10 per day. Such a prosecution would be in the District Court.

The claimant may appeal the fine imposed by the District Court either to the Circuit Court or to the High Court (depending upon jurisdiction — see above). Such an appeal is final and is limited to:

(1) The amount of damages awarded by the District Court when an employer is convicted of having failed to implement a Labour Court order relating to a discriminatory dismissal within the two-month period;

(2) The amount of an additional fine imposed by the District Court where an employer is convicted of having failed to implement a

Labour Court order relating to a retaliatory dismissal within the same two-month period.

It has to be generally stated that proceedings under these sections of the equality legislation are extremely rare.

PENSIONS AND EQUALITY

The Pensions Act, 1990 provides for equal treatment between men and women in occupational pension schemes (see Chapter 14 — Pensions). Prior to the operation of this Act all claims in respect of pension schemes were referred under the Anti-Discrimination (Pay) Act, 1974 or the Employment Equality Act, 1977. The procedures in respect of these disputes are now more complicated. The Pensions Board has a role in the resolution of disputes connected with equal treatment in pension schemes, yet there appears to be nothing prohibiting a person bringing a claim under the 1974 or 1977 Acts (as an employee) and under the 1990 Act (as a scheme member), as the 1974 and 1977 legislation has not been amended (see Lynch and Kelly, pages 25–60).

Any person — namely, the trustees, a member or a prospective member of a pension scheme, or the Employment Equality Agency — may refer a dispute to the Pensions Board concerning, *inter alia*, whether the terms of the scheme comply with the equal treatment provisions. The Board considers the matter and issues a written determination which may be appealed to the High Court on a point of law.

The 1990 Act provides that an employee or the Employment Equality Agency may refer a dispute to an equality officer who issues a recommendation which may be appealed to the Labour Court. That determination may only be appealed to the High Court on a point of law. There are also similar procedures, as under the 1974 and 1977 Acts, for implementation of Labour Court determinations.

GENERAL REFERENCES

Lynch, C. and Kelly, R., *Pensions Act, 1990, Irish Law Statutes Annotated, 1989–1990*, Sweet and Maxwell.

Second Commission on the Status of Women, *Report to Government*, Stationery Office, Dublin, January 1993.

SCHEDULE 1

EMPLOYMENT EQUALITY ACT, 1977 (SECTION 28)

QUESTIONNAIRE OF EMPLOYEE

Name of person   To ....

to to be questioned

(respondent);   ....

Address of   of ....

respondent   ....

                         ....

Name of Employee   1. I, ...

                         of ....

Address of Employee   ....

                            ....

                         believe that you have discriminated

                         against me contrary to the

                         Employment Equality Act, 1977.

Date, time, place   2. The following is the act believed by me

and factual   to have constituted such discrimination

discription of the

act believed by

employee to consti-

tute discrimination

3. I wish to ascertain from you the
    reasons for the act described in
    paragraph 2 above

Address to which   Signature of Employee ....

a reply should   Present Address ....

be sent   ....

                                          ....

                          Date ....

_____

Note: Under Section 28 of the Employment Equality Act, 1977, a
person may ascertain from another person the reasons for an act
done by that other person and believed by the first-mentioned
person to have constituted discrimination under that Act, and
that other person is obliged by that section to state the
reason in writing to the first-mentioned person.

SCHEDULE 2

EMPLOYMENT EQUALITY ACT, 1977 (SECTION 28)

Reply to Questionnaire

Name of Employee   To ....

Address of Employee of ....

....

Name of respondent 1. I, ...

Address of   of ....
Respondent   ....,.......

Complete as   hereby acknowledge receipt of the
appropriate   questionnaire signed by you and dated
                      .... which was served on me
                      on (date) ....

#Delete as   2. I *agree/disagree that the statement in
 appropriate   paragraph 2 of the questionnaire is an
                      accurate description of what happened.

If you disagree
give reason.

Complete as   3. The following are the reasons for the
appropriate   act referred to in your Questionnaire
                     and believed by you to have constituted
                     discrimination under the Employment
                     Equality Act, 1977.

                  Signature of respondent ....

                  Date ....

Note: Under the Employment Equality Act, 1977 (Section 28)
Regulations, 1977, the time-limit for the completion and return
of this reply is 21 days from the date on which the
questionnaire was served.

ANTI-DISCRIMINATION (PAY) ACT, 1974
SAMPLE FORM FOR REFERRING DISPUTES FOR INVESTIGATION
BY AN EQUALITY OFFICER

1. The claimant(s) listed on this form are in dispute with the employer named hereunder under the terms of the Anti-Discrimination (Pay) Act, 1974 and request an investigation by an Equality Officer of the dispute.

2. THE NAME AND ADDRESS OF THE EMPLOYER IS:

3. THE NAME(S) OF CLAIMANT(S) ARE AS FOLLOWS:

4. THE NAME(S) OF PERSON(S) OF THE OPPOSITE SEX WITH WHOM THE SAME RATE OF REMUNERATION IS BEING CLAIMED ARE AS FOLLOWS:

5. The claimants claim that they

- perform the same work as the comparator(s) or are interchangeable with the comparators |_____|

        and/or

- perform work of a similar nature to that performed by the comparator(s) and any differences occur only |____| infrequently or are of small importance

        and/or

- perform work which is equal in value to that |____| performed by the comparator(s)

6. THE NAME AND ADDRESS OF THE PARTY REFERRING THE DISPUTE FOR INVESTIGATION IS:

7. SIGNATURE OF PERSON WHO HAS COMPLETED THIS FORM:

DATE:

To: Head of Equality Officer Service
The Labour Court
Haddington Road
Dublin 4

SAMPLE NOTICE OF APPEAL WHERE THE APPEAL IS BROUGHT AGAINST A
RECOMMENDATION OF AN EQUALITY OFFICER, OR FOR A DETERMINATION
THAT SUCH RECOMMENDATION HAS NOT BEEN IMPLEMENTED

Anti-Discrimination (Pay) Act, 1974, Section 8(1)
OR
Employment Equality Act, 1977, Section 21 (delete where inapplicable)

NOTICE OF APPEAL

TAKE NOTICE that   (Name of Appellant) hereby
appeals to the Labour Court pursuant to Section 8(1) of the Anti-
Discrimination (Pay) Act, 1974/Section 21 of the Employment Equality
Act, 1977 (delete where inapplicable) against the Recommendation No.
     of an Equality Officer/for a determination that Recommendation
No.   has not been implemented (delete where inapplicable).

1.   The Appellant is (state name, address and occupation)

2.   The Respondent is (state name, address and occupation)

3.   The dispute between the Appellant and the Respondent was referred
     to an Equality Officer by   on (date)

4.   The Equality Officer issued a Recommendation on (date)
     The terms of the Recommendation are appended hereto.

5. The appeal is made against the Recommendation for the following
    reasons:

                                OR

    The   Respondent has failed to implement the terms of the
    Recommendation as follows:

6. The grounds on which the Appellant appeals to the Court are the
    following:

Dated the   day of   19

                        Signed _____
                                Appellant/on behalf of Appellant

To: The Chairman
    The Labour Court
    Tom Johnson House
    Haddington Road
    Dublin 4.

<u>SAMPLE ANSWER TO AN APPEAL</u>

Anti-Discrimination (Pay) Act, 1974, Section 8(1)
Employment Equality Act, 1977, Section 21

Appellant:

Respondent:

<u>A N S W E R</u>

TAKE   NOTICE that   (Name of Respondent) disputes
the appeal made pursuant to Section 8(1) of the Anti-Discrimination
(Pay) Act, 1974/Section 21 of the Employment Equality Act, 1977 (delete
where inapplicable) which said appeal was served on the Respondent on
the   day of   19

AND TAKE NOTICE that the Respondent will rely upon the following
matters in disputing the said appeal (set out in numbered paragraphs
the grounds on which the appeal is disputed including the facts relied
upon and the arguments which are made by the Respondent, including the
arguments in answer to the Appellant's arguments)

The Respondent seeks the following relief:

Dated this   day of   19

Signed _____
Respondent/On behalf of Respondent

To: The Chairman
    The Labour Court
    Tom Johnson House
    Haddington Road
    Dublin 4

<u>SAMPLE NOTICE OF COMPLAINT WHERE A DETERMINATION OF THE</u>
<u>LABOUR COURT IS ALLEGED NOT TO HAVE BEEN IMPLEMENTED</u>

Anti-Discrimination (Pay) Act, 1974, Section 8(4)
OR
Employment   Equality   Act,   1977,   Section   24(1)   (Delete   where
inapplicable)

Complainant:

Employer/Respondent:

<u>NOTICE OF COMPLAINT</u>

TAKE NOTICE that   (Name of Complainant) hereby
complains to the Labour Court pursuant to Section 8(4) of the Anti-
Discrimination (Pay) Act, 1974/Section 24(1) of the Employment Equality
Act, 1977 (delete where inapplicable) that a determination of the Court
has not been implemented.

1.   The Complainant is (state name; address and occupation)

2.   The Employer/Respondent is (state name and address)

3.   The Court on the   day of   19   decided an appeal under
     Section 8(1) of the Act of 1974/Section 21 of the Act of 1977
     (delete where inapplicable) and gave the following determination:

4. The Employer/Respondent has failed or neglected to implement the
    said determination in the following particulars:

5. The Employer/Respondent would implement the said determination if
    the following were done:

Dated the   day of   19

                            Signed _____
                                    Complainant/On behalf of Complainant

To: The Chairman
    The Labour Court
    Tom Johnson House
    Haddington Road
    Dublin 4

SAMPLE ANSWER TO A COMPLAINT THAT A DISMISSAL HAS
OCCURRED BECAUSE A PERSON SOUGHT HER/HIS RIGHTS
UNDER EITHER OF THE ACTS

Anti-Discrimination (Pay) Act, 1974, Section 10(1) as amended by
Section 31 of the Employment Equality Act, 1977,
Employment Equality Act, 1977, Section 26,
Employment Equality Act, 1977, Section 27.

Complainant:

Employer:

A N S W E R

TAKE NOTICE that   (Name of Employer) opposes the
complaint made pursuant to Section 10(1) of the Anti-Discrimination
(Pay) Act, 1974 as amended by Section 31 of the Employment Equality
Act, 1977/Section 31 of the Employment Equality Act, 1977/Section 26 of
the Employment Equality Act, 1977/Section 27 of the Employment Equality
Act, 1977 (delete where inapplicable) which was served on the Employer
on the   day of   19

AND TAKE NOTICE that the employer will rely upon the following matter
.n opposing the said complaint (set out in numbered paragraphs th
reasons why the dismissal occurred; if the Employer disputes the clai
that a dismissal occurred, specify what did .occur in relation to th
Complainant]

Dated this   day of   19

                              Signed _____
                                     Employer/On behalf of Employer

To: The Chairman
    The Labour Court
    Tom Johnson House
    Haddington Road
    Dublin 4

FORM FOR REFERRING A DISPUTE UNDER SECTION 19 OF THE EMPLOYMENT EQUALITY ACT, 1977 TO THE LABOUR COURT

1.   I, (State name and address)

_____

_____

_____

_____

_____

_____

      refer a dispute concerning whether or not a person has discriminated to the Labour Court.

2.   The name and address of the person alleged to have suffered the discrimination are as follows:-

_____

_____

_____

_____

_____

_____

3.   The name and address of the party alleged to have discriminated are as follows:-

_____

_____

_____

_____

_____

_____

4.   The alleged discriminatory act took place on (the date):-

_____

5.   The alleged discriminatory act is as follows (give details of act concerned on the attached sheet):-

6.   (Please tick appropriate box or boxes.)

  (i)   The complainant was treated less favourably, because
         of her/his sex, than a person of the other sex:

         YES ☐   NO ☐

  (ii)   The complainant was treated less favourably than a
         person of the same sex because of her/his marital
         status:

         YES ☐   NO ☐

  (iii) The complainant was obliged to comply with an
         inessential requirement relating to employment which
         is such that the proportion of persons of the other
         sex, or of the same sex but of a different marital
         status, able to comply is substantially higher:

         YES ☐   NO ☐

  (iv)   The complainant was penalised for taking action in
         pursuance of an entitlement under the Act of 1977 or
         the Act of 1974:

         YES ☐   NO ☐

I confirm that the party alleged to have discriminated has been
notified of and disputes the above complaint(s).

Signed:_____   Date:_____

To: The Chairman
      The Labour Court
      Tom Johnson House
      Haddington Road
      Dublin 4

DETAILS OF ALLEGED DISCRIMINATORY ACT

SAMPLE NOTICE OF COMPLAINT CONCERNING A DISMISSAL
WHICH IS ALLEGED TO HAVE OCCURRED BECAUSE A PERSON
SOUGHT HER/HIS RIGHTS UNDER EITHER OF THE ACTS

Anti-Discrimination (Pay) Act, 1974, Section 10(1), as amended by Section 31 of the Employment Equality Act, 1977,
OR
Employment Equality Act, 1977, Sections 26 and 27 (delete where inapplicable)

Complainant:

Employer/Respondent:

NOTICE OF COMPLAINT

TAKE NOTICE that   (Name of Complainant) hereby complains to the Labour Court pursuant to Section 10(1) of the Anti-Discrimination (Pay) Act, as amended/Section 26(1) of the Employment Equality Act, 1977 (delete where inapplicable) in respect of a dismissal.

1. The Complainant is (state name, address and occupation)

2. The Employer is (state name and address of former employer)

3. The Complainant was until the   day of   19   employed by the Employer as (state position held, or capacity in which employed) at a weekly/monthly gross wage/salary of £

4. The Complainant was on the   day of   19   dismissed from
    the said employment.

5. The   said   dismissal   occurred   solely   or   mainly   because   the
    Complainant   had made an equal pay claim.   The equal pay claim was
    made on the   day of   19

                                  OR

    The   said   dismissal   occurred   solely   or   mainly   because   the
    complainant   did the following (specify the thing done by reference
    to Section 2(d) of the Act of 1977)

                                  OR

    The   said   dismissal   occurred   in   circumstances which   contravene
    Section 3(4) of the Act of 1977

6. (If   applicable)   No   prosecution   has   been   brought   or   is   being
    contemplated against the Employer.

7. The   Complainant will   rely upon the following matters in support of
    the said complaint:

Dated the   day of   19

                        Signed _____

                                Complainant/On behalf of Complainant

To: The Chairman
    The Labour Court
    Tom Johnson House
    Haddington Road
    Dublin 4

SAMPLE ANSWER TO A COMPLAINT THAT A DETERMINATION
OF THE LABOUR COURT HAS NOT BEEN IMPLEMENTED

Anti-Discrimination (Pay) Act, 1974, Section 8(4)
Employment Equality Act, 1977, Section 24(1)

Complainant:

Employer/Respondent:

ANSWER

TAKE NOTICE that   (Name of Employer/Respondent)
opposes the complaint made pursuant to Section 8(4) of the Anti-
Discrimination (Pay) Act, 1974/Section 24(1) of the Employment Equality
Act,   1977 (delete where inapplicable) which was served on the
Employer/Respondent on the   day of   19

AND TAKE NOTICE that the Employer/Respondent will rely upon the
following matters in opposing the said complaint (set out in numbered
paragraphs the grounds on which the Employer/Respondent relies to show
that   the   determination   has   been   implemented   or   reasons why

the determination cannot be implemented. The Reply may also set out
the Employer's/Respondent's response to suggestions made by the
Complainant   as   to   what   would   achieve   implementation   of the
determination)

Dated this   day of   19

                              Signed _____
                                      Employer/Respondent/On behalf of
                                            Employer/Respondent

To: The Chairman
     The Labour Court
     Tom Johnson House
     Haddington Road
     Dublin 4

CHAPTER TWENTY-FIVE

Employment Equality Agency

The Employment Equality Act, 1977 states that the Employment Equality Agency (EEA) has the general function of promoting equality of opportunity between men and women in relation to employment, and overseeing the operation of the equality legislation, namely the 1974 and the 1977 Acts.

The Board of the EEA consists of a chairperson and 10 members who represent trade unions, employers' organisations, women's organisations and other interested parties. All are appointed by the Minister for Equality and Law Reform and are voluntary appointments. There is a full-time executive staff headed by a chief executive. Most of the staff are drawn from the public service, usually from the former Department of Labour (now the Department of Enterprise and Employment). The Agency has an annual allocation of funds from the Department of Equality and Law Reform.

ADVICE/ASSISTANCE TO CLAIMANTS

The Agency may provide assistance to a person who considers that there has been a breach of the 1974 and 1977 Acts, but the wording of the 1977 Act limits the assistance that the Agency can offer; it only refers to "assistance" in making a reference to the Labour Court or an equality officer. There is no reference to financial assistance.

Invariably, the Agency's assistance takes the form of advice prior to the reference of the claim; if a claim is brought, then assistance would include the drafting of submissions and subsequent representation before equality officers and the Labour Court. For many years the Agency has had legally qualified staff who represent claimants before equality officers and the Labour Court. However, the Agency must be satisfied that the proposed claim raises an important matter of principle and that the person would not be in a position to represent themselves adequately. Typically, such claimants are pursuing alleged discriminatory practices where their trade union may have been a party to an agreement wherein the alleged discriminatory practice arose. Agency representation has been used by claimants in cases concerning the appointment of "twilight" shift workers to full-time positions on foot of a trade union/management agreement, alleged discrimination concerning the non-granting of a union card, and in several cases concerning alleged discriminatory interviewing.

CODES OF PRACTICE

The 1977 Act provides that the Agency "may draft and publish for the information of employers guidelines, or codes of practice relating to discrimination in employment".

The Agency issued a Code of Practice in February 1984 in respect of the Elimination of Discrimination in Employment. The Code is not legally binding but it is admissible in evidence before the Labour Court and equality officers and, of course, the courts In practice, the use of the Code in the hearing of discrimination cases is rare. The Code of Practice is comprehensive but it has not been fully updated since 1984.

The Agency recently published a Model Equal Opportunities Policy which includes draft management statements for a commitment to equal opportunities, selection, advertising, application forms, shortlisting for interviews, testing, interviewing, promotion, training, placement, mobility, work experience, work and family responsibility, pay and benefit-in-kind, leave and other matters. Incorporated into this document is a guide to assist in the monitoring of an Equal Opportunities Policy.

A Model Policy has also been published which may be used by employers to recognise that sexual harassment will not be tolerated in that particular employment. The Model provides a positive statement that sexual harassment will not be tolerated, definitions of sexual harassment (defined by the Agency as behaviour which includes "unreciprocated and unwelcome comments, looks, jokes, suggestions or physical contact which might threaten a person's job security or create a stressful or intimidating working environment"), an outline of the responsibility of management and staff, and procedures should an employee consider that they have such a grievance.

It is anticipated that there will be a voluntary Code of Practice on Sexual Harassment under the proposed new equality legislation to give effect to the EC Recommendation on Sexual Harassment.

REVIEW OF THE LEGISLATION

The Agency may carry out a review of existing legislation if it considers that it is impeding the elimination of discrimination. However, the Minister must give it permission to do so. Over the years, the Agency has reviewed the 1974 and 1977 Acts, and has made detailed recommendations for their amendments. It has also submitted its views to the National Pensions Board on the appropriate manner of implementation of EC Directive 86/378 on equal treatment in occupational benefit schemes.

A Bill consolidating and amending the equal pay legislation and equal treatment legislation is expected in 1994. Amended legislation has been promised for years and a government commitment was made as part of the Programme for Economic and Social Progress in January 1991. In addition, the Second Commission on the Status of Women reported to government in January 1993 and its recommendations will be taken into account in the drafting of new legislation.

RESEARCH

The Agency may undertake research and other activities relating to the dissemination of information. To date it has commissioned research on women working in the electronic sector, and has produced a video mainly directed at schoolgirls. A major report on women in the labour force was produced in June 1989: The Agency has clearly been hampered by the lack of necessary financial resources.

The Agency also publishes a quarterly newsletter *Equality News* and has advanced public awareness of equality issues through regular press releases and considerable coverage in the media.

INVESTIGATIONS

The Agency has power to conduct investigations which may be either requested by the Minister for Equality and Law Reform or be carried out with the Minister's approval. In summary, an investigation may only be carried out if the Agency or the Minister considers, that there has been discrimination in the employment concerned, or if there has been discriminatory advertising or an attempt to procure discrimination.

The Agency has certain statutory powers to obtain information and documents and to summon witnesses. A person who does not comply with such a request shall be guilty of an offence and liable to a fine.

When an investigation has been completed, the Agency prepares a report and makes recommendations. If the Agency is satisfied that there has been discrimination in the employment, it may serve a non-discrimination notice on the employer or other persons in question. The non-discrimination notice must detail the alleged discriminatory practice. The Act provides for time limits, etc. for response to such notices and also for an appeal to the Labour Court against them. If the notice has not been appealed, its contents will come into effect — discontinuation of the discriminatory practice, for example. The Labour Court has power to hear the views of both sides on the appeal.

It should be noted that these investigations are very rare, and they have only been carried out in two large employments to date.

The Agency can request the High Court to grant an injunction against such a discriminatory practice if the Agency considers that within five years of the operation of the non-discriminatory notice there is a likelihood of the discriminatory practice recurring.

AGENCY MONITORING

The Agency continuously monitors rates of pay and equal treatment in all the industries and also in the public service. It is obviously not feasible to monitor each individual employment relationship.

SECOND COMMISSION ON THE STATUS OF WOMEN

The Commission's *Report to Government* in January 1993 recommended that there be equal status legislation providing for equal treatment between men and women in respect of goods, facilities and the provision of services. At present, the equality legislation prevents discrimination in employment, which is enforced through the EEA. In order to enforce the proposed legislation, the EEA's mandate would be extended to cover all equality issues and it would be renamed "The Equality Commission". The board of the new Agency should be extended to reflect its wider role than that which is currently constituted in favour of employment related bodies. The Commission considered that the EEA as currently constituted should be under the aegis of a Department of Women's Affairs, which in effect has already happened as it is now under the aegis of the Department of Equality and Law Reform.

In summary, the proposed Equality Commission should:

(1) Be an independent semi-state body,

(2) Have sufficient resources to carry out its functions,

(3) Be independent in relation to staffing and structures and be free to appoint its own staff, and

(4) Have functions to include research, legal enforcement, monitoring and the provision of information and advice in respect of all rights covered under the proposed legislation.

The Commission also recommended that the procedure for the enforcement of rights under the proposed legislation should include an informal conciliation procedure and, if necessary, a hearing before an equality tribunal whose awards would be legally enforceable.

GENERAL REFERENCE

Second Commission on the Status of Women, Report to Government,
Stationery Office, Dublin, January 1993.

Select Bibliography

Callender, Rosheen, and Meenan, Frances, *Equality in Law between Men and Women in the European Community — Collection of Texts and Commentary on Irish Law*, Martinus Nijhoff Publishers and Office for Official Publications of the European Communities, 1994.

Clark, R., *Data Protection Law in Ireland*, The Round Hall Press, 1990.

Collins, Hugh, *Justice in Dismissal*, Oxford, 1992.

Curtin, Deirdre, *Irish Employment Equality Law*, The Round Hall Press, 1989.

Data Protection Commissioner, *Guide to the Data Protection Act, 1988*, Dublin December, 1988.

Dickens, Linda and Others, *Dismissed*, Blackwell, 1985.

Federation of Irish Employers, Kerr, T. and Madden, D., *Unfair Dismissals Cases and Commentaries, 1990*.

Forde, Michael, *Employment Law*, The Round Hall Press, 1992.

Harvey on Industrial Relations and Employment Law, Butterworths, ongoing supplements.

Hepple and O'Higgins, Hepple. B., *Employment Law*, 4th ed. Sweet and Maxwell, 1981.

Industrial Relations News.

Industrial Relations in Ireland, *Contemporary Issues and Developments*, Department of Industrial Relations, UCD, 1989.

Irish Centre for European Law, *Acquired Rights for Employees*, Papers from Conference, November, 1988.

Journal of the Irish Society of Labour Law, Volumes 1-8.

Kerr, A., *The Trade Union and Industrial Relations Acts of Ireland*, Sweet and Maxwell, 1991.

Kerr, A. and Whyte, G., *Trade Union Law in Ireland*, Professional Books, 1985.

McCarthy, C., *Trade Unions in Ireland, 1894-1960*, Institute of Public Administration, 1977.

McCarthy, C. and von Prondzynski, F., *Employment Law in Ireland*, 2nd ed., 1988.

Redmond, Mary, *Dismissal Law in the Republic of Ireland*, The Incorporated Law Society of Ireland, 1982.

Subject Index

Note: The method of alphabetisation used is word by word.
Statutory forms are listed under "Forms".
Abbreviations: EAT: Employment Appeals Tribunal;
EO: Equality Officer